VOLUME 1

WOMEN'S HISTORY IN GLOBAL PERSPECTIVE

VOLUME 1

PUBLISHED WITH THE
AMERICAN HISTORICAL ASSOCIATION

WOMEN'S HISTORY

IN GLOBAL PERSPECTIVE

Edited by Bonnie G. Smith

UNIVERSITY OF ILLINOIS PRESS

URBANA AND CHICAGO

© 2004 by the American Historical Association
All rights reserved
Manufactured in the United States of America
1 2 3 4 5 C P 6 5 4 3 2
∞ This book is printed on acid-free paper.

Library of Congress Cataloging-in-Publication Data
Women's history in global perspective
/ edited by Bonnie G. Smith.
p.   cm.
"Published with the American Historical Association."
Includes bibliographical references and index.
ISBN 0-252-02931-3 (cl. : alk. paper) / ISBN 978-0-252-02931-8
ISBN 0-252-07183-2 (pbk. : alk. paper) / ISBN 978-0-252-07183-6
1. Women—History. I. Smith, Bonnie G., 1940–
HQ1121W88585   2004
305.4′09—dc22   2003024938

Contents

Introduction

BONNIE G. SMITH

This volume, and the two that follow it, testify to an exciting new stage in teaching women's and gender history: the development of a global perspective on the past. For several centuries scholars in the West have produced world history textbooks, including those of Johann-Christophe Gatterer (1761) and Johann Gottfried von Herder (1784–91). These usually began with the appearance of the human species as an advance over animal life and followed what can be called a Christian trajectory that saw other civilizational groups in relationship to the unfolding of the Judeo-Christianity. There were also parallel efforts by earlier historians of women—Lydia Maria Child's *History of the Condition of Women* (1835) is just one among many possible examples—to investigate the experience of the world's women.

As imperialism, debates over the slave trade, more rapid communication and transport, and global trade itself brought people into greater contact with one another, histories of women in the Middle East, China, Africa, and elsewhere poured from the pens of amateur scholars in the nineteenth and early twentieth centuries. The professionalization of history and the cataclysmic wars from 1914 on curtailed some of those efforts. Recently, the vast new evidence of global connectedness has revived the imperative to understand the world better, especially the worldwide history of women. These volumes are devoted to surveying the most recent findings on women and gender in the hope of bringing teachers at all levels a practical introduction to the new data, historical issues, and historiographical debates from all regions of the world.

The volumes are part of the evolution of women's history since the 1960s, and many authors of these chapters were pioneers in that development. The 1970s revived and professionalized the study of women's past, particularly in the form of social history, in which the experience of women as workers, mothers, outcasts, prostitutes, and homemakers took center stage. Historians of women during these and subsequent years quantified many aspects of women's past, often looking at such new issues as the female life-cycle. Investigations of the workplace and the household were primary, but there were also forays into issues of reform and women's participation in great national events such as war. In addition to concern for class as a determinant of women's experience, the women's history written in the 1970s and 1980s brought the study of race to the fore. Work in this field focused on difference and incommensurability, especially as it traced African American women's unique past as slaves, reformers, and free workers. One culminating moment in this development was the appearance of a groundbreaking biographical dictionary, *Black Women in America: An Historical Encyclopedia* (1994).

During the mid-1980s, gender theory emerged to reorient and even contest the path that women's history was taking. In brief, this theory proposed looking at masculinity and femininity as sets of mutually created characteristics shaping and even producing the lives of men and women. It replaced or at the very least challenged ideas of masculinity and femininity and of men and women as operating in history according to fixed biological determinants. Many established historians observing the emergence of the history of women had thought it belonged more appropriately to natural history. Women's history, some believed, had to be told in conjunction with the history of the family and women's biology. Gender history changed all that. By removing these categories of men and women from the realm of biology, it made a history possible.

For some, the idea of "gender history" was but another term for women's history, but serious students of gender theory transformed the ways in which they approached writing and teaching about both men and women. To some extent it may be hypothesized that the major change gender theory offered was to problematize the study of men, making them as well as women gendered historical subjects who operated in a culturally constructed universe of symbols developed around the issue of gender. The leading proponent of gender theory, Joan Wallach Scott, pointed to the ways in which the operation of gender produced hierarchies of meaning and value, which were part of the operation of power in the world. The subsequent investigation of gender in history took on an enhanced variety of subjects under the expanded mandate of gender theory.

As these developments continue to play themselves out in the form of important new scholarship, the last decade of the millennium vividly highlighted the need for more global and comparative perspectives in teaching and scholarship. World and global history appeared more insistently in the curriculum of schools and universities owing to the rapid unfolding of world events such as migration, communication technology, wars, and increased global trade. Because of the expanded subject matter teachers had to convey, attention to women and gender dropped by the wayside. This material was seen as secondary to the more important subject matter of global politics directed by men or of global economic systems such as the Silk Road or routes on the Indian Ocean. In the first forays of a new world history, as in the earlier textbooks in German universities or Arnold Toynbee's extension of their paradigm, women were rarely to be seen. Even when making an appearance, it would be to extend an earlier paradigm. Books introduced unique topics— foot-binding, for example—to point to the barbaric treatment of women outside the (Christian) West. This situation had to be changed, many educators felt.

In the midst of the development of a modern version of world history in the academy, activists from around the world were also at the forefront of highlighting the importance of a fresh, global perspective in women's and gender history, and their insights contributed to developing the new scholarship on women and gender in global perspective. Almost two centuries ago Lydia Maria Child's work on women in various parts of the world was born of her commitment to abolitionism, and it allowed her to see slavery as part of a world system—a perspective reborn in the decades since World War II. More recently, the international meetings of women connected with second-wave feminism inspired participants, especially those from Central and South America, Africa, and Asia, to insist on a more encompassing and diverse global perspective. Issues taken as normative by U.S. and West European feminists had little relevance from the vantage point of activists in Africa, South Asia, and Latin America. Outside the prosperous northern tier of countries, family, work, politics, and nation had different meanings and entailed different political strategies. Gender was multiply constructed, non-Westerners maintained. Western ignorance and U.S. dominance were called into question during these meetings, and an entire system of scholarly priorities and values was thrown into question as well. Nowhere was that more evident than in the study of history.

The dissolution of the Soviet Union and the collapse of state socialism in Eastern Europe and Central Asia have also challenged the orientation of traditional historical research in the United States. As scholarship on women and gender emerged from that region, it raised an alternative array of historical questions, particularly concerning democratization, the free market, and citizenship. In what was euphemistically called the "transition," women suddenly found themselves both without jobs and without the social services that had provided health care for them and their children. Following free-market values meant unemployment for women, and belief in women's equality was equated with a failed and often brutal socialist system. Women's equality became prized in these countries because of its association with American and Western European success, inspiring bursts of feminist activism from women in the post-Soviet world. As nongovermental organizations sponsored women's and gender history programs in Budapest and Moscow, scholars and activists both used the insights of Western scholars and devised many new questions of their own, often contesting the would-be hegemony of U.S. feminists and their scholarly concerns. Historians in eastern and east central Europe helped shift attention to issues of citizenship and democratization as global process-es. Eastern European scholars have helped their counterparts elsewhere ad-dress issues of historical evidence and feminism from a fresh point of view.

These events alone have shown that a global perspective calls for exam-ining the past from more than one point of view. Beyond that, however, ques-tions of what constitutes world history and global studies still remain open to zestful debate. As Margaret Strobel and Marjorie Bingham describe so well, world history has had many metamorphoses and will probably have many more. Orthodoxies have come and gone while the field of knowledge about women and gender in world history has expanded exponentially. For some, a global perspective has meant examining and integrating the history of all countries except the United States. According to this view, global history is best taught by specialists in the Chinese, African, or similarly non-U.S. fields. Others have seen global history as best when it additionally excludes Europe, which is perceived as so hegemonic in historical narrative that studying it ir-remediably distorts attempts at understanding the global past. In these two versions of global history, such a history means "the rest" and has led to a much-criticized pedagogy: While Americanists and Europeanists have focused on relatively specialized scholarship and teaching, specialists from outside those fields have been charged with teaching the world in its entirety.

In contrast, this book and those that follow try to integrate both North America and Europe into the global perspective in the belief that such inclu-sion is necessary for a holistic history that encompasses the world. Similarly, the most innovative textbooks in the field have increasingly rejected this strat-egy. The initiator of the volumes, the Committee on Women Historians of the American Historical Association, envisioned a wide-ranging series that would make available the insights and information from recent scholarship from *all* geographic regions. Moreover, it aimed for inclusive topical chapters that would bring into play women's experience of such large-scale institutions and movements as nation-state, feminism, and religion from around the world and that would be written by specialists in a variety of geographic fields. We see the virtues of inclusiveness, for example, in the chapter on work, which es-tablishes discernible patterns, topics, and analytical themes that can unify the study of work in many parts of the world over the centuries. Material on women in the United States and Europe helps establish those themes and patterns, but it does not dominate the analysis. More important, the global sweep of this analysis of work prevents the omission of the United States and Europe

4

from distorting our understanding. Instead the centrality of gender to the organization, remuneration, and conditions of work globally comes into true focus.

Because of the vast amounts of potential historical coverage in both topical and geographical volumes, the distinguished authors have been ruthlessly selective, providing a usable model to teachers who also must prune their classroom presentations. Understanding that there are many world religions, the chapter on religion, written by a specialist in North Africa, has focused on Islam, Christianity, and Judaism while omitting other systems of belief that are treated in other chapters and volumes. Regional and national presentations of women's and gender history are also pared to the most central and useful topics and themes. These are not necessarily uniform across the volumes because each region's history and central concerns differ. The chapter on China, for example, provides a detailed overview of the family system as a prelude to the more general treatment of women and gender in Chinese history. The early history of Latin America, in contrast, brings into play the impact of contact on indigenous women and on the evolution of gender. The author of the early history of North America emphasizes the interaction and diverse lives of the multiple ethnicities there, offering excellent material for teachers wishing to establish a background to the complex gendering of North American history.

Several classroom uses are intended for this volume and those that follow—and we stress again the practical intent of these overviews. First, they allow more material on gender to be introduced into the study of any particular area of the world. The regional volumes that follow this one are designed to help teachers and students of Chinese history or Latin American history, for example, learn more about the gendered aspects of that history and add the history of women to their understanding. Women are present in the evolution of classical Chinese thought and the nation-building processes of modern Latin America. The regional histories provide an overview of women's history from around the world and can enrich the gendered component in national and regional courses. A second step, one that has shaped the world history course, is to encourage comparisons among the historical experiences of women from various continents, regions, nations, and religious traditions. The topical chapters on family, religion, race, and ethnicity and other basic subjects allow nearly any course to have a comparative gendered component. Critical insights develop when the study of such phenomena as nationalism or work contains material on women and gender. Material from the regional volumes, however, also allows for comparative study and teaching.

As mentioned earlier, women's activism has led to seeing history in a more inclusive, comparative manner. That activism brings to light still another perspective on globalism that involves thinking about the very nationalist bias of women historians in the United States in the writing and conceptualization of history. A substitute way of thinking considers the histories that crossed borders. Transnational women's movements parallel contemporary phenomenon such as global migration, multinational corporations, global communications, and transnational ruling structures like the World Bank. These developments, however, have been accompanied by new findings in world history that suggest the enduring nature not of nations but of global contact.

The surprising constancy going back tens of thousands of years of global migration, cultural exchange, and the spread of disease and epidemics opens new vistas for the history of women and gender. Among these phenomena are women's relationship to overland and overseas trade, their variegated participation in migration and diasporas, and their contributions to culture both nationally and internationally. Women throughout time have been part of regional and transregional slave systems and international prostitution; they have also participated in international movements against slavery and forced prostitution. The transregional spread of religion has involved women, and it has simultaneously often been a highly gendered process.

The chapters in this book and successive others include material that allows teachers to focus on the place of women and the role of gender in the transnational aspects of world history. Various components of women's work have implications beyond national and regional borders, and information on their labor appears in the chapters on sexuality, race, and work, among others. Women's relationship to world religions and philosophical systems appears in multiple chapters, including most of the regional chapters and topical ones such as sexuality. Women's transnational activism is also prominent, especially in the investigation of feminism and nationalism. The books are intended to encourage gendered study in the exciting evolution of world history as it comes to examine processes that operate across current national and regional boundaries.

A "global perspective" allows for several different approaches to women's and gender history in the classroom. First, it can mean simply bringing to the fore historical material from most of the discrete areas of the globe—what might be called a "civilizational approach" that many teachers find important. Reading the two volumes of regional chapters will provide an overview of women's history from around the world and permit teachers to enrich the gender component in national and regional courses. It also permits cultural literacy in women's history that is worldwide. A second step in developing a global perspective would be to encourage comparisons among the historical experiences of women from various continents, regions, and nations. The seven topical chapters on family, religion, race and ethnicity, and other subjects allow courses based on a topical approach to have a gender component. Many teachers find that organizing a course by topic allows for clear organization that students can follow. Insights develop when a study of such phenomena as nationalism or work contains material on women and gender. If the study of women and gender has helped to transform historical study, we believe that there is still more to be done—namely, opening for students a still wider window on the historical world using multiple strategies.

As historians of women struggle to meet the need to inform students and themselves more broadly about both global processes and pressing international issues, the sheer mass of information in the ever-expanding historical field seems overwhelming. The chapters that follow provide economical coverage of basic themes and facts. In the face of our current information overload, however, the greater danger is to continue to claim only marginal importance for issues of women and gender and omit any coverage at all. In the face of great world events and the need to understand major cultural influences, women's importance can appear to shrink. The chapters also demonstrate a distinctly opposite historical world in which issues of gender and the presence of women have been pivotal to political, economic, and cultural development.

From the opening salvos of this volume, where women appear as critical players in Islam, to the final chapters on women in the twentieth-century Americas, there are perils to accurate understanding if women's experience and the construction of gender are omitted from the historical account. Both have been central to the development of nationalism, the economy, and religious life, and individual regions and nations have mobilized both women and gender to advance political and economic agendas.

Responsible and accurate historical understanding depends on considerations of women and gender, and these volumes seek to provide a usable overview of the latest issues, central facts, analytical tools, and current scholarship. In sponsoring this volume and the two that follow it, the Committee on Women Historians of the American Historical Association seeks to enrich the connection of all teachers and students to the vital world of women's and gender history.

1

The Theory and Practice of
Women's History and Gender History
in Global Perspective

MARGARET STROBEL AND

MARJORIE BINGHAM

Women's history, gender history, and world history emerged from the social movements and political and economic dynamics of the last third of the twentieth century. Earlier cohorts of historians had found new questions to ask from both the inadequacies of existing explanations and new challenges in their contemporary world. The post–World War I academics at Columbia College (now Columbia University), for example, developed the survey course in Western civilization in response to "the national wartime policy to strengthen moral and emotional bonds between Americans . . . and their military allies in democratic Europe [and] to assimilate new immigrants by teaching 'the common and deeply rooted heritage that bound them together.'"[1] The resulting course sequence oriented world events around a North American and European axis.

By the 1960s, new issues captured the attention of some academics. As participants and observers in the social movements questioned the exclusion of some people from the benefits of citizenship and equal treatment in law and society, history teachers and graduate students began to ask where were the women in the historical narratives they read.[2] In a similar development, feminism and the revolution in sexual mores of the 1960s created circumstances for the emergence of the gay and lesbian movement, which generated new questions about the role of sexuality in history and the hidden history of sexual practices and sexual identities outside the mainstream.[3] Out of this social, political, and intellectual ferment came the fields of women's history and gender history, fields whose further development is discussed later in this essay.

If the notion of studying the history of women seems fairly straightforward initially, what is meant by the "history of gender" calls for clarification. Gender is understood as the meanings assigned to the biological givens of sex. That is, women and men have certain biological differences expressed in genitalia, other secondary sex characteristics, hormones, and genes. In various times and places, however, societies have attached different meanings, significance, and content to maleness and femaleness.[4] As a field, gender history explores these social and cultural constructions of masculinity, femininity, and, where present, other genders.[5] Furthermore, gender history often includes the history of sexuality and sexual orientation.

Parallel to the development of women's history and gender history, the study of world history has expanded in recent decades in the United States. Developing initially in high schools and two-year colleges, world history now challenges the primacy of Western civilization in the curriculum. Post–World War II decolonization and the cold war contributed substantially to dislodging Western civilization courses. Both trends contributed to the rise of "area studies programs," for example, federally funded university programs to foster the study of Africa, Asia, Latin America, the Middle East, and the Soviet Union and Soviet-block countries. Such programs generated the scholarship necessary to understand these areas on their own terms, while high school and college curricula of the 1970s formulated approaches for teaching an intellectually unified world history survey.[6] To promote research and teaching, high school and college teachers formed the World History Association (WHA) in 1982 and founded the *Journal of World History* in 1990.[7]

Although the fields of women's history and gender history have developed as areas of both research and teaching, world history has typically been primarily a teaching field.[8] Because of the large number of courses offered yearly across the country, the development of world history is driven significantly by centralizing forces. Along with U.S. history, for example, world history was the subject of an intensive exercise to develop national standards for grades five through twelve, identifying what historical thinking skills and historical understandings should be expected of and taught to precollege students.[9] In addition, the large market attracts textbook publishers. In the academic year 2001–2, the College Board introduced an advanced-placement (AP) examination for world history, furthering pressures for standardization. WHA President Carter Vaughn Findley expected about thirty thousand students to enroll during the first three years it was offered.[10]

Because school districts measure and report to school boards and parents the numbers and proportions of students who take and do well on advanced-placement tests, teachers tend to "teach to the test." The test itself becomes an instrument toward the codification of an approach to the subject matter. The problem is not so much unwillingness on the part of designers of the test to include material on women and gender as it is the difficulty of doing so. Although the fields of women's and gender history each have their own complexities, which are explored in the next section, the challenge of world history is especially daunting, requiring instructors to find a coherent approach and narrative that nonetheless respects the particularity of periods, cultures, and societies. The ease with which the principal different approaches to teaching world history accommodate an analysis of women and/or gender is discussed later in this essay.[11]

Women's History and Gender History

DEFINITIONS AND EXPLANATIONS

Women's history is an older specialized field than gender history.[12] Interest in the history of women has been closely linked to political agitation around women's rights in centuries past.[13] It has also been tied to the rise of second-wave feminism in the United States during the 1960s.[14] In part, the legitimacy of women's history drew upon that of social history, with the latter's emphasis on those excluded from formal power (e.g., peasants and laborers). Quantitative social historians explored households and families by digesting data from, for example, birth and death records. Others, influenced by anthropology and other social sciences, explored kinship networks and households by using ethnographic studies or personal narratives. Despite these shared approaches and interests, historians of women questioned the invisibility of women within the households and long-term forces studied by social historians.[15]

Historians of both women and gender generally hold a social-constructionist view of gender; that is, they see gender as the culturally and historically varied meanings given to the biological facts of sexual difference.[16] The emphasis on gender emerged in the mid-1970s with Joan Kelly's invocation of the "social relations of the sexes" (1976) and Natalie Zemon Davis's call (1976) to examine "the significance of the sexes, of gender groups in the historical past."[17] Gender history gathered steam with the rise of deconstruction/postmodernism in the writing of history and with interest in the history of sexuality. In her germinal article "Gender: A Useful Category of Historical Analysis" (1986), Joan Scott defines gender more elaborately and in a particular way: "Gender is a constitutive element of social relationships based on perceived differences between the sexes, and gender is a primary way of signifying relationships of power." The first component of her definition involves "four interrelated elements: culturally available symbols . . . [;] normative concepts that set forth interpretations of the meanings of the symbols . . . [;] a notion of politics as well as reference to social institutions and organizations . . . [; and] subjective identity."[18]

Although historians of women would appear to have been dealing with gender, deconstructionist historians of gender often believe that many historians of women have not problematized the category of "woman/women." Historians of gender argue that not to problematize "women"—to assume that all women share characteristics such that it makes sense to talk about them together—is to essentialize women, to reduce them to a fixed, ahistorical, biological category. The concept of a common identity of women was challenged by the growing number of studies of the diversity of women. Within second-wave feminism, lesbians and women of color within the United States, and women internationally, also challenged the notion of a homogenous category of "women."[19] As Scott says, feminist history has provided both a subject (women) and a lineage (a long line of foremothers) for contemporary feminist political movements as well as ways of analyzing the emergence of such subjects and movements in the past. It has posited "women" as a social category that preexists history and, at the same time, demonstrated that the very existence of the social category of "women" varied according to history.[20]

In addition to calling into question the validity of the category of "women," historians of gender addressed femininity and, eventually, masculinity.[21] Scott contends that "gender is a primary way of signifying relationships of power[,] . . . a primary field within which or by means of which power is interpreted."[22] It is this feature that enables gender as a concept to move the discussion beyond "add women and stir," because "when historians look for the ways in which the concept of gender legitimizes and constructs social relationships, they develop insight into the reciprocal nature of gender and society and into the particular and contextually specific ways in which politics constructs gender and gender constructs politics."[23]

While deconstructionist proponents of gender history criticize practitioners of women's history for assuming "women" as a valid category, nondeconstructionist historians of women claim that a focus on discourse and texts such as Scott advocates disables women, removing them from the possibility of agency. As Louise Tilly argues, "The focus on method and text (whether a formal statement or language or binary oppositions expressed in everyday phrases) seems to me, however, to downplay human agency and tip the scales towards an overemphasis on social constraint."[24]

The preceding account best describes developments in the United States.[25] Elsewhere, contemporary women's movements also have spurred the development of women's history, although the timing and particular nature of the relationship vary according to each country's culture and structure of politics, the academy, and national historiographic traditions.[26] Although the notion of gender has been taken up by some historians in the Netherlands, Britain, Australia, and Canada, the concept is less useful or easily employed for many European historians writing in European languages other than English.[27] Gisela Bock notes that the Romance languages have no such term. The German term *Geschlecht* refers to gender in grammatical constructions, sexual physiology, and other terms, such that its use does not convey the distinction found in English "sex" and "gender."[28]

APPROACHES TO WOMEN'S HISTORY AND GENDER HISTORY

One can illustrate several different approaches to including women in history—and with different results. Mary Kay Thompson Tetreault describes five stages in doing women's history: male-defined history, contribution history, bifocal history, histories of women, and histories of gender. The final stage calls for "a multifocal, relational, gender balanced perspective . . . that weaves together women's and men's experiences into multilayered composites of human experience."[29] The approaches to women's history that are least critical of traditional, androcentric history and are the least transformative, are Tetreault's contribution phase, or what Gerda Lerner has defined as "compensatory" and "contributory" history.[30]

Compensatory history studies "women worthies" (Lerner's term), those women who left written evidence of their individual achievements and whose breakthroughs in the public sphere often did not differ significantly in kind from those of men—leaders of labor unions, for example, or the first woman to go to medical college. Such women can be found through traditional historical sources and tools. Contributory history is another form of "we, too" history, emphasizing what women have done, typically under the constraint of male domination within household structures and the larger economy, society, and polity. Emphasizing women's agency, contributory history may focus on notable individual women or on women acting collectively. In the latter case, traditional sources may yield new information about women that earlier scholars overlooked. Some histories emphasize women as victims, dissecting the structures and processes that restrained and limited their activity. Finally, the most difficult task is that of writing transformative women's history in which the fundamental understanding of a period (or periodization) is reshaped by taking women into account. The difference between contribution and transformation is the difference between "add women and stir" and reconceptualizing history.[31]

It is possible to illustrate these different types of women's history by examining events in southeastern Nigeria in the late nineteenth and early twentieth centuries. Omu Okwei (1872–1943) is a good candidate for a worthy woman characteristic of compensatory history.[32] She amassed a fortune trading European imported goods for palm products by using a vast network of female pawns and traders in the hinterland. She wielded considerable power and legitimate authority, although certain indigenous cultural and structural features constrained her activities and those of other female traders. Among the Igbo ethnic group in southern Nigeria along the Niger delta, women could rise to occupy the position of *omu* (the office held by a woman), who controlled the markets where women traded and adjudicated disputes among women. In contrast to her limited authority, however, the male officeholder, the *obi*, had authority over the entire society, both women and men. (And when the British conquered the territory, they salaried the obi and let the omu's authority atrophy.)[33]

Historians find evidence of "victimhood," inequality, in other realms besides the comparative scope of the obi and omu's authority. Both men and women could buy titles that signified their success and influence, but because women moved to their husbands' villages when they married, men were more likely to wield influence within the patrilineally defined village. Nonetheless, women exercised agency collectively through an institution called "sitting on a man" in which the women of a village would, by singing insults, collectively sanction a man who had broken behavioral rules that both women and men agreed upon.[34]

Moving into contributory history, we find the "Women's War of 1929," which affirmed that women, too, challenged colonial authorities.[35] In 1929, protesting a rumored extension of men's hut tax to women as well, upward of ten thousand women protested in southeastern Nigeria. Drawing on their networks as traders, wives within patrilineal villages, and members of their own natal patrilineages, women congregated at district towns where they "sat on" local African warrant chiefs. These warrant chiefs were men appointed by the British colonial authorities to collect taxes and carry out other colonial administrative tasks. In sitting on the warrant chiefs, the women translated the institution of sitting on a man into an anticolonial expression. (They also had specific complaints against a particular warrant chief who had sexually harassed some women.)

How does knowing about the Women's War change our understanding of Nigerian history? By the 1960s these events had entered the traditional historiography as triggering a "reform" in British colonial policy in Nigeria. From women's perspective, however, the changes did not signal unambiguous improvement. The Igbo and Ibibio of the southeastern region of Nigeria, unlike the Igbo of the Niger delta, had no indigenous institution of chiefship; hence the colonial-appointed warrant chiefs were seen as illegitimate. In the wake of the women's demonstration, the Colonial Office authorized a complete study of the situation and adopted recommendations to withdraw warrant chiefs and put in their place councils of elders who ran local courts. In removing the illegitimate and abusive warrant chiefs, the "reforms" benefited women as colonized individuals and, to some extent, as women because women were allowed to play a role in selecting these elders, and a few women even served on the courts. The new policies, however, also outlawed the sanction of "sitting on a man," instructing women instead to direct their complaints to the male-dominated courts for adjudication. In fact, from the perspective of women, this "reform" represented a diminution of women's collective power and authority. Although it is not transformative in terms of our approach to history overall, a feminist reading of the Women's War challenges the traditional interpretation of its aftermath as "reform."[36]

If we examine the language used to describe these events, we see the manipulation of meaning. The Igbo, Ibibio, and other ethnic groups in the region refer to the uprising as the "Women's War of 1929." British colonial authorities, however, called the events the "Aba Riots" after one of the towns, thereby both removing women's agency and delegitimating the action, "riots" being out-of-control, illegitimate events.[37]

One can examine these same events and this region historically in terms of gender and gender identity, not just in terms of women as historical actors. Indeed, Caroline Ifeka-Moller sees the Women's War as resulting when "local, short-term events (in particular the introduction of taxation for women) exacerbated a long-term and general contradiction that had developed between the way women saw themselves as producers and reproducers."[38] In the forty to fifty years before the 1929 war, women had made economic gains; over all, they were generating and controlling cash from the sale of palm oil. Their gains exceeded those of men, who still controlled land and labor.

The vigor of women's economic roles as producers, however, contradicted their continuing subordinate position within the gender ideology, which stressed gender complementarity while manifesting inequality in terms of formal authority. Moreover, the women perceived that their fertility was declining. Examining the symbolism used in the protest, Ifeka-Moller notes the presence of sexual and reproductive symbolism among the protestors, some of whom were naked or wore vegetation and whose gestures were reported in the subsequent inquiry to be "obscene." The basis of women's solidarity was their reproductive role, and the protest capped a decade of concern about women's declining fertility. The protestors, Ifeka-Moller argues, "expressed the conscious fear that they were becoming 'as men' in the language of reproduction which was associated with the female body and the land. They feared that they were becoming infertile, that more of their children died than in olden times, and that the land itself was 'dying.'"[39]

The study of this region illuminates complexities of gender that are absent in Euro-American society. In Igbo society, Ifi Amadiume argues, "The fact that biological sex did not always correspond to ideological gender meant that women could play roles usually monopolized by men, or be classified as 'males' in terms of power and authority over others. As such roles were not rigidly masculinized or feminized, no stigma was attached to breaking gender rules."[40] Thus, there existed "male daughters," for example, female members of a patrilineage who would occupy the necessary male ritual role in a lineage if there were no living son to do so.[41]

Moreover, the Igbo (and ethnic groups in other parts of Africa) had (and continue to have) the role of "female husband" in the practice of woman-woman marriage.[42] In that institution, a wealthy woman marries another woman, who conceives children via a male lover. The female husband married a wife by doing what male husbands did, namely paying bridewealth. Bridewealth is goods and/or money paid to a bride's family to compensate for the loss of their daughter's labor and to gain rights to children born to a husband and wife. The children belong to the female husband, who is thereby able to start her own lineage and pass on her wealth to her children rather than marrying a man and losing her autonomy and rights to her biological children, who would normally belong to her male husband's patrilineage. Woman-woman marriage, which has been examined more from an ethnographic than a historical perspective, doubtless has been affected by economic and ideological forces.

Pressing the analysis of gender even further, Nigerian scholar Oyeronke Oyewumi argues that before the imposition of European categories, "'Woman' as a social category did not exist in Yoruba communities" (the Yoruba occupied the southwestern part of what is now Nigeria). By that she means, "The body was not the basis of social roles, inclusions, or exclusions; it was not the foundation of social thought and identity."[43]

The preceding example addresses gender from the perspective of women. But men and masculinity are equally critical and interesting subjects of gendered history. Conventional military history that studies battles, technology, and diplomacy is a classic example of writing about men without looking at the social construction of gender. Warfare can be more richly understood, however, if gender is considered. Take, for example, the Dakota War of 1862 in present-day Minnesota. In 1862, in the midst of the U.S. Civil War, some Dakota bands began a war against white settlers. Their reasons for doing so generally are given as the tardiness of annuity payments, starvation due to poor harvests and hunting, and the perceived weakness of Union forces after a series of costly battles.

Historians of gender history might include other causes as well. One of Jerome Big Eagle's reasons for going to war, he said in an 1894 interview, was that the U.S. government had tried to stop the conflict between the Dakota and the Ojibwae, in which young men could gain recognition for bravery.[44] More traditional Dakota men may have been particularly eager to show their courage because, in the summer of 1862, a group of mixed-blood "cut hair" Dakota had enlisted in the Union Army as the Renville Rangers. Just four days after the Rangers left for the front, the Dakota War began. Although the Rangers' departure left a "security vacuum" in the Minnesota River Valley, it also seemed to shift core Dakota male values as warriors to a group formerly accused of being mere "farmers": Christianized males reluctant to pursue traditional warfare. The soldier society within the Dakota became, under the somewhat reluctant leadership of Little Crow, the driving force to reclaim not only Dakota lands but also their warrior identity.

The Dakota conflict was in many ways an intimate war. Both commanders sent to put down the Dakota, Henry H. Sibley and Alfred Sully, had in their early lives been involved with Dakota women. The commanders represented a generation of fur traders and army officers who had often partnered with Indian women. The Renville Rangers included many mixed-blood sons of these alliances, particularly with French fur traders. Later, as fur trade diminished and more white women came to Minnesota, connections to Indian families became less an asset. Further, some whites came to turn their backs on their Indian children and relatives, a violation of another part of the Dakota male's responsibility to family welfare. One of the first men killed in the war, Andrew Myrick, had been involved with a Dakota woman; his abandonment of her and their children, especially in such harsh times, made him a likely target for Dakota anger.

Gender roles also played a part in the way Dakota and white women related to each other. Taken captive, such mixed-blood women as Nancy McClure Huggan often reestablished ties with their Dakota relatives. Some of the traditional values of Dakota women were to farm, harvest rice, gather fruit, and share their collected food supplies with those in need. Accounts taken from captive white women describe such sharing and the protection Dakota women gave in moderating Dakota warrior anger against whites. The accounts of Snana, a Dakota woman, and German immigrant Mary Schwandt also testify to the lasting friendships that also occurred in the midst of war.[45]

Nonetheless, many Dakota women supported the war. They made bullets, carried supplies, and were present at battles to act as "quartermasters." White males, however, did not consider them as combatants. Thirty-eight male Dakota were hanged and 303 shipped to Davenport, Iowa, for imprisonment, but Dakota women faced a different sort of tragedy. The forced removal of most to winter encampment at Fort Snelling, and then from the fertile Minnesota River Valley to Crow Creek and the harsh plains of South Dakota, was a trek mainly made by women and children. Casualties from disease, exposure, and despair were considerable, estimated at more than three hundred Dakota women. One of Good Star Woman's most vivid memories of the journey concerned the angry white women whom the group encountered when they passed through New Ulm, Minnesota, which had been hard-hit by the war.[46] White soldiers' accounts also mention the "harridans" they had to subdue to protect the Dakota as their wagons went through the town.

The reactions of women in New Ulm illustrate how formerly quiet homemakers could react to the killing of settlers and family members. About a hundred white women were killed in the war and others were raped, acts white society viewed as particularly chilling violations of "civilized" warfare. Some women made bullets for the soldiers at Fort Ridgely and helped in defense; several had terrible stories of survival, both from attack and from scrounging food for themselves and their children.[47]

White women could look to reestablishing their former lives, but Dakota and other Sioux women faced years of anguish, resettlement, and the thirty-year Plains War. Such considerations complicate our understanding of women and gender, women's history, and gender history. Teachers, however, must select and simplify in order to make history comprehensible. We now turn to the task of simplifying—indeed, oversimplifying—that same understanding.

Integrating Women and Gender into World History

Just as women's and gender history have developed as fields, so, too, has world history.[48] The "old," Eurocentric world history gave way to a "world studies" approach that stressed contemporary global issues, which itself is being supplanted by the "new" world history that stresses comparative and thematic approaches. But revisions of the world history curriculum are somewhat problematic for women's and gender history. In part the difficulty stems from the fact that historians of women and gender tend to work with individual societies, whereas "new" world historians typically focus on themes that transcend individual societies.[49] This section examines in greater detail some major ways of organizing world history, with some possible advantages and disadvantages of each for women's history or gender history.

THE "OLD" WORLD HISTORY

The "old" world history reflected its roots in, and was often, in effect, the Western civilization course that emerged in the wake of World War I and in the midst of the final stages of European colonialism. Decolonization and cold war competition for the hearts and minds of the people of newly independent former colonies introduced a perceived need to attend to the histories of Africa, Asia, Latin America, and the Middle East. Such scholars as William H. McNeill, Leften Stavrianos, Marshall Hodgson, and Fernand Braudel developed approaches to view the world not merely from a European vantage point.[50] Nonetheless, Peter Steams criticizes the "old" as too Eurocentric and as mainly a history of "the West and the Rest."[51]

Confronted with pressure to include at least women (if not gender), the "old" world history typically adjusted by adding women without changing the narrative. The result has been the insertion of sidebars and photographs of women without a change in the conceptualization of the historical narrative—a quintessential example of "add women and stir."

WORLD STUDIES HISTORY

Generally, world studies as an approach to a world history course focuses on a few "major" cultures or regions and is based on the premise that knowing a few cultures well is better than trying to do "all" of world history (appendix A). In public schools the world studies movement largely began in the 1960s and 1970s, in part as an answer to the charge of Eurocentered world history courses. The "old" history courses were also seen as being so laden with information that teachers never got much past World War I. Therefore, new world studies courses often had a large contemporary issues component, and history was seen as largely informing present circumstances. As with the "New Social Studies" from the University of Chicago that had proponents such as Jerome Bruner, John Patrick, and Thomas Fenton, there was also greater emphasis on inquiry and analysis. The focus on contemporary issues often meant that including women's history was relatively easy; the women's movement of the 1960s and 1970s and the drive for the Equal Right Amendment furnished examples of on-going struggles.

Internationally, issues of genital cutting in Africa, the statistical scarcity of women in India compared to men, and a lack of woman suffrage in such places as Switzerland could all be used as entry points into world studies. Further, because only one area was studied for a quarter or a semester, there was the "luxury" of teaching more "marginal" subjects—such as women. Students could conduct research on one culture using the rich sources developed for women's history in that particular area. For teachers overwhelmed with trying to teach "all the world" and probably having marginal preparation for doing so, a focus on one area meant they could specialize and keep up with one academic field.

Critics of the world studies approach emphasized the lack of global connections, the narrow focus of only a few world regions, and, at times, the neglect of history because courses could tend toward being contemporary problems classes. In addition, the focus on a few cultures was also problematic for women's history. Some instructors using books from the "Women in World Cultures" series produced by the Upper Midwest Women's History Teaching Center, for example, found that footbinding in China seemed so terrible to students that it colored their view of the entire culture. Cross-cultural attention to the ways in which other societies "crippled" women through isolation, tightly laced clothing, or exclusion from education might have given some balance to China's discrimination. Yet regional studies sometimes means identification with a culture and a protective attitude toward it. Issues such as genital cutting for African studies courses and *sati* (the ritual self-immolation of widows) for courses on India were sometimes resisted by teachers who wished to present the "best" side of the foreign culture being taught. Given that only a few world cultures would be part of a student's experience, the necessity for encouraging a positive worldview sometimes came at odds with the realities of women's historical experiences.[52]

THE "NEW" WORLD HISTORY: COMPARATIVE, THEMATIC, AND INTEGRATIVE

The field of world history is undergoing a major shift, as the title of Ross Dunn's text declares: *The New World History*.[53] The "old" world history has been described by WHA Past President Heidi Roupp as a "parade of cultures," a series of segregated "forests." Instead of these courses, she termed the "new" world history an "ecosystem." Much as U.S. history is not a state-by-state curriculum but an integrated U.S. history, so world history, she argued, should involve comparative points of contact and focus on interregional movements.[54]

Comparison has emerged as a useful teaching device and analytic tool for world history (appendix B). Pedagogically, comparative study can underscore key variables in the development of historically common and important structures and processes, for example, slavery, industrialization, state formation, or colonialism. Also the domain of historical sociologists, comparative analysis across disparate regions and periods involves a methodology that demands "the systematic selection of case examples and the mastery of the historical materials relevant to each of these."[55] For example, Louise A. Tilly, who compares Britain, France, Germany, the United States, Japan, and China, sets as her task "to compare both patterns of large-scale structural change and social groups at the micro level, seeking regularities in variation of the forms of gender inequality as they are articulated with the process of industrialization." She admonishes that "such comparisons must take history seriously, examining the ways in which what happens at one point in time may constrain what comes after."[56]

Asking comparative questions can generate new areas of research on the one hand and make more manageable the vast array of information to be covered in a world history course on the other. In this approach gender may be one of the variables analyzed (as in, for example, changes in women's and men's roles and in constructions of femininity or masculinity), or the comparative question may address women's experiences directly. Two major books that use these thematic approaches are Peter Stearns's *Gender in World History* (2000) and Merry E. Wiesner-Hanks's *Gender in History* (2001). Stearns is more concerned with sweeping historical themes: "Westernization and Gender" and "The Chinese Influence." Wiesner-Hanks, however, uses more sociological analysis, beginning with "The Family" and exploring cultural universals such as politics, economics, and education.

In addition to employing comparative analysis, practitioners of the "new" world history focus on selected organizing themes, perhaps trade, disease, cultural diffusion, or citizenship. The issue becomes how to fit women into them. An instructor doing trade and the early Silk Road, for example, could select histories of women from various societies along the route. Looking at the supplying societies, students could explore women's central role in producing silk, whether feeding mulberry leaves to worms, gently unraveling the cocoons, or organizing textile workshops. Often such female rulers as seventh-century C.E. Queen Sondok of Korea or Empress Wu of China were instrumental in encouraging silk production. On the consumption side of the equation, as Pliny complained, Roman women were wearing see-through garments that "render women naked" and straining the economy of Rome with their desire for silk.[57] Between the producers and consumers were the women of Central Asia, who not only produced many of the foodstuffs, such as cheese, that kept caravans going but also fabricated other trade goods, such as rugs. Traders who set out for the deserts of Central Asia encountered shrines to the Chinese goddess Guan-Yin, established by women rulers to give good fortune on the perilous trips. Using such a global theme as trade, an instructor can highlight women's participation in major events.

But, as Sarah S. Hughes points out, if gender is not one of the major themes at the heart of the course, women are difficult to "'add and stir' . . . into an impersonal batter.'"[58] More recent scholarship, for example, has suggested that exogamy, marrying women out of the kinship unit, was a factor on the Silk Road. The use of women as an "exportable commodity" to fashion alliances is an old trading practice, although perhaps most notable in the "women's tribute" the Mongols forced on countries such as Korea. But to understand how women became so "exportable," students also need to understand Confucian values, class, and nationalistic circumstance. Further, it may not be in trading statistics that students find a sense of reality of the silk trade but rather in poetry. Here is Qian Tao's eleventh-century C.E. poem "Written at a Party Where My Lord Gave Away a Thousand Bolts of Silk":

> A bolt of silk for each clear toned song
> Still these beauties do not think it is enough
> Little do they know of a weaving girl
> Sitting cold by her window
> Endlessly throwing her shuttle to and fro.[59]

Although the poem could be included in a general discussion of the silk trade, without Hughes's insistence on "gender as a base," the more likely prospect is of an emphasis on the ruggedness of male travelers' lives on the road. Further, without a sense of the complexity of women's roles in China, students would be unlikely to understand that the poet's criticism of the "beauties" does not take into account their own entrapment as entertainers of rich men. The use of global themes provides a clearer framework for students, but it is often the poetry of specifics that brings them meaning (appendix C).

One problem in integrating women into the "new" world history is that the major themes chosen may impact men and women differently. Although women's roles in warfare increasingly are being documented, a focus on battle formation, generalship, and the creation of military weapons might limit the time allotted to women's history. The use of vernacular language and growth of literacy, however, is not generally a major focus in world history. In the transition from court languages of the largely male elite—such as Latin, Mandarin, Greek, and classical Arabic—to the vernacular, however, women created an important artistic corner. While eleventh-century C.E. Japanese men, for example, struggled with the strictures of the Chinese literati, Murasaki Shibuku and Sei Shonagon were creating Japanese literary classics.[60] Although there were women like Ban Zhao in China and Hildegaard of Bingen in Europe whose scholarship in the languages of the intellectual elite challenged men of the time, the use of the vernacular meant that ordinary women, over time and in increasing numbers, could become literate, perhaps the most liberating force in challenging notions of their inferior nature. What it means to be literate—and who has access to literacy—is not generally a major theme in world history courses, yet for women's history it would be.

The commitment to social history in the "new" world history is probably more promising for the inclusion of gender issues than the "old," politically oriented world history or "world cultures" had been. In the latter, women were usually relegated to a chapter section entitled "The Family," and questions such as those on nationalism were rarely raised. But, over time, the "parade of cultures" did have the advantage of chapters on the culture itself. Students might connect the early Laws of Manu in India, for example, to later issues of gender discrimination and caste. Instead of seeing Catherine the Great as part of a group of generic enlightened despots, students might puzzle over why almost all eighteenth-century Russia was ruled by women. The long-standing attitudes toward machismo and *marianismo* could be used to understand the ways in which Eva Perón defined herself during the 1950s in Argentina and why the myth continues. In some ways, world studies history, by focusing on separate cultures, mirrors the most accessible ways in which academic fields of research are organized, emphasizing national or area histories.

Although college-level courses in world history are increasing, the kind of syncretic scholarship in women's history that could inform "new" courses is still in beginning stages. The series "Restoring Women to History" from Indiana University Press is promising, but even there the emphasis is on regional rather than thematic women's history.[61] For teachers who use primary source documents, Sarah Shaver Hughes and Brady Hughes's edited two-volume *Women in World History* offers excellent readings, as does *Women Imagine Change,* edited by Eugenia Delmotte, Natania Meeker, and Jean O'Barr.[62] While the Hugheses' book follows more regional and national designation, *Women Imagine Change* provides selections in thematic categories broadly defined, such as "Work and Education" and "Identifying Sources of Resistance."

The explosion of women's and gender history means that an integrative history of women is still in process. It would be much easier for a teacher to find good sources on women in Japan, India, Africa, or Central America than sources for cross-national comparisons of women and nationalism, economics, or religion. Even the issues of woman suffrage, despite Leila Rupp's promising beginning in *Worlds of Women: The Making of an International Women's Movement,* lack the kind of analysis similar to work on the silk trade, or the Columbian exchange, or other economic themes.[63]

PIVOTAL INDIVIDUALS: BIOGRAPHICAL WORLD HISTORY

A focus on the "worthies" of history, male or female, has largely fallen out of fashion. Yet history is often taught to young people who are in the process of reenvisioning themselves. For them, the heroines, heroes, and villains of history are often more intriguing than global themes or "habits of mind." In U.S. history and European history courses, such specific people as Abraham Lincoln, Elizabeth Cady Stanton, Isaac Newton, or Elizabeth I have central roles.

If world history emphasizes themes, systems, and movements, the underlying assumptions students may receive is that the West has individuals whereas the "non-West" has masses.

Although not many history courses have biography as a central organizing principle, the concept does offer ways into women's history that may prove useful. The point is not to view an isolated person but the networks and influences that surround that individual. The benefits of such an approach are to re-engage students in the "story of history" and make issues more vivid. T. S. Eliot discussed the "objective correlative" in poetry—that is, how a specific image becomes a symbol intertwined with all sorts of responses.[64] Teachers have taken Alexander the Great, Akbar, Ghengis Khan, Mao Zedong, or Adolph Hitler as beginning points for the "old" world history. Seeing these individuals in relation to gender issues also puts new slants on their stories. For example, Alexander could hardly have traveled about the world had he not known that his mother, Olympias, and sister, Cleopatra, were keeping an eye on the generals back home. Similarly, in Central Asia the mother of the Khan maintained networks by calling leaders together.

There are also women whose stories spread a wide net over history, such as Elizabeth I of England, Sondok of Korea, Tayto of Ethiopia, and Wu of China (appendix D). A nonroyal person such as Pandita Ramabai of India, however, can also raise a wealth of issues. A nineteenth-century reformer, Ramabai (1858–1922) worked for women's education and the end of child marriage and for better health conditions. A scholar of the Hindu religion, she had strong ties to her country's past although she was also connected to Western reform. Helping to support her financially was a circle of women that in Boston included Julia Ward Howe. As a widow in India, Ramabai's personal life illustrated a single woman's range of choices.[65] Her example, of course, cannot tell us everything about Indian women, although her life may provide the sort of "objective correlative" that makes issues lastingly memorable.

The limitations of focusing on a relatively few people in history are significant, and it takes a very skillful educator to balance major themes with illustrative individuals. Yet this way of entering world history has the advantage of easier accessibility to students, a concrete focus on specific women, and the treatment of individual people as ends in themselves rather than a means to understand trade, expansion, nationalism, or imperialism. The guidelines for the new advanced-placement world history course identify information that students should know but do not need for the test, for example "women's emancipation movements but not specific suffragists." What a loss not to become acquainted with such feisty women as Alexandra Kollantai (Russian), Huda Sharawi (Egyptian), Ichikawa Fusae (Japanese), Halide Edip (a Turk), Emmaline Pankhurst (English), or Susan B. Anthony (from the United States).

The way in which world history courses are organized has bearing on the ease of including women's and gender history. Gender history, with its emphasis on systems and analysis, may fit the "new" world history more easily than women's history. But there may be ways of handling a course to take advantage of the attributes of different kinds of history. Instructors may take a "rest" to do three weeks on one culture, discussing, for example, the importance of women in Muhammad's family as role models for later Muslim women. They include Khadijah, his first wife, a trader who financially supported his work, and 'A'ishah, his youngest and favorite wife, whose reports of the Prophet's words and actions helped build the key foundational texts in Islamic law and practice and who helped organize political opposition to the caliph Ali. Fatimah, Muhammad's daughter and wife of Ali, is venerated by Shiis. In the period of warring factions following Muhammed's death, the courage of Zaynab, Fatimah's and Ali's daughter, led her to be claimed later as a model by Iranian women's organizations.[66]

Pivotal women such as Malinche, Hernan Cortes's translator, political informant, and guide in the conquest of the Aztecs, and Ines Suarez, whose participation in the conquest of the New World included donning armor to save the Spanish settlement of Santiago in present-day Chile from Indian attacks, furnish fine topics for historiographical analysis on the issue of Spanish colonialism.[67]

Questions to Consider from a Gender History and Women's History Perspectives

The following represent some of the questions instructors might ask themselves before organizing a history course that has to accomplish so much, either in incorporating women and/or gender into world history or in internationalizing a women's or gender history course. What approach to world history makes it easier to include women's or gender history? If I choose a style that presents problems for bringing in women and/or gender, how will I compensate? Will some themes prove more promising for women's history than others? Is a chronology for women's issues different than for men's? Is it different for some areas of the world more than others? Who are the students in the class? What sort of history will they have had, and what sort can I offer to expand their sense of history? What kind of resources can my students and I expect to find to add new perspectives to a world history course? How will I best do gender history or women's history? How can material on men's roles be used in the same sort of analytical ways as for women's roles? Will gender be equated with "family" and abstract "roles"? How will testing affect the way I teach—or should it?

The answers to these questions will be determined by individual teachers, but knowing the questions will enable those teachers to anticipate problems and develop strategies to address them.

A Women's History Chronology

What follows is a brief, and tentative, chronology that may suggest some organizing themes for a world history course. There can, of course, be many other ways that emphasize a thematic approach. But the aim of this chronology is to suggest that teachers sit down and develop their own set of themes based on gender issues parallel to those developed by other thematic formulas. Constructing such a chronology may help engender the familiar narrative and keep the "big themes" from engulfing what really needs to be said about women.

Generally, the currently accepted chronology for world history, based on national standards and other sources, follows the following pattern:

1. Rise of Civilizations to 1000 B.C.E.
2. Creation of Empires: 1000 B.C.E. to 500 C.E.
3. Development of Interregional Contacts: 500 to 1450 C.E.
4. Rise of the West and the Transformation of World Trade: 1450 to 1918.
5. Emergence of the Contemporary World: 1918 to the Present.

Within these eras, the following suggests topics that integrate women and/or gender:

1. Rise of Civilizations to 1000 B.C.E.
   a. Agricultural revolution: women; neolithic farming; property laws.
   b. Rise of political elites: ruling families access to power; Hatshepsut of Egypt; Ku-Bau of Sumer; Puduhepa of the Hittites.
   c. Segregation of gender roles: women in textiles; household economies.
   d. Religion: female deities as showing diversity of women's attributes or power; gendered roles of women and men as religious leaders.
   e. Arts versus craft division (i.e., architecture vs. quilt making).

2. Creation of Empires: 1000 B.C.E. to 500 C.E.
   a. Military; wars; slavery (kidnapping of women weavers, farmers).
   b. Imperial family support networks: Hellenistic queens; trading partners.
   c. Rise of cultural diffusion, religious conversion: Isis cult; shamans.
   d. Economics: early silk trade; women in local markets; weaving.
   e. "Golden Ages" solidification of attitudes, often negative, toward women: Laws of Manu (India); Confucianism (China); Solon (Greece).

3. Development of Interregional Contacts: 500 to 1450 C.E.
   a. Women as cultural ambassadors: Olga; Christianity to Russia; Toltec/Aztec marriages; Ottoman *valides* (the sultan's mother).
   b. Rise of literacy: women's various roles as vernacular writers (Murasaki [Japan] and Al-Akhana [Arabia]); women as "enlightened" rulers (Queen Sondok [Korea] and Eleanor of Aquitaine).
   c. Displacement: from subsistence to cash-crop economy
   d. Disease: Black Death and women.
   e. Religious dissent and leadership: women as heretics, witches, saints, or defenders of faith (Muslim Sufi saint Rabiah al-Adadawiyyah).

4. Rise of the West, Colonialism, and the Transformation of World Trade: 1450 to 1918.
   a. Cultural views of women imposed on other nations.
   b. Economics: industrialization (women's textile production as producing "take off eras" [Japan, U.S., Russia]); gendered transformation of subsistence economies with the introduction of cash crops.
   c. Immigration: women as preservers of culture.
   d. Educational shifts: women writers producing for women audiences.
   e. Democratic ideas: citizenship; suffrage; nationalism; revolution.

5. Emergence of the Modern World: 1918 to the Present.
   a. Self-determination: women in nationalist movements.
   b. Global links among women: suffrage; peace; missionary reform; League of Nations.
   c. Personal defined as political: redefining the family; issues of domestic violence; sexual abuse.
   d. Labor and the shift to a market economy: "outside home."
   e. War: civilian casualties outnumber military in World War I and II; political and economic mobilization of women.

If the emphasis on systems and global themes represents the future of world history, it is increasingly important that historians of women and gender think through what sort of emphasis should be made.

Conclusion

Historians face myriad challenges in conceptualizing each of the major subjects of this essay: gender history, women's history, and world history. Gender (along with age) is a fundamental organizing principle of human society. All societies, past and present, have recognized and differentiated women from men (and some have identified additional genders). The task of a historian of gender is to identify what meanings, roles, and statuses attach to different genders; what constitutes gender identity in a particular place and time; the salience of gender as a factor in people's lives; and how constructions of gender change over time. Also explaining change, historians of women identify the constraints and opportunities that women encounter and demonstrate the variety of meanings, roles, and statuses assigned to the female gender, mindful that such other identities as nationality or religion interact with being a woman and may at times be more salient. Historians of the world who care about women and gender must make pedagogical sense while respecting both the particularities and patterns of historical events and encounters. Historians who seek to cover the globe and significant, large expanses of time, whether or not they are world historians or women's/gender historians, must posit meaningful periodization and identify compelling principles for the inclusion and exclusion of data.

These challenges are daunting. In the College Board booklet describing the advanced-placement world history test, the inclusion of women's history is shown in the sample documents test with a series of excerpts on the topic of women and nationalism. The selections of these documents enforce the comparative emphasis of the "new" world history. Selections include ones on Mannohine Zutshi Saghal (India), Sung Ching-Ling (China), Huda Sharawi (Egypt), Teodora Igancia Gomes (Guinea Bissau), and Marie Aimee Helia-Lucas (Algeria) in roughly the period from 1920 to 1950. The question asked about these documents is, "Has the rise of nationalistic movements and the modern nation state broadened or restricted women's political and economic participation and social freedoms?"[68]

The question is certainly a significant one. A student taking the test, however, faces a very difficult task: five different revolutions on two continents and three points of analysis (economic, political, and social views). Ironically, the advanced-placement test may ask tenth- and eleventh-graders to do what few, if any, academic historians have done across major geographic regions: provide an integrated, cross-cultural and cross-national analysis of whether and how women have benefited from the rise of the modern nation state and from nationalism.

For younger audiences, particularly those in kindergarten through the sixth grade, contributory, narrative history is more the norm. One of the best models for serious women's history and the use of role models to engage students is the *Young Oxford History of Women in the United States,* edited by Nancy Cott.[69] Unfortunately, there is not yet a similar series for world history, although Cobblestone Publishing Company's *Calliope Magazine* deals with world history topics for young children. Although women appear frequently in these and there are separate issues on some notable women, this is not the integrative "new" world history.[70]

Few have thought through what a kindergarten through graduate school world and gender history curriculum might be. Where might it be best to teach about the struggles of women of color? Are some cultures more telling in showing the diversity of women's lives? How soon can curriculum on women and religion be introduced? Instead of a somewhat arbitrary fitting women into national history standards, what would a curriculum on women's history contain—and when and why?

In the rush to create an academic field of women's and gender history, there has been less attention to the ways in which the scholarship is actually used. The National Women's History Project (NWHP) has been a leader in providing materials and workshops for teachers to speed new scholarship into the curriculum.[71] But the major focus of the NWHP is U.S. history. The Upper Midwest Women's History Center for Teachers produced a Women in World Area Studies series directed at high school students but useful to teachers of lower grades who wish to develop their own materials. The center closed in 1999, however. The CLIO Project, a new Internet source, will continue to distribute lessons on women and world history. A more ambitious project, funded in 2003 by the National Endowment for the Humanities, is "Women, World History, and the Web," located at George Mason University. Part of the Center for History and the New Media Web site (http://www.chnm.gmu.edu/chnm), it will include lesson plans, documents, bibliographies, and scholarly essays for students and educators.

World history teachers who wish to address women and gender in a meaningful way, and historians of women and gender who seek to do cross-regional or comparative analyses, face similar but not identical challenges. Each must strive for meaningful levels of generalization without doing injustice to historical specificities. A dialog between world historians and historians of women and gender can be fruitful. Louise Tilly calls upon historians of women to "make their methodology more analytical on its own terms and to show how their results contribute to the explanation of other, more general problems either already on the historical agenda or readily understandable in terms of central historical concepts."[72] In turn, Jerry H. Bentley, editor of the *Journal of World History* and author of a world history textbook, notes that "methods and insights from women's history and gender analysis hold unusual promises for global historical studies."[73] From such a dialog will come better women's history, gender history, and world history.

Notes

We thank Jerry Bentley, Bonnie Smith, Mary Todd, Judith Zinsser, and the participants in Bonnie Smith's 2000 NEH summer institute for their comments on earlier drafts of this essay. Maria Teresa Fernandez Aceves provided information and sources for Sor Juana.

1. Ross E. Dunn, ed., *The New World History: A Teacher's Companion* (Boston: St. Martin's Press, 2000), 14, citing Lawrence Levine, *The Opening of the American Mind* (Boston: Beacon Press: 1996).

2. For insight into the relationship of personal experience and politics to the development of the field of women's history, see "Introduction: Standpoints on Hard Ground," in *Voices of Women Historians: The Personal, the Political, the Professional*, ed. Eileen Boris and Nupur Chaudhuri (Bloomington: Indiana University Press, 1999), xi–xx. Darlene Clark Hine describes how teachers and members of the local chapter of the National Council of Negro Women challenged her to write about the history of African American women in Indiana. "Editor's Preface," in *Black Women in America: An Historical Encyclopedia*, ed. Darlene Clark Hine (Brooklyn: Carlson, 1993), xix–xi. See also Bonnie G. Smith, *The Gender of History: Men, Women, and Historical Practice* (Cambridge: Harvard University Press, 1998).

3. Martin Duberman, *Cures: A Gay Man's Odyssey* (New York: Penguin, 1991), chronicles the emerging gay consciousness of a historian. See also *Hidden from History: Reclaiming the Gay and Lesbian Past*, ed. Martin Baml Duberman, Martha Vicinus, and George Chauncey Jr. (New York: New American Library, 1989); John D'Emilio, *Making Trouble: Essays on Gay History, Politics, and the University* (New York: Routledge, 1992); and John D'Emilio and Estelle B. Freedman, *Intimate Matters: A History of Sexuality in America* (1988, repr. Chicago: University of Chicago Press, 1997).

4. For elaboration in a U.S. context, see *Engendering America: A Documentary History, 1865 to the Present*, ed. Sonya Michel and Robyn Muncy (Boston: McGraw-Hill, 1999), 1–7.

5. For a thorough discussion of biological research on gender and sex that argues against gender dualism, see Anne Fausto-Sterling, *Sexing the Body: Gender Politics and the Construction of Sexuality* (New York: Basic Books, 2000).

6. Dunn, ed., *The New World History: A Teacher's Companion*, 2–4 and parts 1–3 traces the development of the field.

7. Gilbert Allardyce, "Toward World History: American Historians and the Coming of the World History Course," in *The New World History*, ed. Ross E. Dunn (Boston: St. Martin's Press, 2000), 26.

8. This exclusive teaching emphasis is changing. The World History Association (WHA) has sponsored sessions at professional conferences on world history as a research area. See http://www.thewha.org.

9. National Center for History in the Schools, *National Standards for World History: Exploring Paths to the Present* (Los Angeles: University of California, Los Angeles, 1994; rev. ed. 1996), see also http://www.sscnet.ucla.edu/nchs/guide.html.

10. Carter Vaughn Findley, "The World History Association," *Perspectives* 37 (Dec. 1999): 14.

11. The leadership of the WHA is firmly committed to integrating women and gender into world history. Dunn, ed., *The New World History: A Teacher's Companion*, contains a section on women and gender, including two excerpts by Judith Zinsser, a former WHA president. *Journal of World History* editor Jerry Bentley's essay in Dunn (562–63) notes the importance of women's and gender history for comparative and cross-cultural analyses.

12. For a useful survey of the development of women's and gender history, see Manuela Thurner, "Subject to Change: Theories and Paradigms of U.S. Feminist History," *Journal of Women's History* 9 (Summer 1997): 122–46.

13. Scholars and amateur historians wrote about women before the rise of women's history as a field in the 1960s. Examples include Mauriel Joy Hughes, *Women Healers in Medieval Life and Literature* (New York: King's Crown Press, 1943); Eileen Power, *Medieval English Nunneries* (Cambridge: Cambridge University Press, 1922); Dorothy

Gardiner, *English Girlhood at School* (London: Oxford University Press, 1929); Ellen McArthur, "Women Petitioners and the Long Parliament," *English Historical Review* (1909); Annie Abram, "Women Traders in Medieval London," *Economic Journal* (1916); Marian Dale, "The London Silkwoman of the Fifteenth Century," *Economic History* (1933); Lina Eckenstein, *Woman under Monasticism* (1896); Dorothy Whitelock, *Anglo-Saxon Wills* (Cambridge: Cambridge University Press, 1930); Annie Forbes Busch, *Memoirs of the Queens of France* (Philadelphia: Cary and Hart, 1847); Doris Stenton, *The English Woman in History* (1947, repr. New York: Macmillan, 1957); Nabia Abbott, *Two Queens of Baghdad* (1946, repr. London: Al Saqi, 1986) and *Aishah* (1942, repr. London: Al Saqi, 1985); D. Amaury Talbot, *Women's Mysteries of a Primitive People* (1915, repr. London: Cass, 1968); Lydia Maria Child, *The History of the Condition of Women* (Boston: J. Allen, 1835); Mary Agnes Cannon, *The Education of Women during the Renaissance* (1916, repr. Westport: Hyperion Press, 1981); Elizabeth Aldridge, *These Splendid Women* (New York: J. H. Sears, 1926); and Grace Macurdy, *Vassal-Queens and Some Contemporary Women in the Roman Empire* (Baltimore: Johns Hopkins University Press, 1937).

14. Reflecting these developments, the women's caucus of the American Historical Association was founded in 1969 and named the Coordinating Committee on Women in the Historical Profession/Conference Group on Women's History. Judith P. Zinsser, *History and Feminism: A Glass Half Full* (New York: Twayne, 1993); Hilda Smith et al., *A History of the Coordinating Committee on Women in the Historical Profession—Conference Group on Women's History* (Chicago: Self-published by CCWHP-CGWH, 1994).

15. Zinsser, *History and Feminism*, 23.

16. See, for example, the "sex gender system" in Gayle Rubin, "The Traffic in Women: Notes on the 'Political Economy' of Sex," in *Feminism and History*, ed. Joan Wallach Scott (1975, repr. New York: Oxford University Press, 1996), 105–51.

17. Joan Kelly, "The Social Relations of the Sexes: Methodological Implications of Women's History," reprinted in *Women, History and Theory*, ed. Joan Kelly (Chicago: University of Chicago Press, 1984), 1–18; Natalie Zemon Davis, "'Women's History' in Transition: The European Case," reprinted in *Feminism and History*, ed. Joan Wallach Scott (New York: Oxford University Press, 1996), 79–104.

18. Joan Wallach Scott, "Gender: A Useful Category of Historical Analysis," in *Feminism and History*, ed. Joan Wallach Scott (New York: Oxford University Press, 1996), 167–69.

19. Chandra Mohanty, "Under Western Eyes: Feminist Scholarship and Colonial Discourses," in *Third World Women*, ed. Chandra Talpade Mohanty, Ann Russo, and Lourdes Torres (Bloomington: Indiana University Press, 1991), 51–80.

20. Joan Wallach Scott, introduction to *Feminism and History*, ed. Joan Wallach Scott (New York: Oxford University Press, 1996), 5.

21. See Robert Morrell, "Of Boys and Men: Masculinity and Gender in Southern African Studies," *Journal of Southern African Studies* 24 (1998): 605–30, for an excellent survey of masculinity studies in general as well as in the context of Southern Africa, and R. W. Connell, "The Big Picture: Masculinities in Recent World History," *Theory and Society* 22 (1993): 597–623. See also a review essay, Anna Davin, "Historical Masculinities: Regulation, Fantasy and Empire," *Gender and History* 9 (April 1997): 135–38; and Judith Kegan Gardiner, ed., *Masculinity Studies and Feminist Theory: New Directions* (New York: Columbia University Press, 2002).

22. Scott, "Gender," 169.

23. Ibid., 170–71.

24. Louise A. Tilly, "Gender, Women's History, and Social History," *Social Science History* 13 (Winter 1989): 452.

25. Boris and Chaudhuri, "Introduction."

26. Karen Offen, Ruth Roach Pierson, and Jane Rendall, eds., *Writing Women's History: International Perspectives* (Bloomington: Indiana University Press, 1991), xx–xxvii.

27. Offen, Pierson, and Rendall, eds., *Writing Women's History: International Perspectives,* xxxiv. The following articles appear in the same volume: Francisca de Haan, "Women's History behind the Dykes: Reflections on the Situation in the Netherlands" (259–77), Jane Rendall, "Uneven Developments: Women's History, Feminist History, and Gender History in Great Britain" (45–57), and Ruth Roach Pierson, "Experience, Difference, Dominance and Voice in the Writing of Canadian Women's History" (79–106).

28. Gisela Bock, "Challenging Dichotomies: Perspectives on Women's History," in *Writing Women's History: International Perspectives,* ed. Karen Offen, Ruth Roach Pierson, and Jane Rendall (Bloomington: Indiana University Press, 1991), 9.

29. Mary Kay Thompson Tetreault, "Rethinking Women, Gender, and the Social Studies," *Social Education* 51 (March 1987): 173.

30. Gerda Lerner, *The Majority Finds Its Past: Placing Women in History* (New York: Oxford University Press, 1979), 145–46.

31. Tilly calls upon historians of women to "make their methodology more analytical on its own terms and to show how their results contribute to the explanation of other, more general problems either already on the historical agenda or readily understandable in terms of central historical concepts" ("Gender, Women's History, and Social History," 447).

32. Felicia Ifeoma Ekejiuba, "Omu Okwei of Osomari," in *Nigerian Women in Historical Perspective,* ed. Bolanle Awe (Lagos/Ibadan, Nigeria: Sankore/Bookcraft, 1992), 89–104.

33. Kamene Okonjo, "The Dual-Sex Political System in Operation: Igbo Women and Community Politics in Midwestern Nigeria," in *Women in Africa: Studies in Social and Economic Change,* ed. Nancy Hafkin and Edna Bay (Stanford: Stanford University Press, 1976), 45–58.

34. Judith Van Allen, "'Aba Riots' or Igbo Women's War? Ideology, Stratification, and the Invisibility of Women," in *Women in Africa: Studies in Social and Economic Change,* ed. Nancy Hafkin and Edna Bay (Stanford: Stanford University Press, 1976), 59–86.

35. This episode was one of the few places in which women could be found in African historiography in the late 1960s. Material in this paragraph comes from Van Allen, "'Aba Riots,'" and Nina E. Mba, "Heroines of the Women's War," in *Nigerian Women in Historical Perspective,* ed. Bolanle Awe (Lagos and Ibadan, Nigeria: Sankore/Bookcraft, 1992), 73–88.

36. Van Allen ("'Aba Riots'") is more critical of the outcome; Mba ("Heroines") stresses what women achieved.

37. Van Allen, "'Aba Riots.'"

38. Caroline Ifeka-Moller, "Female Militancy and Colonial Revolt: The Women's War of 1929, Eastern Nigeria," in *Perceiving Women,* ed. Shirley Ardener (London: J. M. Dent and Sons, 1975), 127.

39. Ifeka-Moller, "Female Militancy," 142.

40. Ifi Amadiume, *Male Daughters, Female Husbands: Gender and Sex in an African Society* (London: Zed Books, 1987), 185.

41. Amadiume, *Male Daughters,* 31–32.

42. Joseph M. Carrier and Stephen O. Murray, "Woman-Woman Marriage in Africa," in *Boy-Wives and Female Husbands: Studies of African Homosexualities,* ed. Stephen O.

Murray and Will Roscoe (Boston: St. Martin's Press, 1998), 255–66. Wairimu Ngaruiya Njambi and William E. O'Brien argue that woman-woman marriage, at least contemporarily, is an option selected not just for reasons of establishing rights to children but also out of affection and to escape male control. "Revisiting 'Woman-Woman Marriage': Notes on Gikuyu Women," *NWSA Journal* 12, no. 1 (2000): 1–23.

43. Oyeronke Oyewumi, *The Invention of Women: Making an African Sense of Western Gender Discourses* (Minneapolis: University of Minnesota Press, 1997), x.

44. Jerome Big Eagle, "A Sioux Story of the War," *Collections of the Minnesota Historical Society* 6 (1894): 382–400.

45. Alan R. Woolworth, "The Significance and Challenge of Camp Release, 1862–87," speech given Sept. 15, 1987, in Alan Woolworth Papers, Minnesota Historical Society.

46. Good Star Woman, "A Sioux Woman's Account of the Uprising," transcript in Frances Densmore Papers, Minnesota Historical Society.

47. The most accessible information on accounts of the Dakota War is in *Through Dakota Eyes*, ed. Gary Clayton Anderson and Alan Woolworth (St. Paul: Minnesota Historical Society, 1988).

48. Allardyce, "Toward World History," describes the early period.

49. We thank Jerry Bentley for this insight.

50. Dunn, ed., *The New World History: A Teacher's Companion*, 2–3.

51. Statements from WHA Past President Heidi Roupp and Peter Steams made at the National Council of Social Studies Conference, AP World History Session, Nov. 16, 1999, Orlando, Fla.

52. Stanlie M. James and Claire C. Robertson, eds., *Genital Cutting and Transnational Sisterhood: Disrupting U.S. Polemics* (Urbana: University of Illinois Press, 2002). Comments from teachers reflect those made in the pilot teaching of "Women in World Area Studies," a Title IV Project of the St. Louis Park and Robbinsdale (Minnesota) schools and subsequent workshops. Upper Midwest Women's History Center Papers, Minnesota Historical Society.

53. Dunn, ed., *The New World History: A Teacher's Companion*. For a discussion of the varieties of the new world history, see Jerry H. Bentley, *Shapes of World History in Twentieth-Century Scholarship* (Washington: American Historical Association, 1996).

54. Statement made at the National Council of Social Studies Conference, AP World History Session, Nov. 19, 1999, Orlando, Fla.

55. Michael Adas, introduction to *Islamic and European Expansion: The Forging of a Global Order*, ed. Michael Adas (Philadelphia: Temple University Press, 1993), ix.

56. Louise A. Tilly, "Industrialization and Gender Inequality," in *Islamic and European Expansion: The Forging of a Global Order*, ed. Michael Adas (Philadelphia: Temple University Press, 1993), 245.

57. Quoted in Peter Hopkirk, *Foreign Devils on the Silk Road* (Amherst: University of Massachusetts Press, 1980), 20–21.

58. Sarah S. Hughes, "Gender at the Base of World History," in *The New World History*, ed. Ross E. Dunn (Boston: St. Martin's Press, 2000), 471.

59. Quoted in Susan Hill Gross and Marjorie Wall Bingham, *Women in Traditional China* (Minneapolis: Glenhurst, 1980), 38.

60. Ramusack and Sievers, *Women in Asia*, 178–81.

61. Iris Berger and E. Frances White, *Women in Sub-Saharan Africa: Restoring Women to History* (Bloomington: Indiana University Press, 1999); Ramusack and Sievers, *Women in Asia;* Navarro and Korrol, *Women in Latin America and the Caribbean;* Guity Nashat and

Judith E. Tucker, *Women in the Middle East and North Africa: Restoring Women to History* (Bloomington: Indiana University Press, 1999).

62. *Women in World History*, ed. Sarah Shaver Hughes and Brady Hughes (Armonk: M. E. Sharpe, 1997); *Women Imagine Change: A Global Anthology of Women's-Resistance from 600 B.C.E. to Present*, ed. Eugenia Delmotte, Natania Meeker, and Jean O'Barr (New York: Routledge, 1997).

63. Leila J. Rupp, *Worlds of Women: The Making of an International Women's Movement* (Princeton: Princeton University Press, 1997).

64. T. S. Eliot, "Hamlet and His Problems," in *The Sacred Wood: Essays on Poetry and Criticism*, ed. T. S. Eliot (London: Methuen, 1920).

65. Ramusack and Sievers, *Women in Asia*, 49; Antoinette Burton, *Burdens of History: British Feminists, Indian Women, and Imperial Culture, 1865–1915* (Chapel Hill: University of North Carolina Press, 1994), passim.

66. Nashat and Tucker, *Women in the Middle East and North Africa*, 34–49.

67. Navarro and Korrol, *Women in Latin America and the Caribbean*, 21–29.

68. College Board, *Advanced Placement Program Course Description: World History* (Princeton: Educational Testing Service, 1999).

69. Nancy Cott, ed., *Young Oxford History of Women in the United States* (New York: Oxford University Press, 1994).

70. Cobblestone Publishing, P.O. Box 9306, La Salle IL 612301, or http://www.cobblestonepub.com/pages/callmain.htm.

71. National Women's History Project, 3343 Industrial Dr., Suite 4, Santa Rosa CA 95403, available at http://www.nwhp.org. (Accessed Nov. 18, 2003.)

72. Tilly, "Gender, Women's History, and Social History," 447.

73. Jerry H. Bentley, "New Directions," in *The New World History: A Teacher's Companion,* ed. Ross E. Dunn (Boston: St. Martin's Press, 2000), 563.

Appendix A. World Studies as an Approach to World History: Female Genital Cutting and Kenyan/Gikuyu Nationalism

Control of women's sexuality is a common feature in many societies, both in the present and historically. Critiques of such practices come from a feminist perspective and, increasingly, from a human rights perspective grounded in the principles of the United Nation's Convention on the Elimination of All Forms of Discrimination against Women (CEDAW). Since the 1990s, the issue of female genital cutting (FGC, also referred to as female genital mutilation, female genital surgery, or female circumcision) has appeared with increasing frequency in the U.S. media, from the *New York Times* to *Marie Claire,* and in novels, films, and medical and legal journals. Rarely is it addressed as a practice with a history (as opposed to current practice) in Africa, although its practice in the United States and Europe during the nineteenth century is noted.

One excellent way to teach about the practice historically is to examine FGC among the Gikuyu (or Kikuyu) of Kenya, formerly a major British colony in Africa. The "female circumcision controversy" played a critical role in Gikuyu nationalism. The missionary criticism of the practice and the nationalist defense of FGC in Kenya during the 1920s and 1930s provide an excellent frame of reference for discussing current debates about the role of external, Western critics of FGC. Many African societies' beliefs about female sexuality did not conform to Christian (especially Victorian and Edwardian Christian) preaching. Puberty initiation rites, for example, often included instructing girls in how to achieve sexual pleasure; some included having an older woman massage the girl's labia to stimulate such pleasure. In Kenya, Gikuyu custom approved of sexual play between young women and men who had been initiated as long as the play did not result in pregnancy; indeed, in oral histories Gikuyu women remark on this period as the best time of their lives. In addition to seeing sexual pleasure as an aspect of femininity, the vast majority of Gikuyu women and men during the colonial period saw clitoridectomy, known among the Gikuyu as female circumcision, as central to female identity.

The practice, however, became a major arena for conflict. During the late 1920s, missionaries criticized clitoridectomy, and some congregations deter-

From *Women's History in Global Perspective, Volume 1,* edited by Bonnie G. Smith. Copyright 2004 by the Board of Trustees of the University of Illinois.

mined that those families who circumcised their daughters would be excommunicated. The conflict eventually lead to Parliamentary hearings in Britain, before which Jomo Kenyatta testified that clitoridectomy was essential for a Gikuyu girl to be considered an adult. Kenyatta's defense reappeared in his *Facing Mount Kenya,* the first ethnography written by an African of his (or her) own society. In defense of the practice, the majority of Gikuyu families withdrew their children from mission schools and enrolled them in independent schools organized by Kenyatta, which moved him into the nationalist spotlight. Oral histories from *Voices from Mutira* document the perspectives of older women who remember their own "circumcision" and see it as "buying maturity" and developing solidarity among women of their age group. By the 1990s, the practice had been outlawed (when forcibly performed) in Kenya, reflecting changes in Gikuyu women and men's sense of the centrality of clitoridectomy to female identity.[1]

Note

1. Nahid Toubia, "Female Genital Mutilation," in *Women's Rights, Human Rights: International Feminist Perspectives,* ed. Julie Peters and Andrea Wolper (New York: Routledge, 1995), 224–37. In colonial Tanganyika, T. O. Ranger argues, female missionaries' revulsion at such local practices indeed limited the ability of the mission to involve Masasi women in the church. Terence Ranger, "Missionary Adaptation of African Religious Institutions: The Masasi Case," in *The Historical Study of African Religion,* ed. T. O. Ranger and Isaria Kimambo (London: Heinemann, 1972), 221–55; Jean Davison, with women from Mutira, *Voices from Mutira: Change in the Lives of Rural Gikuyu Women, 1910–1995* (Boulder: Lynne Rienner, 1996), 90–91, 144–45; Jomo Kenyatta, *Facing Mount Kenya* (New York: Vintage, n.d. [1938]); Bruce Berman: "Ethnography as Politics, Politics as Ethnography: Kenyatta, Malinowski, and the Making of Facing Mount Kenya," *Canadian Journal of African Studies* 30, no. 3 (1996): 313–44; Jocelyn Murray, "The Church Missionary Society and the 'Female Circumcision' Issue in Kenya, 1929–1932," *Journal of Religion in Africa* 8, no. 2 (1976): 92–104; Susan Pedersen, "National Bodies, Unspeakable Acts: The Sexual Politics of Colonial Policy-Making," *Journal of Modern History* 63 (Dec. 1991): 647–80; Claire Robertson, "Women, Genital Mutilation, and Collective Action, 1920–1990," *Signs* 21, no. 3 (1996): 615–28.

Appendix B. Comparative World History: Women and Gender in Nationalist Movements and Discourse

India, the jewel in the crown of British colonial possessions, is a major site for exciting and innovative studies of colonialism and nationalism. Partha Chatterjee argues that male Bengali nationalists, educated and middle class, were faced with British challenges to Indian Hindu culture involving family, marriage, and the status of women—challenges of "modernizing the nation on Western terms while at the same time retaining an essential national identity as the basis for a political claim to nationhood."[1] These nationalists resolved that contradiction by "separat[ing] the domain of culture into two spheres— the material and the spiritual. . . . What was necessary was to cultivate the material techniques of modern Western civilization while retaining and strengthening the distinctive spiritual essence of the national culture."[2] These domains were mapped spatially as the outer and the inner, the world and the home. Essential to the anticolonial struggle was the preservation of the home as uncolonized space and the creation of a new female, a new femininity, to guard and nurture that space. This new vision combined various items from a reform agenda (e.g., Western secular education or widow remarriage) with conjugal marriage, Victorian domesticity, and female self-sacrifice that kept the wife/mother within a home, safe from British colonial influence.[3]

The interaction between notions of gender and nationhood can be seen in various other colonial situations. Joanna de Groot traces the dynamics of the development of a "gendered nationalist politics" in Iran. De Groot argues that gender is central to understanding Iranian nationalism in several ways. First, discussions of European women's status were a critical part of male Iranian nationalists' confrontation with European culture and ideas, whether they saw European influence as positive or dangerous. Second, they debated the treatment of Iranian and European women, again, from opposing perspectives. Some saw ancient Iranian practices as debased by foreign Arab influences; others saw current practices as evidence of Iran's failure to meet Europe's standards of modern society; still others argued that Iranian culture manifested Islam's honoring of women. For all of these men, despite their political perspectives as reformers or conservative revivalists, issues of women and gender relations held a primary place as measures of Iranian society.

From *Women's History in Global Perspective, Volume 1*, edited by Bonnie G. Smith. Copyright 2004 by the Board of Trustees of the University of Illinois.

Finally, male Iranian nationalists formed "their own identities as male patriots, Muslims, reformers, or 'authentic' Iranians" through these debates.[4]

De Groot traces "the construction of cultural meanings whereby notions of 'the nation' were gendered and notions of 'women/womanhood' were ethnicized." For example, she analyzes the rhetoric of late-nineteenth-century male figures:

> Malkom Khan's exhortations to fellow Iranians to take up the cause of national political and legal reform were couched as encouragement to find or learn *manliness,* just as he identified the political role of women as promotion of that cause and as inspiration for men . . . Both Mirza Malkom Khan and Mirza Aqa Khan Kermani represented foreign domination or influence through the image of Iranian women raped, enslaved, or abused, making the "nation" itself a gendered/feminized entity and women the signifiers of national integrity and security. Beyond that, Mirza Malkom Khan spoke of Iranian subjugation or backwardness as *loss of manliness* among Iranian males.[5]

She also notes how the language of male-female relations came to be used in discourse about national integrity: "honor," "corruption," "modesty," and "respectability." A few decades later, during the period of the constitutional revolution (1906–11), gendered rhetoric continued: "Attacks on the autocracy and on foreign intervention used the discourse of violated family/sexual honor and of the oppression of women. Protection of women defined as the wives/responsibility/possessions of men from such abuse was a key indicator of patriotic, progressive *manliness,* a term frequently used by both men and women in their exhortations to (male) Iranians to be active in the national/constitutional cause."[6]

De Groot maintains that reforms related to women ended by constraining in new ways, not merely emancipating women. Similar to the case of *bhadralok* (educated, middle-class) women in Bengal whom Chatterjee discussed, the old mechanisms for policing women's sexuality—veiling and seclusion—were supplanted by modesty achieved through self-control and commitment to being a patriotic wife, mother, or "asexual associates of male nationalists."[7]

Why is this important? Because women became the terrain of political struggles again later, during the period of the Pahlavi dynasty and during its overthrow in the Islamic revolution of 1979. Just as women's gains and losses in these later periods are rooted in earlier rhetorics and struggles, so, too, the later movements redeployed comparable rhetorics and images of acceptable (e.g., sexually controlled) women activists as chaste daughters, wives, mothers, and comrades. Following Joan Scott's phrase, "Politics constructs gender and gender constructs politics."[8]

Notes

1. Mrinalini Sinha, "Gender in the Critiques of Colonialism and Nationalism: Locating the 'Indian Woman,'" in *Feminism and History*, ed. Joan Wallach Scott (New York: Oxford University Press, 1996), 482 (first quotation, summarizing Chatterjee); Partha Chatterjee, *Nationalist Thought and the Colonial World* (Delhi: Zed Books for the United Nations University, 1986). See also Prasenjit Duara, "The Regime of Authenticity: Timelessness, Gender, and National History in Modern China," *History and Theory* 37 (1998): 287–308.

2. Partha Chatterjee, "Colonialism, Nationalism, and Colonialized Women: The Contest in India," *American Ethnologist* 16, no. 4 (1989): 622–33, quotation on 623; Barbara Ramusack and Sharon Sievers, *Women in Asia: Restoring Women to History* (Bloomington: Indiana University Press, 1999), 42–43.

3. This tension is the theme of "The Home and the World," a story by Rabindranath Tagore (which was made into a film by the same name by Satyagit Ray and is distributed by Facets [1984]). The film works well pedagogically.

4. Joanna de Groot, "Coexisting and Conflicting Identities: Women and Nationalisms in Twentieth-Century Iran," in *Nation, Empire, Colony: Historicizing Gender and Race*, ed. Ruth Roach Pierson and Nupur Chaudhuri (Bloomington: Indiana University Press, 1998), 143. The introduction to this volume notes parallels with Lata Mani's discussions of sati and Indian nationalism and cites Mani's "Contentious Traditions: The Debate on Sati in Colonial India," in *Recasting Women: Essays in Indian Colonial History*, ed. Kumkum Sangari and Sudesh Vaid (New Brunswick: Rutgers University Press, 1989), 88–126..

5. de Groot, "Coexisting and Conflicting Identities," 144–45, emphasis in the original.

6. Ibid., 146, 151, emphasis in the original.

7. Ibid., 152.

8. Joan Wallach Scott, "Gender: A Useful Category of Historical Analysis," in *Feminism and History*, ed. Joan Wallach Scott (New York: Oxford University Press, 1996), 171.

Appendix C. Thematic World History:
Women in the Atlantic Slave Trade

Women and gender are critical to understanding the Atlantic slave trade, whether as slaves, as slave traders, as textile workers who made the cloth traded to Africa, as craftswomen whose crafts were eclipsed by European imports, as abolitionists, as those who resisted abolition, as traders of the palm oil that constituted the "legitimate" postabolition trade, or as consumers of such palm oil products as soap.

WOMEN AS SLAVES

In the demographics of the slave trade, more African men than women were transported to the New World; overall, the ratio of men to women was about 2:1 or 3:1.[1] The imbalence had more to do with African demand for women's labor than for New World preference for male laborers. (After all, in the New World both men and women worked on plantations, and women could reproduce the slave population in those areas where reproduction as opposed to replacement was a strategy for ensuring sufficient labor.) In most societies in sub-Saharan Africa, especially those from which slaves for the Atlantic trade were drawn, women did the majority of agricultural and horticultural work. They could also be incorporated as wives or concubines, thereby producing children for a patrilineage. Because labor was scarcer than land—and controlling labor (laborers who were kin, wives, children, slaves) was key to power and wealth—patrilineages liked to retain and incorporate slave women. Hence African slaving societies had incentives to retain and incorporate women rather than export them.

WOMEN AS SLAVE TRADERS

Women have played a substantial role in sub-Saharan Africa as traders, especially in the West African areas of the Atlantic slave trade. Hence it is not surprising that women traded slaves. The most famous of these was Madame Tinubu in western Nigeria.[2]

WOMEN AS ENGLISH/EUROPEAN TEXTILE WORKERS

The slave trade brought wealth to England and Europe. The goods traded in Africa for slaves included metal goods (especially guns), liquor, and cloth. Women were employed in textile mills that produced the cloth traded for slaves.

WOMEN AS AFRICAN CRAFTSPEOPLE, SLAVE AND FREE

Imports of English cloth undercut African craft production of cloth.[3] West Africa had a particularly well-developed cloth industry. In some societies women were weavers; in other societies men were weavers; in still others both men and women wove, but they wove different kinds of products. Women were involved in various stages of cloth production. In some cases slave women grew indigo and dyed thread or cloth for male and/or female owners.[4]

WOMEN AS ABOLITIONISTS

Women in Europe and the New World were part of the abolitionist movement. Involvement in abolitionism, in some cases, led women to think about the ways in which they, too, did not have rights to their persons. The exclusion of women delegates from participation in the World Anti-Slavery Convention in England in 1840, for example, led Lucretia Mott and Elizabeth Cady Stanton to organize the women's rights convention in Seneca Falls, New York, in 1848, and the resulting Declaration of Sentiments called for, among other rights, enfranchisement for women. Thus, abolitionism encouraged the women's rights movements in the United States and England.[5]

WOMEN AS TRADERS OF "LEGITIMATE" PRODUCTS

Once the Atlantic slave trade was abolished, trade in other items replaced slaves. Important among these items was palm oil, which was used to lubricate industrial machines and make products such as soap (hence Palmolive brand soap). Often, palm oil was produced by slave labor within Africa, where slavery was abolished only long after the Atlantic slave trade was abolished. Even though women slave owners did not have the same options and access that African male slave owners had, in some places (e.g., the eastern part of Nigeria) women were very actively involved in the palm oil trade. Wealthy women traders along the Niger delta used extensive trading networks in the interior and, through them, accumulated palm oil, which they then traded as middlewomen to Royal Niger Company representatives in exchange for trade goods (e.g., cloth, pots, and pans) that they exchanged for palm oil from women farmers and processors in the interior. These were the trade networks and the markets through which the Women's War of 1929 occurred.

WOMEN AS THOSE WHO RESISTED THE ABOLITION OF SLAVERY

Within Africa, slave owning was an important source of wealth and power for freeborn women. Men had various ways to recruit labor, some of which were unavailable to women (e.g., women did not typically marry wives who would work in their fields, although in some areas woman-to-woman marriage accomplished this labor recruitment for rich women who wished to set up their own lineages in an otherwise pafrilineal society). Moreover, women did not have the same options available to them in the economic structures of the postslavery period, where the British men of the Royal Niger Company often preferred to do business with African men or where literacy and a command of English were increasingly important skills in doing business. Hence, women slave owners, in many cases, resisted the abolition of slavery within Africa longer than did African male slave owners (who had other options available to them).[6]

WOMEN AS BRITISH CONSUMERS OF AFRICAN PRODUCTS

The industrial revolution in England led to an increased living standard among the middle class and to improvements in health and other aspects of life. Soap made from African palm oil was important to these improvements and to a middle-class lifestyle that emphasized cleanliness as a measure of good morals. Women in middle-class families had increased importance as consumers (the person responsible for buying the soap) as production moved from the home to the factory and as married women's roles then moved from being a producer to being a homemaker and consumer.

WOMEN AND RACIAL STRATIFICATION

Racial stratification is a major element of the history of the Western hemisphere after European conquest. The gender dynamics of racially stratified New World societies are complex, and women of different social classes play varying roles. Among Iberian elites in South America, for example, it was essential for upper-class women to maintain the "purity of blood" that marked high status. Such purity required not having sexual relations with men of non-European ancestry. For slave women, the opposite sexual role was expected. They were to be sexually available, whether as concubines or as the victims of rape.[7]

Notes

1. Herbert S. Klein, "African Women in the Atlantic Slave Trade," in *Women and Slavery in Africa,* ed. Claire C. Robertson and Martin A. Klein (Madison: University of Wisconsin Press, 1983), 32.

2. Claire C. Robertson and Martin A. Klein, eds., *Women and Slavery in Africa* (Madison: University of Wisconsin Press, 1983), 15.

3. Kevin Shillington, *A History of Africa* (Boston: St. Martin's Press, 1989), 178.

4. Richard Roberts, "Women's Work and Women's Property: Household Social Relations in the Maraka Textile Industry of the Nineteenth Century," *Comparative Studies in Society and History* 26, no. 2 (1984): 48–69.

5. Vron Ware, *Beyond the Pale: White Women, Racism, and History* (London: Verso, 1992).

6. Robertson and Klein, eds., *Women and Slavery in Africa,* 17.

7. Marysa Navarro and Virginia Sánchez Korrol, *Women in Latin America and the Caribbean: Restoring Women to History* (Bloomington: Indiana University Press, 1999), 41–42.

Appendix D. Biography in World History: Queen Sondok (Silla Dynasty, Korea) and Sor Juana Inés de la Cruz (Mexico)

QUEEN SONDOK

One of the more remarkable—but less known—women leaders in world history is Queen Sondok, who ruled Silla (Korea) from 632 until her death in 647 C.E. Only scattered anecdotes describe her personality, but her father the king was so impressed with her wit and intelligence that he made her his successor. Her success as ruler paved the way for two later women rulers of Silla, Chindok and Chinsong. Sondok's reign was central to the "Golden Age" of Korean history and major cultural and religious change. Several themes of both women's history and world history can be seen in examining her life.

One theme is the way in which Asian women have circumvented Confucian limitations on female rule. Although Sondok did not overtly challenge the ideas of Confucianism, she came to power as the result of Silla's system of "bone rank." Aristocratic family connections, being "close to the bone" of a ruler, could carry more weight than gender. Silla family law meant that women would inherit position and wealth. Therefore, as her father's heir, Sondok could lay claim to the throne. But to bolster this connection she made further political and religious choices. Politically, she allied herself with the T'ang Dynasty in China in an era when Empress Wu and talented women poets had shown significant roles for women. In religion, Sondok fostered a tolerant mix of old and new. The new was Buddhist ideas coming from China and India that seemed to give more spiritual credence to women and gave place to the role of nun. The old was an ancient Korean tradition of shamanism in which women were often seers. Sondok sent monks to China to learn and bring back more information about Buddhism, and she built various temples and the famous nine-tiered pagoda of Hwangryongsa. Although her religious interests in Buddhism seem sincere, Sondok's support of it reflects that of other Asian women looking for alternatives to Confucian restrictions.

The mixing of foreign ideas and Korean tradition can also be seen in Sondok's involvement with the military. The alliance with China was a somewhat uneasy one because there was always the possibility that China would encourage conflicts among the warring states in Korea as a way of taking over the peninsula. With that as a prospect, Sondok showed strong support for the Hwarang ("flower knights"). Although Sondok did not found this organization, she is credited with personal attention that led to its expansion and improvement. The Hwarang might be most easily described as forerunners of the Japanese samurai, warriors with a strong spiritual and loyalty code. Sondok saw these men as a major defense not only against rival Korean states but also, eventually, in Silla's defense against China. She had members sent to China to study military tactics and appointed some particularly able generals, including Kim Yu-sin. According to legend, she also had good military instincts herself, interpreting unusual reports of frogs croaking, for example, to forewarn enemy invasion. The modern-day Korea Military Academy near Seoul, with its hill called Hwarang-sa, honors the organization Sondok fostered.

Sondok's wide-ranging interest in new ideas was also evident in her support for science. In an age of relative lack of interest in science in Europe, Asian astronomers and astrologers were trying to rationalize a system of stars. Sondok had Chomsong-dae (Nearer the Stars Place) built, the oldest existing observatory in Asia. Exactly how the observatory worked is still unclear, but its stones number 365 and the twenty-seven tiers match the number of Sondok's place (the twenty-seventh) on the roll of Silla monarchs.[1] The interest in the zodiac, astrological signs as determining factors and future, is a significant part of many cultures, both modern and past. But the fact that Sondok's observatory still stands after thirteen centuries of warfare and conflict on the Korean peninsula is a mark of cultural respect for her vision.

Still existing also is Sondok's tomb, although it is rarely visited by tourists, unlike the other Silla tombs at Kyongju. Her wish evidently was that she be buried away from the main "thoroughfare" of Silla tombs. For Koreans, the choice of a burial site is particularly important because it should fulfill a sense of the place and person. Located on a rise and in the midst of pines, Sondok's tomb reflects Buddhist and shamanist beliefs about the links between spirit and beauty in nature. It may also represent some quiet after such an active life.[2]

SOR JUANA INES DE LA CRUZ

Famed as a poet and intellectual, Sor Juana created, within the institutions of the court and church that defined colonial Mexico, space to think and write in ways available only to men. In so doing she became "the major poet of the Spanish colonies" and, more recently, a feminist icon.[3] Although she was hardly typical, her life reveals the circumstances under which *criollas* (American-born Spanish women) lived. Born illegitimate (although of Spanish blood) in 1651 (or perhaps 1648), she was brought as a child, because of her unusual intellect, to the Spanish viceroy's palace and became a protégé of the vice-roy's wife, the Countess of Mancera. She amassed the largest library in the Viceroyalty of New Spain (e.g., parts of present-day Mexico and Central America), including books prohibited by the Inquisition. She also acquired the most advanced technology of the time for her research, for example, a telescope and a globe.

She became a nun in 1667, choosing the convent over marriage as a more likely place to be able to study and write. Later in life, she described her zeal for learning: "I began to study Latin, in which I had barely twenty lessons; and so intense was my application that although women (especially in the flower of their youth) cherish the natural adornment of their hair, I would cut off four or six fingers' length of mine, making a rule that if I had not mastered a certain subject by the time it grew back, I would cut it off again . . . for it did not seem right to me that a head so empty of knowledge, which is the most desirable adornment of all, should be crowned with hair."[4]

Indeed, convents were the alternative selected by young women of "pure blood," or forced upon them by circumstance. Their families paid a dowry to the convents, which provided a female-ordered space where, within the limits set by the Church, women could express their talents. Those limits included a prevailing notion that associated leadership with men. Nuns were to practice obedience, chastity, poverty, and self-mortification. Writing was common among them, but before Sor Juana such writings were not published. Instead, the writing of a nun, like the rest of her spiritual life, was controlled by the man who was her confessor. Among the ways in which Sor Juana was unusual is that she dismissed her confessor, Father Antonio Nuñez de Miranda. At the end of her life, however, and facing a religious crisis, she recalled him.

Sor Juana's *villancicos* (writings in a popular genre) posit "the Virgin Mary as a model of feminine power and wisdom."[5] In these pieces she writes in multiple voices—Indians speak in Nahuatl and black figures in a dialect of Spanish—just as her other writings voice an alternate view of women than what prevailed among the clergy.

Sor Juana argued for intellect at a time when the path to sainthood for women was mystical experience. She was well aware of her gifts and, apart from "rhetorical disclaimers," exhibited them until approaching death.[6] Then she wrote (or merely signed, there is debate), "I, the worst one in the world, Juana Ines de la Cruz." She died in 1695, caring for other nuns during a plague.[7]

Notes

1. Committee for the Compilation of the History of Korean Women, *Women of Korea: A History from Ancient Times to 1945* (Seoul: Ewha Woman's University Press, 1976), 25–

28; David Bannon, "Who Were the Hwarang?" *Mudo Dojang Magazine* [Pacific Rim Publishing, 1995?]: 1–6, available online at http://www.hwarang.org/Ancienthistory.html; Edward B. Adams, *Korea's Golden Age: Cultural Spirit of Silla in Kyongju* (Seoul: Seoul International Publishing House, 1991), 45–47;

2. Marjorie Bingham, "Silla Queens: A Golden Age," in *Korea: Lessons for High School Social Studies Courses,* ed. Yong Jin Choi (New York: Korea Society, 1999), 134–38.

3. Georgina Sabat-Rivers, "Juana Ines de la Cruz, Sor," in *Encyclopedia of Latin American History and Culture,* ed. Barbara A. Tenenbaum (New York: Simon and Schuster, 1996), 3: 331–33 (quotation on 331); June Hahner, *Women in Latin American History: Their Lives and Views* (Los Angeles: University of California Latin American Center Publications, 1979); Asuncion Labrin, "'Unlike Sor Juana?' The Model Nun in the Religious Literature of Colonial Mexico," in *Feminist Perspectives on Sor Juana Ines de la Cruz,* ed. Stephanie Merrim (1983, repr. Detroit: Wayne State University Press, 1991), 61–85; Jean Franco, *Plotting Women: Gender and Representation in Mexico* (New York: Columbia University Press, 1989); Sor Juana de la Cruz, *A Sor Juana Anthology,* trans. Alan S. Trueblood (Cambridge: Harvard University Press, 1988). A biographical video, *I, the Worst of All* directed by Maria-Luisa Bemberg, is available and distributed by Facets (1993).

4. Hahner, *Women in Latin American History,* 23.

5. Sabat-Rivers, "Juana Ines de la Cruz, Sor," 331.

6. Lavrin, "'Unlike Sor Juana?'" 70.

7. Ibid., 71.

2

Family History as
World History

ANN B. WALTNER AND
MARY JO MAYNES

Family, Kinship, and Social Organization
around the Globe, ca. 1500

The dynamics of family history are simultaneously local and global. The household is a key site where world-historical processes unfold. These two simple observations provide a starting point for an approach to world history that accommodates family history. World historical change involves the activities of families—that is, small groups linked by ties of marriage, descent, or adoption, normally constituting fluid coresidential households. Global encounters and major processes of global development are structured by systems of kinship—that is, socially recognized relationships between people in a particular culture who are (or are held to be) biologically related or who are given the status of relatives by marriage, adoption, or other ritual. Many common themes of world history can link family and kinship systems with political, socioeconomic, and cultural dimensions of history. We have made family history a central part of a world history course we have taught at the University of Minnesota since 1995.

A key distinction among societies of the precapitalist world demarcated kinship-based from tributary modes of production. In kinship-based societies (around the year 1500 these were located mainly in Africa, the Americas, and Central Eurasia), relations of kinship, economic production, and political authority largely overlapped. In many of these regions, topographical or ecological factors discouraged the level of population density and long-distance trade upon which more highly centralized polities were based. There was little recourse to either highly elaborated mechanisms of political domination or routine processes of extraction of resources to finance and sustain domination. Except for the distinctions along the lines of gender and age, which were pervasive throughout the world, social distinctions were minor. Competition for access to resources tended to occur among groups defined through kinship—clans, lineages, and the like.[1]

In regions where tributary modes of production prevailed (around the year 1500 these were located in Europe, East Asia, and parts of Central and South America and Africa), classes of nonproducers held control over some key element of production such as land or water supply. They also often commanded a military force or other coercive capacity needed to control these resources and collect products from direct producers, mainly peasants, in the form of rents or taxes. This key distinction—at base, one resting on connections between the realm of kinship and the realms of economy and polity— would prove critical in many ways during the era of increasing global contact.

Feminist anthropologists spell out how kinship and gender relations have informed the division of labor and power relations in both kinship and tributary societies. They also have amassed evidence about how the historical process of building tributary states involved renegotiating gender relations as well as economic and political dimensions of family organization. A fairly egalitarian kin-based indigenous society in Mesoamerica, for example, became a "predatory empire" under the Aztecs during the course of the fifteenth century. Women did not play a central role in the emerging economy of war and tribute, and hence the new order of society was dominated by males in a way the earlier societies had not been.[2]

These insights remind us that however convenient it may be to start with cross-regional comparisons, regional differences apparent in 1500 were themselves a product of ongoing historical developments. Tributary states often relied on preexisting kinship relations and by no means erased their significance. Even where new forms of organization had been superimposed on kinship structures, people still called on kin relations in everyday life. Moreover, they created and thought about political relationships in ways that were inseparable from kinship.

The Family, the Economy, and Social Structure in Comparative Perspective

In 1500 the world's economies, whether kinship-based or tributary, rested largely on household-level production. Most people drew their livelihoods

49

from agrarian or pastoral pursuits. Most farming units were small in scale and oriented toward subsistence or barter rather than a market. Work devoted to the production of goods other than foodstuffs, or to trade or services, was also primarily organized at the level of the household. All of these characteristics of economies would change at varying paces in different parts of the world in the centuries after 1500. But to understand economic history and social stratification around the world in this era it is important to explore the micro-level of the family and household.

Household-level decisions determined work processes and specified how individuals would spend their time. The transitions individuals made at various points in their life-cycles (birth, marriage or divorce, and death) also entailed entering or leaving work units. It was primarily in families that wealth was accumulated and transmitted from generation to generation. Anthropologists and feminist theorists long ago pointed to pervasive reciprocal movements of women and goods that were exchanged among kin groups headed mainly by men.[3] Family capital (bride-wealth or dowries, inheritances, and wedding gifts) was impossible to distinguish from business capital.

In addition, principles of land tenure in the tributary societies of both Europe and China privileged kin-based households as the locus of economic decision-making and cross-generational transmission of resources. Peasant families in both regions laid claim to the most significant economic resource— arable land—even if their claims were never exclusive and were often contested. Conditions of land tenure varied widely, but peasant household heads generally strove to secure their claims to tenancies for themselves and their descendants, thus moving toward identifying particular lineages with particular farms and even "houses." To some extent, land tenure reinforced patrilineal tendencies in much of China and many regions of Europe because land, more frequently than other resources, passed through male lines.

Land was worked primarily by household labor composed of family members and other dependents. Labor was organized according to age- and gender-based divisions of labor that presumed the family as the normative work unit. In many regions of Europe, service days owed to landlords as part of the rent (associated with the system of serfdom and still in place throughout Europe until the French Revolution) were specified in "men's days" and "women's days," depending on the task at hand. Land use rights and associated dues were transmitted through family mechanisms in both places, even if the particulars varied. In China, household divisions were overseen by go-betweens employed by the family.[4] In Europe, inheritance following locally variant customs was the main mechanism of transfer. Chinese lineages, where they existed, also held a corporate stake in some of their resources, but for the most part land under production was farmed by small households (of owners or tenant farmers) based on stem families who regulated land use and intergenerational transmission.

These links between family and economy in China and Europe produced some striking parallels in marriage transactions. Marriage in both regions was the result of family deliberations informed by land availability and strategies regarding heirship as well as by community-enforced norms that evolved to maintain the local balance between land and population. Certain marriage rituals echo each other in these two different cultures. In China, wedding norms prescribed that a bride be transported in an enclosed sedan chair from her father's house to that of her groom's family. Woodblock prints depict bridal processions that include bearers carrying the bride's dowry items.[5] Similarly, in early modern Germany the bridal wagon (*Brautwagen*) carried the bride and her dowry goods to her new home. Notarial documents and family records list the wagon's contents, often in great detail. An early-eighteenth-century listing of the contents of a Brautwagen in Diepholz, Germany, begins with "a bed cover with 10 pounds of feathers" and ends with "six pigs" whose individual values were specified.[6] The dowry—which with the land that so often came from the groom's side formed the economic basis of a family—was thus on display.

Along with these striking parallels we should also note a significant difference regarding rules of household formation in the peasant societies of China and Europe. Briefly, a new couple in China typically moved in with the groom's family, whereas in many regions of Europe it had come to be expected by the early modern era that the new couple would set up a household of their own. Moreover, because the young couple was not expected to begin a new independent household enterprise but rather join an existing one, marriage could and did occur at a younger age in China than in most of Europe. This particular variation would hold consequences for long-term economic development patterns despite an overall similarity that made much of China and Europe resemble each other in the realm of household economy—at least until the modern era—more than either did other world regions.

The logic of wealth accumulation, and thus of social stratification, in these two peasant-based tributary societies was also related to the household and family basis of agrarian organization. State authorities and other elites had ultimately to acquire their wealth at the base, through extraction from peasant households, in a fashion that made China and Europe again more similar to each other than either was to much of Africa or the Americas. Social structure and patterns of stratification resembled each other in China and Europe. Over the course of generations, peasant families and their farms could prosper or fall into poverty because of the working out of changing demands for rent and taxes, successive property divisions and inheritances, demographic and environmental hazards, managerial skills, and dumb luck.

Over time, then, increasing differentials in wealth, farm size, and well-being evolved. Imagined visually, the social structure of the peasant-based tributary society took a bulbous form. The visual representation originally drawn by anthropologist G. W. Skinner for traditional China strongly resembles an onion, and an analogous diagram for the early modern German Empire would be strikingly similar.[7] At the base is a huge mass of peasant families, their bulge narrowing slightly toward the top to accommodate the peasant elites and narrowing even more at the long tip for the few wealthy landlords, high state authorities, and members of ruling dynasties. Arguably, family-economic strategies at the peasant base, combined with state-building, shaped social structure in these two world regions.

A variation on the tributary-state model can be seen in the complex societies of pre-Conquest Mesoamerica. Historians note the similarities between European and Nahua culture as well as the differences. Commonalties include "sedentary life, intensive agriculture, dynastic rulers and tax systems, territorial polities, a well-developed religious apparatus of pantheon, priesthood and ritual calendar associated with those polities, and social distinctions between nobles, commoners and intermediate groups."[8]

There were, of course, differences as well. The various kingdoms and empires of Mesoamerica on the eve of the Conquest were organized in loose and shifting alliances. Although the household was the primary unit of labor and consumption, less attention was paid in Mesoamerica than in either Europe or China to whether or not residents of a household were related. (Indeed, this can be seen in Nahuatl kinship terminology, which stresses co-residence rather than blood ties.)[9] Land was transmitted to both children and siblings, and males and females could inherit from both fathers and mothers. All heirs were not equally important; the eldest son often acted as a guardian for the sibling set.[10] Still, the somewhat dispersed inheritance patterns common in Mesoamerica may have been less favorable to wealth accumulation than the patrilineal patterns found in either Europe or China.[11] Marriage differed as well. The average age at marriage was probably about fifteen for women and a few years older than that for men—therefore younger than in either Europe or China.[12] Property and residence would be among the items negotiated at the making of the marriage.[13]

In ordinary agricultural households, as elsewhere, a gendered division of labor prevailed. Women were in charge of domestic tasks. In addition to childbearing and child rearing, that included food preparation (especially the many hours spent pounding maize into flour) and textile production. Men did most agricultural labor. In times and places where warfare was important, they were also warriors. As was true elsewhere, the distinction in gender roles was seen as natural and was encoded in birth rituals. After the birth of a boy, his umbilical cord was buried on a battlefield; after the birth of a girl, by the hearth. The midwife's words at the hearth foretold the future woman's tasks: "Thou wilt be in the heart of the home . . . thou art to provide water, to grind maize, to drudge, thou art to sweat by the ashes, by the hearth."[14] In contrast, midwives would tell infant boys, "Thy home is not here, for thou art an eagle, an ocelot. . . . Here are only thy cradle, thy cradle blanket, the resting place for thy head. . . . War is thy desert, thy task . . . thy real home, thy lot is the home of the sun in the heavens."[15]

Other features of pre-Conquest Mesoamerican marriage systems also distinguished them from both the Chinese and Central European cases in the mid-fifteenth century. In the Yucatan Peninsula and in parts of the Aztec region of Mexico, pre-Conquest customs required a young man to go and live with his bride's father for a few years and earn the right to a wife and children. His labor in the fields earned him adult status and the right to marry. (Europeans who later noted this practice objected to it; to them, it seemed as if the bride was being "bought.")[16] As was true elsewhere, marriage required resources, and wealthier men had an advantage in marriage negotiations. Powerful men would often have a number of secondary wives and concubines—so, as in China (and more covertly in Europe), polygamy was practiced among the upper classes.

As in Europe and China, then, marriage was a clear economic and social status marker among men, but the typical route to (and timing of) marriage varied, as did the younger generation's reliance on the older for the necessary transfers of capital that marriage entailed. The Mesoamerican system nevertheless placed less emphasis on the transfer of accumulated resources from generation to generation.

In many regions of Africa and much of North America extended family groups, clans, and lineages collectively regulated access to land and other resources through mechanisms and technologies that were even less conducive to accumulation. In East Africa the labor required for family subsistence was typically organized at the household level. But the long fallows and the itinerant and collective nature of usufruct in a situation of relatively low population density meant that claims to particular houses and plots of land so critical in much of Europe or China were irrelevant to family strategy in East Africa. Moreover, there was little political support for accumulation of wealth in the absence of highly developed mechanisms of extraction of taxes or rents by state authorities or landlords. In envisioning social structure in these regions, one needs to imagine different shapes—much squatter than the "onions" depicting stratification in China and Germany—to reflect the relatively egalitarian distribution and redistribution of resources within and across the generations.[17] Still, if a certain equality prevailed among adult men in many

East African societies, status and power differentials privileged them over younger men and most women. In most cultures, senior men controlled more valued resources, such as cattle used for trade and bride-price, even where accumulation was limited. Thus, even where class formation was minimal, gender and age hierarchies still could be pervasive and significant.

In the largely kinship-based and relatively decentralized societies of East Africa, a wide range of marriage systems often coexisted in the same locality.[18] That was especially true in areas such as the Swahili Coast, where coastal traders (often Muslims) lived among people who depended on agriculture, hunting, and fishing and practiced a variety of local religions. Swahili Coast Muslim communities derived many of their marriage and family practices from Islamic law. With respect to the economic implications of marriage, some of the most significant Islamic rules and practices stipulated that a bridegroom's family had to make a ritual payment to the bride in order for a marriage to be deemed valid. A bride was assumed to be under the command and protection of her husband, who owed her and her children a livelihood; a woman could have but one husband although a man could have up to four legal wives and concubines as well (provided he could afford them all).

The complex economies of the Coast also were reflected in marriage systems. Among Islamic mercantile elite families who inhabited the "stone house" neighborhoods of coastal cities such as Lamu and Kilwa, particular local variations on the more general Muslim customs were emerging before the arrival of Europeans in the sixteenth century. The wealthy merchant clans of these towns claimed descent from ancestral intermarriages between male traders from the Red Sea and Western Indian Ocean coastal trade cities and indigenous women. These trade families came to control municipal offices in the towns where they lived. Their wealth was based on control over trade goods, often held corporately by the patrilineal clan.

Among these elite families, particularly strong links between business and family resulted in a marked tendency toward cousin marriage. Betrothals were arranged by the father of the bride and the father of the groom, who were also brothers, when their children concerned were still quite young. The actual marriage took place as soon after the girl reached puberty as it was practical for the families.

These marriages involved substantial transfers of wealth. In addition to the token bride-wealth (*mahari*) specified in Islamic law, a larger bride gift (*kitu*) was paid by the groom's family to the bride's. Many smaller gifts would also go to the bride's various kin. In addition, the *hidaya* was a gift to the bride from her father. Somewhat like the European (and Chinese) dowry, it was understood to belong to the bride rather than to her husband and might include household and personal goods, gold, and jewelry as well as personal

slaves. More unusually, the brides in these families also received accommodation in the paternal stone house—a new apartment or wing. This uxorilo-
cal arrangement (that is, the couple lived with the bride's natal family) was
highly unusual in a patrilineal system, logical only because in these marriages
the fathers of both bride and groom, as brothers, were members of the same
patriline.

These particular marriages doubly secured the patriline in that the bride's
sexual purity until marriage was safeguarded by both father and future father-
in-law and the property transferred at marriage was preserved within the lineage. The son of one of the brothers thus was groomed to take over the family business, married to the daughter of the other brother who eventually took
over the house and its management.

In the very same region of Africa, other forms of marriage, regulated by
custom rather than written law, prevailed among the non-elites, both along
the Coast and in the interior. Most commonly, marriages were understood as
exchanges between clans or lineages. They were secured by the exchange of
either bride-wealth—that is, payment from the groom's family to the bride's—
or bride-service—that is, work performed by the young man for the bride's
family. Most East African systems tended to be patrilineal, although some more
matrilineal systems of reckoning kin were also to be found (for example, the
Kaguru and Zaramo people in the hinterland west and southwest of the island
of Zanzibar) as well as some bilateral systems.

Whether more heavily matrilineal or patrilineal, kinship relations determined how people reckoned their ancestry and tracked the relatives on whom
they could call for various services or to whom they owed services. Relationships of kinship were the basis of claims to access to key resources such as land
for farming or herding, cattle or goats, and hunting and fishing rights. Indeed,
it appears from more modern evidence that marital strategies among the non-
elite multiplied kinship claims whereby children could have access to different sources of livelihood—both farming and fishing rights, for example.

This East African example makes explicit another critical dimension of
marriage systems hinted at in all of the cases: their relationship to status hierarchies and accumulation. The first-cousin marriages of Swahili Coast merchants, as well as the marital strategies of the coastal poor, were practices rooted in particular different social milieus. In the case of mercantile elites, who
like their counterparts in merchant communities around the globe were interested in accumulation of the goods and cash necessary for prosperity,
marriages maximized the containment of wealth within a lineage. In the milieus of farmers, pastoralists, and fisherfolk more typical of the region, marital strategies focused on enhancing chances for survival (as in the case of
marriages linking farming and fishing families) through creating alliances and

claims for children to collective resources. Wealth—usually in the form of animals or cloth—did move from family to family and generation to generation at marriage. But in East Africa, only the family strategies of the mercantile elite were conducive to the accumulation of considerable marketable wealth.

The point is clear: Regional variations in patterns of wealth accumulation, social structure, and status hierarchy were inseparable from family systems. The rules governing family and kinship strongly marked the shape of social structure. Families everywhere were understood to be created by "blood" or biological ties of marriage and parenthood (supplemented to varying degrees by alternative ways of acquiring kin such as adoption and god-parentage). But whatever the immensely flexible and varied rules according to which biological kinship were reckoned, in every case, kinship relations brought culturally specific sets of *material claims* based on kinship ties. The particular things transmitted through the family connections invoked at marriage and on other occasions—whether property, usufruct claims, personality characteristics, legal rights, or privileges—varied immensely, but such transmission always held utmost significance for the social order. Moreover, family mechanisms for transferring wealth, as well as notions of property and accumulation, eventually would play a role in positioning regions differently with respect to the global order.

FAMILY AND POLITY IN COMPARATIVE PERSPECTIVE

Political authorities hold a stake in kinship and family relations because of their implications for reproduction and the transfer of property, the models they provide for forms of authority, and their connection with religion and moral beliefs—in short, because family relations have the capacity to uphold or undermine social and political order. But the precise ways in which political authorities expressed interest or intervened in families have differed greatly in time and place. World history courses, whatever approach they take, concern themselves with varied and changing political systems and with processes of state formation. They often examine contrasts among different political systems and varying ways in which political authorities interact with other powerful entities—religious institutions, social elites, and so on.

The family can also be a fruitful site for the historical exploration of varying forms of political authority and varying definitions of political community. Discussion here will focus on just two aspects of the early modern family-polity nexus—how political power was legitimated and political legitimacy related to thinking about the family (and family practices) in different world regions, and the different degrees and forms of political involvement in marriage.

Throughout much of Europe, East and South Asia, and Mesoamerica around 1500, the kinship basis of rule persisted in the context of an ongoing process of development of large and complex states. State bureaucracies emerged without eradicating older associations between legitimate rule and claims based in kinship. Moreover, whatever the form of rule, metaphors of kinship still permeated ideas of political authority in all these regions. In other areas, including much of North America and Africa, political authority was more exclusively tied to kinship. Rule in these societies was never just a matter of kinship, but the role kinship played in ideas about legitimacy was strong and direct. In discussing political authority and political community it is useful to consider both kinds of cases—those where claims based on kinship are direct and those where such linkages are more submerged.

In China, kin linkages played a role in political legitimacy, although kinship alone was not sufficient to confer it. The Chinese Empire was the most durable of the political communities under discussion here. The empire was first unified in 221 B.C.E., and durable structures of legitimating rule persisted although subsequent centuries saw disunion, social transformations, and even political conquest. Dynastic legitimacy and bureaucratic legitimacy were strong components of political legitimacy. Dynastic legitimacy could be transferred from one dynasty to another through the Mandate of Heaven; bureaucratic legitimacy, however, had to be validated through the process of civil service examinations.

Political and family authority were connected through a series of powerful metaphors known as the "Five Relationships." Confucian social theorists regarded these relationships (ruler-minister, father-son, husband-wife, elder sibling–younger sibling, and friend-friend) as the fundamental dynamics of human society. The authority of a ruler was thus in a sense naturalized by analogy to kinship relations. But that is not the only implication of the analogy: A loyal minister should serve only one ruler, and a loyal wife should have only one husband. Discussions about widow remarriage, for example, took on added urgency during the Ming and Qing periods because of the correlation between political loyalty and sexual fidelity.[19]

A dynasty held legitimacy through the Mandate of Heaven. Heaven would endorse a dynasty's rule through good crops, fine weather, and so on and show displeasure through disasters such as flood and famine. If a ruling family lost the Mandate, it could be replaced with a new claimant. Rebels (even unsuccessful ones) routinely claimed that the Mandate had passed to them. Even ethnically non-Chinese dynasties such as the Mongol Yuan and the Manchu Qing dynasties used the Mandate of Heaven as a legitimating theory. Within a ruling family, emperorship followed lines of patrilineal transmission. In the Ming dynasty, detailed succession rules were prescribed in the founding emperor's Ancestral Instructions: The heir to the throne was the eldest son of the emperor's principal wife, and should she have no sons his younger brother would inherit. The Manchus did not practice primogeniture, and Qing dynasty succession procedures did not systematically prescribe which son would inherit. Although the mechanisms varied, both the Ming and the Qing dynasties used the principle of heredity to select an emperor. But the transmission of authority from the Ming to the Qing was achieved by military conquest. It was a negotiation among the principles of merit (the Mandate of Heaven), heredity, and military might.

The civil service bureaucracy also navigated between the principles of merit and heredity. The emperor did not rule alone. He ruled in the company of bureaucrats who were selected on the basis of civil service examinations. Although the details of the examination structure varied, in essence the examinations tested a man's knowledge of the Confucian classics. There was an aristocracy formed by imperial relatives, but the aristocracy was normally not nearly as powerful as the bureaucracy. Success in the examination system was not only a route to political office but to social prestige. Clearly, the sons of scholar-officials had advantages over boys from other classes of society in preparing for the examinations, but even they had to pass. Some high officials were granted what was called the *"yin* privilege," which enabled the sons to enter the bureaucracy but at a much lower rank than their fathers had held. Here again is a negotiation between the principles of merit and heredity, this time with merit (at least theoretically) gaining the upper hand.

In the centuries between 1500 and 1750 most European dynasties undertook state-building projects that paralleled in some respects the older Chinese model. Many European states had begun to build permanent modern bureaucracies to organize and fund their administration of law and their standing armies and navies. State-building projects would dominate political life on the continent between 1500 and 1750. By the late seventeenth century, many had even begun to define "the economy" as a site of deliberate state activity.[20] The new bureaucratic forms of authority, however, coexisted, often uneasily, with older principles based on the notion of inherited kingship. With few exceptions, European states continued to be ruled by dynasties. Moreover, the inheritance of the right to rule was part of a larger system of aristocratic notions of hierarchy. At its very core, political authority was closely tied to family position.

In practice, political systems were more complicated. Notions of legitimacy were, as in China, tied to religious sanction as well as lineage and even at times to notions of effective rule or popular acclaim. The right to rule over the Holy Roman Empire, which dominated Central European political formation around 1500, entailed multiple claims of legitimacy. Ceremonies marking the accession of a new emperor involved dynastic affiliation, to be sure. (In effect, the Habsburg dynasty provided all but one of the Holy Roman Emperors between the mid-fifteenth century and the empire's end under Napoleon.) But the bestowal of legitimacy also required election (often oiled with bribes) by the imperial electors (lesser princes and prince-bishops of the empire) as well as anointing by a bishop who symbolized the ultimately divine sanction of all authority. The German Empire, then, was a dynastic state based on kin relations but not exclusively or unambiguously so.

The Lutheran Reformation, which began shortly after 1500, held important consequences for both political legitimacy and family-state relations. As historians have long recognized, Luther's challenge to the Catholic Church necessarily involved him in political rebellion as well, because state and Church authority were so closely bound together. More recently, scholarship has highlighted the Reformation's implications for the history of family and gender relations.[21] Reformation-era creation of official state churches under bureaucratic authority built upon and exacerbated patriarchal models. Under the slogan "Gottesvater, Landesvater, Hausvater" the Christian God, the territorial prince, and the male household head were linked in a hierarchical and explicitly patriarchal order.

Arguably, the Lutheran critique of clerical celibacy and Catholic views of marriage opened a new approach to gender relations. In contrast with Catholic teachings, Lutheran writings exalted marriage as superior to celibacy; marital sexuality was seen as natural and not sinful. But the abolition of female religious orders also removed an honorable alternative to marriage for women. According to the Protestant gender order henceforward enforced in the Protestant states of the empire, adult women belonged in male-headed households under the supervision of a husband whose authority reflected divine and princely authority. Ironically, even where Catholicism prevailed, women were also brought under tighter male authority, and churches moved closer to the state. In the wake of Catholic Reform, nuns had to be cloistered and their convents supervised by male spiritual authorities. In other words, state-church bureaucracies not only took over many functions previously performed by the Catholic Church but also brought state authority into many more aspects of everyday life. The innovations subjected the population of Central Europe to unprecedented state discipline and brought family life under tight control.

By the end of the sixteenth century, then, German states and their lay and religious bureaucracies had created a form of rule that penetrated everyday family life to a historically unprecedented degree. The lightly governed polities of East Africa, a region of the globe deemed "stateless" around 1500, offer a stark contrast in the form of political community. Nevertheless, kinship, spiritual authority, and political authority were closely bound together, although in strikingly different and varied forms.

In East Africa, the boundaries of political community and the bases for the exercise of legitimate political authority drew on both Bantu and Arabic influences. Like many other Bantu people, those of East Africa linked political authority with lineage and rule with lineage elders, usually although not always male elders. Rulers—whether kings, chiefs, or elders—buttressed political authority with spiritual power. That usually meant the capacity to demonstrate a special relationship to the ancestor spirits identified with the locality. Family, political, and spiritual authority were superimposed on one another and difficult to separate.

Political communities were relatively decentralized. Only in the region around Buganda (roughly present-day Uganda), in Ethiopia, and to the south around Zimbabwe was there evidence of kingdoms that ruled over an extensive territory. The realms of most political authorities were far smaller, encompassing several dozen rather than hundreds of villages. The most relevant political and spiritual authorities were kin—the living and the ancestors. Their powers centered on the cluster of villages associated with a given lineage. Many East African people recognized a more distant supreme deity, but local ancestor spirits, except among the nomadic herders of the northern Rift Valley, were the most significant forces in everyday spiritual life.

On the Indian Ocean Coast, Bantu people mingled with the trading people who had been sailing the East Coast of Africa south from the Horn of Africa and Arabia since at least the seventh or eighth century C.E. Through shared settlements and intermarriage they together established a political culture that reflected these dual origins. Forms and symbols of power mix Bantu and Arabic, ancestor-based and Muslim practices. Oral traditions for the coastal cities clearly locate political authority in a family saga of union. The central metaphor of these origin myths is a primordial marriage between a foreign trader and a local king's daughter. The following excerpt from a Swahili oral tradition about the ruling family of the city of Kilwa offers one example:

> Then came Sultan Ali bin Selimani, that is, the Persian. He came with his ship, and brought his goods and his children. . . . They disembarked at Kilwa . . . went to the headman of the country, the elder Mrimba, and asked for a place in which to settle at Kisiwani. This they obtained, and they gave Mrimba presents of trade goods and beads. . . . Sultan Ali married Mrimba's daughter. He lived on good terms with the people. He gave them presents, each according to his standing. These presents were cloth and beads. . . . Sultan Ali had a child by Mrimba's daughter, a son, who was called Sultan Mohamed bin Sultan Ali. He lived at home until he reached manhood, and then set off and went to the Ruvuma to visit his grandfather, the Elder Mrimba. When he arrived, his grandfather handed over his power to him, his grandson.[22]

Political authority was thus directly linked to genealogical fusion and its accompanying exchange of wealth. Family positions and rituals continued to reinforce political position and power.

Around the year 1500, stronger states tended to prevail in regions where tributary arrangements provided the resources necessary for exerting authority on a basis other than kinship over widely separated groups of primary producers (families, clans, lineages, villages, or tribes). Among the cases we have discussed, these would certainly include China and many European states as well as the Aztec confederation in Mesoamerica.

These states had established at least forms of organized domination over wide territories and institutionalized control through a combination of offices based on kinship claims, to be sure, as well as on personal loyalties, bureaucratic relations, and military power. They financed themselves and funded institutions of rule through the extraction of tribute. And, of tremendous significance for world-historical dynamics, they developed a far greater capacity for expansion and domination than localized kinship-based systems, although, of course, not all would use this capacity to expand and dominate to the same extent. Conversely, in regions of localized, mainly kinship-based polities such as East Africa (where even on the Coast rule rarely extended beyond a city-state and its immediate hinterland) no such capacity existed. Instead, these societies would find themselves vulnerable to conquest. Thus, very significant distinctions among polities around the globe on the eve of global contact turned precisely on the extent to which they rested on kin versus tributary authority and had developed mechanisms for the accumulation and political deployment of wealth. This basic distinction, strongly rooted in kinship dynamics, held world-historical implications.

To move to another very significant point of contact between family and political authority, the institution of marriage provides another good (and, for undergraduate students, compelling) focus for a discussion. Although the specific characteristics of marriage systems vary tremendously across time and space, community and political authorities virtually everywhere intervene to some extent in marriage. In both Europe and China, parents around 1500 held the legal and customary authority to arrange marriages for their children. Supra-local tributary regimes also staked claims over productive and reproductive forces in both regions. But the evolving landscapes of authority in the two societies differed greatly. In the long run of European history, a three-way contest among family, church, and state set the conditions under which legitimate marriages could be contracted. Women and children held little power in comparison with adult men. But the Catholic Church's insistence that both partners in a marriage enter into the marriage willingly gave some women an out—namely, an appeal to the Church in ecclesiastical courts that had won political backing, claiming that the marriage their parents wanted was being forced upon them without their consent. Surprisingly, there is historical evidence that some young women won battles with their fathers over marriage decisions through resort to Church courts.[23]

In China, by way of contrast, state, religion, and family were less institutionally distinct. Paternal authority echoed and reinforced the political and the moral order. Religious authorities could rarely be called upon to intervene in a family dispute. Therefore, young women (and young men, for that matter) had no clearly established institutional recourse in a situation of an unwanted marriage.[24] Despite the fact that paternal power was very strong in both early modern Italy and early modern China, specific institutional differences put different constraints on that paternal power and set the family in differing relations to state and religious authorities.

This comparison isolates some of the particular features of marriage systems that are significant in addressing family and gender relations in a world-historical context. In China, the rules of family formation and family governance were generally enforced within the bounds of each extended family group. Family leaders enforced state law and religious norms on behalf of the wider community; only rarely did disputes over marriage reach the state legal system.[25] In Europe, the institution of marriage was altered first by the effort of the Catholic Church to wrest some control over marriage from the family by defining it as a sacrament and then eventually by the struggle between churches and state authorities to regulate families.[26] The historical contest among church, state, and family authorities over marriage decisions turns out, in comparative perspective, to be a particular feature of European history (and of the history of some European colonies) that would have consequences for many aspects of social life. The contest would eventually find ramifications in European colonies where the influence of the Catholic Church was particularly strong, as in Mexico.[27]

In East Africa, relationships were different. Family and political authority overlapped and remained decentralized. A historical admixture of older Bantu practices and imported religious ideas about marriage influenced the institution, although in this case the imported religion was Islam. Its introduction to the coast of East Africa dates as early as the twelfth century. Islamic states were (and are) characterized, at least ideally, by an identity of interest between religious and political authorities in marriage and other matters as well. State marriage law and the prescriptions of the Koran and later traditions are supposed to coincide.

For most of East Africa's history, however, Islamic rules were not enforced by a powerful Islamic state but rather were followed locally and selectively by communities of believers. Religious and municipal political offices often overlapped, and the two forms of authority typically reinforced each other as male heads of elite trading families monopolized both religious and political offices, although the extent of their authority was usually quite localized. (This would change only in the mid-nineteenth century when the sultan of Oman moved his capital to Zanzibar in a process of political consolidation that also brought a stronger and more politicized Islamic presence to the Coast.) East Africans followed a wide variety of spiritual belief systems that intersected in different ways with political authority. For many Africans on the Swahili Coast and in East Africa more generally, marriages were governed by customary law derived from various and intermingling Bantu cultures. As is true with much customary law elsewhere in the world, that law was unwritten and varied tremendously from one village or ethnic group to another.

In all of these cases marriage choice was never left up to the young couple, but the constellation of interested parties that participated in the decision—family, state, and religious authorities—varied. The degree to which political authorities were involved in family life varied as well from case to case and changed over time. State involvement in marriages is thus a revealing mechanism through which to track political variations. Moreover, the examination of marriage also offers a route for exploring the changing role of religious authorities and the varying relationships between religious and state authorities. Focusing on the moment of marriage presents opportunities, then, for understanding the historical connections between the operation of family and gender relations in everyday life and the broader realm of political structures.

KINSHIP AND RELIGION IN COMPARATIVE PERSPECTIVE

Our discussion of family and polity highlighted their interconnections. Moving into the realm of religion reveals deep and pervasive commitments to kinship ties that had spiritual as well as material and political dimensions and that continued beyond death. Family and religion were closely interconnected around the globe in 1500. Sometimes surprising similarities across regions in religious practices stem from the focus of many systems of religious belief on cosmic questions such as the origin and meaning of human existence, the nature of life after death, and connections between the living and the dead across time. Family metaphors play a central role in religious practices aimed at addressing these concerns. In ways that vary across religious traditions, religious festivals and practices link generations. Through religious metaphors, concerns about the past and the future of the individual, the family, and indeed human society can be formalized in rituals that link the living with ancestors and descendants.

The concern with ancestors in China has been more overt and explicit than in many other societies. Ancestors were honored with sacrifices of food and specially produced paper money ("spirit money"). Humans communicated with the other world and its residents in a variety of ways, one of which was transmission of objects to the spirit world through the mechanism of burning. People also buried their dead with grave goods that represented objects of daily use that would be needed in the next life.

When death was properly managed, the dead became ancestors. Ancestors concerned themselves with their living descendants only to a minor degree and in a generally benevolent fashion. The dead who were not treated appropriately, however, were potentially very dangerous, and a ritual structure was designed to propitiate them. One festival day in particular became the focus of concerns with ancestors. The fifteenth day of the seventh lunar month (that is, in late summer or early fall) is the Ghost Festival. As with religious festivals in so many societies, it was a syncretic creation. Buddhist festival practices were superimposed upon an earlier, Taoist, celebration. According to Taoist traditions, on this day the gates that separated the world of the living and the world of the dead were thrown open, and the dead and the living might wander in one another's realms, terrifying to both. Later, the Buddhist Festival of the Hungry Ghost (Ullambana) was celebrated at the same time. (A hungry ghost is someone who did not receive proper sacrifices at death or someone who died a violent or untimely death.)

The foundational story of the Buddhist festival is interesting for its explicit kinship dimensions. The monk Mulian gave his mother money to distribute to other mendicant monks before he himself went off to beg. She spent the money on banquets and musicians, and when she died she went to hell. Mulian, distraught, went to hell to find his mother. Once he did so, the king of hell, Yama, told him that she could be saved if Mulian would institute a festival to feed all hungry ghosts.

The Mulian story has been told and retold, and dramatic representations of it were (and still are) a common feature of funerals. It and the Ghost Festival were essential components in the historical process of the sinification of Buddhism, for it reconciled Buddhist notions of individual salvation with Chinese concerns with family and filial piety. It is further noteworthy that it is Mulian's *mother* whom he saves; she is the beneficiary in this key moment of Buddhist mythmaking about filial piety.[28]

Such stories were critical in the Chinese adaptation of Buddhism and thus in the broader history of religion. Chinese criticisms of Buddhism had revolved around the antifamilial nature of its monasticism and elevation of celibacy. The story and its festival, centered on filial piety as a Buddhist virtue, made Buddhism more acceptable in China even while it claimed that filial piety is a duty owed both parents by all children rather than just a duty a son owes his father.

64

Chinese beliefs about ghosts and ancestors resonate to a surprising degree with beliefs found in the very different social context of East Africa. There, some pastoral groups such as the Masai of what is now southern Kenya devoted religious attention to a single creator god, a practice Christian missionaries would later encourage as analogous to Christian monotheism. But most people who lived throughout East Africa also believed that the spirits of dead ancestors looked over the prosperity and morality of the kin group and community. Ancestors, for those who revered and feared them, were often thought of as elders of the very eldest sort who remained intimately connected with the affairs of their lineages—busybodies who were never too far away, even in death. Ancestors were the proprietors and guardians of the land, and it was their attentions that kept it fertile and watered.

If descendants neglected the ancestors, or if burial rituals were not properly carried out, then ancestors could become vengeful spirits, wreaking havoc on the land and its people. Proper attention to ritual, including feasts shared with the ancestors, helped maintain proper relations with ancestors so they remained benevolent. If a family member were ill, for example, the family might send a representative to a medicine man to determine which ancestor was displeased. The family would then prepare a ritual meal (often, in the pastoral cultures, featuring a sheep, goat, or bull) to which friends and neighbors would be invited. Some of the food would be consumed by living guests, and some would be buried near where the ancestor had lived. A prayer such as the following would be spoken: "If you are disturbing me or causing this trouble in my home, now today I have given you food. Eat it with your friends who have also died, as much as you can, and then do not disturb me again."[29] This prayer makes very clear the relationship between the festive feeding and the desire for rectifying a cross-generational relationship gone sour.

One category of deaths that provided particular problems from the perspective of both the East African and Chinese worldviews was the death of people who had not yet married. If the purpose of death ritual was to transform the deceased into a proper ancestor, and if the cosmological order rested on the maintenance of respectful relations between the living and the dead, then a person who died unmarried presented a vexing problem. He or she would have no progeny to carry on the relationship. In both China and East Africa, special rituals could be performed for those who died unmarried. In China, "spirit marriages" permitted a deceased unmarried man to marry in a posthumous ritual. Usually he was married to a deceased woman, although on rare occasions a living woman might be married to a dead man.[30] In some regions of East Africa there could be ritualized simulation of intercourse at the funeral of a dead unmarried girl to dispel fears that her failure to bear a child would make her an unhappy (and hence, dangerous) spirit.[31]

Christian societies managed relationships with dead ancestors in a different way. The most specific and famous Christian celebration of the dead—the period encompassing All Hallow's Eve, All Saints' Day, and All Souls' Day (October 31 through November 2) apparently originated in the Celtic festival of Samhain. On the night of October 31 the souls of the dead were supposed to visit homes that had been theirs when they were living. At that moment in the ritual calendar it was necessary to placate the supernatural powers controlling the processes of nature.

This pre-Christian observance obviously influenced the Christian celebration of All Hallows' Eve, just as the Taoist festival affected the newer Buddhist Ullambana Festival. Although the Christian version of All Saints' and All Souls' Days came to emphasize prayers for the dead, visits to graves, and the role of the living in assuring the safe passage to heaven of their departed loved ones, older notions never disappeared. The less benevolent side of relations between living and dead continues to figure into religious and secularized versions of All Hallows' Eve. The European Christian festivals surrounding it found particular resonance in Mexico, where they, too, were added to an earlier, indigenous festival. There is some evidence that in autumn the pre-Conquest Nahua culture celebrated a festival to the War God (Cloud Snake) to honor those who had died in war. At this festival, food was offered and music was performed to propitiate the dead. These festivals were eventually combined with the imported Christian celebrations to become a focal point of the Mexican ritual calendar—the Day of the Dead, featuring elaborate home shrines to ancestors, replete with very material goods such as rich and expensive food and decoration along with the more orthodox prayers.[32]

In each of these spiritual traditions, then, important moments in both the individual life-cycle (especially the transition from life to death) as well as in the communally celebrated ritual calendar emphasized ongoing ties that link ancestors and descendants. Ties and metaphors of kinship permeated religious beliefs and practices and helped place people in the cosmic and eternal as well as the social and temporal order.

These ties and metaphors of kinship, however much they shaped relations among the living and addressed cosmic questions about life and death, were never just benign. Kinship maps operated both in practice and metaphorically to structure not only family but also the economic, political, and religious communities and hierarchies within them. Family ties transmitted genetic matter, names, and identities (some and not others), political authority and subjecthood, unequal claims to land or dowries, and protection provided by and duties toward ancestors. Framing these all were deep understandings of attachment to place and belonging, impulses to mark boundaries between insiders and outsiders, and spoken and unspoken exclusions. Religious festivals that celebrated and maintained the chain of connections between the living and the dead marked and reinforced community membership among the living. By the same token, however, kin-based religious practices (and the notions of community through time that underlay them) also reinforced differences among community members along the lines of age, gender, and status and excluded individuals and groups perceived as marginal or alien to the celebratory community. The degree to which kinship shaped these rights, positions, and boundaries varied with time and place, but nowhere was kinship irrelevant to defining communities and identities.

In kin-based societies, political inclusions and exclusions were naturalized by reason of the close association between political community and lineage. But in tributary societies—those organized on a larger scale and often ruled bureaucratically—kinship metaphors did not disappear. They often continued or were reintroduced to justify forms of dominance no longer based explicitly on kinship. Indeed, thinking about political ties through kinship metaphors would eventually provide a basis for modern racialist and nationalist conceptualizations of political community. Such conceptualizations sharpened and took concrete form in the centuries of European overseas conquest, colonization, enslavement, and imperialism.

Family and Global Dynamics in the Era of Global Contact, 1500–1750

Comparisons among regions illustrate the range of patterns of social organization around the globe as accelerated global contact commenced in the late fifteenth century. Sketching out these broad regional patterns of political authority, economy, social hierarchy, kinship, and belief systems sets the stage for the next era of world history. These broad regional patterns fed into the subsequent dynamics of global contact and conflict. Family relations contributed in important but rarely acknowledged ways to the dynamic and interconnected processes of world historical change that figure so centrally in world history. These processes include:

— the conquest, or attempted conquest, and colonization by various European powers, of New World empires and strategic trade bases in the Pacific and Indian Oceans;
— the associated expansion of Christianity, primarily in the New World, and the continued expansion of Islam in Africa and around the Indian Ocean;
— the development of the institutions of merchant capitalism in regions of Europe and Asia;
— the establishment of commercial plantations on the rims of the Atlantic and Indian Oceans;

67

— the expansion of slave-taking and other forms of coercion to provide labor for these plantations;

— the growth of demand for marketed foodstuffs, including both staples and luxuries, in urban areas, primarily in Europe;

— the creation of grain-producing commercial plantations in Eastern Europe worked primarily by enserfed landless labor; and

— the development of extensive cottage industries, especially textile industries, in Europe and Asia to supply mass-produced handicraft goods for domestic and overseas markets.

In this section we discuss changes in family life that occurred in disparate regions of the world as merchant entrepreneurs reorganized agricultural and craft production across the globe. Plantations in the New World and the Indian Ocean, large-scale commercial grain farms in Eastern Europe, and protoindustrial systems in many regions of Europe and Asia all reflected the new growth and profitability of long-distance trade. The incorporation of agricultural commodity production into the system of merchant capitalism altered peasant family life. Moreover, the family-polity nexus held consequences for global dynamics. Varying forms of kin-based and tributary societies were positioned differently with respect to the introduction of early capitalist relations into local economies, the capacity to conquer, and the vulnerability to conquest. The newly emerging inequalities among global regions were based in part on preexisting family and kinship systems.

CONQUESTS AND FAMILY SYSTEMS

Conquest is a social and political dynamic that operates on many levels, but perhaps the most basic one is the level of the family.[33] In the period from 1492 to 1700 Europeans colonized the Americas and some outposts in Asia and Africa. Conquest disrupted and reconfigured family life in a number of ways. The devastation of conquest had effects on family formation, and the conquerors brought with them laws, religious systems, and other social formations that differed fundamentally from those of the people they were conquering. In the most fundamental way, intermarriage and other sexual unions produced offspring who are colonial—neither indigenous nor completely of the culture of the colonizer. Thus the processes of social formation in colonial settings—accommodation, resistance, transformation, and even racial formation—work themselves out at the level of the family.

Mexico is in many ways an exemplary case study of the familial dynamics of conquest and colonization. Family and kin systems figured in the establishment of the Spanish colonial empire in Mexico in several important ways. The brutal facts of the Conquest itself, with warfare and even more devastating disease, caused a demographic catastrophe. Scholars disagree on what the pre-

Conquest population of the area that was to become New Spain was, but most estimates fall in the range of ten to twelve million people. In the wake of the Conquest, the population plunged to around 750,000 by the early seventeenth century.[34] By 1793 the population was only 3.8 million. Some scholars have suggested that the depopulation was severe enough that women were more likely to inherit, although the theoretical possibility that a woman could be an heir was to some degree undercut by the fact that an elder brother served as guardian.[35] But as the population began to recover, women were less frequently heirs. Moreover, the introduction of Spanish law increased the power of male heads of household.[36]

The most obvious impact of the Conquest on Mexican family formation was in the realm of ethnic and racial formation as a consequence of marriages and other sexual unions across the cultural frontier. Some of the original Conquistadors married high-ranking Indian women; many other Spaniards had sexual liaisons of varying sorts with Indian women. The offspring of these unions were known as *castas*.[37] Race became a principle of social hierarchy. The changing racial composition of the population shows the demographic evidence of family formation and transformation. At the end of the eighteenth century there were an estimated 2.8 million Indians, 685,000 whites, 788,000 castas, and 6,000 blacks.[38] Of course, these categories themselves evolved, as did the claims individuals made about their racial identity. Some women, for example, who registered as mestiza on baptismal certificates were registered as white on marriage certificates when they married white men, an illustration of how racial imagination interacted with family strategy.[39]

The family systems of Central America were dramatically altered by the Conquest. One important demographic index—age at marriage—apparently rose because unions with very young girls were proscribed following European customs. Not surprisingly, the transplantation of the Catholic Church, and the particular relationship between Church and state, from Europe to Mexico was reflected most clearly in the institutions surrounding marriage.

The importation of Catholicism was part and parcel of the Spanish conquest of Mexico. By the sixteenth century the Catholic Church was already a power to be reckoned with. The first Christian marriages were performed in the 1520s.[40] It is clear from census records later in the sixteenth century, however, that such marriages still remained rare.[41] As in Europe, the Council of Trent (1547–63) gave the Mexican Church enhanced power to intervene in marriage choices. The interventions were, in fact, most apparent in the historical record of the colonial era, when religious conversion and associated attempts to "colonize" family life were most intense. Evidence from early colonial Mexico suggests that young couples being coerced into marriage could appeal to clergy as they could in Europe. In Mexican history as in many regions of Europe, a centuries-long tug of war between state and church affected the extent to which each regulated marriage.[42] Still, marriage according to the prescriptions of Church or state was predominantly an upper-class institution; the remainder of the population formed consensual unions.[43] There were obstacles to marrying in the Church, even if one had wanted to. Both parties, for example, had to produce baptismal certificates, which could be hard to obtain in a context where there was much migration.[44]

In addition, European, specifically Catholic, rules about consanguinity were introduced. For example, cross-cousin marriage, which had been practiced among the Maya, was conceptualized as incest (and hence prohibited) under Church rules.[45] The Laws of Toro, based on Spanish law and introduced into Mexican courts in the sixteenth century, formed the core of family and inheritance law throughout the colonial period and tended over time to supplant pre-Conquest indigenous practices, at least in urban areas.[46] The introduction of a dowry system as an alternative to the bride-service that Europeans found objectionable had strong implications for gender and the generational pattern of wealth. The colonial government also attempted to institute monogamy. In 1551, for example, a royal decree was issued that punished a man for marrying a second wife while the first wife was still alive.[47]

Thus the changes introduced by the Spanish colonial regime in Mexico attempted to impose some of the same constraints on marriage that prevailed in much of early modern Europe, one effect of which was to put further upward pressure on the age at marriage.[48] In addition, the reconstruction of the racial and social stratification system that accompanied colonization, along with the immigration of many thousands of Spanish settlers, had a profound effect on indigenous marriage patterns. Still, changes should not be exaggerated.[49] The Church seems to have made inroads in its campaign against upper-class polygamy, for example, but one effect of efforts to regulate marriage was that many lower-class people simply ignored Church prescriptions and lived in consensual unions. Village life in particular seems to have been only lightly affected. Indigenous rural communities continued to organize household life according to their practices, most of which were not in direct conflict with Spanish Catholic ideas.[50] In short, the post-Conquest Mexican family system, like so many other Mexican institutions of this historical era, was hybrid and complex. Its class, racial, regional, and generational variation echoed and helped constitute other dimensions of post-Conquest society.

In contrast with the rather thoroughgoing colonial project characteristic of the Spanish Conquest of Mexico, the Portuguese presence in East Africa was superficial if nonetheless destructive. The contrast shows up well through the lens of family history. In East Africa, the Portuguese focused on the attempt to profit from existing Swahili Coast trade and establish way stations for the lucrative Indian Ocean spice trade. They burned and pillaged cities whose rulers refused to acknowledge their dominion, and they interfered in preexisting trade to such an extent that it was driven underground. But they met with little success in efforts to establish a permanent Portuguese presence and administrative center in this part of their empire. In contrast with the Spanish in Mexico or Islamic traders from the Red Sea and the Arabian Peninsula who had sailed the Swahili Coast for centuries and intermarried there, the Portuguese who arrived in East Africa at the very end of the fifteenth century brought little deep change. Virtually no intermarriage or any alteration of indigenous family practices can be ascribed to this phase of Portuguese colonialism in the region.[51] Even attempts to establish Christian missions were half-hearted and mostly unsuccessful.

The relative superficiality of early modern Portuguese colonial projects on the Swahili Coast compared with other contemporaneous European projects thus has a family-historical dimension. The more decentralized, kinship-based societies of East Africa were certainly more vulnerable to conquest but at the same time more difficult for outsiders to infiltrate and govern as conquerors. The dense and urbanized population of Mexico, with its relatively centralized tributary polity, was both more powerful and more vulnerable to European diseases and actual takeover.

Once the conquest of Mexico was completed and the indigenous population decimated by rapidly spreading epidemic disease, repopulation perforce involved reconstruction of family life. But it was not reconstructed as it was before the Conquest. The combination of substantial immigration from Spain, intermarriage between the Spanish and indigenous people, and efforts by both state and Church to transform the family practices of the resulting population provided the basis for its colonial governability. These two cases present contrasts as colonial projects; they also represent contrasting histories of the family during the first phase of European overseas colonization.

MERCHANT CAPITALISM, THE PLANTATION SYSTEM, SLAVERY, AND FAMILY LIFE

To reiterate: In 1500 all of the world's economies were predominantly household-based. One of the most significant transformations that unfolded between 1500 and 1750 was commencement of the move of productive activities, even the conceptualization of "the economy" as a terrain of human action, to arenas outside the household. The process did not occur at the same pace in all sectors of the economy nor in all the world's regions. Moreover, the transformation has been neither linear nor unidirectional. Still, the changing historical relationship between mostly kin-based communities of reproduction, consumption, and residence, on the one hand, and the sites of production and distribution of goods, on the other, provides focus for meaningful analysis of global economic history.

This section will discuss how the varying degrees to which economies of different regions of the world were organized according to kin-based or tributary logic played a role in their ultimate position in the emergent capitalist world order after the fifteenth century. In addition, even within the realm of tributary societies, varying patterns of family organization, gender relations, and household activity shape the ways regions have involved themselves in the global economy, as is well illustrated by the economic divergence between Europe and China beginning in the nineteenth century.

No world history course can neglect the role of world market development as an engine of historical change, however such development is discussed or evaluated. Patterns of trade that were becoming apparent by the sixteenth century were already hinting at the regional inequalities that would become more fully developed in ensuing centuries. For a start, people who deployed predominantly kinship-based modes of production would find themselves at a serious competitive disadvantage in a world economy increasingly dominated by accumulators whose wealth rested on large-scale tribute collection or the control of private property. This disadvantage was, in turn, related to political dimensions of tributary systems as opposed to kin-based polities. Conditions favoring accumulation were more likely to be present in centralized tributary systems than in more dispersed and localized kin-based systems. Moreover, the mercantile elites most successful at implanting and dominating market systems in their own regions, and eventually throughout the globe, relied in many ways on the power of the states that backed them and supported their ventures.

Historians now recognize that the key shifts defining the emergent global economy occurred long before Europe's Industrial Revolution. The increasing domination of traders and entrepreneurs over aspects of the global economy owed more to the reorganization of agriculture, handicraft production, and trade than to industrial technology. Beginning in the fifteenth century, merchant entrepreneurs linked to an ever-expanding global trade network increased intervention into the household production of industrial and agricultural goods in such a way as to transform family labor systems throughout the world.

The growth of merchant capitalism is by now a familiar story for world historians. Our aim here is to emphasize the family-historical dimensions of this development. Initially, much of the booming world trade that enriched merchants, especially but by no means exclusively in Europe, and altered consumption patterns by the eighteenth century involved agricultural commodities. Production of most of the boom crops—spices, sugar, tobacco, cotton, coffee, and tea—had moved to large-scale Indian Ocean or New World plantations during the sixteenth and seventeenth centuries. The move held huge implications for agricultural labor systems because plantation owners needed to recruit large and concentrated labor forces. They met labor needs by buying slaves rather than relying on labor service from households of farmers.

The New World, both North and South America, had an insatiable appetite for labor. Disease remained a problem in the tropical New World, and Africans were regarded as ideal laborers in such a context. They were regarded as having—and, indeed, they may have had—more immunity to tropical diseases than did Europeans. Transportation of Africans to plantations along the coast of South America, the Caribbean, and North America as far north as the Chesapeake Bay provided labor to produce the crops, many of them tropical, for which there was growing European demand.

During the course of the eighteenth century, about sixty thousand Africans entered the Western Hemisphere each year as slaves. Only about 10 percent of the total entered the United States, yet between one-third and one-half of the descendants of those who came from Africa as slaves live in the United States. The North American slave population reproduced itself; other slave populations in South American and the sugar islands of the Caribbean did not. The nature of the plantation system and climate are both relevant here. Crops such as sugar were lucrative enough that planters calculated it cheaper to buy a slave than to raise a child. Calculations were different in the cotton economies that predominated in the slave areas of North America. There, it was in the planters' interest to encourage slave reproduction. The climate in North America may have helped—cold climates with killing frosts limit the devastation of disease. By 1850 only 1 percent of the slaves who lived in the United States were African-born. That is in sharp contrast to a place like Brazil, where there was steady traffic back and forth with Benin and hence strong elements of Yoruba culture remained present there.

Slaves who lived on plantations in North America developed durable kinship networks that differed in some aspects from the kinship systems of planters. Most slave families were founded on durable marriages despite the constant threat (often realized) of families being disrupted through the sale of one or more members. Some marriages, called "abroad marriages," were between slaves who resided on different plantations. Despite the fact that slave marriages were not recognized in law, weddings were important for plantation communities. Planters often promoted marriages because they regarded doing so as part of their task as Christians; moreover, they wanted to encourage reproduction among their slaves. Prenuptial pregnancy does not seem to have been stigmatized, but marriage normally followed such pregnan-

73

cies. There seems to have been a strong taboo on cousin marriages among slaves, although planters frequently married their own cousins. Slave women bore their first children, on average, earlier than did other women in the United States. Most data on slave families in the United States come from the last years of slavery, and it is difficult to reconstruct what slave families would have been like during the early years of the institution. It is clear, however, that kinship among slaves was neither an importation of African kinship nor an imitation of planter kinship but rather a new system.[52]

We associate plantation agriculture primarily with areas of the New World that Europeans colonized. But it is important to note that parallel and related changes came to other regions of the globe at around the same period as the establishment of the Atlantic rim plantation economy. In the seventeenth century mercantile elites of southern Arabia, newly ascendant politically after the overthrow of Islamic religious rule, established a plantation regime attuned to the expanding world demand for products such as dates and spices. Soon they, too, were relying heavily on slave labor brought from East African caravan routes.[53] The increasing migration of Omani and Islamicized Swahili mercantile elites to East Africa in the nineteenth century, in the context of a growing European demand for plantation goods, resulted in the spread of slave plantation agriculture to the Swahili Coast.

The slavery associated with East African plantation agriculture was not identical with the system that took West Africans to the New World. The crops the plantations produced—such as cloves and dates—were less labor-intensive than most New World plantation crops.

Slaves were thus occupied in varying activities over the course of the year and often had time to themselves. Moreover, the system was originally built upon prior forms of slavery permitted under Islamic law. The demands of the global plantation economy eroded the protections that that law stipulated for slaves. Nevertheless, certain features differentiated Swahili Coast slavery from the chattel slavery under which West Africans were captured to work the European plantations of the New World.

Some distinctions emerged from the location of slaves in Islamic kinship. Under Islamic law, free men who married slave concubines were required to free them at death if they bore children. The children of free fathers were deemed free. Thus servitude was not considered a perpetual and inheritable status as it was in many other forms of slavery. Some historians argue that Islamic law discouraged the enslavement of "peoples of the book"—that is, Christians and Jews as well as Muslims. Africans who practiced local religions were thus favored targets of the slave-raiders who increasingly plagued the Coast beginning in the late eighteenth century, but prior conversion to Islam did at least hypothetically protect one from enslavement. As was the case among free people, the social status and condition of slaves was bound up with particular forms of kinship law and family practices.

FAMILY AND HOUSEHOLD IN THE DEVELOPMENT OF PROTOINDUSTRIAL WAGE LABOR SYSTEMS

Merchant capitalism took many forms and adapted to different political circumstances and market niches in addition to slave plantations. Grain production controlled by aristocratic landowners in Eastern Europe, for example, also evolved in the face of market opportunities created by the growth of urban populations in Western Europe fed by Baltic shipping routes. Beginning in the fifteenth century, and facilitated by political compromises between landlords and state-builders, formerly free peasants in the Baltic and trans-Elbian regions of the Holy Roman Empire were subjected to the "new serfdom" on plantationlike grain estates. New rules of labor discipline tied peasants to particular estates, put them more tightly under the juridical control of estate-owning Junkers, and eroded their ability to own and work land in their own right. In many regions of the East, a new family economy evolved that was based not on household production but on family wage labor on large estates.

Further to the West, merchant entrepreneurs followed still a different strategy for creating and capturing new markets—those for mass-produced textiles. Densely settled regions of peasant agriculture in the Rhineland and parts of Switzerland emerged as classic zones of protoindustry or "putting out"—a form of industrial organization whereby merchants advanced raw materials such as wool to rural households, whose members would then work them up into finished products for sale by the merchant. State authorities throughout Central Europe became interested in the increasing productivity and wealth that markets promised. Seconding the efforts of entrepreneurs, they drew on the advice of men of academic education to found "industry schools" that taught rural children work discipline and handicrafts. Some governments even granted monopoly concessions to entrepreneurs to establish and regulate rural putting-out industries. They also established state "manufactories"—large-scale handicraft workshops—for the production of luxury goods such as porcelain, tobacco, and silk to sell on the world market and prevent their own people from buying expensive imports.

Growth in the agricultural and industrial sectors brought wealth visible in new consumption habits documented, for example, by research on the Württemberg weaving village of Laichingen, where even girls from weaving households brought the occasional silk item along with their dowry.[54] But these changes brought new tensions as well, often manifested in family relations. The intensification of agricultural labor and the introduction of putting-out work disrupted traditional gender and generational divisions of labor and brought increasing conflict to overcrowded households and communities. On the one hand, the intense labor that these new industries required could be provided by peasant sons and, especially, daughters needing a portion to marry. On the other hand, the very availability of income outside of the traditional peasant household economy seems, in some regions at least, to have loosened family and community regulation of marriage.[55] Even though some peasants, artisans, and putting-out workers prospered during the economic expansion that peaked in the late eighteenth century, the unevenly distributed social costs of economic growth were manifested in rising rates of infant mortality, divorce, and the pilfering of firewood and fodder.[56]

Again, there are some interesting parallels between Central Europe and China in the era of protoindustrialization. Historians now argue that there were rough parallels in the dynamics of demographic expansion and economic growth in China and Europe throughout the early modern period. Both economies were expanding on the basis of growth of rural industrial enterprises in which peasant families supplemented agricultural work and income with part-time industrial production. In the Chinese case, this protoindustrial form of development was an alternative route to industrialization rather than a precursor of factory production. Indeed, a prescient observer of the European economy in 1750 would likely have predicted such a future—that is, "a countryside with a growing proletariat working in both agriculture and manufacturing."[57]

We address the question of the eventual divergence between Chinese and European forms of economic development and its relation to family history in the following section. The point here is that early modern world market growth had far-reaching and uneven consequences for families in many different regions of the globe—from slave plantations on the rims of the Atlantic and Indian Oceans, to those regions of Africa from which slaves were taken, to East European estates and Central and West European protoindustrial villages.

Families in Industrial Capitalism and Imperialism, 1750–1920

The following section discusses how regional differences in kinship, family, and gender relations were significant for the development of the system of global industrial capitalism by the second half of the eighteenth century. We then discuss the role of family ideologies and family practices in the global encounters structured by imperialism around the end of the nineteenth century. We take up three aspects of imperialism: family historical dimensions of European imperialist ventures in Africa and Asia; the role of family ideals and ideas in the encounters between European Christian missionaries and prospective converts, especially in East Africa; and the impact of indirect imperialism and attendant political reforms on gender relations in China.

INDUSTRIAL CAPITALISM AND FAMILY LIFE

Historians and social theorists have long been interested in the relationship between the emergence of modern industrial capitalism and the history of family life. Pioneering works on the history of the family and women's history in Europe and the United States were structured around questions of how the disappearance of productive labor from households affected family life and women's status.[58] Although the long-term improvement in living standards brought about by increases in productivity is clear, many historians nevertheless point to a long period of increased class and gender inequality that industrial capitalism brought with it. These issues are important but fairly familiar terrain. We take on the somewhat different task here of examining evidence about how specific variations in family-kinship systems in different areas fed into regional paths to economic development and, ultimately, contributed to varying regional positionalities with respect to the industrial capitalist world system.

The comparison between Chinese and European patterns of industrial development from the nineteenth century onward offers one illustration of how family and gender arrangements played a role in the development of global industrial capitalism.[59] Important, and more recent, comparative analysis of economic and demographic development in these two regions lays the groundwork.[60]

Attention to family and household dynamics makes the logic of the different "paths to the present" followed in Europe and China increasingly clear.

One of the striking peculiarities of Central and Western European history that had developed by the seventeenth century was its pattern of relatively late marriage—that is, relative to other regions of the world where some form of marriage, at least for women, usually occurred shortly after puberty and was nearly universal. A substantial minority of men and women never married. The European practice of relatively late marriage was closely connected with particular family-economy links already described. There were widespread customs preventing marriage before a couple commanded the resources required for economic independence. In the case of artisans, that traditionally meant having a shop and master status. In the case of peasant couples, that meant having a house and land and the basic equipment required to farm it. It was the responsibility of the family and the community to oversee courtship, betrothal, and marriage to assure that these conditions were met. Late marriage, recall, was also rooted in the practice of *neolocality* (that is, expectation that a bride and groom would set up their own household at or soon after marriage) common in much of Northern and Western Europe.

As a result of relatively late marriage, European young people of both sexes experienced a relatively long hiatus between puberty and marriage.[61] Unmarried youths played a distinctive role in economic life (as well as social, cultural, and political life) through such institutions as guilds, rural youth groups, domestic service, and universities. The contrast between early modern Europe and other world regions meant that teenaged girls were available for employment outside the familial household (either natal or marital) to a degree uncommon elsewhere. Household divisions of labor according to age and gender meant there was constant demand for servants on larger farms. In Europe this role was typically filled from the pool of unmarried youths who could be hired in as servants from neighboring farms or land-poor families. A period of service in a farm household, as an apprentice, or as a domestic servant in an urban household was a characteristic experience for both male and female European youths in the life-cycle phase preceding marriage.[62]

The traditional Chinese family system was characterized by early age at marriage, nearly universal marriage for women, and *virilocal* residence (that is, a newly married couple normally resided with the groom's parents). From the sixteenth through the twentieth centuries, Chinese couples married much younger on the average than did their European counterparts. According to Chinese historical demographers "In China, females have always married universally and early . . . in contrast to female marriage in Western Europe, which occurred late or not at all."[63] Whereas in the nineteenth century all but 20 percent of Chinese young women were married by age twenty, between 60 and 80 percent of young women among European populations were still unmarried at that age. In traditional China, only 1 or 2 percent of women remained unmarried at age thirty, whereas between 15 and 25 percent of thirty-year-old Western European women were still single. (For men, the differences, although in the same direction, are far less stark.)[64] Because the new couple in China would ordinarily reside in an already-existing household, that of the groom's family, it was not necessary for an artisan to become established or a peasant to own a farm before marrying. The newly married couple participated in an ongoing domestic and economic enterprise. New households were eventually established through a process of household division. That typically happened at the death of the father rather than the moment of marriage, although it could happen at other points in the family cycle as well.

Early marriage in China meant that the category of "youth," which was so significant for European social and economic history, has no precise counterpart in Chinese history. A young Chinese woman labored, to be sure, but the location of her work was domestic—either in the household of her father or her husband. There were female domestic servants in China, but their servitude seems to have been of longer duration that the life-cyclic servitude so common in Europe.[65] The domestic location of young women's labor in the Chinese context also had implications for the particular way in which Chinese cottage industries were organized and for how early modern economic development occurred in the two regions.

Analysis of economic development in Europe and China suggests explicit connections between economic and demographic growth. In particular, the link between marriage and economic opportunity meant that "in both China and Europe, rural industry supported lower age at marriage and higher proportions of ever married than would have been plausible in its absence."[66] But despite apparent similarities on the eve of industrialization, regional differences of both the timing and residency of young people before and after marriage persisted and held particular significance for subsequent forms of development.

In a comparative account of why Chinese industrial development relied so heavily on domestic production, the fact that the young female labor force in China was to an extent far greater than that of Europe (both married and "domesticated" within a male-headed household) needs to be part of the story. This pattern of female marriage and residency held implications for entrepreneurial choice that helped determine the different paths toward industrialization in Europe and China. A comparison that takes into account aspects of gender relations and marriage and kinship systems highlights their possible significance for economic development, a significance that economic historians have not, until recently, given proper attention.[67] Indeed, the family and marital status of the young women who played so significant a role in the workforce (in particular, in the textile industry that was key to early industrial development in both Europe and China) was a major factor in determining the varying paths to development followed in China and Europe in the centuries of protoindustrial growth and early industrialization. In China a young woman remained in the domestic realm, moving at marriage from her father's household to that of her husband's family. Young women in Europe, in the period before they married, were increasingly regarded as an available labor pool for work outside the domestic realm, and they were a significant element in the early factory labor force.

Another difference between European and Chinese textile development that is key to understanding divergence involves the gender division of labor in household production. In particular, "The lower Yangzi and some other regions were full of rural weavers and spinners but not of couples composed of two textile workers, as one so often found in Western Europe, and not of great landlords interested in settling such people on their land as cottagers in order to gain access to their labor. In short, what we might call the 'proletarian migration option' was difficult in China because the normative spinner or weaver was not a proletarian—she was part of a household that had, if not its own land, at least the money for a tenant's rent deposit."[68]

Here, too, an important feature of the protoindustrial labor force is related to agrarian household structure and its gender division of labor. Both dimensions—the young woman's domestic containment through the marriage transition and her continued connection to a peasant household—made her less available to become a factory proletarian. One might argue that European factory industrialization could have proceeded without young female laborers, but in fact it relied heavily on them. In China, encouraging domestic manufacture was a more apparent option.

FAMILY AND IMPERIALISM

The economic and political stories of imperialism, relatively well known, are mainstays of most world history courses. The ways in which family and gender relations were implicated in the imperialist project are just beginning to be recognized. More recent innovative scholarship suggests the extent to which imperialist projects aimed to reconstruct family life as much as political and economic life in the Colonies. Moreover, they demonstrate how, in the context of imperialism, global power systems and race relations, and family/gender history (of both colonizers and colonized) are bound together. Critical reading of the sources has debunked the once-prevalent myth that sexual liaisons between colonizing men and colonized women provided a humanizing side to imperialism until the arrival of white women in the Colonies. More recent research has shown how family policies were intrinsic to the management of colonies and racial relations in Africa and Asia and demonstrated the intersection of gender identities, family dynamics, and imperial politics in India.[69]

In East Africa, as in other colonized regions of the globe, imperialism brought European ideals of family along with colonial rule. Conflicts between various indigenous people and European colonizers about gender and family relations were subsequently an important dimension of colonial regimes and anticolonial struggles. Moreover, these struggles inserted themselves into ongoing gender and generational tensions implicit in precolonial family systems. In the era of imperialism, no one system of gender relations prevailed in East Africa; there were regions of matrilinear, patrilinear, and mixed systems of accounting for kin relations. Moreover, different degrees and types of power were associated with men and women, old and young, although certainly most prevalent normative systems placed men over women and older men over younger men in terms of power in both the political and the kinship realms.

With respect to such authority and control over wealth, Europeans, mis-

sionaries in particular, disrupted prevailing gender and generational hierarchies in several ways. In Gikuyuland (now central Kenya) the disruption became evident with the first cohorts of converts in the early twentieth century,
especially at the point of marriage.[70] Missionaries maintained that proper virtuous marriages were the basis of the Christian society. According to a Scot-
tish missionary in Gikuyuland, writing in 1923, "The very first principle of
Christian teaching is the endeavor to make the home life here something that
it has not been—namely 'home' life where health, purity and love—between
man and wife, and between parents and children—reign. . . . The foundation
of Christian homes is the missionary aim."[71]

But this missionary reform of marriage ran up against rule by male elders
and their prerogatives, polygamy and control over bride-price (which was
perceived by missionaries, as previously in Mexico, as "selling" daughters). In
places like Gikuyuland, marriage was often an occasion for conflict between
men and women and between older and younger generations even before
serious intervention by Christian missionaries at the beginning of the twentieth century. Christianity in the context of imperialism exacerbated structural tensions within such elder-dominated societies. With the encouragement
of Christian missions, both Christian women and younger men mounted
opposition to polygamy. More broadly, the control over timing and arrangement of marriages by elders, powerful because of their authority and their
control over the wealth needed for bride-price (in Gikuyuland paid in goats
and beer), came under attack. Not surprisingly, then, the tendency to con-
vert reflected family position. The earliest converts were younger men, followed by younger women and then older women. Male elders were the least
interested in Christianity in the early years of the missions. Converts saw Christianity as an ideological and institutional basis for challenge to the power of
male elders, and of particular use were the missionaries' teachings about family
relations.

Thus the religious conversion of young Gikuyu during the 1910s and
1920s was also a form of rebellion against their fathers' culture and power.
Through their conversion to Christianity, negotiation of their own marriages,
and refusal to drink beer (they preferred tea), they broke with key elements
of the Gikuyu family-economic and cultural nexus. Meanwhile, their fathers,
whose accumulated wealth (in goats) and control over wives and the wives'
fertility (symbolized by control over the production and distribution of beer),
resisted this challenge. According to a contemporary newspaper account, at
the first Christian marriage conducted at Tumutumu Mission, between two
students at the missionary boarding school in 1916, the parents refused to
attend. Older Christian converts stood in for them at the ceremony. At the
conclusion of the ceremony, tea was served.[72] As Christianity became institu-

tionalized, elders complained the Gikuyu men no longer drank beer to cement relationships and distinguish elders from children, men from boys, and males from females. "How is a man to be recognized as an elder nowadays?" one Gikuyu asked in a newspaper article of the 1920s.[73] Here again we see the familiar interconnection among political authority, family structure, and religion.

Imperialism disrupted gender and generational relations in other ways as well. European styles of dress, with their particular connotations of gender and status, came to signify forms of compliance with, or resistance to, European rule and also European family gender and sexual norms. One clear example of this is provided by a political movement of Luo men (in contemporary Kenya) in the first half of the twentieth century. In songs and political protests, the adoption of European male dress was represented as a threat to Luo masculinity. Resistance took many forms, including men's assertive nakedness in the fact of European efforts to promote the wearing of "civilized" clothing.

This sense of colonial demasculinazation also came up, of course, in conflicts over the gendering of labor. Colonial powers were interested in extracting labor and taxes from their colonies as required by the demands of the mother country and the settler population. But Europeans found that African patterns of labor violated their norms of female propriety—women did much of the agricultural labor after the initial clearing of the land and digging, which was men's work. When Europeans set up plantations and farms, they wanted male laborers; they also wanted labor for their households and other enterprises. In addition to pushing people into kinds of jobs and forms of work that they weren't accustomed to often under forced-labor systems, they also thus attacked masculine prerogatives by asking men to do what was regarded as women's work.

European labor demands were problematic because they were disruptive of household patterns and the ability of households to sustain themselves and because they called into question indigenous gender norms and gender divisions of labor. In areas such as German East Africa, cotton plantations operated with resort to forced labor.[74] Because adult men were conscripted to do this labor, women and children had to make up for the lost labor time of the family's food crops, and those often suffered. According to oral traditions, "If you left the chasing of the pigs to the women she could not manage well at night . . . if you did not have children it was necessary to help your wife drive away the birds, while at the same time you cleared a piece of land for the second maize crop, because your wife would not have time . . . and during this period they still wanted you to go and work on the *jumbe*'s plantation. This was why people became furious and angry."[75] As the forced cotton regime spread through more and more of German East Africa, it brought with it increasing work for everyone, decreasing food production and disruption of the household economy. This added fuel to the hatred for the colonial regime, ultimately feeding into anticolonial insurrections such as the Maji Maji revolt of 1905–7 against the German colonial regime in East Africa.

THE MAY FOURTH MOVEMENT, GENDER RELATIONS, AND GLOBAL POLITICS

By the early twentieth century, anticolonial movements and revolts began to undermine the imperialist world order, which would finally topple after World War II. Examples of such movements—the Maji Maji revolt, the Indian nationalist movement, or the May Fourth movement in late imperial China—bring us to revisit connections between political authority and kinship and family relations. The May Fourth movement provides an example.

The fall of the Qing dynasty brought an end to the old order, but it did not produce a new order. One attempt to imagine and enact a new order was the May Fourth movement, one of a series of movements that were part of the political restructuring of China in the early twentieth century. The movement took its name from a political demonstration in the Chinese capital on May Fourth 1919. It refers broadly to a time period and a cultural movement that extended well into the 1920s. The political movement began as a demonstration of three thousand students at Peking University to protest the Treaty of Versailles, particularly those provisions of the treaty that gave the former German possessions in Shandong to the Japanese. It spread to other campuses, and by the time it was suppressed it had involved workers as well as students. It was a movement that was from its very inception anti-imperialist, but it was also vehemently critical of most of the Chinese tradition of authority. What began as a nationalist awakening culminated in a cultural critique of China's past. Anti-imperialist sentiment did not prevent May Fourth thinkers from advocating the teachings of "Mr. Science" and "Mr. Democracy" as remedies for the position in both the international and the domestic arenas.

China was backward, so the May Fourth critique went, largely because of the generational and gender hierarchies that had dominated Chinese cultural and social life for so long. The Five Relationships made the analogy between state and family life clear; a good son or a good wife also stood for a good subject. Because the family was so deeply implicated in the explicit ways the state was imagined, when the old regime was overthrown and a new regime was imagined, new ways of imagining families and gender relations came to the forefront. Customs such as footbinding, prostitution, and concubinage were regarded as being both causes and symptoms of China's weakness. The perceived weakness was, of course, weakness with respect to Western powers, which presumably were free of such vices. Movement leaders were predominantly male, but they championed women's rights.[76] The movement also questioned generational hierarchies.

The thinkers of the May Fourth movement were young (Li Dazhao, at thirty, was the old man among them), and they celebrated youth. It is perhaps not overly cynical to suggest that these criticisms of the usual gender and generational hierarchy did not emerge out of any interest in the political rights of women and youth per se. Rather, the movement leaders understood that gender and generational subordination was key to the social structure of the old regime, and if they wanted to challenge the old regime, then there was no more fundamental place to start than by challenging the traditional family structure. Thus, at the end of the course we reinvoke connections among family, gender, kinship, and political legitimacy with which the course began.

Conclusion

World history in the twentieth and twenty-first centuries continues to demonstrate the multiple ways in which family and gender relations are connected with broad economic, social, and cultural dynamics. One example from the realm of international politics is provided by the transition from socialist to market economies in Eastern Europe in the last decade of the twentieth century. The case of East Germany, and the process of its eventual political reunification with West Germany, provides a particularly telling illustration. Reunification brought many political conflicts that were exacerbated by the fact that between 1945 and 1989 the two Germanies had developed different systems of gender relations along with their different economic systems. East German women who were involved in the democratization movement of the 1980s expected to continue their full participation in the labor market supported by generous maternity leaves and state-supported child care. They sought political reform but not the loss of what they had regarded as women's rights under the socialist gender regime. Not surprisingly, then, some of the bitterest political struggles of the 1990s revolved around divergent views on abortion, child care, and female employment—struggles that sometimes even pitted Western feminists against their Eastern "stepsisters."[77]

Closer to home, the global migrations that have been a common feature of world history (and U.S. history) since the fifteenth century provide another recurrent thematic connection between the local and the global, between family-level and global processes. Many of the phenomena we have already discussed—slavery, colonization, and trade—of course involved the movement of individuals with or without their consent and with or without their families. Sometimes, these migrations were small in scale, but they sometimes involved huge numbers of people. Many West Africans, for example, were brought as slaves to the Americas—on the order of eleven million between the sixteenth and the early nineteenth centuries. During the period from 1850 to 1920, there were massive international migrations of a more voluntary sort, although some of this later movement involved unfree labor, and much was driven by economic marginality. One massive migratory stream brought 34.5 million people from Europe to the Americas. During the same period, about thirty-two million Asians (eighteen million from China and fourteen million from India) migrated to Southeast Asia (this in addition to perhaps another eighteen million Chinese who migrated to relatively underpopulated regions such as Manchuria).[78]

One advantage of discussing global migration as a family-historical process is the opportunity this presents for making direct connections between history and the present by discussing how new migrations are reshaping global family connections, identities, and racial and ethnic formations in our contemporary world. Undergraduate student populations are themselves products of the history of global migration, some more recent than others. The growing diversity of world history classrooms, and the varying family histories represented in them, can through discussions of familial institutions and relationships become part of the story being told. Whether this means lecturing about veiling with veiled young women in the audience or having classroom discussions informed by student descriptions of how their families celebrate Chinese New Year or the Day of the Dead, it becomes obvious that "our" family history of the present has been altered by migrations past and ongoing. In this sense, world history classrooms are natural laboratories for the study of family dynamics in a global-historical frame.

Notes

Earlier versions of this essay were presented at the University of Minnesota's Comparative Women's History Workshop, the 2001 World History Association meeting in Salt Lake City and the University of Illinois Department of History. We thank the audiences at those sessions for their helpful feedback. In addition we thank Patrick McNamara and Derek Peterson for commenting on an earlier draft.

1. Eric Wolf, *Europe and the People without History* (Berkeley: University of California Press, 1982), ch. 3.

2. June Nash, "The Aztecs and the Ideology of Male Dominance," *Signs* 4, no. 2 (1978): 349–62.

3. Gayle Rubin, "The Traffic in Women: Notes on the 'Political Economy' of Sex," in *Toward an Anthropology of Women,* ed. Rayna Rapp Reiter (New York: Monthly Review Press, 1975), 157–210.

4. The classical anthropological account is Myron Cohen, *House United, House Divided: The Chinese Family in Taiwan* (New York: Columbia University Press, 1976); see also

David Wakefield, *Fenjia: Household Division and Inheritance in Qing and Republican China* (Honolulu: University of Hawai'i Press, 1998).

5. Convenient reproductions of such images can be found in Susan Mann, *Precious Records: Women in China's Long Eighteenth Century* (Stanford: Stanford University Press, 1997).

6. Ingeborg Weber-Kellermann, *Die Familie: Geschichte, Geschichten und Bilder* (Frankfurt am Main: Insel Verlag, 1976), 238.

7. The onion was part of a presentation, "The City in Imperial China," at the conference on Urban Society in Traditional China sponsored by the ACLS-SSRC Subcommittee on Research on Chinese Society, Aug. 31–Sept. 6, 1968.

8. See James Lockhart, "Sightings: Initial Nahua Reactions to Spanish Culture," in *Implicit Understandings: Observing, Reporting, and Reflecting upon Encounters between Europeans and Other Peoples,* ed. Stuart Schwartz (New York: Cambridge University Press, 1994), 218.

9. Lisa Mary Sousa, "Women and Crime in Colonial Oaxaca," in *Indian Women of Early Mexico,* ed. Susan Schroeder (Norman: University of Oklahoma Press, 1997), 210.

10. Susan Kellog, "Tenochca Mexican Women, 1500–1700," in *Indian Women of Early Mexico,* ed. Susan Schroeder (Norman: University of Oklahoma Press, 1997), 125–26, and Susan Kellog, "Cognatic Kinship and Religion: Women in Aztec Society," in *Smoke and Mist: Mesoamerican Studies in Memory of Thelma D. Sullivan,* ed. J. Kathryn Josserand and Karen Dakin (Oxford: British Archaeological Reports Press, 1988), 666–81.

11. For a discussion of how lateral ties seemed to have been more important before the Conquest, and lineal ties more important after, see S. L. Cline, *Colonial Culhuacan 1580–1600: A Social History of an Aztec Town* (Albuquerque: University of New Mexico Press, 1986), 164.

12. Robert McCaa, "Marriageways in Mexico and Spain, 1500–1900," *Continuity and Change* 9, no. 1 (1994): 14.

13. Susan Schroeder, "The Mexico That Spain Encountered," in *Oxford History of Mexico,* ed. Michael C. Meyer (New York: Oxford University Press, 2000), 71; Asunción Lavrin, "Sexuality in Colonial Mexico: A Church Dilemma," in *Sexuality and Marriage in Colonial Latin America,* ed. Asunción Lavrin (Lincoln: University of Nebraska Press, 1989), 68; and McCaa, "Marriageways," 13, 15.

14. Fray Bernadino de Sahagún, *Florentine Codex: General History of the Things of New Spain,* trans. Charles E. Dibble and Arthur O. J. Anderson (Santa Fe: Monographs of School of American Research, 1979), 14, pt. 6, 172.

15. Sahagún, *Florentine Codex,* 171.

16. Inge Clendennin, "Yucatec Maya Women and the Spanish," *Journal of Social History* 13 (1982): 428.

17. Of course, there is the problem that these diagrams of social structure account primarily for men. How to fit women (and children) into them is always problematic.

18. Historical evidence about marriage and family systems is much more difficult to come by for East Africa than for cases where written records were more common. Coastal Muslim communities left written legal and genealogical records, but for most of the interior, historians rely on sources such as archeological evidence, oral traditions, and travelers' reports. What one can know about the past thus varies from case to case, an issue we discuss explicitly with students. Our account here and elsewhere draws on Juhani Koponen, *People and Production in Late Precolonial Tanzania: History and Structures*

(Helsinki: Finnish Society for Development Studies, 1988); Madelain Farah, *Marriage and Sexuality in Islam: A Translation of al-Ghazali's Book on the Etiquette of Marriage from the Ihya'* (Salt Lake City: University of Utah Press, 1984); Marja-Lisa Swantz with the assistance of Salome Mjema and Zenya Wild, *Blood, Milk, and Death: Body Symbols and the Power of Regeneration among the Zaramo of Tanzania* (Westport: Bergin and Garvey, 1995); Margaret Strobel, *European Women and the Second British Empire* (Bloomington: Indiana University Press, 1991); and John Middleton, *The World of the Swahili: An African Mercantile Civilization* (New Haven: Yale University Press, 1992).

19. For an exploration of these issues, see Katherine Carlitz, "The Social Uses of Female Virtue in Late Ming Editions of *Lienü Zhuan,*" *Late Imperial China* 12, no. 2 (1991): 117–48.

20. A more recent study of the gendered character of Central European state-building and economic thought and policy appears in Marion Gray, *Productive Men, Reproductive Women: The Agrarian Household and the Emergence of Spheres during the German Enlightenment* (New York: Berghahn Books, 2000).

21. On gender and confessionalization, see Lyndal Roper, *The Holy Household: Women and Morals in Reformation Augsburg* (New York: Oxford University Press, 1989), and Ulrike Strasser, *State of Virginity: Gender, Religion and Politics in an Early Modern Catholic State* (Ann Arbor: University of Michigan Press, 2004).

22. Derek Nurse and Thomas Spear, *The Swahili: Reconstructing the History and Language of an African Society, 800–1500* (Philadelphia: University of Pennsylvania Press, 1985), 70–71.

23. Lucia Ferrante, "Marriage and Women's Subjectivity in a Patrilineal System: The Case of Early Modern Bologna," in *Gender, Kinship, Power: A Comparative and Interdisciplinary History,* ed. Mary Jo Maynes et al. (New York: Routledge, 1996), 115–30. For related evidence about gender and patriliny in early modern Italy, see the work of Christiane Klapisch-Zuber, *Women, Family and Ritual in Renaissance Italy* (Chicago: University of Chicago Press, 1985).

24. Rubie S. Watson and Patricia Buckley Ebrey, eds., *Marriage and Inequality in Chinese Society* (Berkeley: University of California Press, 1991), esp. Susan Mann, "Grooming a Daughter for Marriage: Brides and Wives in the Mid-Ch'ing Period," 204–29.

25. Recent scholarship shows that Chinese families made recourse to courts in matters of property far oftener than was once thought. See Philip Huang, *Civil Justice in China: Representation and Practice in the Qing* (Stanford: Stanford University Press, 1998), and Matthew Sommer, *Sex, Law and Society in Late Imperial China* (Stanford: Stanford University Press, 2000).

26. Jack Goody, *The Development of the Family and Marriage in Europe* (New York: Cambridge University Press, 1983); Michael Mitterauer and Reinhard Sieder, *The European Family: Patriarchy to Partnership from the Middle Ages to the Present* (Chicago: University of Chicago Press, 1982); Marion A. Kaplan, ed., *The Marriage Bargain: Women and Dowries in European History* (New York: Institute for Research in History, Haworth Press, 1985).

27. Patricia Seed, *To Love, Honor and Obey in Colonial Mexico: Conflicts over Marriage Choice, 1574–1821* (Stanford: Stanford University Press, 1988).

28. For a translation of the Mulian story, see (anon.), "The Great Maudgalyayana Rescues His Mother from Hell," in *Traditional Chinese Stories,* ed. Y. W. Ma and Joseph S. M. Lau (Boston: Cheng and Tsui, 1994), 443–55. On the story and the ghost festival, see Stephen Teiser, *The Ghost Festival in Medieval China* (Princeton: Princeton Uni-

versity Press, 1987); Robert Weller, *Unities and Diversities in Chinese Religion* (Seattle: University of Washington Press, 1987); and David Johnson, ed., *Ritual Opera: Operetic Ritual: "Mu-lien Rescues His Mother in Chinese Popular Culture,* Publications of the Chinese Popular Culture Project no. 1 (Berkeley: University of California, distributed by IEAS Publishers, 1989).

29. Hans-Egil Hauge, *Luo Religion and Folklore* (Oslo: Universitetsforlaget, 1974), 82.

30. For a brief discussion of spirit marriage and a more general discussion of the difficulties faced by the spirit of a young woman who died before marriage, see Emily Ahern, *Cult of the Dead in a Chinese Village* (Stanford: Stanford University Press, 1973), 127ff.

31. Richard Nzita and Mbaga-Niwampa, *Peoples and Cultures of Uganda* (Kampala: Fountain Publishers, 1993), 48.

32. Juanita Garciagodoy, *Digging the Days of the Dead: A Reading of Mexico's Dias de Muertos* (Boulder: University Press of Colorado, 1998).

33. For a useful discussion of the two waves of colonialism/imperialism, see Philip W. Porter and Eric S. Shepherd, *A World of Difference: Society, Nature, Development* (New York: Guilford Press, 1998), esp. ch. 14, "The Historical Geography of Colonialism and the Slave Trade." See also Maria Beatriz Nizza da Silva, ed., *Families in the Expansion of Europe, 1500–1800: An Expanding World: The European Impact on World History,* vol. 29 (Aldershot, U.K.: Ashgate, 1998).

34. Mark Burkholder, "An Empire beyond Compare," in *The Oxford History of Mexico,* ed. Michael C. Meyer and William H. Beezley (New York: Oxford University Press, 2000), 127. For a brief discussion of the debates, see Elinor Melville, "Disease, Ecology, and the Environment," also in *The Oxford History of Mexico,* 226.

35. Cline, *Colonial Culhuacan,* 164ff.

36. Kellog, "Tenochca Mexican Women," 134–35.

37. In eighteenth-century Mexico there appeared a genre of paintings known as *casta* paintings, which portrayed husband, wife, and offspring of various racial blendings. Ilona Katzew, *New World Orders: Casta Painting and Colonial Latin America,* ed. John A. Farmer and Ilona Katzew, trans. Roberto Tejada and Miguel Falomir (New York: Americas Society, 1996).

38. Burkholder, "An Empire beyond Compare," 144.

39. Elizabeth Ann Kuznezof, "Ethnic and Gender Influences on 'Spanish' Creole Society in Colonial Spanish America," *Colonial Latin American Review* 4, no. 1 (1995): 164.

40. Arthur O. J. Anderson, "Aztec Wives," in *Indian Women of Early Mexico, Indian Women of Early Mexico,* ed. Susan Schroeder (Norman: University of Oklahoma Press, 1997), 65.

41. Sara Cline, "The Spiritual Conquest Re-examined: Baptism and Christian Marriage in Early Sixteenth-Century Mexico," *Hispanic American Historical Review* 73, no. 3 (1993): esp. 477–80.

42. Seed, *To Love, Honor, and Obey;* see also Patricia Seed, "The Church and the Patriarchal Family: Marriage Conflicts in Sixteenth and Seventeenth-century New Spain," *Journal of Family History* 10 (Fall 1995): 20–38.

43. Asunción Lavrin, "Lo femenino: Women in Colonial Historical Sources," in *Coded Encounters: Writing, Gender and Ethnicity in Colonial Latin America,* ed. Francisco Javier Cevallos-Candau et al. (Amherst: University of Massachusetts Press, 1994), 155–57.

44. Maria Beatriz Nizza da Silva, introduction to *Families in the Expansion of Europe,*

1500–1800: An Expanding World: The European Impact on World History, ed. Maria Beatriz Nizza da Silva (Aldershot, U.K.: Ashgate, 1998), 29: xix.

45. Pete Sigal, *From Moon Goddess to Virgin: The Colonization of Yucatan Maya Sexual Desire* (Austin: University of Texas Press, 2000), 33–38.

46. Seed, *To Love, Honor, and Obey.*

47. Edith Couturier, "Women and the Family in Eighteenth-Century Mexico: Law and Practice," *Journal of Family History* 10, no. 3 (1985): 294–304.

48. McCaa, "Marriageways," 12.

49. See, for example, Louise Burkhart, *The Slippery Earth: Nahua-Christian Moral Dialogue in Sixteenth-Century Mexico* (Tucson: University of Arizona Press, 1989).

50. Lockhart, "Sightings," 218.

51. The Portuguese did undertake a more intensive and far-reaching colonization further south, in Mozambique, where the colonial government and economic policy resembled the Spanish administration of Mexico.

52. The classic work on the slave family in North America is Herbert Gutman, *The Black Family in Slavery and Freedom, 1750–1925* (New York: Pantheon Books, 1976). For more recent work, see Leslie Schwalm, *A Hard Fight for We: Women's Transition from Slavery to Freedom in South Carolina* (Urbana: University of Illinois Press, 1997), and Marie Jenkins Schwartz, *Born in Bondage: Growing Up Enslaved in the Antebellum South* (Cambridge: Harvard University Press, 2000).

53. For economic history of the Western Indian Ocean, see Abdul Sharif, *Slave, Spices and Ivory in Zanzibar* (Athens: Ohio University Press, 1987), and Michael N. Pearson, *Port Cities and Intruders: The Swahili Coast, India, and Portugal in the Early Modern Era* (Baltimore: Johns Hopkins University Press, 1998).

54. Hans Medick, *Weben und Überleben in Laichingen 1650–1900: Lokalgeschichte als Allgemeine Geschichte* (Göttingen: Vandenhoeck and Ruprecht, 1996).

55. On the highly debated relationship between economic and demographic change in Europe, see *The European Experience of Declining Fertility, 1850–1970: The Quiet Revolution,* ed. John R. Gillis, Louise A. Tilly, and David Levine (Cambridge: Blackwell Publishers, 1992).

56. For an excellent local analysis, see David W. Sabean, *Property, Production, and Family in Neckarhausen, 1700–1870* (New York: Cambridge University Press, 1990), and David W. Sabean, *Kinship in Neckarhausen, 1700–1870* (New York: Cambridge University Press, 1998).

57. Charles Tilly quoted in R. Bin Wong, *China Transformed: Historical Change and the Limits of European Experience* (Ithaca: Cornell University Press, 1997), 40.

58. The classic work is Louise A. Tilly and Joan W. Scott, *Women, Work, and Family* (New York: Holt, Rinehart and Winston, 1978). See also Mitterauer and Sieder, *The European Family.* More recently, Louise Tilly's pamphlet *Industrialization and Gender Inequality* (Philadelphia: Temple University Press, 1993, repr. American Historical Association) takes up these historical arguments in the different contexts of Europe, the United States, Japan, and China. Her summary provides a useful introduction to questions of family history and gender relations as they were affected by industrialization.

59. For a more fully developed version of this argument, see Mary Jo Maynes and Ann Waltner, "Women's Life-Cycle Transitions in a World-Historical Perspective: Comparing Marriage in China and Europe," *Journal of Women's History* 12 (Winter 2001): 11–21.

60. Wong, *China Transformed;* James Z. Lee and Wang Feng, *One Quarter of Humani-*

89

ty: Malthusian Mythology and Chinese Realities, 1700–2000 (Cambridge: Harvard University Press, 1999); Kenneth Pomeranz, *The Great Divergence: China, Europe and the Making of the Modern World Economy* (Princeton: Princeton University Press, 2000). See also the "Forum," *American Historical Review* 107 (April 2002): 425–80, which includes an introduction by Patrick Manning, as well as Kenneth Pomeranz, "Political Economy and Ecology on the Eve of Industrialization: Europe, China, and the Global Conjuncture" (425–46), R. Bin Wong, "The Search for European Difference and Domination in the Early Modern World: A View from Asia" (447–69), and David Ludden, "Modern Inequality and Early Modernity" (470–80).

For two critiques of Pomeranz, Lee, and Wang Feng as well as their responses, see Philip Huang "Development or Involution in Eighteenth-Century Britain and China: A Review of Kenneth Pomeranz's *The Great Divergence: China, Europe, and the Making of the Modern World Economy*" (501–38), Kenneth Pomeranz, "Beyond the East-West Binary: Resituating Development Paths in the Eighteenth-Century World" (a response to Huang, 539–90), James Lee, Cameron Campbell, and Wang Feng, "Positive Check or Chinese Checks?" (a response to Huang, 591–608), and Robert Brenner and Christopher Isett, "England's Divergence from the Yangzi Delta: Property Relations, Micoeconomics, and Patterns of Development" (a response to *The Great Divergence*, 609–62), all in the *Journal of Asian Studies* 61 (May 2002): 539–662.

61. The classic work on the Western European marriage pattern is John Hajnal, "European Marriage Patterns in Perspective," in *Population in History: Essays in Historical Demography,* ed. D. V. Glass and D. V. Eversly (Chicago: Aldine Publishing, 1965), 101–40. The essay generated a debate among Europeanists that is ongoing. More recently, Kenneth Pomeranz points out that despite this difference, in terms of birthrates, life expectancy, and other variables, the European pattern does not differ markedly from China, Japan, or Southeast Asia (*The Great Divergence,* 11). See also Lee and Wang, *One Quarter of Humanity.*

62. Women's work has been the focus of much innovative and important scholarship in European history, but the emphasis tends to be on connections between women's work and family and gender relations rather than on the particular issue of the role of the female labor forces in economic change. For an excellent summary of this historical literature, see Tilly, *Industrialization.* One exception is Maxine Berg's research, which takes this as a major problem: *The Age of Manufactures, 1700–1820: Industry, Innovation, and Work in Britain* (New York: Routledge, 1994).

63. Lee and Wang, *One Quarter,* 65.

64. Ibid.

65. Knowledge about the recruitment and labor conditions of female servants in Ming-Qing times is still rather fragmentary. For a discussion of what is known, see Mann, *Precious Records,* 38–44. For a discussion of women and work, see Mann, *Precious Records,* 143–77. See also Rubie Watson and Maria Jaschok, *Women and Chinese Patriarchy: Submission, Servitude and Escape* (Hong Kong: Hong Kong University Press, 1994) for more recent times.

66. Wong, *China Transformed,* 37–38.

67. Jack Goldstone, "Gender, Work, and Culture: Why the Industrial Revolution Came Early to England but Late to China," *Sociological Perspectives* 39, no. 1 (1996): 1–21.

68. Pomeranz, *Great Divergence,* 85.

69. Margaret Strobel, *European Women and the Second British Empire* (Bloomington: Indiana University Press, 1991); Margaret Strobel, *Gender, Sex, and Empire* (Philadelphia:

Temple University Press, 1993, repr. American Historical Association); Margaret Strobel and Nupur Chaudhuri, *Western Women and Imperialism: Complicity and Resistance* (Bloomington: Indiana University Press, 1992); Ann Stoler, *Race and the Education of Desire: Foucault's History of Sexuality and the Colonial Order of Things* (Durham: Duke University Press, 1995); Lora Wildenthal, "Race, Gender, and Citizenship in the German Colonial Empire," in *Tensions of Empire: Colonial Cultures in a Bourgeois World,* ed. Frederick Cooper and Ann Laura Stoler (Berkeley: University of California Press, 1997); Lora Wildenthal, *German Women for Empire, 1884–1945* (Durham: Duke University Press, 2001); Mrinalini Sinha, *Colonial Masculinity: The "Manly Englishman" and the "Effeminate Bengali" in the Late Nineteenth Century* (New York: St. Martin's Press, 1995).

70. This account of gender and generational dynamics in Gikuyuland is based on Derek Peterson, "Writing Gikuyu: Christian Literacy and Ethnic Debate in Northern Central Kenya, 1908–1952," Ph.D. diss., University of Minnesota, 2000. A revised version has been published as *Creative Writing: Translations, Bookkeeping, and the Work of Imagination in Colonial Kenya* (Portsmouth: Heinemann, 2004).

71. Peterson, "Writing Gikuyu," 86.

72. Ibid., 82–83

73. Ibid., 90.

74. On forced cotton cultivation, see Allen Isaacman, *Cotton Is the Mother of Poverty: Peasants, Work, and Rural Struggle in Colonial Mozambique, 1938–1961* (Portsmouth: Heinemann, 1996), and Thaddeus Sunseri, "A Social History of Cotton Production in German East Africa, 1884–1915," Ph.D. diss., University of Minnesota, 1993.

75. From "Records of Maji Maji," in *East African History,* ed. Robert O. Collins (Princeton: Markus Wiener, 2001), 2: 125.

76. Wang Zheng, *Women in the Chinese Enlightenment: Oral and Textual Histories* (Berkeley: University of California Press, 1999). For a recent analysis of women and gender at the end of the Qing dynasty, see Joan Judge, "Talent, Virtue and the Nation: Nationalisms and Female Subjectivities in the Early Twentieth Century," *American Historical Review* 106, no. 3 (2001): 765–803.

77. For discussion of the gender politics of postsocialism and German reunification, see Myra Marx Ferree, "Patriarchies and Feminisms: The Two Women's Movements of Unified Germany," *Social Politics* 2, no. 1 (1995): 10–24; Ingrid Miethe, "From Mothers of the Revolution to Fathers of Unification," *Social Politics* 6, no. 1 (1998): 1–23; Elizabeth Rudd, "Reconceptualizing Gender in Post-socialist Transformation," *Gender and Society* 14, no. 4 (2000): 517–39; Joyce Mushaben, Sara Lennox, and Geoffrey Giles, "Women, Men and Unification: Gender Politics and the Abortion Struggle since 1989," in *After Unity,* ed. Konrad Jarausch (Providence: Berghahn, 1997), 137–72; and Elizabeth Wesuls, "Wo wir doch jetzt die Freiheit haben," and Katrin Rohnstock, "Die verschwiegene Ostfrau," both in *Stiefschwestern: Was Ost-Frauen und West-Frauen voneinander denken,* ed. Katrin Rohnstock (Frankfurt am Main: Fischer Taschenbuch Verlag, 1994), 115–26.

78. *Migration in Modern World History,* CD-ROM, Wadsworth Thomsen Learning, 2001.

3

Exemplary Women and Sacred Journeys:

WOMEN AND GENDER IN JUDAISM, CHRISTIANITY, AND ISLAM FROM LATE ANTIQUITY TO THE EVE OF MODERNITY

JULIA CLANCY-SMITH

Women have been central, not marginal, to the founding
and shaping of many of the world's religious traditions.
The task ahead for the history of women and religion is
the development of multiple narratives that document a full,
inclusive historical vision of the female presence.

—Sue Morgan, "History,"
Encyclopedia of Women and World Religion

The notion of religion as a nontheological field of inquiry developed during the nineteenth century as part of a larger scientific interest in human societies. By definition, this perspective is Eurocentric and, when applied to non-Western belief systems, can deform the spiritual experiences of other religious communities, cultures, and cosmologies. The first lesson for students is that the category *religion* has its own history in modern Western intellectual thought. Moreover, students bring a number of unexamined assumptions to the study of religion. The most frequently encountered is that the historical processes identified with modernity—capitalism, secularism, and nation-states—have banished religion to the quiet backwaters of private belief or unbelief. Related to that, many have little formal instruction in the history of religions, comparative religions, or religious studies in general. Thus, mysticism, monasticism, or asceticism are unfamiliar concepts; notions basic to the sociology or anthropology of religion, such as ritual or pilgrimage, need explanation.

The women-gender-religion nexus poses another set of complications. Many students remain unclear as to what issues, approaches, and relationships are subsumed under the rubric *gender.* They assume that all religions, no matter how defined, have always and everywhere oppressed women, denying them agency because of the close imbrication between patriarchy and religion. Therefore, "The suggestion that Christianity can empower women seems implausible to many Western feminists. Some have concluded that Christianity is irredeemably patriarchal and have moved to a post-Christian stance."[1]

Nevertheless, scholars continue to debate whether religion is primarily to blame for women's oppression, given that religions have permitted varying degrees of female participation and allowed some women access to sacred knowledge. These questions are further complicated by the fact that women have historically been victors as well as victims, although the dichotomy is overly simplistic because empowerment and subordination are often simultaneous within a single religious tradition. In addition, scholarship on women, gender, and religion remains uneven. World religions practiced on a global scale receive more attention than ancient religions no longer in existence or contemporary micro-traditions.

Research since the 1980s has irrevocably transformed the way we think about women and world religions and religion in general. Scholarship on Christianity in medieval and early modern Europe is a case in point. Not only has it produced new appreciation of gender's significance to religion but it also has made substantial theoretical contributions to a number of related disciplines and subfields.[2] For example, nuanced research on the gendered significance of the body and food-related practices during the Middle Ages, by demonstrating that women's religious experience as such should be the point of departure for research, has produced a disciplinary shift. In contrast, research on gender in the medieval Greek Orthodox Church, for instance, is still relatively scanty, although studies on Byzantine women and hagiography exist. Succinctly stated, at present more scholarship is available on women than on gender in world religious traditions. Employing a comparative feminist approach, the two-volume *Encyclopedia of Women and World Religion* (1999) attests to concerted efforts to redress the situation.

The relationship between world history and gender history also merits reflection. As Ross E. Dunn sees it, "World history and gender related history have thrived during the past quarter century but until recently they have not had much influence on one another."[3] Since the early 1990s, the world history movement has achieved noteworthy success in globalizing curricula. Yet macro-level world systems approaches—Big History—tend to write women and gender relations out of the story. Indeed, the integration of women into the historical narrative is often inversely related to the scale of analysis. For the modern era, religion as a force in world history drops out of textbook narratives because deep shifts in political economies or new cosmologies of science and technology are deemed more significant. If religion lies partially within the realm of the history of ideas, its powerful role in social praxis, organization, and legitimation—above all, in matters pertaining to gender—needs emphasis. Most important, when gender theory informs the study of religion, however defined, other seemingly self-evident verities become less certain.

Definitions and Approaches

A universally valid definition for religion across historical time and cultural space does not exist. Nevertheless, scholars of women and gender history have complicated the notion of religion which is now viewed as inseparable from patriarchy and patriarchal systems of domination in most, if not all, world traditions. These assertions serve as provocative starting points but do not solve the problem of where to begin or what to include or exclude. To better tame an unwieldy topic, I draw upon my own classroom experience and scholarship that suggest a theme: "exemplary women and sacred journeys in Judaism, Christianity, and Islam from late Antiquity to the eve of modernity." Combining these two related, although not coterminous, dimensions of the religious experience opens windows into complex spiritual beliefs, religious ideologies, and social practices—sacred journeys, pilgrimages, shrine cults, and pilgrims, on the one hand, and exemplary women and their sociohistorical constructions as objects of pilgrimage, saints, pious women, patronesses, or good wives and mothers, on the other.

In addition, representations of pious women were invariably constructed in relation to exemplary men—Abraham, Moses, Jesus, or Muhammad—whose memory was commemorated by scripture or by sacred travel and accounts of those travels, composed mainly by men. Virtuous women have not only been defined implicitly or explicitly against male exemplars but also against insubordinate, disorderly, or dangerous females—the Jezebels and Mary Magdalenes of history. Together these themes open onto a wide range of related topics appropriate for studying other religious systems.

The shared similarities as well as differences between the three traditions are sufficiently numerous to justify the comparative methodology. All are monotheistic with revealed scriptures, a masculine deity, purity-pollution taboos, and pilgrimage traditions, yet neither Judaism nor Islam have ordained clergies as such. Mysticism is present in all three religions, but both Islam and Judaism reject monasticism. It is significant that they share three fundamental assumptions undergirding the notion of divinely ordained male superiority and female inferiority: Man—and not woman—represents God's primary creation; woman was primarily responsible for the Fall; and, finally, "Woman was created not only *from* man but also *for* man, which makes her existence merely instrumental and not fundamental."[4]

Monotheism has identified God with maleness, an identification that has held significant social, cultural, and historical consequences for women and men. Detecting transformations in gender ideologies ostensibly sanctioned by divine favor is difficult because they are usually depicted as eternal and thus not subject to change. Subordinate female status has historically been legitimized by appeals to core religio-spiritual beliefs and legal dictates—even when a specific unfavorable gender norm may have been originally "exterior" to a particular religious tradition. Nevertheless, even the masculinity of the divinity was not immutable. The relative gender equality suggested by the early gospels or the notion of "Jesus as mother," for example, contrast with the unambiguous masculinity of God. Thus, the discourses on gender have been "contradictory, internally riven, and at odds," and the resultant social constructions and practices far from static.[5]

My principal objectives here are, first, to demonstrate how and why religious ideologies as well as social practices can, in some contexts, empower women and yet in others subordinate them and, second, to understand how larger historical forces alter the balance between subordination and empowerment, provoking shifts in the constructions of exemplary women as well as in sanctioned forms of female religiousity, particularly sacred movement or pilgrimage. At the same time, local variations within all three religious traditions—the idea of religion as locally understood and lived—are considered to avoid essentialized views of complex historical and cultural phenomena.

WOMEN AS RELIGIOUS EXEMPLARS IN THE CLASSROOM

Juxtaposing female religio-spiritual exemplars with and against the masculine character of the divinity introduces provocative questions into classroom discussion. The topic also leads to the issue of extraordinary versus ordinary women and men in history and how to recover their pasts despite class and other distinctions and status-gender hierarchies. Many paragons of virtue began life as humble or even reviled individuals—sinners or prostitutes—and although the monotheistic religions profess spiritual equality, sharp class and gender differences have always existed. Collective historical memory, and the political armature expressing that memory, privileges some individuals' lives over others. Patronesses have been important in nearly all religious traditions, although philanthropic activities frequently, but not exclusively, are recorded and thus remembered for women of elevated social rank.

Because the generosity of patronesses often found expression in physical landmarks such as buildings or monuments, the historical record of their munificence has been retained. This contrasts with charity associated mainly with the domestic sphere. As Leslie C. Orr observes, "Much of women's patronage and sponsorship of religious activity in the domestic or community setting—a Buddhist, Jain, or Hindu woman's offering of food to a mendicant at her doorstep, Muslim woman's distribution of alms during Ramadan or her hosting of a gathering of women in her home to hear stories of the saints, a Jewish woman's visit to a sick person or her embroidering of Torah covers for the synagogue, a Christian woman's mending and laundering of the clothes of the poor—goes virtually unnoticed."[6]

Saints, uncommonly holy men and women, represent another category of exemplary individuals present in most religious traditions and cast in roles of mystics, ascetics, miracle workers, and healers. Catholicism's institutionalized procedures for recognizing saints and its official saint "list" would appear to render sainthood somewhat unique. Islam and Judaism, like Protestantism, have historically been uneasy with devotions to the very special dead, which can compromise God's unity. Due to popular consensus from below, however, persons regarded as exceptionally close to God have been venerated and remembered in Judaism and Islam. Until the rise of modernity in the Middle East and North Africa, Jews, Muslims, and Christians held saints in common, honoring them in shared shrines and pilgrimages frequently condemned as "popular" by disapproving observers. Local Catholic communities have always revered persons, living and deceased, blessed with heroic piety without the Church's validation. Finally, holy persons raise the issue of subaltern or "populist" beliefs and practices that were frequently identified by male religious authorities with suspect female religiosity to discredit or devalue their spiritual importance.

Mystics and visionaries, at times conflated with saints, are found in all three traditions and pose roughly similar problems, although mysticism has offered relatively more outlets for female religiosity in Christianity and Islam than Judaism. A mystic's heightened spiritual enthusiasm suggested that salvation could be achieved without benefit of clergy and sacraments or of the sacred law and its interpreters. The mystical path to enlightenment and unity with the divine has theoretically been open to men and women, but female mystics provoked disquiet because the spiritually empowered sometimes transgressed gender norms. Whether punitive measures were directed against overly enthusiastic mystics and saints, male and female, was a function of historical context and social circumstance.

Exemplary individuals also haunt the realms of the heretic and heresy. Often the lines between witch and holy person, cunning women, wise men, and malevolent beings were blurred. Because women have historically been considered more prone to doctrinal error and heretical belief, their exclusion from religious authority has been justified on that basis. In some cases the label *heterodox* has been applied to movements solely because women occupied leadership positions. In large measure, the early Church secured the boundaries between orthodox and non-orthodox communities by progressively excluding women from sacerdotal offices. Finally, the lives of pious men and women have been recreated through pilgrimage of one kind or another. Spiritual experience as performance becomes more visible through participation in saint cults, whether expressed in collective veneration or individual supplication. Ordinary people have always made sacred journeys, although traveling less frequently and widely due to economic or other constraints. Sacred journeys signify breaks in time or liminal moments when rules governing ordinary life might be temporarily suspended, in turn illuminating partially concealed gender ideologies and practices.

SACRED JOURNEYS AND TRAVEL IN THE CLASSROOM

Most religions have a culture of sacred movement. Pilgrimage, a spatial, temporal, and spiritual displacement of mind and body, also entails acts of imagination. Because pilgrimage functions as a huge intake for diverse people, pilgrims, like migrants or invaders, carry new or different ideas, skills, commodities, and information. States and ruling elites have always sought to control pilgrims as well as objects, spaces, and places of pilgrimage. Profane motives inspired even the most pious pilgrims, who might, under certain conditions, turn into holy combatants or warriors for the faith; sacred travel could also be manipulated for political or personal ends. And pilgrimage has always been (and is today) very much about identity.

In the past, pilgrimages to the exemplary centers of Judaism, Christianity, and Islam represented "hemispheric" events because individuals and groups from across Afro-Eurasia made the journey. That pilgrimage, commerce, and trade have always been closely associated is well documented. Trade diasporas, inevitably linked to religious minorities like the Armenian Christians and Jews in the Middle East, were connected to local and translocal pilgrimages, often facilitating them.

Looking at pilgrimage comparatively over time also raises the issue of changes in modes of transportation for travelers to Mecca, Jerusalem, Lourdes, Rome, or Compostela and the related question of gender and movement. Did women travel and perform pilgrimage in the same way that men did? When considering the scriptural-theological imperatives for ritual voyages, it is important to consider how gender norms historically shaped cultures of religious journeys and, conversely, how cultures of sacred travel have defined women's relationship to the transcendent.

97

Because most societies have historically controlled and limited women's physical movements and activities, female religiosity often found fuller expression in local pilgrimage and cults. These provide windows into religion as received by women and men as well as sites for recovering the sociocultural values of ordinary people. Various types of sacred objects—for example, portable shrines containing statues or relics and carried in procession—were associated with local cults. In many societies, women create, maintain, and pray at household shrines within the confines of the home.

Female-dominated religious activities have at times been denounced as "profane" or "unorthodox" because they were performed in domestic settings, largely outside clerical or male control. Currently, feminist scholars are questioning rigid dichotomies between the sacred and profane, between the sacred and domestic, precisely because these marginalize women's religious experience.

Finally, sacred journeys and holy persons are directly linked to hagiography, biography, and autobiography. The performance of pilgrimage sometimes occasioned a personal narrative of the soul, resulting in social recognition of individual spiritual virtuosity. For women, the matter of voice, authorship, authenticity, and censorship immediately arises when considering these genres. Many pious women's lives were narrated exclusively by men and largely for male audiences in certain periods.

CHRONOLOGICAL AND GEOGRAPHICAL LIMITS

This essay deals mainly with the periods from late Antiquity to the eve of modernity, a chronological choice that demands some explanation. From roughly the seventh century C.E. onward, monotheistic traditions coexisted more or less side by side in the Near or Middle East, Africa, the Mediterranean world, parts of Europe, and (to a lesser extent) in Asia. These centuries witnessed expanding networks of communication and exchange produced by migrations, the extension and consolidation of trade routes, and the proselytizing of missionaries of new faiths or "heretical" offshoots of established faiths (such as the Nestorians). What resulted was transregional, hemispheric borrowings unprecedented in scale. The elaboration of the Silk Road, trans-Saharan routes, and the Indian Ocean system meant that people, products, and technologies circulated ever more widely and, with them, philosophies, cosmologies, ideas, practices, and customs. I will focus on the geocultural regions of Western Asia, Northern Africa, and Western Europe.

I chose to concentrate on the period from late Antiquity to the eve of modernity because material for classroom use is more difficult to find for women, gender, and religion in premodern societies. Sources for the modern, and particularly the contemporary, era are abundant and fairly easy to access for teachers; I list some in the bibliography. Moreover, the centuries from late Antiquity to the cusp of modernity are important in and of themselves. Religious and secular authorities have historically appealed to the distant past—often portrayed as a golden age—to justify women's continued subordination. Feminists and others seeking to change prevailing gender norms now carefully scrutinize these same distant epochs to rebut the notion that earlier core beliefs and "unchanging" practices sanctioned women's inferior position.

The essay ends on the threshold of the modern era, although scholars contest the notion of modernity because it represents a highly uneven set of processes whose origins, meanings, and impact varied widely across geocultural regions. The nature of the state and political economy, social class structures, levels of education and literacy, resource structures, and patriarchal systems either fostered or impeded—or both—the complex historical processes known as modernity. Thus, the historical narrative ends in slightly different periods for each community of faith. In any case, the methodology that follows can be usefully applied to historical periods and religions not dealt with here.

The Problem of Eve

Shared by all three traditions is the exemplary mother, Eve, and father, Adam, although each offers differing versions of the creation story. As important, however, the tale of the first man and woman has been employed by interpreters of Judaism, Christianity, and Islam to vindicate women's subordination to men—and less frequently to justify gender equality. Initial creation accounts in Genesis 1 present human beings as either male or female but created at the same time. In subsequent accounts, Eve is fashioned by God from one of Adam's ribs. Moreover, in Genesis 3, Eve is the first to be seduced by the serpent, partaking of the forbidden fruit that she presses upon her spouse. Punishment by expulsion is visited upon both Adam and Eve, but God's retribution is gendered. Adam will labor in the fields, and Eve will suffer the pains of birth, of reproductive labor. In the Quran, the story is somewhat different. Eve does not spring from Adam's rib; both are equally culpable of yielding to temptation and shoulder equal blame for paradise lost. Nevertheless, interpretations of the creation story—as opposed to the narrative itself—have shown remarkable convergence over time in the three religious traditions.

In Judaism, "Rabbinic exegesis connects the Hebrew name for Eve with the Aramaic word for serpent (*hewya*), suggesting that the serpent was Eve's undoing as Eve was Adam's."[7] Early Church fathers held that humankind's fall from grace was specifically due to Eve's sinful actions. Indeed, when theologians met at the Council of Orange in 529 C.E. to expound the doctrine of original sin, Eve was cast not only as the one who caused Adam's downfall but also as the first sinner. Despite the Quranic account, later Muslim thinkers, perhaps under the sway of Judeo-Christian thinking, reinterpreted the creation story to maintain that woman, responsible for the loss of paradise, was created from the most crooked part of Adam's rib.

Traditionally, female nature has been portrayed as the antithesis of male nature and female sexuality in negative opposition to male sexuality. That had important ramifications, because societies have always linked religious duties with specified sexual practices. Judaism, Christianity, and Islam shared similar—in some cases, identical—views of female nature until recently, which is hardly surprising given their common origins. Religious texts as well as widely held customs, beliefs, and ideologies from the ancient Near East and pagan or Hellenic Mediterranean world conflated woman with the realms of nature, the body, the physical, and, above all, pollution, temptation, and the irrational. Early Christian authorities, especially Augustine, reproduced the opinions of classical philosophers who believed that "only the male is the true image of God."[8] Jewish, Christian, and Muslim religious authorities as well as ordinary people, male and female, believed that women were sexually insatiable, lacked self-mastery over desire, and, in consequence, would entertain sexual relations with any man if not controlled by various means.

This construction of the "bad woman" whose voracious appetites demand constant male surveillance by fathers, brothers, husbands, and sons serves as a counter-model to the notion of the good woman or exemplary female. Given the majority opinion regarding women's innate sexual irresponsibility, chastity was a major component in the construction of the ideal woman, particularly in view of widespread concerns with purity of lineages. Islam and Judaism, however, differ markedly from Christianity in one important dimension of sexuality. Both are hostile to the notion of celibacy, particularly for women (but also for men) because only marriage guarantees social order and procreation. For Christian women (as also in Buddhist thinking), chastity, institutionalized through vows of celibacy associated with membership in a religious order or community, paradoxically liberated women from male control expressed in marriage. The fundamental reason for the pre-Reformation Church's exaltation of virgin martyrs and chaste females should be seen for what it was—a manifestation of long-standing contempt for, and fear of, women's sexuality.

The social fear of female sexuality and reproductive functions undergirded elaborate pollution and purity codes surrounding the female body. Indeed, Orthodox Judaism, Orthodox Christianity, and Islam still maintain strict taboos concerning ritual uncleanliness during menses that limit women's participation in religious activities. Finally, dissident religious groups have employed purity-pollution taboos to more sharply delineate their movements from mainstream thinking. Some North African Jewish micro-communities, for example, evinced exaggerated concern with female ritual purity to signal their difference from the Jewish majority, and Jewish communities in Eastern Europe have observed extremely rigorous requirements for female purification. In Islam, certain Shi'ite groups have interpreted and observed purity-pollution codes for women in ways that distinguish them as dissenters.

Negative views of female nature and sexuality are found in most of the world's religious traditions and have been deployed to justify the naturalness of women's subordination. By representing women as dangerous, weak, evil, lustful, and disorderly, their exclusion from positions of religious authority or from full participation in society is justified. Although the Jewish Eve differs from the Christian Eve—and the Quran does not specifically name Eve—biblical accounts of creation have been continually drawn upon throughout the centuries to enjoin patterns of social order and enforce the "nature of maleness and femaleness."[9]

Exemplary Women and Sacred Journeys in Judaism

HISTORICAL OVERVIEW: THE EXPERIENCE OF EXILE

Political subjugation, exile, and dispersion have shaped gender relations in Judaism because local Jewish communities were inevitably influenced by the dominant states and cultures under which they lived. Between 63 B.C.E., when Judea was incorporated into the Roman Empire, and the twentieth century, no politically independent Jewish states existed. Following the Temple's desolation in 70 C.E., the centers of Jewish religious and communal life were synagogues, courts, rabbinic academies (yeshivot), ritual baths (mikva'ot), and the household; the home represented a particularly important space for female religious observance. Between Jerusalem's final destruction and the fourth century, Jews were forbidden to set foot in the city, renamed Aelia Capitolina by the Romans. One consequence was that pilgrimage to the exemplary center of Judaism was impossible for several centuries, and local pilgrimages grew in importance. In addition to Palestine, communities of Jews long resided in Arabia, Central Asia, China, India, and Africa. In view of the vastness and longevity of the Persian empires, Iran was second only to Palestine in importance because Jews have resided there for some 2,700 years. From Persia, they moved to India and China or north to Russia.

Jews residing along the Mediterranean Coast from Egypt to Spain represented one of the largest diaspora groups, although some African Jews traced their roots to the Punic or Carthaginian period (ca. 814 B.C.E.–146 B.C.E.).

Under Roman, Byzantine, Vandal, and subsequent Islamic rule (i.e., from the seventh century c.e. on), Jewish communities were found in the countryside and in cities. After the Arab-Islamic conquests, many Jews gradually became Arabized, retaining their faith and cultural uniqueness as well as developing a vernacular language. In North Africa, a smaller number, mainly those who lived in the mountains or in deserts, spoke Berber.

During the Byzantine Empire, Jews appear to have made up 1 to 2 percent of the population, and they continued to do so under early and classical Islamic states. They fared much worse under the Orthodox Church and Byzantine rule compared to the situation under most Islamic empires or states. Thus, diversity marked Jewish communities in the Middle East and elsewhere; nowhere did they form a monolithic group. In that diversity the gender norms and relations in force in a particular local Jewish community helped distinguish among diasporic groups.

During the High Middle Ages (ca. 900–1200 c.e.), sustained interactions between North African and Middle Eastern Jews produced complex ties linking Muslim Spain and the Mediterranean Basin with South Asia. Jewish trading diasporas facilitated commerce between the Mediterranean, Black Sea, and Indian Ocean and Central Asia. One principal element structuring these communities was marriage; the exchange of Jewish women as marriage partners assured that far-flung families remained tightly knit and networks operated. Contacts with Muslim states, elites, and ordinary people were also close and, in cities, occurred on a daily basis, extending even into Islamic law courts.

The fortunes of Jews of the Middle East, Northern Africa, and Spain were heavily influenced by events in Europe, particularly the Crusades (1095–1291) and the Reconquista (1085–1492). The situation of Spanish Jews (and Muslims) began to deteriorate in 1391 with the persecution of the Jews of Castile, Catalonia, and the Balearic Islands, which provoked a wave of emigration to North Africa. During the fifteenth century, Muslim kingdoms in Algeria and Tunisia provided havens for Spanish Jews, as did parts of Europe such as Dutch cities. With the fall of the kingdom of Granada in 1492, Morocco and the Ottoman Empire became sites for Iberian Jewish settlement due to massive expulsions and persecution.

In Europe, it appears that until the eleventh century social mingling across religious lines transpired between Jews and Christians; otherwise, constant denunciations by church officials would have been unnecessary. The situation of European Jews deteriorated due to the Reconquista, Crusades, and Inquisition, all related events. By 1215 and the Fourth Lateran Council, strict regulations forbade intermarriage between Jews and Christians. Sexual relations were severely punished as adultery because such contacts between a Christian and an "inferior" Jew resulted in a doubly polluting act. Increasing legal and professional restrictions, including sumptuary laws, made the position of many European Jews more precarious than ever. In the late thirteenth century, expulsions occurred from England and elsewhere in Europe and continued until 1492.

Global crises such as the mid-fourteenth-century bubonic plague brought catastrophe to European Jewry. As was true elsewhere, in parts of France the outbreak of the Black Death in 1349 was blamed on Jews. In Strasbourg, rumor had it that they had poisoned water supplies; on St. Valentine's Day two thousand were burnt to death on a platform erected in their cemetery. In contrast, the Ottoman Empire welcomed exiled Jews from all over Europe—Iberian, French, Italian, and German—and there they generally flourished until the late nineteenth century.

LAWS, CUSTOMS, AND GENDER RELATIONS IN DIASPORA

Some scholars characterize the practice of Judaism after 70 C.E. as the gradual transition from a temple-based to home-based religion in some respects. The Jewish household became infused with a semisacred importance because women's prayers, key rituals, and legal observances—such as compliance with laws for food preparation—took place within the home and under women's supervision. The separation between Judaism and Christianity occurred gradually during the first centuries C.E., but growing animosity from the era of Justinian (who reigned from 527 to 565) onward brought restrictions on building synagogues as well as public worship and preaching.

Those processes may have hastened the shift from temple to home, with important consequences for women and religion as lived. Of utmost importance to Jewish communities whether in the Middle East, North Africa, or Europe was the meticulous observance of Jewish law (halakhah) and tradition in daily life and during collective celebrations. If a community was numerically small or isolated, careful observance was all the more critical for survival. In contrast to Christian theology, which emphasizes dogma, Judaism emphasizes law, ritual, practice, and exegesis, a concern shared by Islam as well. For women and gender relations in Judaism, revealed scripture, legal codes, and oral traditions present interpretive problems similar to those in other religious systems.

The Mishna is a multivolume legal code produced by rabbis in the first two centuries C.E. from earlier oral interpretations of scripture. Subsequent commentaries on the Mishna formed the Palestinian (ca. 400) and Babylonian Talmud (ca. 500), a vast legal and prescriptive corpus. As the authoritative basis for religious Judaism, this represents the basis for leading a moral and ethical existence. The legal part of Talmudic literature, interpreted in responsa literature, governed ritual, spiritual, and ceremonial observances of individuals and collectivities. Because religious law determined family life, purity taboos, and dietary and sacrificial regulations, it had enormous impact on women and gender relations. In the Middle East and North Africa, religious law generally remained in force until at least the middle of the nineteenth century.

Until the rise of modern Judaism around 1750 in Europe, women were not permitted to lead public worship or interpret Jewish law. Moreover, some authorities understood the Mishna to mean that teaching sacred texts to women was prohibited, although that has been disputed. Rabbinic law does not require women to take part in services held at a synagogue, although they are required to hear Torah reading. In Middle Eastern or North African cities, towns, or villages, the synagogue was the center of community life, and children were sent to rabbinic schools for primary education. Advanced studies for boys were available at the yeshiva, which trained the rabbinical elite.

Before the modern era in both Sephardi and Ashkenazi synagogues, women participated in public prayer only if a space apart was provided—a partition, balcony, or separate room. This was due to the belief, found also in Islam, that any female presence constituted a sexual presence and thus a distraction to male worship. Yet in Middle Eastern villages, and even in some urban areas, synagogues did not necessarily offer special sections for women. In these cases women and girls observed the festivities of Sabbath or major holidays from the outside, listening through windows or doors.

Scholars now debate the origins of male-female segregation. Some maintain that the enforced separation of the sexes at communal public prayer dates to the Second Temple, whereas others see it as a more recent practice. Women and girls could also gather collectively for pious purposes in cemeteries. (For Muslim women in the same region, weekly outings to cemeteries to honor deceased family members was also an important social occasion.) Directly related to weekly family grave visits were the ritualized visits, accompanied by prayers, to tomb-shrines of the "special dead," observances that Middle Eastern Jewry shared with Christians and Muslims.

Prayer has always been important for Jewish women, although its frequency and form have varied because of obligations to spouses, children, kin, and community. Rabbinic authorities did not obligate women to pray at specified times of the day because of conflicts with family duties, although most held that praying at least once daily was required. Learned women prayed formally in Hebrew; illiterate women memorized prayers read aloud to them from the Hebrew prayer book and followed female prayer leaders in devotions. Prayers always accompanied the rituals—baking challah and blessing Sabbath candles or performing the ritual bath (mikvah)—incumbent upon women. Mundane as well as important life-cycle stages were marked by prayers frequently incorporating biblical figures and finding inspiration for ordinary women's daily travails in scriptural role models. "Indeed," observes Sylvia Barack Fishman, "the biblical Hannah's heartfelt prayer was considered by Talmudic sages to exemplify correct and effective communication with God."[10]

EXEMPLARY WOMEN IN SCRIPTURAL
AND IN OTHER SOURCES

Some of the earliest accounts of exemplary women's lives are found in Hebrew scripture—Sarah, Miriam, Esther, Deborah, and Jael, for example. Although five females are named as prophets in the Hebrew Bible, they predate the period of literate prophecy, and their voices are unrecorded although gender norms are evidenced in their stories. Feminist historians have begun analyzing these stories through the lens of gender theory. Deborah, prophet and judge in the twelfth to eleventh centuries B.C.E., was credited with delivering the Israelites from Canaanite oppression, which suggests female leadership.

Scholars of religion also employ literary and linguistic analysis to reveal new meanings in biblical stories, for example, how and why Deborah and Jael were celebrated as heroines possessed of uncommon courage and virtue. More recent studies of the Book of Judges posit that ancient Israel's political economy—a decentralized, largely agrarian-pastoral society without rigid class structures—explains women's relative freedom and autonomy. Three closely related elements emerge as determinants of women's status within socioreligious systems: the nature of hierarchies, state formation, and political economy. Some argue that limitations on women's participation in religious and social life were written into the Torah later by elite scholars who resided in cities, inevitably associated with complex, bureaucratic states and a high degree of stratification. The establishment of the Temple promoted a religious class—the priesthood—that excluded women and most men from office.

Women are portrayed in the Hebrew Bible almost exclusively in terms of relationships to men, whether as mother, wife, daughter, or sister. Stories of ancient Jewish women in scripture were reproduced and reinterpreted over the centuries as models for ideal social behavior, although we lack ample documentation as to how female audiences understood the stories. A twelfth-century funeral speech honoring a noble Jewish lady from Cairo, for example, extolled the deceased's memory, equating her with the biblical Naomi. The comparison was elicited because the Cairene woman had shown exceptional kindness to her daughter-in-law in the same way that Naomi had nurtured Ruth, "a foreigner from the Land of Moab."[11]

As with other sacred scriptures, the Hebrew Bible is replete with parables about the social chaos created by disorderly women who violated the moral lessons taught by exemplary woman. Biblical gender analysis demonstrates that the term *zonah* (prostitute) was broadly applied to women who were not "relational"—Jezebel, Tamar, and those whose sole fault was being too assertive. They were not, that is, protected by (or subordinate to) men. Because Christian and Islamic scriptures draw upon the Hebrew Bible, many gendered moral tales inform the sacred texts of the two successor traditions.

Documentation on Jewish women and gender in the late Roman and early Christian periods is found in the New Testament, particularly the Gospels. Inscriptions from synagogues of the era offer compelling evidence that women were not only patronesses or donors but also acceded to leadership positions, including *archisynagogue* (head of the synagogue). Despite evidence of women as leaders, the attributes of the exemplary woman—whether in pagan Roman, rabbinic, or patristic literature—were remarkably alike. A first-century Roman woman's epitaph, describing her as "pious, chaste, thrifty, faithful, a stayer-at-home," represented a universal ideal, as did "fruitful as a vine" in view of devastating mortality rates.[12] Survival depended upon the preservation of the Jewish family, which dictated endogamy. Mixed marriages between Jewish men and non-Jewish brides were to be avoided because mothers determined their children's religious identity.

As in other traditions, control over women's sexuality and reproduction was critical and thus the emphasis upon chastity. Although variations existed in Jewish sexual practices, the rabbis approved of the enjoyment of a disciplined sexuality for men and women. Only in marriage, defined as a contractual partnership reflecting God's relationship with Israel, could the disorders of the sexual instinct be tamed. A sacred relationship, marriage constituted a contract and not a sacrament, as in Christianity. Thus divorce was possible, although dissolving a marriage contract was generally only a husband's privilege. Legal and social mechanisms for initiating marriage focused on the consignment of a nubile girl from her father's house to that of her husband, a transaction that normally also entailed an exchange of property.

In Europe, polygyny among Jews was acceptable until the eleventh century, when it was forbidden by Rabbi Gershom b. Judah. It continued in North Africa and the Middle East, as did concubinage. The Jewish (and Muslim) position on human sexuality opposes the early Christian value placed on celibacy as enunciated by Paul and others. Nevertheless, all three traditions viewed ideal womanhood as motherhood; in this way, social constructions of the exemplary woman served patriarchal functions. Fertility was a sign of God's favor; barrenness, a shameful state expressing divine disapproval, could lead to divorce.

An appreciation of the degree of divergence between ideal and real gender relations depends on the nature of available historical evidence, including archaeology, material culture, financial registers, business or personal letters of commercial diasporas in Afro-Eurasia, and the records of non-Jewish states or authorities governing Jewish communities. Social rank, age or generation, and race or ethnicity were determining influences on women's lives, as were marital status and fertility levels. Divorced women or widows often enjoyed more control over their destinies than married women. Times of crisis or unusual historical events often attenuated—even contradicted—ritual, legal, and ethical prescriptions found in biblical and Talmudic literature.

Rebellious groups tend to be well documented. As in other religions, dissident or charismatic sects within Judaism, often embracing organized asceticism and/or mysticism, afforded women more religious space and even leadership roles—if only temporarily. A first-century Jewish community of ascetics, the Therapeutae founded in Egypt, permitted female members to engage in scholarship, and some even formed their own monastic establishments. The movement was similar to a slightly later (the second half of the second century C.E.) Christian millenarian community, the Montanists, which also allowed women to act as prophets.

Although female imagery is preponderant in mystical literature, Jewish women have generally not played a part in creating that literature or in visionary or ecstatic devotions, a contrast with Christianity. An unnamed female celibate, visionary, and mystic from twelfth-century Baghdad, however, was the focal point for a messianic upheaval inspired by her visions during the 1120s. Before the uprising, rabbinical authorities in Baghdad arranged for her marriage because, it was believed, her visions were the product of sexual renunciation and overly rigorous ascetic practices. Once she was wed and forced to abandon self-imposed celibacy, or so it was reasoned, the visions would cease.

WOMEN AND GENDER NORMS IN EUROPE   Early modern Spain offers a striking example of the relationship between crisis and women's access to sacral functions. The centuries-long Reconquista, tied to European state-building and overseas expansion, the Inquisition, and forced conversions of Jews worked to temporarily undermine rabbinic authority. A Portuguese widow, Doña Gracia Nasi (1510–1569), a patroness of rabbinical academies, put her family fortune in the service of crypto-Jews, subsequently taking her family to the Dutch Republic and finally the Ottoman Empire for safety. Because of Judaism's domestic-centered nature, women were especially active in crypto-Judaism, keeping faith and rituals alive in secret within the household. Visionary or messianic movements coalesced around some women-led crypto-Jewish groups in Portugal and Spain, as documents from the Inquisition proceedings have revealed. Iberia during the latter stages of the Reconquista confirms the modification of male religious authority and the gender norms and prescriptions flowing from that authority, ignoring or blatantly disregarding them during times of upheaval. Yet periods of crisis can have the opposite effect.

There are many more cases of women who overcame, flouted, or openly challenged gender restrictions, although once again the problem of historical sources comes into play. Nevertheless, most Jewish women strove to exemplify the ideal of Jewish womanhood while negotiating personal and religious autonomy. Within a highly patriarchal world they carved out spaces as patronesses, organizers of charity, and businesswomen as well as healers, midwives, wise women, and teachers of other women. In twelfth- and thirteenth-century Germany, the wives of rabbis, Dulce and Urania of Worms, achieved considerable learning and acted as prayer leaders for circles of Jewish women, although both were empowered by association with revered religious leaders.

The interpretation of sacred texts and mastery of Hebrew were still reserved for men, but some Jewish women were literate and had prayer books written specifically for them in Yiddish in late medieval and early modern Europe. The printed devotional material suggests that women transformed domestic celebrations associated with Sabbath or holy days, such as the baking of the ritual bread, into sacerdotal acts through their own prayers and readings of scripture.

Some middle-class Jewish women were actively involved in family commerce, which demanded not only business skills but also literacy in various vernacular European languages, and notarized contracts reveal that they had prominent roles in financial operations essential for family survival. A representative example comes from late-fourteenth-century Venice, where Jewish traders were only permitted to engage in money-lending during a period of crisis. Guotela Rapin took part in independent loan transactions: "She and other women obviously had considerable freedom to operate on their own, for we find them coming and going, and granting power of attorney to persons meant to act in their name during their absence."[13] Under certain circumstances, women could appear in court; wife-beating was frowned upon when it was not condemned by rabbis; and marital rape was proscribed. And, in contrast to Christian women, rabbinical rulings permitted the use of contraceptive devices under certain circumstances.

Nevertheless, visions of the bad woman persisted and reflected larger social currents surrounding Jewish communities. The thirteenth-century *Sefer Hasidim* (*Book of the Pious*) written in German provides a fascinating window into medieval male views of woman. Judith Baskin notes that unfavorable representations of female nature long present in Talmudic traditions were "intensified." Women were not only portrayed as "untrustworthy, sources of sexual temptation, and demonic" but also as prone to "sorcery and witchcraft . . . even the most pious women has the potential, however unwitting, to tempt a man to sin or sinful thoughts." Negative images were also found in medieval Jewish mysticism or Kabbalah literature, where the women, unrestrained by male control, and menstrual blood are conflated with "demonic forces responsible for evil in the world."[14]

JEWISH WOMEN IN THE MEDIEVAL MUSLIM WORLD   The social, economic, and cultural lives of Jews living around the Mediterranean Basin, particularly Cairo and Egypt, from the tenth to the thirteenth centuries emerge from the Geniza documents. In these sources of a primarily religio-legal or financial nature, Jewish women rarely speak for themselves because most were illiterate, or, if literate, they normally spoke through male guardians. A close reading, however, reveals that some oversaw not only their children's well-being but also their formal education. Moreover, merchants, Jewish and otherwise, traded in far-flung commercial networks and were frequently away for years at a time, so women were obliged to assume managerial functions at home. Wealthy Cairene women acted as patronesses by furnishing richly made Torah scrolls or designating a share of their inheritance to cemeteries, synagogues, or other religious purposes. Women of ordinary means donated objects, money, time, skills, or their labor to the upkeep of synagogues and shrines, although the record is less abundant. Regardless of class, motherhood, particularly the birth of sons, conferred status and authority.

At the level of ordinary people, the customs, attitudes, and lifestyle of Middle Eastern Jewry hardly differed from non-Jewish neighbors; "superstitions" such as the evil eye were held both by Jews and Muslims. Jews under Islamic rule observed some of the sexual and gender norms and practices of the majority. Some Jewish women enjoyed divorce rights and were even able to initiate divorce proceedings—not always the case elsewhere. Jewish women's freedom of physical movement in public spaces, however, may have been limited compared to Europe, although their sexual segregation was less restrictive than for Muslim women. In large Middle Eastern cities, Jewish and Muslim families resided in the same neighborhoods or even shared domestic compounds, and at times there was discord; the more relaxed attitude toward sexual mixing within Jewish households clashed with Islamic norms about sexual segregation. Some Jewish husbands attempted to impose unusually strict seclusion upon wives, who were allowed to leave the house only for prayers and ritual bathing.

Jewish women of ordinary or middling social ranks frequently played important socioeconomic roles in local communities as healers, midwives, entertainers, small retailers, and brokers, often serving Muslim neighbors and clients. Thus they forged critical patron-client ties, acting as mediators between different religious groups, which might offer some measure of protection during times of crisis. Finally, Middle Eastern Jews and Muslims sometimes participated together in saint cults—a major difference from Europe and one that directly involved female religiosity.

SAINTS (ZADIKIM), PILGRIMS, AND PILGRIMAGE

In Judaism, pilgrimage represents travel to God's presence as embodied in sacred text and place. Pilgrimage to the exemplary center was forbidden until the fourth century, but with Islamic rule from the seventh century onward, Jews were more or less free to travel to Jerusalem. Historical evidence for travel to the Holy Land during the period under consideration exists in the Geniza documents and wills from European Jews during the late medieval and early modern eras. It was common for those nearing the end of their lives, particularly men, to depart for the Holy Land to die and be buried (the same was true for Christian pilgrims). Jewish women who performed the pilgrimage to Jerusalem earned an honorific title after returning, a practice perhaps reflecting Islamic influence.

Pilgrimage to, and residence in, Jerusalem became easier for both Jewish women and men after the Ottoman conquest of Palestine in 1516. Under the Ottomans, Jews from the Middle East and North Africa journeyed to Jerusalem and Hebron in spring, celebrating the festivals of Passover and Shavu'ot. Cairene women participated in this pilgrimage as well.

Because women traveled less freely, more is known about the sacred journeys performed by men, who often left detailed instructions regarding care of their families while absent. One valuable twelfth-century account was the pilgrimage performed by a Spanish rabbi, Benjamin of Tudela (Toledo), who traveled in the 1160s to Palestine as well as to Baghdad and Persia. Like Christian counterparts from Europe en route to the Holy Land, the rabbi visited Jewish communities and sacred places found along the pilgrims' route, discovering Jewish saints, martyrs, and miracles in unlikely places like Rome. In addition, this particular work offers a lesson in historical memory because Benjamin "read" Jerusalem as a Jewish city replete with prophets and matriarchs and not as a site that had been under Muslim rule for more than five centuries or one whose principal monuments recalled Christ and Christianity.

The Spanish rabbi also noted the existence of Rachel's tomb in Bethlehem at a time when the shrine was attracting a transregional following. The mausoleum was situated on the site of a much older structure; a visit to Rachel's resting place was part and parcel of the pilgrimage to Jerusalem. By the seventeenth century a local cult was organized in her honor, and Rabbi Moshe Surait's 1650 account notes that both men and women took part in rituals before Rachel's domed shrine: "And many there pray and made petitions and dance around the tomb and eat and drink."[15] Miracles came to be associated with the tomb, and thus from the end of the nineteenth century the site's importance has increased, particularly—as might be expected given the biblical story—for women seeking help with childbearing problems.

Babylonia (under Persian rule in this era) was next on Benjamin's twelfth-century itinerary. Persian Jews performed pilgrimages to tomb-shrines where the prophets were believed buried—Ezekiel in Baghdad and Mordecai and Esther in Hamadan. Located in Hamadan in western Iran is the ebony tomb of Esther, the queen who spared her people from annihilation some 2,400 years ago. The tomb-shrine was a vaulted crypt adorned with Hebrew inside and surrounded by walls outside. It still functions as a pilgrimage center for Persian Jews, who have observed Purim there for centuries, celebrating their identity as both Jews and Persians simultaneously. Benjamin expressed surprise at Ezekiel's tomb in Baghdad because Muslims, who also revered the prophet, paid ritual visits there, and the shrine's guardians were both Jewish and Muslim.

Judaism as lived in North Africa and the Middle East has a rich tradition of saint cults and pilgrimage. Nevertheless, because of the emphasis upon God's unity and transcendence, the veneration of holy persons has caused disquiet in Judaism, as also in Islam. Prophets and patriarchs were regarded as particularly close to God because of their miraculous gifts and uncommon virtue, but they were not believed to exert supernatural powers from the grave. (An exception is a movement in modern Judaism, "Beshtian Hasidism," which recognizes holy men.)

For many diaspora Jews, journeying to Jerusalem was not only dangerous but also difficult due to financial or family circumstances. Local pilgrimages centered on saint veneration provided an alternative sacred space, no matter how much some rabbinical authorities frowned upon or condemned these manifestations of piety. Indeed, saint cults in memory of uncommonly pious rabbis or unusually learned sages have long represented an important expression of African Judaism. Often the tomb-shrine of a holy man—a zaddik—attracted a following that gradually evolved into a constructed system of rituals as well as shared beliefs in his miracle-working abilities (the *hillula*). As late as the twentieth century, Morocco alone boasted some six hundred Jewish saints, mainly rabbis; their shrines have served as the focal points for local or regional pilgrimages until the present. Charting these sacred geographies in the premodern eras also demonstrates that the same saints and spaces were sometimes venerated by Jews, Christians, and Muslims alike.

The veneration of holy persons expressed in saint cults constituted a prominent feature of Jewish popular spirituality in the region from Morocco to Persian/Iran. One socially admissible reason for Jewish women to travel was pilgrimage to a local saint's center. Jews regarded the shrine of Dammuh south of Cairo, for example, as sacred space; the number of statutes governing female visitors' behavior indicates how common the practice was. Women unaccompanied by male family members were forbidden to take part in festivals, unless the women were very old. Those neither old nor under male supervision must have visited the shrine spot frequently—otherwise the regulations would have been unnecessary.

Local pilgrimages, shrine visits, or celebrations to honor holy persons were occasions when social barriers loosened, if only temporarily, and, more important, where unregulated sociability between the sexes occurred. Jewish women participated in the collective rites, which is why religious authorities condemned these manifestations of populist piety. With several exceptions, Jewish saints in North Africa and the Middle East have been rabbis, honored for erudition while alive and for miraculous powers after death.

The Jews of the island of Jerba off the coast of southern Tunisia date their arrival there from the destruction of Solomon's Temple in 586 B.C.E. They represent their community as "the Jerusalem of Africa" because, in this first diaspora, emigrants brought with them the door of the Jerusalem sanctuary. An annual international pilgrimage is still performed in the island's best-known synagogue, the Ghriba ("the Marvelous"), which houses fragments from the first Temple as well as ancient Torah scrolls. In local lore, however, the site where the Ghriba synagogue now stands has been conflated with pious legends about a young female saint and virgin who sailed to Jerba from Palestine carrying Torah scrolls sometime in the early nineteenth century. Since that time, mass pilgrimages to the Ghriba synagogue have been performed to commemorate the arrival of the female saint from Palestine and honor pious rabbis. In the annals of North African Judaism, the female holy person as cultic figure was unusual, because most Jewish saint cults are male-centered although women participated actively in them. Muslims have also recognized the sacredness of the Ghriba over the centuries.

A final example demonstrates women's tenacity in local shrine visitations, even in the face of male disapproval, as well as the power of popular forms of Judaism. Located in Tripoli in Libya are the tomb-shrines of two close disciples of Shabbetai Zevi (1626–76), the "false messiah." An Ottoman subject born in Izmir, Shabbetai studied Kabbalah and Jewish law with the intent of becoming a rabbi but declared himself the Messiah in 1648. Local tradition had it that after the movement was suppressed, two of Shabbetai's followers emigrated to Tripoli, where they died. Libyan Jews, male and female, honored the memory of the false messiah and his disciples by performing pilgrimages to their tombs as well as keeping candles lit in the ancient synagogue, al-Thalithah, in Tripoli. The local Muslim population also venerated the holy men's shrines. Until the twentieth century, Jewish women not only made offerings of oil for the synagogue's lamps but also sang (in dialectical Arabic) from the "Song of the Book," praising the movement's leaders with "you are the Merciful and Forgiver, send the Messiah together with Nathan."[16]

As some North African Jews came into contact with reform movements of European Judaism in the nineteenth century, they denounced saint cults as heterodox, all the more so because illiterate women of ordinary status often were the main participants. During the 1860s, Rabbi Abraham Adadi of Tripoli attempted to end collective veneration of Shabbetai Zevi and his disciples but to no avail. Women in particular persisted in their devotions until well into the next century. When Rabbi Khmus Fallah heard them singing in honor of the false messiah on the eve of World War II, he broke their synagogue candles as a reprimand.

Even ordinary women, however, unlettered and of humble circumstances, did not always obey communal religious leaders when it came to saint cults. As was true in Europe, North Africa, and the Middle East, Libyan Jewish women, often widows, endowed synagogues. In at least one case a female-endowed synagogue was also named after a woman, although that broke with tradition.

For Jewish communities in exile, pilgrimage to Jerusalem became entwined with a sense of collective banishment tempered by messianic expectations for future redemption. Thus, diaspora Jews practiced pilgrimage to places other than the holy city while preserving a sense of spiritual and emotive continuity with the exemplary center, its Temple, and its mythologized landscape. For the nascent Church, pilgrimage traditions, although heavily influenced by Judaism, followed a somewhat different path, one marked by the spiritual activism of pious women and men as well as the growing imbrication between state or empire and religion.

Exemplary Women and Pilgrimage in Christianity

HISTORICAL OVERVIEW: THE EARLY CHURCH

The lines between the "Jesus movement" or nascent Christianity and Judaism remained blurred until the fifth century, when religiously syncretic communities were still found in parts of Syria and Palestine. From the second century, however, Jewish and Christian authorities began erecting boundaries between their respective traditions and barriers around their followers. As is often true of radical socioreligious movements, "gender roles and expectations were temporarily transcended as women and men worked together to spread the gospel message" beyond the community coalescing around Jesus in the decades immediately after his death.[17] Some of the earliest written sources suggest female leadership, including women who exercised prophecy. Nevertheless, Roman law and customs exerted an enormous impact upon Christianity

113

(as upon Judaism). In part, scholars attribute shifts from the relative gender egalitarianism of early dissident or millenarian Christianity to the later subordination of women to the adoption of household codes inspired partially by pagan Roman models as well as by gradual changes in Church-state relations.

By the end of the first Christian century, bishops and laymen increasingly restricted women's church roles. Orthodoxy rested upon eliminating female preaching and teaching, an idea found in the contested Deutero-Pauline letters, which also negatively portray woman's nature. The early third century saw another change reflected in patristic literature—the church hierarchy's growing concern with the spiritual, social, and physical control of women. Most historical evidence from this and later periods comes from male authors and was largely prescriptive. Nevertheless, "Writings *about* women often provide glimpses of conflicts between male ecclesiastical leaders and laywomen in Christian churches."[18]

During the last Roman persecutions (from 303 to 311 C.E.), the number of women whose spiritual quest for union with Christ brought public humiliation, torture, and martyrdom was remarkable. Because man was in the image of God, female martyrs and ascetics strove to emulate men. Perpetua of Carthage, author of the earliest Christian text by a woman, was imprisoned and condemned to death; before her execution she dreamed of assuming a male body. The virgin Thecla dressed like a man so as to travel freely without fear of rape, and Pelagia, too, wore men's clothing to join an all-male monastery. From this period on, "Women of surpassing spiritual achievement had been masculinized, as the female rulers and scholars and fictitious heroines of the Renaissance would be later."[19]

Gender transgressions were disturbing both to early Christians and pagan Roman societies. Martyrs, mystics, and ascetics have always posed problems to religious authorities, females even more so because the renunciation of earthly pleasures constituted an implicit critique of male control. In its earliest stages, the ascetic movement exalted virginity, which complicated the notion of marriage as the Christian ideal for woman. Theological debates over the issue demonstrate the enduring influence of older, pagan Graeco-Roman views of sexuality, particularly of Hellenic asceticism. With the eclipse of martyrdom as the path to salvation, Christians embraced asceticism as a means of redemption, although self-denial was, by its very nature, highly gendered. Withdrawing from the world, often in communities, ascetics employed veneration of the Eucharist as "a trigger for contemplation and absorption, ever closer to an immersion in God."[20] The Eucharist remained the central devotion until the late medieval period and constituted an important construct for imagining and defining symbolic power for Christian Europe.

The Sacraments render Christianity distinct from both Judaism and Islam. Baptism was a rite for men as well as women. It replaced circumcision, which, as a sign of belonging in Judaism, was fixed upon the male body and masculinity as well as conferring superior identity and status on boys. Moreover, the fact that marriage was a sacrament—rather than a contract as in Judaism and Islam—meant that ending a Christian marriage was difficult if not impossible. In Judaism and Islam, marriage is a commandment for men and women; the celibate life was only possible for those few Jewish scholars who entirely devoted their lives to studying Torah. All three religions prize chaste women and, in varying degrees, silent and submissive women. By joining institutionalized celibacy and some education with the silence of prayer and mystical devotion, however, the monastic movement paradoxically created a sociospiritual space for women.

MONASTICISM

After the 313 edict of toleration and the establishment of Christianity in 391, the era of heroic virgin martyrs more or less ended. Subsequently, aristocratic women acted as patronesses, endowing shrines, building churches, or donating to monasteries. In Europe, Christian women of high rank married to pagan rulers were instrumental in converting barbarian princes. Despite important roles in conversion and patronage, women were restricted to the office of deaconess by around 400—a change attributed to elaboration of an exclusively male, ordained priesthood and widespread acceptance of the notion that female nature was inherently weak and lustful.

The growth of monasticism, first in Egypt and the Eastern Mediterranean and then in Western Europe, offered new opportunities for women, particularly those of the upper class, to assume leadership of all-female congregations as canonesses and abbesses. The idea of being the brides of Christ, introduced by Tertullian before 200 C.E., evolved into organized communities of virgins and widows dedicated to celibacy, prayer, and good works. In Bethlehem, the Roman pilgrim Paula (347–404) established a monastery with two hundred women under vows. From the Eastern Mediterranean, the system spread into Spain and to southern France and elsewhere.

Perhaps the first convent where manuscripts were copied was in the city of Arles, France, where a large community of virgins was established in 506 by Caesaria, sister of the bishop, Caesarius, who wrote the "Rule of Arles." This rule was superseded by the Latin Rule of St. Benedict (480?–547?), which rendered monasticism a rural movement less concerned with enclosure and more with missionary activity and manual labor. Functioning as centers of teaching, learning, prayer, and communal social service for surrounding populations, particularly the poor, monasteries multiplied for males and females.

As such, they played a powerful role in conversion along the shifting borders between paganism and Christianity in Germany and the British Isles.

During this period, monasticism had fewer gender differences than it did later. Monasteries that had both men and women in close proximity were common. Although theoretically under the authority of an abbot, some monastic establishments were run by abbesses, often of high social birth, who were allowed to hear nonsacramental confessions from the women under their spiritual guidance. During the ninth century, however, Benedictine reformers under imperial patronage—and in the tenth century the abbots of Cluny—sought not only to enclose women more firmly but also to separate them from male communities. At the same time, monks were made superior to sisters through ordination.

The same pattern began to emerge in the historical evolution of Christianity that did in other religions. During the turbulent centuries of invasions in Europe, when the state was weak or decentralized and Christianity represented a rural, frontier missionary faith, women were accorded greater public roles in religious, cultural, and political life. The reemergence of stronger states, urban-based elites, and highly stratified ecclesiastical authorities narrowed women's range of options, imposing more gendered differences upon male and female piety. Nevertheless, high social rank frequently conferred considerable religiosocial authority upon individual women, as did literacy.

In Christianity as in Judaism and Islam, men have monopolized religious knowledge and the interpretation of sacred scriptures until very recently. Yet some women achieved literacy and composed spiritual literature, such as didactic poetry, lessons, and saints' lives. Not surprisingly, most female intellectuals of the period were nuns and tended to be from privileged classes. The tenth-century Saxon canoness Hrotsvitha, for example, wrote dramas in Latin and composed biographies of female saints and martyrs to counter the misogyny of such classical authors as Lucan. Narrating exemplary lives for imitation constituted a critical process in consolidating the Church's social and moral authority; paradoxically, it also gave voice to, and legitimated, female spirituality.

The later Middle Ages (from the twelfth to the early fourteenth centuries) saw a significant increase in female participation in the Church, whether as religious or lay members. Along with a spectacular growth in the number of monasteries or convents and the emergence of reformed orders, new saints and visionaries appeared. Aiming at stricter discipline, the Cistercians arose from a reform movement within the Benedictines. Established in France around 1098, the Cistercian Order played a major part in promoting spiritual activism. By 1150 three hundred Cistercian houses were scattered throughout Western Europe. Simplicity in all its manifestations represented the order's ideal, and that inspired similar orders, especially mendicants such as the Franciscans and Dominicans.

Hildegard of Bingen (1098–1179) of western Germany was a member of a reformed Benedictine convent. Placed in a convent when still a child, she experienced visions from an early age but prudently revealed them only after attaining the rank of abbess around the age of forty. She is best known for three books of visions (*Scivias, Book of Life's Merit,* and the unfinished *Book of Divine Works*) and also composed, in Latin, an autobiography and liturgical music as well as works on theology and medicine. Hildegard oversaw the creation of illuminations depicting her visions and devised specifically female spiritual symbols, for example, the egg. Her mystical and prophetic gifts were widely recognized by secular and religious authorities, yet her criticism of Church abuses created conflict with the ecclesiastical establishment, which opposed Hildegard's claims that God spoke directly through her.

Associated with "exaggerated" poverty and mysticism, the Penitential and Third Orders were sometimes accused of heretical leanings, although their appeal to believers of all social ranks may have been as threatening to religious authorities. Popular sociospiritual movements often offer an expanded (if only briefly) space for women who joined these religious houses in droves.

Communities known as Beguines represented a new manifestation of female religiousity in this period; some scholars view them specifically as a women's movement whose impact upon forms of piety was enormous. Taking vows of poverty, chastity, prayer, and service, Beguines did not adhere to formally organized, church-approved orders, which made them suspect. Found mainly in urban areas in northern Italy, France, Germany, and the low countries, the Beguines included solitary seekers of spiritual perfection as well as small groups that resided together; still others, such as the Grand Beguinage of Paris, collected hundreds of women for communal spiritual life.

The movement produced a number of prominent visionaries, such as Marie d'Oignies (who died in 1211) and Mechtild of Magdeburg (who died around 1290), and also posed the problem of "women without men" not under direct male protection or supervision. The Beguines' lack of institutionalization, their "more informal arrangement for giving religious significance to ordinary life seemed odd and dangerous to male sensibilities."[21] One solitary itinerant Beguine, Marguerite Porete, was burned at the stake as a heretic in 1310 because she disobeyed the bishop of Cambrai's injunction against women teaching in public and preaching, inspired by her book *The Mirror of Simple Souls.* The year following her execution Church hierarchy launched an attack against the Beguine movement.

These centuries constituted a golden age of female mysticism and mystics, whose enthusiastic spirituality sometimes troubled male clerics or society at large. Frequently ecstatic experiences centered around Christ as Man, encountered as the divine lover—"bridal mysticism"—or the suffering redeemer on the cross.

As the Church made the Eucharist its central sacrament, identification with the suffering Christ grew since the twelfth century into a popular form of devotion in which women played a major role. Through eucharistic devotions, a believer could become one with the body of Christ, regardless of gender; female images and representations of relationships with Christ as human are explicitly physical. Loving union with Christ remained the spiritual goal of mystics for centuries. Indeed, female visionaries and mystics, often blessed with miraculous powers, have appeared during the modern and contemporary eras in Christian communities worldwide. It should be kept in mind, however, that "the received view of women as weaker and less rational than men paradoxically functioned both to certify the authority of women mystics and to impugn it."[22]

Women of uncommon piety, and their lives and spiritual journeys, provided inspiration for other female visionaries. Hildegard was a model for many pious women in the Rhineland, and Bridget (or Birgitta) of Sweden (who died in 1373) and Elisabeth of Hungary (who died in 1165) were exemplars for the fifteenth-century English visionary Margery Kempe. Kempe (ca. 1373–ca. 1440), a noblewoman from Norfolk, bore some fourteen children before taking a vow of chastity in 1413. Matrimony and motherhood prevented intense devotional lives. Beset by visions after the birth of her first child, it was only later that Kempe realized her spiritual quest and experienced Christ in mystical encounters as the bridegroom whom she loved passionately and whose sufferings she shared. She came to Church attention not only due to her religious experiences but also because she openly condemned the hypocrisy, lewdness, and unchaste lives of some clergy. Although she was exonerated of charges of heresy, the archbishop of York rebuked Kempe for violating Paul's interdiction against female preaching.

Kempe's exposure of vice among male clerics, as well as Christine de Pizan's (ca. 1364–ca. 1430) spirited defense of the female sex, provides evidence that some women during the late medieval period contested the prevailing religious and social order. Indeed, Kempe's vision of an alternative Christian social order suggested that she regarded prevailing gender norms as constraining women's true spiritual life. The list of ecstatic women whose extraordinary encounters with the divine were committed to writing is a long one indeed. Yet class or social rank need to be taken into account. Had Hildegard, the "prophetess of the Rhineland," been of common origins—or worse, had she lost the support of those in power—she might have been condemned as a witch or heretic, the fate of the virgin visionary and military leader Joan of Arc, who was burned at the stake in 1431.[23]

EXEMPLARY WOMEN

Christian scripture is ambiguous about woman's nature and thus on her proper role in religion. Modern interpretations of the New Testament have sparked debates not only on female leadership in the early Church but also the dating, authorship, and authenticity of some sources. The Deutero-Pauline letters (e.g., Colossians or Ephesians) paint an especially negative view of female nature as inherently impure. Essentially weak and given to sin and base desire, women are therefore incapable of learning. In consequence, the ideal woman was silent as well as subordinate. The wife's surrender to her husband symbolized the church's submission to Christ. Chaste, modest, and fertile, the exemplary woman could only achieve sanctity through child-bearing and motherhood as well as obedience to husband or other males. Noncanonical writings, mainly the Apocrypha, as well as canonical writings, such as some of Paul's uncontested letters, have been interpreted in ways that partially offset these negative images and offer women limited spiritual authority. From some books of the Apocrypha and canonical sources come the legends and lore informing the cult of the Virgin Mary, female symbol of goodness and benevolent power.

Although many women saints are remembered either as virgins or mothers, Mary claimed special status because she alone was both virgin and mother of God. The cult in her honor developed over centuries from popular veneration as well as pre-Christian beliefs. Some scholars detect earlier pagan practices in the emergence of Marian piety. Imperial concerns also shaped the Virgin's cult. For example, the notion of "Mary Mother of God" (Theotokos) was encouraged by the Empress Augusta Pulcheria (399–453) to buttress her own power. From about 1150 on, veneration of the Virgin as Jesus' human mother "exploded in new forms of prayer, scriptural exegesis, song, art, pilgrimage, drama, church dedication, and social organization."[24]

In medieval Christian piety, Mary earned the exalted title of "Our Lady," which placed her on the same spiritual plane as Jesus Lord, although she is revered as a powerful intercessor rather than a ruler. Her cult was not static but evolved over time in response to social, cultural, and other changes; moreover, significant regional variations existed. In Mediterranean and southern European Christianity, imitation of the Virgin for both men and women was the norm. During the thirteenth century the emphasis on Mary and motherhood shifted in Italy toward a new focus upon Jesus as infant and child, mirroring perhaps larger transformations in attitudes toward childhood and the family.

Devotions to the Virgin Mary were highly developed in pre-Reformation Christianity and now exist primarily in Roman Catholic, Orthodox, and other Eastern Rite Churches in the Middle East. Her cult has always attracted men as well as women because Mary has been seen as the exemplary Christian although the reception of the Marian ideal, as well as participation in the Virgin's cult, has displayed gender differences. In modern time, Marian apparitions worldwide have frequently been claimed by young women or girls. Until very recently among the Melkite Christian communities of northern Syria, the composition of poetry in honor of the Virgin was largely a male activity. Finally, Mary, the mother of Jesus, is also revered in Islam.

Older scholarship on female religiousity during the Middle Ages propounded the "virgin-whore" polarity. More recent research, however, has shown that although these extremes existed, literary and legal sources offered a more subtle view of women, real and imagined. Mary Magdalen, the patron saint of repentant fallen women, is a case in point. Indeed, after the Virgin, Mary Magdalen was the most popular female saint during the Middle Ages. Now, scholarship argues that the Magdalen's biography was constructed over the centuries from possibly three different women mentioned in the Gospels. Moreover, feminist biblical exegesis posits that the historical Mary Magdalen was an active preacher and spiritual associate of Christ, the "apostle of the apostles," and that historical memory of her as a prostitute was a later clerical invention. Venerated by women and men in the early and medieval church, she became the focal point of penitential practices because, as the paradigmatic sinner, Mary Magdalen offered hope of salvation to all. Devotions to her gave rise to a genre of literature—narratives of converted prostitutes. The tale of the redeemed harlot was a favorite trope in Byzantine hagiography, legends, and sermons. Despite the complexity of the legends and devotions surrounding the reformed prostitute, "The harlot in the extremity of her chastisement bore the full weight of the abhorrence of sexuality that the church focused upon women."[25] Historically, devotions to Mary, heroic virgins, pious visionaries, or bad but repentant women were part of the impetus for organized saint veneration, including pilgrimage.

Even as examplars, holy persons or saints represented gendered socioreligious constructs. Saintly vocations for male and female followed different "career paths," mirroring distinct social opportunities and constraints. Women were assigned a more passive, interior role, whereas men were portrayed as actively engaging in the world. It must always be kept in mind, however, that the most vitae for holy persons were written by men, following hagiographical conventions. The double standard for aspiring holy women was unmistakable: "The virtuous girl might demonstrate her virtue either by heroically insisting on chastity (and thereby rebelling against her family) or by obediently marrying at her parent's command (and thereby retreating from what the church argued to be a higher good)."[26]

Variations in eucharistic devotions, miracles, and ascetic or meditation practices suggest differences between male and female piety as portrayed in the lives of saints. Historical circumstance combined with social class frequently determined whether a woman was accused of being a heretic or a sorceress or, conversely, whether she was regarded as uncommonly virtuous and thus worthy of emulation. Inquisition handbooks such as the *Malleus maleficarum,* issued in 1486 by two Dominican inquisitors, Krämer and Sprenger, defined "demonic" female behavior to detect and punish witches, most of them from the lowest social orders. Saint Catherine's (1347–80) visions, for example, were first seen as demonic influences. Yet being of high rank meant that she was exonerated and eventually venerated for special piety. Indeed, as Caroline Bynum has argued, by 1500 the model of a female saint, both in popular belief and Church doctrine, was a mirror image of a witch.

SACRED JOURNEYS: PILGRIMAGES AND SAINT CULTS

With a zeal and courage unbelievable in a woman she forgot her sex and her physical weakness, and longed to make there, amongst those thousands of monks, a dwelling for herself [from St. Jerome's account of Paula's travels to the holy places].[27]

In contrast to the duty for pilgrimage to Mecca for the Muslim faithful, Christianity does not require this act, although the example of Jewish devotions at the prophets' tombs played a formative role in pilgrimage traditions in Christianity and later Islam. Only after Constantine's victory of 324 C.E. did public pilgrimage to Jerusalem become feasible for Christians. Still, some theologians and Church fathers opposed the practice because Jesus Christ had made statements that seemingly discouraged it. That changed when Constantine's mother, Helena, undertook a journey through the holy places. Her discovery of the remains of the true cross and the construction of majestic basilicas in Bethlehem and Jerusalem provided inspiration for future pilgrims and pilgrimages. "Helena's trip was to have fundamental consequences for the history of Holy Land pilgrimage . . . and became the model for many."[28] It also generated new religio-literary genres as well as a praxis whereby the pious imitated the life of Christ through various kinds of sacred journeys, both physical and interior.

Generally, Christian women of high social rank narrated or inspired pilgrimage accounts. In 385 the Roman noblewoman Paula traveled to Jerusalem with her daughter, eventually becoming a model for pilgrims, male and female, to the city. As late as the nineteenth century, English Protestant pilgrims to Jerusalem consulted her account. Yet we only know about Paula through the intervention of a male author. She was accompanied by St. Jerome, who subsequently composed the narrative and thus her spiritual experiences in the exemplary center were refracted through the prism of his words. The first autobiography of a sacred journey was composed in the 380s by Egeria, who was either from Gaul or Galicia in Spain. Apparently well educated (she knew scripture by heart), Egeria journeyed to Jerusalem, spending three years there. Her invaluable account provides details on gender differences and how worship services, rituals, and liturgies were performed in the fourth century.

Paula's and Egeria's examples helped render the act of sacred travel an ideal of piety and holiness. Egeria was later made a saint because of her sacred voyage. Her firsthand account of the "labours of pilgrimage" inspired other sojourners to journey to the Holy Land; to other centers such as Rome that served as symbolic alternatives; or to undertake an interior, life-long pilgrimage of the soul, a pilgrim's progress. Whether spiritual travels constituted actual physical displacements or internal spiritual states, pilgrimage became integral to a holy person's biography and a fundamental element in hagiography, mainly composed by men living in monastic orders. Some Church authorities, however, continued to believe that actual pilgrimage to Jerusalem might result paradoxically in "moral mischief," a fear focused upon women, who in their travels might engage in sexual impropriety with the males accompanying them.

Pilgrimage might afford a credible reason for disobeying family patriarchs in matters of life choices. The aristocratic sixth-century Syncletica of Constantinople, for example, avoided an undesirable marriage by persuading her father to grant permission for pilgrimage to Jerusalem. By the twelfth and thirteenth centuries, more and more laywomen traveled to the Holy Land to perform penitential acts, visiting other pilgrimages cities like Compostela on their way East. Margery Kempe made the pilgrimage to Jerusalem during the early 1400s. The narrative she later dictated to a priest is regarded as the first autobiography in English and the second book written by a woman in that language. Although women had composed accounts of either real pilgrimages performed or interior spiritual travels for centuries, these were generally penned by celibates who lived in orders. Kempe was different because of her status as wife, mother, and layperson. Moreover, for her journey, she donned male garb, a not unusual act because women of the period often dressed as men when performing pilgrimages to distant lands.

During the first Christian millennium, pilgrimage centers within Europe were mainly focused upon saint veneration. Marian piety grew rapidly during the eleventh century, resulting in new cult centers dedicated to the Virgin that translated local or regional differences in religiosity. In medieval Germany, for example, Marian shrine devotions tended to emphasize the pietà, the suffering mother of Christ. Major centers boasted relics, images, exuberant iconography, and votive gifts. Minor shrines were often embellished by rural artisans, who drew upon rich folk art traditions in which ordinary women and men participated fully. Women's shrine offerings were invariably the products of the household economy—food, clothing, and handicrafts expressing the domestic sphere in the public realm.

For women in particular, local pilgrimage and the liminal state it entailed offered respite, a legitimate opportunity to travel if only a short distance. It also reaffirmed their spiritual agency and religious identity. And although the Reformation transformed Europe's saint maps as well as the topography of sacred journeys, it could not entirely suppress pilgrimage, even in predominantly Protestant regions. Western Europe now boasts six thousand active shrines dedicated to various kinds of pilgrimage in honor of the saints or the Virgin, and they attract nearly one hundred million annual visitations.

Exemplary Women and Pilgrimage in Islam

Striking parallels can be detected between early Christianity, when women enjoyed spiritual authority and held religious offices, and the nascent faith community in Mecca coalescing around the Prophet Muhammad after 610 c.e. in which women participated fully. In terms of class and gender, early Christianity was relatively egalitarian—both cause and consequence of the fact that private dwellings served as churches. Paul's first church in Antioch, for example, was in a house in the city's Jewish quarter. In Islam the first mosque was in the Muhammad's modest residence in Medina, where male and female followers worshipped.

Intense persecution of the followers of Jesus and Muhammad, both male and female, also emphasized horizontal bonds of solidarity rather than vertical, stratified relationships. Finally, women in both cases were increasingly marginalized as the two socioreligious movements crystalized into highly institutionalized systems of dogma and praxis implicated in states or empires (which always have a huge stake in patriarchy). This section focuses, for the most part, upon the Near or Middle East and North Africa because core gender values of later Muslim societies situated outside the region were often adopted from this cultural matrix or validated by reference to the birthplace of Islam. Nevertheless, generalizations about women and gender in Islam historically are perilous for the same reasons they are for Judaism or Christianity.

HISTORICAL OVERVIEW: ISLAMIC CONQUESTS, STATES, AND CONVERSION

The spread of Islam across Asia, Africa, and parts of Europe from the seventh century onward produced an enormous range of cultural compromises with preexisting beliefs, institutions, and social organization. Muhammad and his followers explicitly linked Islam to both Judaism and Christianity while claiming to correct their doctrinal errors and thus supersede them. Due to early similarities, Church fathers initially interpreted Islam as yet another Christian heresy after Muslim forces moved from Arabia to the Byzantine-controlled lands of Syria and Egypt in 633 c.e.

With these conquests and the construction of states from remnants of the Persian and Roman Empires, older Arabian gender norms combined with Graeco-Roman, Judeo-Christian, Zoroastrian, and Indo-Persian (to name but a few) gender practices and ideologies. In addition to military conquests stretching to Iberia, France, and India by 732, Islam was also introduced by missionaries, sufi orders, and merchants working the trans-Saharan or Asian trades. Large-scale population displacements and migrations across Eurasia also resulted in conversions. The movement of originally shamanist Turco-Mongolian people westward during the tenth century into Persia and, subsequently, Byzantine and some Arab lands not only brought mobile pastoral societies into contact with established Muslim and Christian societies but also introduced other gender customs. The greater freedom of movement permitted to Turkic or Kipchak women, as well as the public power wielded by Mongol princesses even after conversion to Islam, shocked prudish urbanites such as the fourteenth-century Moroccan scholar Ibn Battuta as he traveled through Anatolia and across the Steppes.

In Central Asia or sub-Saharan Africa, introduced to Islam later than the Middle East and Mediterranean world, Islamic and pre-Islamic indigenous belief systems continuously interacted, which in turn shaped women's situations. Conversion was frequently accomplished in phases, with some elements of Islamic culture—purity and pollution taboos, for example—initially being accepted. Later conversion introduced considerable sociolegal changes such as the shift from matrilineal to patrilineal succession, although not always and everywhere. Old Nubia, on the Nile between Egypt and Ethiopia, had ancient traditions of female public authority that were not erased after Islam's acceptance, and a marked preference for matrilineal inheritance and succession remained despite Quranic and legal injunctions to the contrary.

Bureaucratic states, cities, and highly stratified social hierarchies are often associated with increasing restrictions upon women in the religious and/ or public spheres. Veiling, seclusion, and polygamous households (or harems) were practiced in the Middle East before Islam's advent. These practices may have been gradually adopted by Muslim elites after the Umayyad Caliph Walid (who ruled from 705 to 715) secluded royal women within palace confines and took numerous concubines in addition to four legal wives. The Abbasids (750–1258), whose elaborate courts and palaces were relocated to former

Sassanian lands in Iraq, imitated Persian ancient statecraft and generalized seclusion and veiling among the upper classes. The Abbasid Caliph al-Mansur (754–75), for example, commanded that bridges over the Euphrates near Baghdad be sexually segregated, and a separate bridge for women was constructed.

Yet implementation of gender segregation varied widely over time and space. In medieval Egyptian cities, women "went out in the streets and mingled with men at various celebrations and public prayers, as well as for visits to cemeteries and holy tombs, where they would sometimes spend the entire night."[29] Constant condemnations of sexual mixing by moralists confirm that the practice existed. Although seclusion represented a powerful norm legitimated by appeals to religion, particularly for certain classes of urban women, it was, in reality, subject to limitations. Thus, as in Judaism and Christianity, Islamic laws, beliefs, and practices governing gender relations have varied greatly in time and place and also in accordance with social rank, age, ethnicity, or race.

QURAN, LAW, CUSTOM, AND GENDER

Both Judaism and Islam place heavy emphasis on sacred law in ordering human societies. Most studies of Muslim women evoke female status as defined in the Quran and sharia. The Quran consecrates an entire chapter to women, containing regulations for marriage, divorce, inheritance, and ritual purity. Interpretations of Quranic passages, however, differed according to the various legal schools emerging during the first two centuries. Varying interpretations of female inheritance and property rights were espoused by the main law schools; for example, temporary marriage was permitted by some jurists, particularly Shiite, but not by others. The extensive Hadith literature that supplements the Quran was fundamental to Islamic law and represents an important source for ideal gender roles and conduct.

In many places, however, customary law held sway and was applied in conjunction with, or instead of, sharia. When the two systems conflicted, customary law might take precedence over the opinions of Muslim jurists. Customary law for North African Berbers, for example, had always determined female inheritance; the same was true for some pastoral groups in Iran and Afghanistan. Local systems of patriarchy, customs, and political economies often shaped gender relations as much, or more so, than Islamic law, although Muslim societies have always sought legitimacy for these practices by appeals to sacred texts.

Islam imposed virtually identical religious duties upon women and men. Observance of the five pillars—profession of faith, fasting, pilgrimage, alms, and ritual prayer—was incumbent upon all women and offered hope of salvation. But different culturally constructed behaviors were expected of male and female resulting in distinct sociophysical realms. The most visible expression of this was the segregation of male and female spaces, a direct product of the high sociomoral value placed upon female modesty and chastity.

Sexual segregation meant that women fulfilled some religious duties differently from men. They were, for example, required to perform prayers, but household and family duties often interfered. Moreover, women were either barred from communal services at congregational mosques, performing prayers at home, or participated in specially designated areas away from male worshipers in a manner reminiscent of Judaism. They did appear in religious courts, however, either as litigants or informal legal agents for other women. Sexual spatial segregation was more common in urban areas than in the countryside or among pastoral nomadic societies. Indeed, the morphology of Middle Eastern cities and towns was partially determined by the social demand for family and female privacy.

Menstruation taboos, found in most religions, have limited women's participation in formal religious observances and daily life. For Judaism, Christianity, and Islam, Eve's sin was embodied in menstruation and ritual impurity. Patristic Christian thinkers such as Augustine supported Levitical prohibitions surrounding menstruation. In medieval Christian Europe, the food asceticism practiced by fasting females was invariably accompanied by reported cessation of menses, a sign of purity and thus holiness. In Islam, a menstruating woman is unclean; sexual relations are forbidden, as well as fasting, prayer, entering a mosque, touching the Quran, or involvement in religious rituals. Women can not resume prayer, even at home, until after the cessation of menses and a ritual bath. *Tahara* (ritual purity) obligations thus have prevented Muslim women from fulfilling religious obligations in the same way that men do. Menstruation prohibitions were not in force, however, during the hajj or pilgrimage to Mecca; nor were alms-giving or other charitable acts subject to menstruation taboos.

As in other religions, women's mental and moral deficiencies have been directly linked to the impurities of menstruation and other reproductive functions. Muslim jurists have invoked them over the centuries to justify the fact that a woman's testimony in court is only worth half a man's, to impose male guardians upon women for decision-making affecting their lives, and to ban Muslim women from marrying non-Muslims because they were assumed incapable of raising children properly in their faith. The connection between ritual impurity and exclusion from devotional activities as well as leadership positions remains largely unquestioned among Muslims even now. Many Eastern Christian Churches—Armenians, Assyrians, and Greek Orthodox—held identical views regarding impurity and imposed similar prohibitions upon women. Even now, menstruating women are forbidden from touching icons in Greek Orthodox Churches.

Religious authority in Islam was an exclusively male preserve. Although ordained clergy did not exist, the leaders of communal prayer, the personnel of law courts, and the personnel of other religio-legal institutions could only be men. Expanded literacy was an important consequence of Islam's introduction to some parts of Africa and Asia due to the establishment of mosques, courts, and schools employing Arabic. Religious learning was an exclusively male activity, although educating elite women at home was common. Excluded from the formal spaces of learning such as mosque-schools or universities, a few women nevertheless attained remarkable levels of erudition. Umm Hani (1376–1466), from a Cairene family of notables, studied law and the Hadith in Egypt and Mecca under her grandfather's supervision and personally instructed some of the greatest Hadith scholars of her day. Umm Hani not only achieved a remarkable level of erudition but also performed the hajj thirteen times in her life, married twice, and produced seven named children. Here a pattern emerges that recalls the prominent Jewish women mentioned earlier such as Dulce and Urania of Worms, who hailed from rabbinical families and had been educated at home.

In all religions based upon sacred scriptures, the importance of female erudition is not whether a few women were schooled in those texts but rather whether female-authored works were considered worthy of interest. Hadith scholarship offered a commodious space for learned Muslim females such as Umm Hani in specific historical periods, but the general view of women as weak-willed and mentally incompetent held sway. According to numerous proverbs, woman was synonymous with ignorance: "the 'women's book' (i.e., the corpus of female superstitions) was loaded on a camel, but it was not able to carry the burden."[30] At times, medieval moralists opposed instructing women in all but rudimentary knowledge of their faith. In the Mamluk period (ca. 1250–1516 B.C.E.), a tradition attributed to the Prophet was manipulated to inveigh against female instruction: "A woman who learns [how to] write is like a snake given poison to drink."[31] Similar attitudes were found in both Christianity and Judaism at the official and popular levels.

There are no sacraments in Islam. As in Judaism, marriage is a contract and thus easier to abrogate, particularly for men. Polyandry and temporary marriage were practiced in pre-Islamic Arabia, but in the time of the Prophet polyandry was banned. Temporary marriage, often practiced in pilgrimage or trading cities attracting men without womenfolk, was continued but regulated by law. Under Islam the practice of polygamy expanded, although with legal restraints. Generally, only elites could afford more than one spouse; the incidence of multiple wives appears to have been less pervasive than previously thought. Ordinary people—the bulk of the population—tended toward monogamy. Some groups, such as the Berbers, looked with disfavor upon polygamy, probably due to local resource structures combined with customary inheritance law. And because divorce was common and much easier for men, the recourse to polygamy was not needed—serial marriages replaced concurrent multiple wives. Some Jewish communities under Islamic states practiced limited polygamy in certain regions and periods.

Another direct parallel with Judaism is that Islam discourages celibacy, because the greatest duty of believers is to produce progeny, above all, males. At times pious Muslims embraced sexual renunciation to better serve God. However the reasons impelling Christian ascetics such as Augustine and Muslim ascetics such as the Persian scholar al-Ghazali (who died in 1111) to become celibates were informed by similarly negative views of female nature: "to isolate themselves from women, whose sexuality was viewed as possessing a dangerous power that seduces, an impurity that pollutes, or a physical quality that weakens the will and spirit."[32]

The early Christian notion of marriage as a school for sexual continence—and all the more so the idea of celibacy within marriage—was foreign to Islam because both men and women (theoretically) have right to sexual fulfillment within marriage. Organized monasticism, with convents and monasteries enclosing men and women in vows of celibacy, did not exist in Islam. Muslim moralists rejected monasticism itself, mainly on the basis of Hadiths condemning the practice as well as prophetic example.

In contrast to Christianity, Muslim women did not have recourse to convents or other forms of religious associational life that offered acceptable alternatives to marriage and, for some women at least, an education. Although infrequent, individual Muslim women embraced celibacy as an empowering spirituality. The foremost example was the ascetic Rabi'a of Basra (who died in 801[?]), who adopted the celibate life to achieve union with God.

From roughly the twelfth century onward, organized sufi or mystical establishments for Muslim men grew, probably first in Persia. Membership in a sufi order did not imply sexual renunciation. Many shaykhs or leaders of these establishments were married, often having multiple wives. Some sufi orders accepted women members, but that did not normally result in an associational or communal life independent of marriage, family, or household. Finally, unlike Judaism in diaspora, where the home represented an important site for religious observances, celebrations, and festivals, the domestic unit or household in Islam was not invested with any special religious significance, although the home was where most women performed their daily prayers. The nondomestic spaces deemed appropriate for women regardless of social circumstance were mosques, when equipped with separate sections for prayer;

public baths; cemeteries on Fridays; and, depending upon location, saints' shrines.

One principal point made throughout this essay is that social rank and gender have historically intersected in different ways to shape women's participation in, or exclusion from, religious institutions. Islamic philanthropy represented a critical element not only in the construction of exemplary females but also for women in general, because charity constituted a moral and legal obligation not limited by menstruation taboos. Predictably, we know more about elite and urban philanthropic activities.

In the early Abbasid era, Queen Khayzuran (who died in 789) transformed one of Muhammad's dwellings in Mecca into a glorious mosque. Another queen, Zubayda (who died in 831), had an aqueduct constructed to furnish Mecca with pure water. The significant part that women played in establishing religious endowments (*waqfs*) is well documented for medieval Egypt and Syria, where wives of princes or governors alienated revenue-producing enterprises—bathhouses, mills, factories, oil presses, and stores—for communal religious purposes. Endowed hospitals, mosques, theological colleges (*madrasas*), or fountains often bore female patrons' names.

High social rank offered some women more visible venues for undertaking pious works in the public sector, and other factors, too, played a role—particularly age and generation. Older women, particularly those with sons, wielded enormous authority; female matriarchies and hierarchies that had their own patronage systems greatly shaped religious philanthropy and social charity.

During the sixteenth century elite status combined with the politics of reproduction within royal Ottoman households resulted in women's active involvement in imperial affairs and, indirectly, in the religious sphere of jihad. The Ottoman ulema castigated the "sultanate of women," blaming political decline with respect to Christian Europe on the fact that women had intervened in politics. In 1599 the Ottoman mufti publicly condemned royal women, citing a well-known prophetic hadith: "A people who entrusts its affairs to a woman will never know prosperity."[33] Offered as counter-models were pious, chaste, and submissive females, such as Khadija and Fatima, related to the Prophet. Perhaps the Ottoman ulema also recalled with trepidation 'A'isha, the Prophet's third wife, whose meddling in religion and politics rendered her a problematic example for ordinary women.

EXEMPLARY WOMEN

From the early Islamic era, the women associated with the Prophet, his family, and followers were subjects of extensive hagiographical literature, one of whose major sources was the biographical dictionary, a genre more or less unique to Islam. Composed from the nineth century on, these dictionaries contained the life stories of pious Muslims. Ibn Sa'd's tenth-century *Book of Classes* is one of the earliest surviving works.

Because scholars like Ibn Sa'd drew on oral traditions handed down from Muhammad's time, the compilations contain material about virtuous men and women from the first generation of Muslims. Indeed, the vast majority of female exemplars flourished during Muhammad's lifetime, and some pre-dated Islam. The Quran does not name Abraham's legal wife or his consort, but oral traditions, later collected into the Hadith, celebrated Hagar. When she and her son Isma'il (Ishmael) were banished to unforgiving wastelands near Mecca, Hagar saved her son's life. The event is ritually commemorated during the annual hajj, when pilgrims frantically search for water in the desert.

Muslims also revere Mary, the mother of Jesus, who is cited in the Quran, although Fatima (who died in 633), the Prophet's daughter and only surviving child, is not mentioned. Fatima was the wife of 'Ali, the fourth Caliph or successor to Muhammad. Over the ages she has been exalted as a pious, submissive daughter and mother of two imams in Sh'ism. The Shi'a conferred upon Fatima attributes similar to Mary, for example, as the suffering mother. If the holy family was a focal point of Christian devotion, Shi'ites venerated the holy family of Muhammad, Fatima, and 'Ali. "Fatima is the Mother-Creator figure, not very different from the image of Mary in Roman Catholicism, she is even referred to as 'virgin' (*batul*)."[34] In popular Shiite lore, Fatima was represented as devoid of sexuality; at times she was portrayed as not subject to menstruation and thus perpetually fulfilling obligations of fasting and prayer. In Shiite communities, the cult surrounding the "mistress of the women of the worlds" held the belief that Fatima wielded miraculous powers and even infallibility, something reserved for the Prophet and imams. With time Fatima embodied perfect womanhood and the ideal mother blessed with patience, passivity, long-suffering devotion, and selflessness. Over the centuries, women have sought Fatima's intercession for problems of conception, childbirth, illness, and marital woes.

More ambiguous was 'A'isha bint Abi Bakr (who died in 678), revered by Sunni Muslims as Muhammad's favorite spouse and a learned woman. Yet 'A'isha drew criticism because of her bold, untoward actions as a widow. In Shi'i tradition, she took part in the evil plot to deny to Muhammad's cousin, 'Ali, the office of caliph, and thus Shiite sources tended to vilify her. Classical Islamic literature, however, differed on 'A'isha's role in the Battle of the Camel (656), where she participated in bitter struggles over succession to the caliphate. Nevertheless, women active in political affairs were compared to 'A'isha with negative connotations. As was true of Mary Magdalene, 'A'isha's story was reinterpreted over time. In the later Middle Ages she was "rehabilitated" by

Sunni writers due to her religious knowledge and importance in Hadith transmission, eventually becoming the "Mother of Believers." With the spread of the printing press and print culture in the nineteenth century, the lives of the pious women associated with the Prophet were circulated more widely in editions resembling lives of the Christian saints and recited at women's religious gatherings.

As in other traditions, Muslim scholars regarded women in authority as an "unnatural state of affairs." Chastity, modesty, and submissiveness constituted highly prized behavioral characteristics; moralists such as al-Ghazali legitimized that by appeal to the Quran, Hadith, and the Prophet's women. As paragons of virtue, women became guardians of family honor. Female public and private comportment brought either collective humiliation or dignity to the lineage. Fathers, sons, and particularly brothers ensured that womenfolk did not violate honor codes. In tempting men and leading them astray, women wielded powers commensurate with those of Satan; they were represented as inherently lustful, sexually irresponsible, and dangerous. Regarded as a source of disorder and chaos (*fitna*) due to their mental and moral deficiencies, women required not only constant male supervision but also concealment. These views of female nature closely resembled those of Christian clerics and Jewish rabbis during the same period. Ideologies of sexual honor and shame have existed in most societies to various degrees and were directly related to notions of sexual purity, reproduction, lineage, and, ultimately, patriarchy.

Profane literature, composed for male elites, also portrayed women as sexually insatiable. The best-known examples are in the *Arabian Nights,* where wives sexually betray husbands and cause misfortune to all around them. Destructive female lust structures the tales' narratives, which offer portraits of the "bad woman" as opposed to the "good chaste wife" In addition, medieval Muslim scholars produced an enormous corpus of prescriptive works— marriage manuals, instruction books for rulers, and treatises on health—containing gendered moral messages. Al-Ghazali's advice manual for kings opined that "a woman's piety and seclusion are favors from God" and urged readers to avoid contacts, physical or even aural, between unrelated men and women.[35] Censuring the moral laxity of Cairo's women, Ibn al-Hajj repeated a well-known Hadith: "A woman is permitted three exits: one to the house of the husband when she is married to him; one when her parents die; and one when she is carried to her grave."[36] Ibn al-Hajj drew from a larger ideology of sexuality interpreting the female body as dangerous to the "order of the male world."[37]

Female and feminine signified corruption because women, ignorant of religious knowledge, believed in vile superstitions due to innate physical and mental deficiencies. Social class also undergirded moral treatises because the popular socioreligious practices of ordinary men and women were frequently condemned as un-Islamic and as provoking anarchy and natural calamity.

PILGRIMAGE AND SACRED JOURNEYS

The Muslim ideal in human behavior was patterned upon the "perfect human," the Prophet Muhammad, who unlike Christ never claimed divine attributes, although later followers associated him with supernatural events and quasi-divine status. Muhammad, the "seal of the prophets," was regarded as the supreme guide for all men and women, the sure path or right way to salvation. Throughout the ages, pious Muslims have imitated the Prophet's way (or sunna), including norms governing gender. Female veneration of Muhammad did not approach the ecstatic forms of women's devotion to Christ as expressed in bridal mysticism during the medieval Christian era. Some Muslim mystics, such as Rabi'a, employed similarly ecstatic discourse in their mystical poetry, but it was often directed primarily at God as the ultimate lover and less to his prophet.

Muhammad's life has been recreated during the pilgrimage to Mecca, which ritually celebrated sociospiritual and political events in a way somewhat reminiscent of the stations of the cross for Christians. Pre-Islamic figures such as Hagar or Abraham were also commemorated, but Muhammad's biography provided the fundamental structural narrative for the pilgrimage. Pilgrims frequently visited tombs associated with Muhammad's family; mausoleums in Medina contain the remains of daughters, wives, paternal aunts, and even his wet-nurse, Halima. Significantly, during the hajj, some gender prescriptions were lifted, for example, women were not required to veil their faces. The "Great Pilgrimage" has been performed for more than 1300 years and represents a central event not only for Muslims but also for world history. Its annual occurrence brought large numbers of diverse people from the Afro-Eurasian ecumene together for worship as well as trade and other exchanges.

Unlike Judaism, both Christianity and Islam are imbued with strong missionary imperatives. Performing the annual pilgrimage to Mecca sometimes entailed crossing tremendous expanses of territory, resulting in conversions to Islam because pilgrims proselytized along their journey. As in Christianity, the act of pilgrimage became a paradigm for piety and thus a standard feature in the lives of Muslim holy persons. And as in both Judaism and Christianity, the hajj maps out revelation and scripture topographically onto a sacred landscape. Shi'i Muslims also performed the hajj to the Holy Cities, although they held other spaces as sacred, especially the pilgrimage cities of Karbala and Najaf, which house the tombs of the imams.

One of the five pillars, pilgrimage is incumbent upon women if their social condition permits. For reasons of safety and moral probity, Muslim women traveled less frequently than men. As was true for Christian or Jewish women on long-distance pilgrimage, Muslim women had to be escorted by male family members. Umm Hani may have performed the hajj thirteen times, but she did so with male relatives and was greatly assisted by family wealth. Pilgrimage accounts by women comparable to those of Paula or Egeria do not exist, although pilgrims' instruction manuals were produced. The earliest known female-authored work was written by a Mughal princess, Gulbadan Begum, who made the hajj from India in the sixteenth century. Her account does not provide detailed information, however, perhaps because it was deemed impious to reveal too much about the most sacred of journeys. Contemporary Muslim women have written accounts, yet there is little historical evidence about how Muslim women in the pre-modern period experienced the hajj— a journey to the exemplary center.

Nevertheless, completing the hajj meant that a woman's social status changed; as for a man, she added the honorific *hajja* to her name. Women unable to travel compensated through philanthropy facilitating others' journeys to Mecca. In addition to the great pilgrimage, women and men visited saints' shrines, participated in annual celebrations of the Prophet's birthday, or in urban public rituals such as those in Cairo when the hajj caravan departed for the holy cities in Arabia, Mecca, and Medina. Local pilgrimages involved more women more fully in collective rites and rituals, but those manifestations of religiosity tended to be less well documented.

As in Judaism and Christianity, Muslim women's daily religiosity found fullest expression in "popular" rites, rituals, observances, and festivals preserved chiefly but not exclusively in oral traditions. Much of what we know about ordinary people and their past religious practices comes from those charged with suppressing them. The most visible embodiment of these beliefs was the saint's shrine or sufi center located in the village, urban quarter, or some remote corner of desert or mountain. Indeed, the religious topography of the Middle East and Africa was deeply marked by saints and their shrines and the broader social networks based upon them. Often excluded from the mosque, women's communal spiritual life was institutionalized by intense involvement in saint veneration and/or sufism. As in Christianity, there were fewer holy women than men, although both men and women venerated powerful female saints. Within saint cults and sufism, women constructed their own sacred spaces and religious hierarchies. Until nineteenth-century Islamic reform movements, mosque-centered Islam coexisted more or less harmoniously with saint and sufi.

Although overlapping, sufism and devotions to holy persons should not be conflated nor was the Muslim "saint" identical to Christian saints. There is no canonization process in either Judaism or Islam, and Muslim holy persons can be living or deceased. At the level of "popular" practices, however, differences among the three religions were attenuated. Many sacred sites or holy persons were venerated by Jews, Muslims, and Christians. Throughout the centuries, West European observers were shocked by the religiocultural promiscuity of Middle Eastern or North African saint cults that attracted believers from all three religions.

As was true in Christian Europe, popular rituals were also boisterous and profane. In 1388 venerations at Shaykh Inbaba's shrine near Cairo included not only the prodigious consumption of wine by night—some 150 jugs—but also large numbers of women, or so those condemning the festival claimed. Small wonder that rumors of orgies ran riot through the city and the ulema protested vehemently. Irreligious behavior, equated with public immorality, was often used to explain natural disasters. When plague and famine hit Egypt in 1438, the ulema opined that "women in the streets" had provoked these catastrophes. Orders were issued for them to remain inside their home.

Saint cults depend upon successful shrines where miracles, "the essential signs of the power of the saint," occur with "adequate frequency."[38] The supernatural events produced by extraordinary individuals attracted daily supplicants and visitors to neighborhood shrines or "corner saints" for succor. In sixteenth-century Istanbul, female supplicants tied themselves to the saint's powers through diverse rituals, including "the lighting of candles, the driving of nails, the knotting of rags to nearby trees or window-bars, the rubbing of stones, the eating or drinking of earth or water from the holy site."[39] Talismans to cure sickness, ward off evil, or confer blessings constituted concrete expressions of a saint's healing grace. At Koyn Dede's shrine in Ottoman Istanbul, custodians provided lamp oil to parents who believed that as long as the flame endured progeny would thrive. For centuries, Helvaji Baba's tomb, also in Istanbul, was much frequented by barren women who "unwound cotton and laid it out in great loops as they prayed for the gift of a child."[40] Holy persons served as spiritual patrons for large-scale entities such as guilds, urban quarters or towns. The thirteenth-century female ecstatic Lalla 'A'isha Manubiya (who died in 1267) was venerated as the patron saint of Tunis due to her miraculous powers.

Sufism or Islamic mysticism, emerging in the late eighth or early ninth centuries C.E., celebrated women known for spiritual virtuosity. Sufism drew its original inspiration from the Prophet and his companions, whose lives were marked by ardent mystical sensibility. One historical impetus to mystical Islam was the very fact of military and state expansion. Ruling elites in the Abbasid Empire engaged in extravagant lifestyles and profane behavior that alienated the devout, providing impetus for ascetics and mystics.

During the twelfth and thirteenth centuries, branches of sufi brotherhoods expanded across Persia, Mesopotamia, and, subsequently, the entire Muslim world. Scholars view the Mongol conquests as another major force in sufi expansion because the brotherhoods offset the devastations provoked by the invasions. Sufism developed institutionalized rituals, initiation rites, and doctrines expressed in literary genres, meditation practices, and artistic traditions. By the early modern era, hundreds of different sufi orders were found from West Africa to Southeast Asia. Before the twelfth century c.e., however, sufism tended toward the asceticism practiced by lone hermits or informally organized communities, including women. After that date in eastern Islamic lands, sufi retreats for women, often poor widows, were established, frequently built and endowed by elite women.

In the realm of sufism, women carved out sociosacred spaces not only as participants but also as exemplars and patrons. Some orders admitted females as members, although participation was normally subject to sexual segregation. Sufi women became focal points of collective venerations, although in medieval biographies they frequently lack a firm identity because many are unnamed. A few have remained paragons of virtue over the centuries. The mystic Rabi'a lived in the early Islamic period but still enjoys an international reputation. Born in Basra to an impoverished family, Rabi'a al-Adawiya (714?–801?) was abducted as a small child and sold into slavery. Her pious nature, however, convinced the slave-master to free her. Embracing celibacy, a somewhat unusual act, she retired to the desert to engage in extreme asceticism, attracting disciples through her holiness and doctrine of pure love. In contrast, contemporary male ascetics such as Hasan of Basra (who died in 728) sought union with a stern, fearsome divinity. Dread of hell informed their acts of self-abnegation. Rabi'a interpreted spiritual journeys as expressions of joy and love, and thus pilgrimage was a recurring theme in devotions to her. When asked if she loved the Prophet, Rabi'a rejoined that her love for God was greater than for any human.

Regarded as a saint, Rabi'a had numerous miracles, often associated with healing, nurturing, and supernatural light, attributed to her. She represented a critical stage in the formation of Islamic mysticism because the notions of divine passion and beatific vision were introduced into devotional practices and literatures. Rabi'a's life served as the model for an Islamic literary genre—an individual truth-seeker's heroic spiritual quest, which is a genre also found in Christianity. The first complete account of her life came from the thirteenth-century Persian writer Farid al-Din Attar, whose collection of sufi biographies included a lengthy entry on Rabi'a, the only woman cited. As with most male-authored works about saintly women, however, Attar molded her life to suit his own purposes. According to Attar (as well as other male Sufi writers), Rab'ia had become a man in order to achieve true spiritual progress: "No she wasn't a woman but a hundred men over."[41]

Yet often sufi women were portrayed, along with being women, as superior to male counterparts in both piety and gnosis. Sometime during the fourteenth century, legends about Rabi'a reached Europe, perhaps through Muslim Spain. The great thirteenth-century Spanish Muslim mystic Ibn 'Arabi wrote biographical accounts of sufi women, including Rabi'a, praising their spiritual powers. Rabi'a continues to have great appeal among Muslims, male and female, across the globe. Numerous biographies were composed about her during the twentieth century, and she was the subject of a feature-length film in Arabic. Most, if not all, contemporary sufi hagiographies contain extended entries on her life, celebrated as an exemplary form of internal, spiritual pilgrimage—a notion found in Christianity as well. Muslim feminists now use Rabi'a and other female mystics or erudites, as well as women from the Prophet's family, to argue for expanded female roles in Islamic worship, ritual, and scholarship.

Conclusion

Dealing with the topic of women, gender, and religion in comparative historical perspective represents an intellectual project of daunting magnitude. Attempts to illuminate a relationship that is this ancient, vast, and complex may seem doomed in advance to defeat—or at best to banal generalizations that flatten the richness of humankind's spiritual quests over time. Still, the theme of exemplary women and sacred journeys in Judaism, Christianity, and Islam offers an aperture into religion as lived, received, taught, and understood.

During the periods under consideration, the ideal woman in all three traditions was remarkably similar—indeed, that immense religiocultural and social construct represented by the exemplary female remained in force until very recently. Beneath the ideology of the passive, silent, obedient, and chaste woman, however, existed historical realities that continually posed problems to theologians, moralists, rabbis, and ulema. Prescriptive literature, almost exclusively written by men, reveals that Jewish, Christian, and Muslim women did not conform to the ideal—far from it; otherwise, the continual reminders of duty and obligation, the constant condemnations of immoral or impious behavior, would have been unnecessary.

In addition, historical conjunctures—crises, upheavals, or subterranean shifts in social hierarchies and political systems—offered opportunities to contest in myriad ways injunctions against women exercising spiritual and moral authority. The Crusades, the Reconquista, Mongol invasions, the disintegration of empires or rebellions against states, as well as movements of religious revival or reform—frequently condemned as heresy—produced breaches in the patriarchal armature of the three monotheistic religions from which both women and men profited, if only momentarily. Nevertheless, social rank and status played a significant role in conferring a voice and historical identity upon individual women. Some methods of spiritual and sociosexual enclosure for women—the home, convent or sufi lodge, and the celibate state—paradoxically created opportunities for learning and acquiring a voice. A few women, such as Margery Kempe, used that voice to openly criticize the practices of specific religious authorities and, although less frequently, male spiritual authority in general.

Finally, pilgrimage of various kinds permitted sacred (and worldly) travel to honor the very special dead or living holy persons. Often, the fact of pilgrimage would enhance an individual woman's sociospiritual status in the community. By undertaking sacred movement, women and men affirmed their identity as spiritual persons, often at nonofficial sites or unsanctioned shrines, and sought to shape their destinies in this world and the next. In some cases the special virtue of female exemplars or the miraculous powers of holy persons have been commemorated over time and preserved through organized rituals and memory.

What distinguishes the premodern historical periods dealt with here is not merely that more and more women today are now educated in scriptures or sacred texts. Rather, these texts themselves are seen as historical constructs and therefore subject to exegetical reinterpretation. More important, women scriptural scholars, along with like-minded male counterparts, now engage in intense debates over the gendered nature of religion, the religious experience, and authority. The acceptance of these reinterpretations, at least in some quarters, represents a fundamental change. The process is underway not only in the religious communities studied in this essay but also in other traditions such as Buddhism. In Thailand, for example, Chatsumarn Kabilsingh, a woman scholar of Buddhism, in the late twentieth century renounced marriage and family to follow Buddha's path. She assumed a new name, Dhammananda (the joy of righteousness) and the novel identity as an ordained monk. Due to enormous opposition in her own homeland, however, she traveled to Sri Lanka for ordination because the Buddhist hierarchy in Thailand maintains that only men can become monks. To attain spiritual fulfillment as well as socioreligious recognition of her spiritual goals, the "joy of righteousness" employed strategies that combined scriptural authority and global feminism with active refusal to submit to national male religious authorities. Perhaps this approach to women, gender, and religion is indicative of what the future can hold.

Notes

Invaluable intellectual sustenance was provided by my colleagues at the University of Arizona: Karen Anderson, Alan Bernstein, Gail Bernstein, Linda Darling, Ruth Dickstein, Esther Fuchs, Donna Guy, Susan Karant-Nunn, Helen Nader, Mary Spiedel, and Charles D. Smith. This essay is dedicated to Nikki R. Keddie of the University of California, Los Angeles, who taught me about women, gender, and comparative history.

1. Elizabeth Isichei, "Does Christianity Empower Women? The Case of the Anaguta of Central Nigeria," in *Women and Missions: Past and Present, Anthropological and Historical Perceptions*, vol. 11 of *Cross-Cultural Perspectives on Women*, ed. Fiona Bowie, Deborah Kirkwood, and Shirley Ardener (Oxford: Berg, 1993), 209–28, quotation on 209.

2. Caroline Walker Bynum, *Holy Feast and Holy Fast: The Religious Significance of Food to Medieval Women* (Berkeley: University of California Press, 1987), 6.

3. Ross E. Dunn, "Gender in World History," in *The New World History: A Teacher's Companion,* ed. Ross E. Dunn (Boston: St. Martin's Press, 2000), 441–45, quotation on 441.

4. Riffat Hassan, "Challenging the Stereotypes of Fundamentalism: An Islamic Feminist Perspective," *Muslim World* 91 (Spring 2001): 55–69, quotation on 59–60.

5. Miriam B. Peskowitz, *Spinning Fantasies: Rabbis, Gender, and History* (Berkeley: University of California Press, 1997), 101.

6. Leslie C. Orr, "Laity," in *The Encyclopedia of Women and World Religion* (hereafter *EWWR*), ed. in chief Serinity Young, 2 vols. (New York: Macmillan Reference, 1999), 2: 567–69, quotation on 567.

7. Diane M. Sharon, "Eve," in *EWWR*, 1: 319–20, quotation on 319.

8. Nancy J. Barnes, "Evil," in *EWWR*, 1: 320–22, quotation on 321.

9. Kristen E. Kvam, Linda S. Schearing, and Valarie H. Ziegler, eds., *Eve and Adam: Jewish, Christian, and Muslim Readings on Genesis and Gender* (Bloomington: Indiana University Press, 1999), 2.

10. Sylvia Barack Fishman, *A Breath of Life: Feminism in the American Jewish Community* (New York: Free Press, 1993), 146, quotation on 143.

11. S. D. Goitein, *A Mediterranean Society*, vol. 5: *The Individual* (Berkeley: University of California Press, 1988), 164.

12. Barbara Geller, "Roman, Byzantine, and Sassanian Judaism," in *EWWR*, 1: 534–38, quotation on 536.

13. Reinhold C. Mueller, "The Jewish Moneylenders of Late Trecento Venice: A Revisitation," in *Intercultural Contacts in the Medieval Mediterranean*, ed. Benjamin Arbel (London: Frank Cass, 1996), 209.

14. Judith Baskin, "Judaism: In the Middle Ages," in *EWWR*, 1: 538–40, quotation on 540.

15. Susan Starr Sered, "Our Mother Rachel," in *The Annual Review of Women in World Religions* (1996) 4: 1–56, quotation on 21.

16. Rachel Simon, *Change within Tradition among Jewish Women in Libya* (Seattle: University of Washington Press, 1992), 157–58.

17. Margaret Miles, *Carnal Knowing: Female Nakedness and Religious Meaning in the Christian West* (New York: Vintage Books, 1989), 22.

18. Miles, *Carnal Knowing,* 54, emphasis in the original.

19. Margaret L. King, *Women of the Renaissance* (Chicago: University of Chicago Press, 1991), 192.

20. Miri Rubin, *Corpus Christi: The Eucharist in Late Medieval Culture* (New York: Cambridge University Press, 1991), 317.

21. Bynum, *Holy Feast and Holy Fast,* 24.

22. Matthew C. Bagger, "Mysticism," in *EWWR,* 2: 699–701, quotation on 700.

23. See Kathryn Norberg's review of two films devoted to the Maid of Orléans, "Joan on the Screen: Burned Again?" *AHA Perspectives* 38 (Feb. 2000): 1, 8–9.

24. Anne L. Clark, "Virgin Mary," in *EWWR,* 2: 1004–6, quotation on 1004.

25. Susan Ashbrook Harvey, "Women in Early Byzantine Hagiography: Reversing the Story," in *The Gentle Strength: Historical Perspectives on Women in Christianity,* ed. Lynda L. Coon, Katherine J. Haldane, and Elisabeth Sommer (Charlottesville: University Press of Virginia, 1990), 36–59, quotation on 46.

26. Bynum, *Holy Feast and Holy Fast,* 25.

27. Simon Coleman and John Elsner, *Pilgrimage: Past and Present in the World Religions* (Cambridge: Harvard University Press, 1995), 82.

28. Coleman and Elsner, *Pilgrimage,* 79.

29. Ruth Roded, *Women in Islamic Biographical Collections from Ibn Sa'd to Who's Who* (Boulder: Lynne Rienner Publishers, 1994), 138.

30. Abraham Marcus, *The Middle East on the Eve of Modernity: Aleppo in the Eighteenth Century* (New York: Columbia University Press, 1989), 227.

31. Jonathan Berkey, *The Transmission of Knowledge in Medieval Cairo: A Social History of Islamic Education* (Princeton: Princeton University Press, 1992), 161–62.

32. Maura O'Neill, "Celibacy," in *EWWR,* 1: 143–45, quotation on 143.

33. Leslie P. Peirce, *The Imperial Harem: Women and Sovereignty in the Ottoman Empire* (New York: Oxford University Press, 1993), 267.

34. Moojan Momen, *An Introduction to Shi'i Islam* (New Haven: Yale University Press, 1985), 235–36.

35. Guity Nashat and Judith E. Tucker, *Women in the Middle East and North Africa: Restoring Women to History* (Bloomington: Indiana University Press, 1999), 62.

36. Huda Lutfi, "Manners and Customs of Fourteenth-Century Cairene Women: Female Anarchy versus Male Shar'i Order in Muslim Prescriptive Treatises," in *Women in Middle Eastern History: Shifting Boundaries in Sex and Gender,* ed. Nikki R. Keddie and Beth Baron (New Haven: Yale University Press, 1991), 99–121, quotaton on 99.

37. Lutfi, "Manners and Customs," 100.

38. Stephen Wilson, ed., *Saints and Their Cults: Studies in Religious Sociology, Folklore, and History* (New York: Cambridge University Press, 1984), 27–28.

39. Rafaela Lewis, *Everyday Life in Ottoman Turkey* (New York: Dorset Press, 1971), 50.

40. Lewis, *Everyday Life.*

41. Marcia K. Hermansen, "The Female Hero in Islamic Religious Tradition," *The Annual Review of Women in World Religions,* vol. 2: *Heroic Women,* ed. Arvind Sharma and Katherine K. Young (New York: State University of New York Press, 1992), 111–43, quotation on 130; Roded, *Women in Islamic Biographical Collections,* 91–113 (a chapter devoted to female mystics).

Bibliography

GENERAL WORKS

Abbott, Elizabeth. *A History of Celibacy.* New York: Scribners, 2000.
The Annual Review of Women in World Religions. Albany: SUNY Press, 1991–92.
Bowersock, G. W., Peter Brown, and Oleg Grabar, eds. *Late Antiquity: A Guide to the Postclassical World.* Cambridge: Harvard University Press, 1999.
Davis, Nathalie Zemon. *Women on the Margins: Three Seventeenth-Century Lives.* Cambridge: Harvard University Press, 1995.
Journal of Feminist Studies in Religion. 1985– .
King, Ursala. *Religion and Gender.* New York: Oxford University Press, 1995.
Sharma, Arvind, ed. *Women Saints in World Religions.* Albany: SUNY Press, 2000.
Sharma, Arvind, and Katherine K. Young, eds. *Heroic Women.* Vol. 2 of *The Annual Review of Women in World Religions.* Albany: SUNY Press, 1992.
———, eds. *Feminism and World Religions.* Albany: SUNY Press, 1999.
Weber, Michael C. "A Humanistic Approach to Teaching Religion in the World History Class," *World History Bulletin* 16 (Spring 2000): 26–28.
Young, Serinity, ed. *Encyclopedia of Women and World Religion.* 2 vols. New York: Macmillan Reference, 1999. Articles consulted by Howard Adelman, Ghazala Anwar; Ellen L. Babinsky, Denise N. Baker, Janet L. Bauer, Lois Beck, Francine Cardman, Mary Rose D'Angelo, Jill Dubisch, Carole R. Fontaine, Erica C. Gelser, Riffat Hassan, Judith Hauptman, Susannah Heschel, Ursala King, Kim Knott, Amy Lavine, Vasiliki Limberis, Ann E. Matter, Jo Ann Kay McNamara, Kathleen O'Grady, Jacqueline Pastis, Jennifer Rycenga, Jennifer; Nikky-Guninder Kaur Singh and Henry J. Walker, Jane I. Smith, Gail Corrington Streete, Francis V. Tiso, and Judith Wegner Romney.

JUDAISM

Ackerman, Susan. *Warrior, Dancer, Seductress, Queen: Women in Judges and Biblical Israel.* New York: Doubleday, 1998.
Baskin, Judith. *Gender and Jewish Studies.* New York: Biblio Press, 1994.
———, ed. *Jewish Women in Historical Perspective.* 2d ed. Detroit: Wayne State University Press, 1998.
———. *Women of the Word: Jewish Women and Jewish Writing.* Detroit: Wayne State University Press, 1994.
Ben-Ami, Ibrahim, S. Morag, and Norman Stillman, eds. *Studies in Judaism and Islam.* Jerusalem: Magnes Press, 1981.
Brenner, Athalya. *The Intercourse of Knowledge: On Gendering Desire and "Sexuality" in the Hebrew Bible.* Leiden: E. J. Brill, 1997.
Brooten, Bernadette. *Women Leaders in the Ancient Synagogue: Inscriptional Evidence and Background Issues.* Chico: Scholars Press, 1982.
Cohen, Mark. *Under Crescent and Cross.* Princeton: Princeton University Press, 1994.
Fuchs, Esther. *Sexual Politics in the Biblical Narrative: Reading the Hebrew Bible as a Woman.* Sheffield: Sheffield University Press, 2000.
———. "Status and Role of Female Heroines in the Biblical Narrative." *Mankind Quarterly* 23 (Winter 1982): 149–60.

Goldberg, Harvey E., ed. *Sephardi and Middle Eastern Jewries: History and Culture in the Modern Era*. Bloomington: Indiana University Press, 1996.

Hirschberg, H. Z. *A History of the Jews in North Africa*. 2 vols. Leiden: E. J. Brill, 1974.

Levy, Avigdor. *The Jews of the Ottoman Empire*. Princeton: Darwin Press, 1994.

Levy, Habib. *Comprehensive History of the Jews of Iran: The Outset of the Diaspora*. Los Angeles: Mazda Press, 1999.

Marcus, Jacob R., ed. *The Jew in the Medieval World: A Source Book*. 1938. Reprint. Cincinnati: Hebrew Union College Press, 1960.

Meyers, Carol L. *Discovering Eve: Ancient Israelite Women in Context*. New York: Oxford University Press, 1988.

Neusner, Jacob. *A History of the Mishnaic Law of Women*. Vol. 5: *The Mishnaic System of Women*. Leiden: E. J. Brill, 1980.

———, Tamara Sonn, and Jonathan E. Brockopp. *Judaism and Islam in Practice: A Sourcebook*. London: Routledge, 2000.

Rodrigue, Aron, ed. *Ottoman and Turkish Jewry: Community and Leadership*. Bloomington: Indiana University Press, 1992.

Udovitch, Abraham L., and Lucette Valensi. *The Last Arab Jews*. New York: Harwood Academic Publishers, 1984.

CHRISTIANITY

Bilinkoff, Jodi. *The Avila of Saint Teresa: Religious Reform in a Sixteenth-Century City*. Ithaca: Cornell University Press, 1989.

Blumenfeld-Kosinski, Renate, and Timea Szell, eds. *Images of Sainthood in Medieval Europe*. Ithaca: Cornell University Press, 1991.

Brock, Sebastian, and Susan Ashbrook Harvey, trans. *Holy Women of the Syrian Orient*. Berkeley: University of California Press, 1987.

Brown, Peter. *The Body and Society: Men, Women and Sexual Renunciation in Early Christianity*. New York: Columbia University Press, 1988.

———. *The Cult of the Saints: Its Rise and Function in Latin Christianity*. Chicago: University of Chicago Press, 1981.

Bynum, Caroline Walker. *Fragmentation and Redemption: Essays on Gender and the Human Body in Medieval Religion*. New York: Zone Books, 1991.

———. *Gender and Religion: On the Complexity of Symbols*. Boston: Beacon Press, 1986.

———. *Jesus as Mother: Studies in the Spirituality of the High Middle Age*. Berkeley: University of California Press, 1982.

Cooper, Kate. *The Virgin and the Bride*. Cambridge: Harvard University Press, 1996.

Hummel, Thomas, and Ruth Hummel. *Patterns of the Sacred: English Protestant and Russian Orthodox Pilgrims of the Nineteenth Century*. London: Scorpion Cavendish, 1995.

Isichei, Elizabeth. *A History of Christianity in Africa: From Antiquity to the Present*. London: SPCK, 1995.

James, Liz, ed. *Women, Men, and Eunuchs: Gender in Byzantium*. London: Routledge, 1997.

Karant-Nunn, Susan C. *The Reformation of Ritual: An Interpretation of Early Modern Germany*. London: Routledge, 1997.

Kempe, Margery. *The Book of Margery Kempe*. Edited by W. Butler-Bowdon. London: Cape, 1936.

Klapisch-Zuber, Christiane. *Women, Family, and Ritual in Renaissance Italy*. Chicago: University of Chicago Press, 1985.

Kors, Alan C., and Edward Peters, eds. *Witchcraft in Europe, 1100–1700: A Documentary History.* Philadelphia: University of Pennsylvania Press, 1972.

Nader, Helen, ed. *Power and Gender in Renaissance Spain.* Urbana: University of Illinois Press, 2002.

Nolan, Mary Lee, and Sidney Nolan. *Christian Pilgrimage in Modern Western Europe.* Chapel Hill: University of North Carolina Press, 1989.

Peers, E. Allison, trans. *The Letters of Saint Teresa of Jesus.* 2 vols. London: Burns, Oates and Washbourne, 1951.

Porete, Marguerite. *The Mirror of Simple Souls.* Translated by Ellen L. Babinsky. New York: Paulist Press, 1993.

Scaraffia, Lucetta, and Gabriella Zarri, eds. *Women and Faith: Catholic Religious Life in Italy from Late Antiquity to the Present.* Cambridge: Harvard University Press, 1998.

Schutte, Anne Jacobson, ed. and trans. *Aspiring Saints: Pretense of Holiness, Inquisition, and Gender in the Republic of Venice, 1618–1750.* Baltimore: Johns Hopkins University Press, 2001.

———. *Autobiography of an Aspiring Saint: The Other Voice in Early Modern Europe.* Chicago: University of Chicago Press, 1996.

Solterer, Helen. *The Master and Minerva: Disputing Women in French Medieval Culture.* Berkeley: University of California Press, 1995.

Staley, Lynn. *Margery Kempe's Dissenting Fictions.* Philadelphia: University of Pennsylvania Press, 1994.

Weinstein Donald, and Rudolph M. Bell. *Saints and Society: The Two Worlds of Western Christendom, 1000–1700.* Chicago: University of Chicago Press, 1982.

Wiesner, Merry E. *Women and Gender in Early Modern Europe.* New York: Cambridge University Press, 1993.

Wilkinson, John. *Itinerarium Egeriae: Egeria's Travels to the Holy Land.* Warminster, Eng.: Aris and Phillips, 1981.

———. *Jerusalem Pilgrimage, 1099–1185.* London: Hakluyt Society, 1988.

ISLAM

Ahmed, Leila. *Women and Gender in Islam: The Historical Roots of a Modern Debate.* New Haven: Yale University Press, 1992.

Boddy, Janice Patricia. *Wombs and Alien Spirits: Women, Men, and the Zar Cult in Northern Sudan.* Madison: University of Wisconsin Press, 1989.

Callaway, Barbara, and Lucy Creevey. *The Heritage of Islam: Women, Religion, and Politics in West Africa.* Boulder: Lynne Rienner, 1994.

Clancy-Smith, Julia. "The Middle East in World History." *World History Bulletin* 9 (Fall-Winter 1992): 30–34.

———. *Rebel and Saint: Muslim Notables, Populist Protest, Colonial Encounters (Algeria and Tunisia, 1800–1904).* Berkeley: University of California Press, 1994.

———. "The Shaykh and His Daughter: Coping in Colonial Algeria." In *Struggle and Survival in the Modern Middle East,* ed. Edmund Burke III. Berkeley: University of California Press, 1993.

———. "A Visit to a Tunisian Harem." *Journal of Maghrebi Studies* 1–2 (Spring 1993): 43–49.

Denny, Frederick Mathewson. *An Introduction to Islam.* 2d ed. New York: Macmillan, 1994.

Encyclopedia of Islam. 2d ed., 8 vols. Leiden: E. J. Brill, 1960– .

Esposito, John L. *Women in Muslim Family Law.* Syracuse: Syracuse University Press, 1982.

Evans, Charles T., and Julia Clancy-Smith, eds. *Studies in Islamic History and Cultures.* Special issue of *The Community College Humanities Review* (1997).

Gulbadan Begum, *The History of Humayun.* Trans. Anne Beveridge. Delhi: Idarah-I Adabitya-I Delli, 1972.

Haddad, Yvonne Yazbeck, and John L. Esposito, eds. *Islam, Gender, and Social Change.* New York: Oxford University Press, 1998.

Haeri, Shahla. *Law of Desire: Temporary Marriage in Sh'i Iran.* Syracuse: Syracuse University Press, 1989.

Hambly, Gavin R. G., ed. *Women in the Medieval Islamic World.* New York: St. Martin's Press, 1998.

Keddie, Nikki R., and Lois Beck, eds. *Women in the Muslim World.* Cambridge, MA: Harvard University Press, 1978.

———. "The Past and Present of Women in the Muslim World." *Journal of World History* 1 (Spring 1990): 77–108.

Keddie, Nikki R., and Beth Baron, eds. *Women in Middle Eastern History: Shifting Boundaries in Sex and Gender.* New Haven: Yale University Press, 1991.

Kenyon, Susan M. *Five Women of Sennar: Culture and Change in Central Sudan.* New York: Oxford University Press, 1991.

Lapidus, Ira M. *A History of Muslim Societies.* Cambridge: Cambridge University Press, 1988.

———. *Muslim Cities in the Later Middle Ages.* Cambridge: Harvard University Press, 1967.

Lifchez, Raymond, ed. *The Dervish Lodge: Architecture, Art, and Sufism in Ottoman Turkey.* Berkeley: University of California Press, 1992.

Meriwether, Margaret L., and Judith E. Tucker, eds. *Women and Gender in the Modern Middle East.* Boulder: Westview Press, 1999.

Nashat, Guity, and Judith E. Tucker, *Women in the Middle East and North Africa.* 2d ed. Bloomington: Indiana University, 1999.

Robinson, Francis. *The Cambridge Illustrated History of the Islamic World.* New York: Cambridge University Press, 1996.

Roded, Ruth, ed. *Women in Islam and the Middle East: A Reader.* London: I. B. Tauris, 1999.

Rosander, Eva Evers, and David Westerlund, eds. *African Islam and Islam in Africa.* Athens: Ohio University Pres, 1997.

Ruggles, D. Fairchild, ed. *Women, Patronage, and Self-Representation in Islamic Societies.* Albany: SUNY Press, 2000.

Shoshan, Boaz. *Popular Culture in Medieval Cairo.* New York: Cambridge University Press, 1993.

Smith, Grace Martin, and Carl W. Ernst, eds. *Manifestations of Sainthood in Islam.* Istanbul: Isis Press, 1994.

Smith, Margaret. *Rabi'a the Mystic and Her Fellow-Saints in Islam.* 1928. Reprint. New York: Cambridge University Press, 1984.

Spellberg, Denise A. *Politics, Gender, and the Islamic Past: The Legacy of 'A'ishah Bint Abi Bakr.* New York: Columbia University Press, 1994.

Stowasser, Barbara Freyer. *Women in the Qur'an, Traditions, and Interpretation.* New York: Oxford University Press, 1994.

Strobel, Margaret. *Muslim Women in Mombasa, 1890–1975.* New Haven: Yale University Press 1979.

Tucker, Judith E. *In the House of the Law: Gender and Islamic Law in Ottoman Syria and Palestine.* Berkeley: University of California Press, 1998.

Wadud-Muhsin, Amina. *Woman and Quran: Rereading the Sacred Text from a Woman's Perspective.* 2d ed. New York: Oxford University Press, 1999.
Walther, Wiebke. *Women in Islam.* London: George Prior, 1981.

AUDIO-VISUAL MATERIALS AND ELECTRONIC SOURCES

Videos

Medieval Women. Twenty-four minutes. New York: Insight Media, 1989.
Religion. Series with more than a hundred titles representing all religious traditions of the world. New York: Insight Media
Socio-Historical Gender Roles. Four videos, each sixty minutes. New York: Insight Media, 1994.
Women in History. Fifty-eight minutes. New York: Insight Media, 1994.
Women in Islam. Sixty minutes. New York: Insight Media, 1997.

CD-ROMs, Databases, Electronic Journals, and Web sites

American Theological Library Association (ATLA) Database [ATLAReligion].
Diotima. Materials for the Study of Women and Gender in the Ancient World Web site.
The Encyclopedia Judaica. CD-ROM edition.
Historical Abstracts. CD-ROM and online.
Fordham University. Internet Modern History Sourcebook Web site at http://www.fordham.edu/halsall/sbook.html/.
Iter Database. Abstracts of three hundred scholarly journal titles on the late Middle Ages and Renaissance.
Matrix. Resources for the Study of Women's Religious Communities Web site.
Renaissance Women Online Web site.
The Witchcraft Bibliography Project [early modern Europe] Web site: http://hist.unt.edu/witch.htm/.
Women in Judaism: A Multidisciplinary Journal at http://www.utoronto.ca/wjudaism/. Published only on the Internet.
Women's History Review at http://www.triangle.co.uk/whr/index.htm/. Electronic journal.
Women's Resources International available in CD-ROM and on the Web.

4

Gender and Work: Possibilities for a Global, Historical Overview

ALICE KESSLER-HARRIS

Jobs, they say, are the first step towards restoring their freedom.

—Ann Garrels reporting for National
Public Radio on women in Afghanistan
after the Taliban, December 4, 2001

Work is a common element of every society. Productive labor and labor that services the household and community can be either paid or unpaid, whether undertaken for the household or for the market, it is, for most people, a requisite for survival. Its organization emerges along with the development of communities. Sometimes it is involuntary, as in the case of slavery, and at others apparently voluntary, as in the case of the proverbial "lady bountiful" of Victorian fame or firefighters who risk their lives in the service of community. Sometimes it is visible, as, for example, when it is organized in workshops or factories; at others it is invisible, as in the case of women whose household labor sustains wage-earners or nurtures the generations to follow. Most often it produces the means for survival, whether through income-generating activities, barter, or by providing the wherewithal for household sustenance. Everywhere, it is a source of identity.

But what kinds of claims can be made for gender and work? Gender relations everywhere are social—neither immutable nor fixed—and they take specific forms under particular historical circumstances. Because work is a common element in almost all gender relationships, its forms and meanings are legion. Yet a surprising number of men and women, over time and space, have organized their activities in recognizably similar ways. Men have tended to do jobs that require upper body strength, to fight, and to govern; women have tended to work in and around households, to feed, and to clothe. If exceptions exist to every pattern of work, still their frequent and repeated parallels speak to larger historical changes like commercialization, industrialization, and urbanization. This essay probes for the commonalities even as it tries to acknowledge and respect the cultural differences. It asks what we can say about gendered relationships to work, risking interpretive hubris in the service of a greater understanding of how gender works.

One approach to capturing a gendered history of work is to focus on the impact of large-scale economic transformations on gender relations. That approach requires close examination of the lives of ordinary women and men in different times and places to find out how they have participated in economic activity and to explore the constraints and incentives for their choices. Although stories of daily lives include some of the exceptional women and men who became leaders in their fields, they much more often rotate around the history of male and female duties and prescribed roles; around the differing and changing cultures of masculinity and femininity, including conceptions of honor, service to the family, and fealty to lords; and the varied demands that political citizenship has exacted of work-related status. The history of work for women then becomes, to quote medievalist Judith Bennett, "in part a history of the constraints of economic disadvantage, familial duty and prescribed social roles. But it is also in part a history of women's agency within and against these constraints."[1] The temptation is, of course, to write about the drama of achievement and resistance—the optimism of accomplishment and agency rather than the limits of prescription and duty.

An alternative approach assumes the shaping impact of gender relations on the organization of production, on the changing nature of the world economy, on the transformation of local economies to national economies, and on their adaptation to a global marketplace. Here the social organization of households and their belief systems influence gendered roles in the workplace, limiting or expanding aspirations and expectations of men and women in particular ways. The economic historian David Landes has noted that "the best clue to a nation's economic growth and development potential is the status and role of women."[2] That perspective provides a sense not only of how ordinary women lived but also of how the shape of their daily lives—their cultures—influenced economic decisions on local, national, and even global levels.

This essay considers both approaches. It explores the influence of historical change on women's work and the complicated meaning of gendered relationships for economic transformation. Holding gender constant, assuming its value as an analytic category, it explores how work is conceived, managed, and implemented in societies at similar levels of economic development, although with quite different political and social contexts.[3] The exploration reveals that a gender-encompassing approach—one that is cognizant of gender's racial, ethnic, and class-based constitution—opens aspects of the history of work that have long remained obscure. It also tells us something about how the history of human progress and regress relates to gender.

My discussion focuses on four points. The first concerns several generalizations about gender and work that seem to transcend time and space. It focuses on the issue of how, acknowledging that there will always be exceptions and respecting the differences among cultures, it is possible to think about women's work comparatively. The second describes how cultural phenomena such as lifecycle, marriage, reproduction, and ideology influence the organization of work. It explores how these stages in women's lives affect opportunities and choices. Third, I investigate how changing modes and means of production alter the relationship of gender to work. In this part, I proceed roughly chronologically, trying to hold moments of economic development constant across time, beginning with a brief excursion into precapitalism and then moving to the moment of proto-industrialization. That occurred during the late medieval or early modern period in Western Europe, at the end of the Ming dynasty in China, and not until the twentieth century in some South Asian countries. From there I follow the effects of the processes of industrialization and urbanization, of colonization and imperialism, and, finally, of the development of a global economy. Finally, I examine the existence of several occupations that seem to have been peculiarly or largely the province of women, including textile manufacture, sexual service, domestic service, and teaching.

The Sexual Division of Labor

Until the present, all known societies have organized themselves around a sexual division of labor. Different societies distribute work between men and women differently, and in any one society economic and technological changes that alter the nature of work can create new patterns of distribution. But, as Maureen Mackintosh notes, everywhere "some tasks are allocated predominantly or exclusively to women, others to men."[4] A few may be done by both men and women. The sexual division of labor precedes and overwhelms other sorts of divisions, including those between slaves and their masters or mistresses, those of lord and serf, and those of class. Thus a mistress and her female slave may occasionally work at spinning thread, and an independent entrepreneur may perform the same tasks as his or her apprentice. But if it is the job of a female to spin, then it is not the job of the master. And if it is the job of a male to be a scholar, then women will generally be denied the kind of education that will enable them to breach those ranks.

The sexual division of labor is as prevalent in unwaged labor (including housework) as it is in waged work. We see it in agricultural societies, where women tend to care for domestic animals and vegetable gardens while men clear and plow fields, and among the clergy of primitive and modern religions, where men and women perform different institutional functions. We observe it in the volunteer labor on which many advanced industrial societies rely, in the charitable acts of women toward their neighbors, in the brotherhoods of male firefighters who protect communities. And it is everywhere evident in the assignment of child-rearing primarily to females.

But the sexual division of labor has rough edges or what in modern jargon might be called permeable boundaries. It changes over time in the same society. The women who brewed beer in the nineteenth-century United States and sold it in their parlors found themselves replaced in a single generation by commercial breweries and male barkeeps. At any given moment, singular men and women could often find ways over seemingly insurmountable barriers. A determined woman could acquire a scholarly education even when most women were consigned to illiteracy, as, for example, the fifteenth-century French/Italian intellectual Christine de Pisan. More women disguised themselves as men and served in the American military—from the Revolution on— than we can now count. Family status often enabled women to breach conventional divisions. The daughter trained by her father, the widow who took over a husband's business, and the female political advisor whose ideas found expression in the voice of a witless lord and master—none of these is unfamiliar. All raise the question of how particular sexual divisions of labor are institutionalized and maintained in place.

ORIGINS

Many scholars attribute the source of a sexual division of labor to essential biological differences. Arguing that women's tasks follow from the necessities of bearing and nursing babies, they contend that women's reproductive duties required them to perform compatible jobs. Men, in contrast, needed to train themselves to provide for and protect vulnerable women. From that it followed that women's work would remain tied, at least metaphorically, to the household, with the preparation of food and clothing at its center, while men could move beyond domestic borders to hunt and fight. Yet the subtleties of food and household provision cannot be explained biologically. Nursing babies and tending infants remained by and large women's work, but providing food called for cultural intervention. African men felled trees to clear fields. After that, some tribes gave women the entire responsibility for preparing the fields and sewing and harvesting grain. In other tribes, men did those jobs, calling on women to pitch in at harvest time.[5] Midwives and healers tended to be female in pre-modern Western societies; barber-surgeons and physicians tended to be men, as did apothecaries. Yet women by no means limited their medical practice to gynecological and obstetrical issues. Small but significant numbers can be found scattered through other medical fields, including the preparation of pharmacological compounds. In the seventeenth century, when Western European men began to arrogate medical knowledge to themselves, they successfully transformed the compounding and selling of herbs into a professional activity, depriving women of jobs they had held for centuries.[6] Ultimately, men effectively pushed women out of most medical practice, including, in many places, delivering babies. In much of Asia men could as easily dominate the healing arts as women, reserving to themselves the skills of pharmacology. But they did not take over the tasks of midwives. Delivering babies remained the province of women.[7]

If the sexual division of labor is not rooted in biology, neither is it rooted in the market although generally the advent of market economies reorganizes and sharpens differences between what men and women do. Primitive markets—which involve the sale or barter of household products and produce—tend to be the provinces of the women who make or produce the items for sale. African women successfully developed such markets to sell the products of their fields, to create wealth, and to build their own power within families and communities. But men dominated markets where cattle were traded or goods were the products of machinery. The more complex and distant the market the more likely it was to be the venue of males who tended, through the trade of animals, to have greater access to even small amounts of capital.[8] The European "Commercial Revolution" of the fifteenth and sixteenth centuries seems not only to have restricted women's access to trade beyond local arenas but it also, in a domino effect, reduced their control over products sold and ultimately constrained their opportunities. The men who went to market and set the prices for goods found themselves in a position to determine production standards and sometimes to select and train the workers they wanted.

Technological changes seem to exacerbate the sexual division of labor but cannot account for its development. The advent of the plow, almost everywhere a machine worked by men, was used by women in Egypt. And although it restrained women from doing one job, it did not forecast their use in other agricultural jobs. Spinning wheels and looms located in homes tended to be the province of women. Factory-based spinning machinery remained largely a woman's arena, but weaving looms could be run by either men or women, depending on cultural constraints. In the global marketplace, where technology has reached its apogee, occupational segregation by sex persists at startlingly high levels "in every region, at all economic development levels, in all political systems, and in diverse religious, social and cultural environments."[9]

Nor can the sexual division of labor be attributed to, or blamed on, capitalism, because it both predates it and persists even in the absence of a capitalist economic system. Feudal societies, whether in Western Europe, China, or nineteenth-century Russia, certainly boasted sharp sexual divisions that were generally motivated by the need for military service. Twentieth-century socialist economies, which made greater use of paid female labor than most other industrial societies, nevertheless continued to subscribe to the notion that women retained primary responsibility for child-rearing and household maintenance. If they did not argue that women were weaker or different, they perpetuated patriarchal male values and maintained hierarchy and order by organizing workplaces that provided little leeway for family responsibilities and social policies that provided women, rather than men, with benefits for child care. Partly in consequence, the Soviet Union, East Germany, and China had among the highest levels of female workforce participation and some of the highest levels of sex segmentation in the labor market.[10]

How work is distributed between women and men seems to hinge at least as much on gendered meaning systems as on economic circumstance. To be sure, what is thought appropriate may derive from and sustain the biological and economic imperatives of particular societies, yet generalizations about what women can and cannot do often outlive economic or biological necessity. Every society has such gendered meaning systems, often rooted in religious faith or in inferences about the natural order and expressed as moral assumptions about propriety or in stereotypes that regulate and control the expectations of both sexes. These stereotypes and assumptions manifest themselves in injunctions to men and women to behave in particular ways—in line with a military ethic, for example, or in conformity with notions of domesticity.

Changing ideas about manliness govern much labor force behavior. Where military prowess is valued, routine daily subsistence activities for men are not. The task of sustaining households then falls within the province of women. Market economies, in which men are not visibly or constantly the protectors of women's bodies, seem to call for sometimes subtle definitions of manhood that can foment turf wars among different kinds of men as well as between men and women. Jobs that require physical strength, dirty and dangerous jobs, and those that demand the use and control of machinery, long apprenticeships, or access to knowledge are variously considered manly and reserved for workers who fit particular cultural or class-based definitions of manliness.

If manliness is often linked to physical and mental strength, womanliness is generally tied to domesticity—whose ideals justify restrictions on women's activities within as well as outside the household—and exclusion from the labor market. Where the household is the locus of production, women tend to have wide responsibilities that govern many phases of its activity, and their diligence, thrift, and competence as managers are called upon. But where some or all production moves out of the household while females are expected to remain within it, women's sustaining, nurturing, and submissive qualities are emphasized. And where female leisure denotes male status, women are often characterized as docile, delicate, and emotional. At every stage, gendered meaning systems are called on to tether women to household economies of one sort or another. In twelfth-century China, a revived Confucianism trumpeted faith in separate spiritual roles for the sexes, calling on women to serve their husbands and do womanly work that would ensure their family's future success. Not incidentally, simultaneous state policies benefited from calling men to the plow while encouraging women to confine themselves to household tasks, where they could perfect skills such as weaving.

CONSEQUENCES

Unlike gendered divisions that seem to be rooted in reproduction, those that govern income-generating tasks do not appear to be natural, at least at first, so they require justification. But most cultures quickly naturalize what men and women do through reciprocally confirming systems of thought and behavior that then govern the jobs to which each sex is assigned. Where men are thought to be competitive, risk-takers, courageous, and physically strong, they are perceived to be ideally suited for the challenges of an emerging capitalist world; where women are said to be submissive, patient, manually dexterous, and nurturing, they appear perfectly suited to jobs performed under close supervision and consisting of repetitive movements. For example, the production of silk, engaged in for two millennia, requires a number of different processes, all of them skilled and some of them extraordinarily demanding. The job has generally been assigned to women, a division of labor often justified by the need to nurture the worms that feed off mulberry trees and the cocoons they produce as well as on the speed and adroitness required to gather spun silk from the cocoons. Despite the skill involved and the value of the final product, silk production has traditionally been neither a well-paid nor a high-status job. Its association with women has rendered it the subject of exploitation rather than reward. Silk weaving, in contrast, often the province of men, has reaped both status and financial reward.

Whether or not a woman's status is improved when she engages in paid work may rest on many things, including whether and how the work counts.

Preindustrial societies that relied on women's income-generating activities tended to value women's labor in the household more highly than those that passed through the industrialization process. When household work no longer generated an income, women's labor in it often went unnoticed (if they were wives) and underpaid (if they were servants and household helpers). Most such women continued, of course, to work, not only by rearing the children who reproduced the labor force but also by sustaining the labor of other household members who brought in income. In the absence of tangible income, women tended to become economically invisible. Writing about West Bengal, Bahnisikha Ghosh notes the continued underestimation of women in labor force statistics. Domestic work (in one's own household) is commonly excluded, as is agricultural labor. Farmer's wives and children (especially students) are assumed to be nonworkers. Small trades and crafts in which women engage seasonally are also not counted.[11]

The delineation of what counts as work is widely applicable. Just as the periodic U.S. censuses failed to count the millions of women who took in boarders, or sewing, or laundry, or sold their butter in local markets, so, Florencia Mallon suggests, much of women's productive work continues to remain invisible in Latin America. "It appears simply as an extension of their domestic activities."[12]

If the assumption that women did not work was illusory, it served the interests of social order in many ways. Generally, males who governed households in which their labor alone appeared to support wives and families, or in which wives did not leave the household to work, reaped the benefits of higher status. Confucians saw such households as following a spiritually guided, logical order. Western Enlightenment thinkers bestowed political voice on their heads. By the nineteenth century, working-class men in industrialized countries began to insist on a "family wage" sufficient to sustain households of their own. The demand fuelled political battles for the distribution of industrial profits.

The notion that manliness inhered in the male who provided for a family soon added another competitive wedge between male and female workers as males learned to fear the low-wage competition of women, who were not expected to support families but only to contribute to them. In contrast to men, whose willingness to support their families generated at least a modicum of approbation, the capacity to earn income outside her household rarely contributed to a married woman's status, and it sometimes diminished community respect for her family. When women did earn wages as part of a family, their imputed location within families justified pay from half to two-thirds that of men. A particular job, assigned to women, thus took on the devalued status of the worker, confirming women's generally subordinate positions. The result, as one historian points out, is that middle-class women like those she studied in Mexico City in the mid-twentieth century, discovered that paid work did not improve their position in society at all.[13]

Yet sexual subordination around wage work is not universal, and women who have benefited from their class and family positions have frequently held important positions that not only increased their individual status but also that of their families. Women teachers, entrepreneurs, and healers all fall into this category, as do occasional political leaders such as Indira Ghandi and Golda Meir. Because economic development, in every phase, takes advantage of women's skills, there are moments when women produce family wealth, sometimes by virtue of their nimble fingers and at others through business acumen and scholarship, and are honored for so doing. The expansion of such activities in recent years has undoubtedly led to greater economic independence for women and greater social and political equality with men. But the jobs of women and men are still sharply divided in most places, and women at any given level of the class structure tend to work at more poorly paid jobs than men.

What then can we say in general about gender and work? We can say that insofar as it affects women, the sexual division of labor (whatever it looks like) is an artifact of three intertwined elements—male efforts to control technology, knowledge, and economic resources; the distribution of reproductive and family responsibilities; and cultural and religious messages about propriety with regard to sex roles. A gendered history of work that tries to compare men and women over time and place will need to comprehend the particular circumstances within which each operates while acknowledging how in practice each incorporates at least these three elements.

The Influence of Culture

Among the many elements that help to explain why we can assume a phrase like "women's work" has similar meanings in places thousands of miles apart and at chronological distances of hundreds of years, sociocultural factors belong in the mix. Life-cycle patterns, demographic trends, the material conditions of family life, and the differential attribution of biological, emotional, and psychological characteristics to men and women all participate in shaping decisions that ordinary women and men make about how to sustain themselves and their families. The relative importance of these elements may vary, but we need to account for them all in order to understand how particular men and women function in the labor force.

HOUSEHOLD ORGANIZATION

Household organization lies at the heart of any explanatory paradigm. For most of recorded time, goods and services were produced within what is sometimes called an extended household, which consisted of a stem family with assorted siblings, their spouses, and children. Sometimes servants and slaves joined the mix as well. In self-subsistence economies where items produced by the household were largely consumed by it or traded for necessary goods, boys as well as girls were inducted early into the roles assigned them. Generally, women nurtured infants and trained girls while men took on the training of boys. In rural, self-sufficient households, girls learned, either from their mothers or mother surrogates, to care for house, garden, and domestic animals, and, in some parts of Africa, to build shelters as well. Girls also developed skills in the production of food, soap, baskets, textiles, and garments. Some of these goods were bartered or sold in local markets that were the province of women. Males and females learned to do complementary work, but wherever women were responsible for both food production and household maintenance, their high economic value was reflected in the custom of paying a young girl's family a brideprice for the woman who entered a man's household. If, in contrast, the female had a lesser role in the economic well-being of the family, she needed to offer a dowry to ensure her marriageability.

In some agrarian societies such as those as in sub-Saharan Africa where property was collectively owned, many wives could make a man rich. Because each wife provided the labor to work more land, and because each was expected not only to support herself and her children but to contribute something to the household, an additional wife brought in far more than her keep. Many wives also enhanced the dignity and standing of their husbands.[14] Division of land into private property prevented most men from marrying more than a single wife lest his property be insufficient to support a large family. But in the absence of hired help, even a single wife who worked in the fields contributed to the well-being of a household. Men customarily paid a bride-price for such women in Southeast Asian countries like Malaya and Laos. In Hindu India, where women tended not to work the fields, a large dowry compensated a husband's family for a woman's support. Poor women and those whose families could only afford insufficient dowries generally found themselves in positions that resembled those of servants. Either way, a woman whose economic usefulness was measured by her dowry could find herself vulnerable if her new family were disappointed with the sum total of her contributions.[15]

Urban households organized around a craft that involved every member in its successful completion tended to be smaller and rely on the skill of the generally male household head for survival. How young men and women developed and honed their skills in this context depended on the kinds of households to which they belonged, but commonly boys and girls were apprenticed to different trades—boys to crafts like metal- or woodworking, and girls to silk and textile production and domestic service. More prosperous families could allow daughters to use their early years to develop skills that made them marriageable or to amass dowries. Chinese girls, for example, learned to spin and weave. Their carefully stored bales of cloth served as essential parts of dowries with which families could bargain for bride-wealth and visible evidence of the skills they would bring to a husband's household. The same families might make a risky but potentially rewarding investment in the education of one or more of their sons for government service or the scholarly professions.

Absent a household with opportunities for learning a trade or money to find an apprenticeship, boys and girls were consigned to serve others. Poverty-stricken families in seventeenth-century New England, who had neither land nor the means to apprentice their sons to a trade, hired them out as farmworkers. Girls frequently learned to do domestic service in other people's families, where they often worked without pay until adulthood. Well into the nineteenth century, young women from poor Chinese households could find themselves sold into slavery—either as concubines or as domestic servants. Worldwide, the most accessible route to survival for unprotected women was that of a servant in a home other than their natal one. There, ensconced behind walls, a woman might live out her life, learning the skills of the household and exercising them in the service of others.

Skills that passed from fathers to sons typically involved wives and daughters in the enterprise. Artisan parents—in China, in India, and in Western Europe—expected daughters who learned at least part of the paternal skill to remain within the trade and arranged marriages accordingly. Wives boarded apprentices, learned the skills of income management and distribution, and often became effective business partners. When widowhood altered the household's composition, knowledgable women carried on a household enterprise either by hiring appropriate workers or by doing the job themselves along with their children.

Depending on economic opportunities and family needs, rural as well as urban labor forces could be more or less transient. Young women as well as men left home to seek work, more often than not encouraged by families in need of income. After the Black Plague in late-fourteenth-century Europe, rural women took advantage of labor shortages to move to urban centers. Japanese women found themselves sold to the emerging textile industry in the mid-nineteenth century, their earnings offered to their families in advance of their labor to ensure their loyalty.[16] New England farm women journeyed to the first textile factories in Lowell, Massachusetts, in order to earn enough to secure their families' independence and sometimes their own as well. French adolescents moved from family farms to nearby towns and cities to find work, returning large portions of their incomes to their families.[17] Single men from Ireland sought their fortunes as canal-diggers in America, Italian men migrated to Argentina and other parts of Latin America as well as to the United States, and married men in many parts of Africa moved from their villages to work on railroads and in mines.

Generally, women more than men sent money home to the households they had left behind, and men established new households in the communities to which they migrated. That pattern of female support for natal families seems to have continued well into the twentieth century, even in the most industrialized societies. Turn-of-the-century immigrants to the United States, for example, relied on the earnings of their young daughters, whose pay packets tended to be turned over to their mothers unopened. More recently, the migration of women from the Philippines to the Middle East and Japan and Latin America to the United States has enabled the families of female migrants to emerge from poverty while fueling the movement of educated professional women into the labor force.

LIFE-CYCLE

If a woman's training and mobility hinged on her family's economic position and the expectation of family responsibilities, her life's experience was conditioned by the fate of her father or husband. Most women and men accommodated their work patterns to the stages of their life-cycles and the vagaries of their partners' fortunes. For men, these remained fairly stable. For women, however, economic options rotated around life-cycles that incorporated unmarried young womanhood, marriage and children, maturity and adult children, and widowhood. Each stage ushered in differences in unpaid work as well as in paid work, and each held the key to the rules by which woman typically lived.[18]

Because family was integral to all preindustrial economies, expectations of marriage guided the rearing of girls in most societies and conditioned expectations of their working lives. The same expectations also provided boundaries for their positions as workers. In seventeenth-century Germany, public officials recognized that some women would have to work outside their own homes, yet they enforced rules and regulations that treated women's work as a temporary or stopgap measure until the women could attain, or return to, their "'natural,' married state." As a result Germany, like most modern societies, had no stake in making employment an attractive alternative to marriage.[19] Because marriage and child-rearing would be a woman's first calling, "'women's work' came increasingly to be defined as that which required little training or initial capital, could be done in spare moments and was done by men only as a side occupation, carried low status, and was informally organized and badly paid."[20]

This placed women without partners, especially those without family position or inherited means, in odd positions. Generally, women who chose not to marry faced two problems. First, living independently was a threat to social order, violating the expectation that women would engage in the reproduction of the labor force. Second, because traditional expectations of marriage gave women less opportunity to acquire sufficient training to be economically independent and successful outside the household (or to accumulate what economists sometimes call "human capital"), they had far fewer economic options than those who married. Often, the options of the unmarried were reduced to marginal, poorly paying jobs, for example, road repair and roof thatching in medieval England or spinning and weaving in Ming China. Nevertheless, women headed their own households in far larger numbers than we have typically imagined. In São Paulo, Brazil, for example, the development process that drew men into the frontier left women to fend for families and themselves. In the first part of the nineteenth century, the female-headed family was the most prevalent family form in São Paulo. Women headed nearly half of all families.[21] To survive, they participated in the cottage industry that paved Brazil's path to industrialization.

Two acceptable alternatives to marriage existed in many areas: religious communities and domestic service. Women could and did join together in Catholic convents or in Buddhist monasteries where their work often consisted of educating the young, ministering to the sick, and caring for the poor. Laywomen sometimes created communities like the Beguinages that originated in twelfth- and thirteenth-century Belgium and spread throughout the region.[22] They tried to counter the discriminations faced by single women living alone by constructing communities of women who shared their wealth and did good works. But they faced open hostility from both the secular and the religious and eventually disbanded. In some respects the early-twentieth-century movement of women into social settlement houses located in poor neighborhoods, especially in Britain and the United States, resembles the Beguinages.

Unlike the fate of single women, that of married women who became widows could vary widely. In numbers of places, widows were discouraged from remarrying, either so they could serve the families of their deceased husbands (China, Japan, India) or preserve their property for the children of those husbands. In China and India, the husband's family was entitled to a widow's labor in perpetuity, so she was frequently reduced to the status of household servant. In parts of Africa, a wealthy widow could be the object of envy and encouraged to remarry in order to control her autonomy. But elsewhere, a widow might be forced to marry a dead husband's brother in order to keep family property intact. In Western Europe, widows could choose to remarry or not, but they faced limited work options. The lucky ones discovered that some jobs, like that of community bathmistress, were reserved for them.[23] The widows of artisans could often continue a deceased partner's business, sometimes by hiring men to do the male's work.[24] Still, there were inevitable restrictions. Some strong guilds limited a widow's right to run her husband's business to a year or so; others allowed her to continue the operation until her eldest son was ready to take over. And widows who became merchants could generally take charge only of local distribution; for long-distance trades, they were forced to rely on men.[25]

In Western Europe, a widow's choices were partly conditioned by whether she was a mother and by the ages of her children. The childless rich often found themselves in control of not only their own dowries but also their husband's property, while those with grown children might find themselves at the children's mercy. Poor but virtuous widows could depend on the resources of the parish, or they might be thrown into the workhouse. In France, Britain, and Germany, among other places, a widow with a young son might negotiate to keep her husband's guild membership, and thus her right to practice his trade, until her son grew old enough to take over. Remnants of this conception of widowhood as an extension of marriage survive in twentieth-century American social policies. For years, these policies suggested that social benefits accrued to a dead father's children (but not to those of a dead mother) by providing benefits only to widows with children—and then only until the children became old enough to support themselves.[26]

The rights of the divorced varied dramatically. In countries where Islam predominated, the shariah granted women exclusive rights over their inheritance and dowry as a hedge against divorce and widowhood. Given the possibilities of living an economically independent life, Muslim women, some scholars argue, "have had a keen sense of property and a good nose for making their assets grow."[27] In rural Morocco, where 55 percent of twentieth-century marriages ended in divorce, certain jobs might be reserved even for women without resources. In the traditional Moroccan village, Susan Schaefer Davis tells us, "A woman does not usually *choose* to take on an activity to earn additional income or enrich her life as a Westerner might; rather she does it out of necessity."[28] In that context the most prestigious women's jobs (those of bathmistress, seamstress-teacher, or seamstress) produced sufficient income to enable a woman to survive a divorce economically and even increase her status. In much of preindustrial Western Europe, however, where divorce was impossible, women abandoned by their husbands had no rights to the husband's trade although they might well possess the privilege of practicing that of their father, which could be the same.

RELIGION AND IDEOLOGY

The practical realities of household organization pale beside the power of ideologies of domesticity, morality, and sexuality to enforce and sustain institutional structures. Unlike life-cycle imperatives that could dramatically change a woman's daily work at a moment's notice, ideas that guided normative behavior provided a consistent foundation for the social relations of the sexes in any community, equally impelling men and women. By illuminating the visions and aspirations of ordinary people, these ideologies or meaning systems provide clues to the tangible and intangible constraints imposed on both sexes.

Take, for example, the idea of a male breadwinner. Until recently, Western women assumed that it was a universal response to the industrialization process, necessary to meet the need for someone to care for home and children while other household members generated income outside the hearth. More recent research has demonstrated just how much the ideal of the male breadwinner "varied greatly over time and space, from one neighboring community to the next, between different parts of the world, and between different families in one and the same locality."[29] It seems not to have been widespread in the preindustrial period, even in Britain and the United States, where it appears in its strongest forms. Rather, the assumption that women would work to extend the prosperity of the household prevailed, best captured by an aphorism popular among the preindustrial British population: "None but a fool would take for a wife a woman who cannot earn her bread."[30]

In countries such as Sweden, which had a tradition of female labor, the advent of industrialization, which required at least one member of almost every household to generate income, did not settle the issue of who would produce that income.[31] That said, it also seems to be the case that, where it existed, a male breadwinner ideology reshaped definitions of manhood from the rugged to the respectable, and it encouraged men to collude across class lines to create and maintain an occupational structure that was self-reinforcing. It exercised powerful pressure on employers to act according to cultural norms, even against their own economic interests, and it could and did bring to bear the institutional forces of the state to sustain it.[32]

Injunctions about women's behavior derive from varying sources, including religious influences, male desire to preserve property, and various forms of nationalism and patriotism. These tend to be justified by means of arguments about women's nature or her biology. Thus women are at various times depicted as morally and physically weak, emotional rather than rational, maternal and uncompetitive by nature, and in need of protection. Such arguments, or domestic ideologies, legitimize constraints on women's participation in the public sphere and have a heavy impact on their aspirations with relationship to work-related goals. They sometimes provide rationales for sequestering women, necessarily confining their economic contributions to work that can be done entirely within households or in the presence of other women. They can also demand from women the entire economic support of family units and therefore their intimate involvement in the marketplace. Although men and women often subtly undermined these injunctions and the belief systems on which they rested—for example, by making exceptions of their own spouses or daughters—historians have uncovered little active rebellion against the seemingly natural divisions of work within and outside the household that they produced.[33]

Domestic ideologies (often religiously informed) seem to emerge most powerfully as regions make their way from agrarian societies into preindustrial modes with more fully developed markets. In the twelfth and thirteenth centuries, for example, the Chinese witnessed a resurgence of Confucianism, with its powerful mandate to segregate the sexes and assign women only internal household duties while giving men control of everything outside the household.[34] Injunctions against women's public appearances that emerged in Tuscany over the course of the thirteenth and first half of the fourteenth centuries were only slightly less restrictive. There, women were meant to obey orders, not give them. They were excluded from publicly visible roles because they were seen as "not merely caretakers of the material welfare of their home, but also as the guardians of its religious and moral values." These attitudes "worked to keep women out of occupations that required mobility and public exposure."[35] They also provided grist to men who resented employment situations that placed women in superior positions. As a result, women's economic options shrank; they could not so easily succeed their fathers or husbands in workshop hierarchies. The municipality banned females from hawking their wares on the streets.

On the other side of this coin were public efforts, prevalent as modernization succeeded traditional societies, to encourage women to choose jobs that affirmed home roles or restricted their personal freedom in order to provide a safe environment that resembled one's own home. These are now familiar in the job-channeling efforts that still persist and account for the large numbers of women in every industrial society who became domestic servants, retail clerks, and elementary school teachers as opposed to engineers, plumbers, and electricians.[36]

Such gender distinctions were frequently tied to class. During the twelfth-century Sung dynasty, women in working-class households ignored the trend to confinement in deference to the need to earn their livings by picking tea or mulberry leaves. Their visibility, however, merely confirmed the elite status of men whose wives were invisible. Other forms of this linked ideology of gender sequestration with class privilege lingered for centuries, and some survive even now. Foot-binding remained a mark of elite status and a sign of limited work possibilities among Chinese women; veiling served the same purposes for women in many Muslim countries. Modified forms of gender sequestration appear as well in familiar protests of working-class men in Britain and the United States of the late nineteenth and early twentieth centuries. Their honor, their manliness, they argued, rested on their capacity to "keep" a wife. That women did not earn their own livings was central to the conception of elite status in the Mexico City of the late twentieth century.[37]

Domestic ideologies have helped maintain racial and caste barriers as well. In turn-of-the-century Bengal, even poor women did not work at rice cultivation. Regional value systems, Mukul Mukherjee tells us, sustained a popular perception of status that "tended to be negatively associated with 'visible' work participation by women, particularly in outdoor agricultural activity."[38] Orthodox mores among Bengalis denigrated exposure to, and contact with, nonfamily males and even certain categories of male relatives. Sociocultural norms therefore discouraged women from participating in many different forms of work and produced strong motivation—on the part of both sexes—to restrict women's economic activities to household industries as far as possible. The employment sphere sustained and supported such gender divisions. Calcutta jute mills hired few women, and when they did so they favored women from families already connected to the mills, using male relatives to supervise women's behavior.[39]

Complicated value systems, including appeals to respectability, have traditionally framed women's factory work. The first generation of female factory workers in the United States—the mill girls of Lowell, Massachusetts—were enticed not only by promises of safety and good wages but also by offers of supervised living in boardinghouses that would protect their reputations. Peasant fathers in Meiji Japan gave up their daughters to the new textile mills in return for a flat fee payable to the family and assurances that the daughters would be safely housed. That the daughters ended up in overcrowded dormitories with inadequate food and locked doors mattered little. In Bengal, "the factory job never quite achieved the status of a respectable livelihood." The factory remained "the last resort for the helpless, most such jobs being usually held by widows or by women of 'doubtful reputation.'"[40] Still, over the years and through space, women have chosen factory work for the income it provided them and their families rather than for reasons of status. With momentary exceptions (as, briefly, during the nationalist experiments of the Meiji years or during wartime, when patriotism provided an inducement to nontratitional female labor), women have forfeited respect in favor of earning their livings.

The Christian emphasis on marriage as the only proper vocation for women also swayed women's choices, leading women forced to earn their livings to choose arenas in which they could have the company of their own sex.[41]

The most dramatic example of how ideologies of domesticity can intertwine with religious faith to create powerful channeling devices for job segregation occurred in Afghanistan during the 1990s. To cement a religious revolution, the ruling Taliban denied women access to both education and wage work— strictly confining women to domestic spaces and insisting that public trans- actions of any kind belonged to men.

Religious practice could combine with domestic ideology to produce the opposite effect as well. Orthodox Jewish injunctions to men to spend their days in prayer and reflection often placed the entire burden of family support on women, encouraging them to learn trades as well as to become skilled mer- chants. In this instance, being a good wife required activity in the world. In others the twin power of religion and domesticity participated in creating hierarchies of desirable jobs. An intriguing example of this comes from a small Moroccan village, where women who came from families of saintly lineages had options other women did not have. This lineage, derived not from hus- bands but from their birth families, entitled the women to a certain degree of respect and enabled those who needed to do so to give advice generally paid for in food or clothing. Women who had contact with the spirit world also found themselves in demand, especially if they were possessed of anoth- er skill, like that of musician or midwife.[42]

Ideologies of gender have historically teamed with racial and ethnic prej- udices to create exclusionary mindsets and perpetuate hierarchies of good jobs. If publicly accepted ideas about women were designed to protect them even as they entered the labor market, they also consigned those without caste or class status to the poorest, most menial jobs a society had to offer. To pro- tect respectability could require more privileged women to exclude the less- er privileged, just as protecting manliness required men to exclude women from men's jobs. Dark skin color or low caste positions marked some women as outside the circle of domestic protection, available for jobs that white or higher-caste women would not do and excluded from those where more priv- ileged women had already staked a claim. Such attitudes led even the poor- est, most oppressed white female factory workers in the United States to refuse to work alongside black women until the labor shortages of World War II forced them to do so. Calcutta jute mills would not hire any but women with- in certain castes for most jobs, but they kept lists of names available for the jobs that higher-caste women would not do.[43]

Where religious and moral injunction proved insufficient to restrain ei- ther demands of capital for female labor or the capacity of women to resist, ideology was frequently translated into coercive agendas. Indeed, domestic ideologies have been called on to legitimize an astonishing variety of restraints on women's mental and physical labor in a great number of regions and cultures. The mechanisms of restraint range from slavery in ancient civilizations to a centuries-long tradition of binding the feet of some Chinese women, to veiling women and secluding them in harems, and to denying women access to education almost everywhere. Each of these acts may have multiple purposes. They may, for example, be intended to restrict the sexual services of a woman to a single male or to make a statement of national determination. Their outcome is not necessarily to reduce the capacity of females to achieve economic independence, although that is often the case. Some sixteenth-century Chinese women took advantage of their seclusion to become teachers, educators, and writers who had broad political influence.[44] Islam's harem tradition gave women a sense of independence from men as the female chiefs of harems became talented leaders in modern professions.[45] But for the most part, gendered restraints have deprived women of the education and training necessary for economic independence. Bengali women, for example, were so routinely deprived of literacy that as late as 1930, less than 3 percent could read. When a modern economy began to demand office and retail workers, few women could fill the bill, leaving those jobs to men.

Modern states have adopted legislative agendas that reinforced customary restraints, offering boys and girls differential access to education and training, segregating women in the labor force, and denying them occupational mobility. Britain's poor laws, for example, incarcerated women in workhouses, where they earned only enough for their keep, thus ensuring perpetual servitude. In the late nineteenth century, some southern states in the United States rounded up black women and treated those who refused to take jobs as vagrants. Spaniards sometimes put poor women to work on public projects regardless of whether or not they wanted the jobs.[46] These acts skirted a fine line between punitive treatment of poverty and vagrancy and social responsibility for dependent women.

Changing Economic Structures

There has probably never been a "golden age" for women—a moment when women participated as equals not only in economic production but also in the structures of power that sustained economic systems. And yet, the social relations of the sexes has not been static. It reflects the transformation of economies from primarily rural and dependent on agriculture, to commercial and urban, and then to industrial and, finally, postindustrial. These large-scale economic processes have affected the distribution of work to men and women and altered the patterns by which the sexes relate to each other as well as the relationship of women to power and authority. If we imagine the sexual division of labor as more than the passive consequence of economic change, as a contributing agent to economic transformation, we can begin to see how gender participates in historical change.

Premodern agrarian communities that assigned (and continue to assign) women a diverse array of tasks provided opportunities to participate in the creation of household prosperity and amass wealth that equaled that of men. Women's jobs in the agrarian economy—cultivating fields, caring for vegetable gardens, attending to domestic animals, and dairy production—often produced the first objects of trade. Women who took grains, vegetables,and cheese to market to barter or sell increased household well-being, often accumulating the cash needed to purchase the livestock that became the source of male wealth production. Those who produced and reared children who would labor for the household, and cleaned and repaired the houses in which they lived, also increased its wealth.

Where land was collectively owned or passed through maternal lineages (as in much of precolonial Africa), the lack of labor, not land, limited production. A female household head could enhance her wealth by encouraging brothers, sons, and sons-in-law to carve out and help cultivate more soil. A male household head might do the same by acquiring several wives to cultivate ever-greater areas. In the absence of a plow culture (the case in most of Southern Africa), women remained the primary cultivators. If each wife produced children who could also work the land, a man might amass a comfortable subsistence. By the sixteenth and seventeenth centuries, women could also achieve wealth by trading. They, like the female entrepreneurs of Senegambia and the Upper Guinea Coast, tended to have both social status and political influence.[47]

Where land was individually owned or worked as part of a feudal arrangement, the products of women's labor tended to accrue to the benefit of the generally male-headed household. In most parts of Asia, where men operated the plow and women performed auxiliary agricultural work or none at all, women's opportunities for amassing individual wealth and exercising influence diminished. In the peasant economies of Europe, women might earn money by marketing the products of family fields. Daughters of smallholders might work as servants in the houses of others until they married, and wives administered their own holdings and weeded the fields while their husbands hired themselves out to bring in the harvest for wealthy landlords. This pattern, common around Seville, Spain, during the Middle Ages, enabled husbands to earn incomes by harvesting the grain and olives of rich landlords while wives tended vineyards.[48]

In such a peasant economy, women worked at a range of jobs, including many that contributed to household prosperity. The production and barter or sale of home manufactures and crafts was often the province of women, whereas men engaged in transactions around livestock. The prosperity of a household determined power and position in the community; every producer earned community approbation. Inheritance patterns reflected and perpetuated women's contributions. Husbands willed their wives, especially those with young children, more than their legally required share of household property and land. But wealth tended to pass through widows to their sons or to their daughters' sons.[49]

Somewhat paradoxically, increasing household wealth generally decreased demands on women to work the fields and frequently resulted in tighter domestic ideologies, including the sequestration of women within the household walls. A good example of this process comes from Bihar, India, where women of low castes, even poorer women from the middling castes, retained historical responsibility for all aspects of fieldwork with the exception of plowing, a job almost everywhere reserved for men. Women followed the plow, sewing seeds, transplanting seedlings, manuring fields, weeding, and reaping. Sometimes they worked with the help of men, but often they recruited only their children while the men hired themselves out as day laborers or to work on the estates of the rich. Women engaged in these processes, as well as in household crafts and spinning, could earn as much as their menfolk, a relative wage equality reflected in their participation in household decision making. But when commercialization and new work opportunities for men concurrently undermined the value of women's crafts, reduced the relative value of women's wages, and provided men with the capacity to support families without the financial help of women, men quickly adopted new notions of manhood. Women found themselves occupying subordinate positions, their work diminished and their bodies sometimes confined to households.[50]

Growing commercialization and the transition to primitive and then full-fledged market economies everywhere altered the sexual division of labor in ways that strained gendered norms and tended to undermine women's independence. The Ming dynasty in China reserved artisanal jobs for selected men, and England's fourteenth-century "Statute of Laborers" required all men to choose a trade and confine themselves to it exclusively. There, and in most of Europe, emerging guilds increasingly restricted membership to men.

Women who did not contribute directly to wealth creation quickly lost influence and voice with relation to their husbands, although they might retain class and family influence. Those who continued to contribute by working as servants and hired laborers found themselves with poorer wages and in inferior positions as a result of embedded ideologies of womanhood. The resulting difference in wages embedded itself in women having a lower status within their families. And the absence of opportunities for wealth creation fostered a transition in many cultures from the groom's payment of bride-price to female payment of dowries—with all the attendant abuses of female infanticide, wife and widow abuse, and in some cultures even dowry deaths.

But where women found ways to participate in wealth creation their status might be improved, and they could earn credit for fostering the well-being of their communities. China offers an illustration of how state policies might influence such processes by shaping gender ideology to conform with economic goals. The Qing dynasty, which came to power in the seventeenth century, inherited from its predecessor Ming dynasty a strong Confucian ideology of women's home roles in which women rarely worked in the fields except under circumstances of dire poverty. But it also had difficulty collecting sufficient taxes from the agriculturally based economy in which wives remained confined to their households. At the same time, it feared rapid expansion of the commercial sector into towns that could become breeding grounds for disobedience and revolt. Adopting a "men plow, women weave" ideology, state officials encouraged women to engage in the production of silk, to spin cotton and silk at home, and to weave fabric for the market as well as for household use. They managed, thus, to reshape ideologies of domesticity to incorporate hard work and the dignity of labor for women, all the while insisting that these tasks remain in the home. Inspired by such mantras, repeatedly told that "where a woman works diligently her family will surely rise; where a woman is lazy, her family is certain to fall," even women of the upper classes learned handicraft arts, wove diligently, and supervised the training and work of children and servants in their households.[51] They dramatically expanded their production of textiles, enabling China to participate fully in commercial expansion, and increased the prosperity of their households and their country without upsetting traditional ideologies of domesticity. The respect women earned as participants to household success may well have enabled them to exercise strong voices in cultural spheres and household management.[52]

On the European continent, men and women who lived in towns before the advent of industrialization also found themselves more equally responsible for their families' prosperity. "In the societies of both classical and barbarian antiquity and in the early Middle Ages," the historian David Herlihy notes, "until as late as the twelfth and thirteenth centuries, women were prominent participants in many forms of productive activity."[53] When the great medieval historian Eileen Power tried to list women's occupations, she could, she writes, hardly find a craft that excluded women. Women were butchers, chandlers, ironmongers, net-makers, shoe-makers, glovers, girdlers, haberdashers, bookbinders, smiths, and goldsmiths. Two kinds of occupations, however, predominated: making cloth, clothing, food, and household provisions.[54] The presence of women was highly visible as well in the brewing of beer; in high administration; and, among other skills, in the arts of healing and the interpretation and dissemination of sacred knowledge. Women tended to learn their skills from their fathers or husbands, ensuring the continuation of family wealth by continuing to function as entrepreneurs and merchants long after a partner's death.[55] Like boys, girls were apprenticed to trades—often for shorter periods—most frequently to cloth and textile artisanship. Women, married and unmarried, also worked as shopkeepers and wage-earners. They negotiated the marketplace when necessary, remained responsible for their own debts, and acted legally in and for themselves. Still, as Barbara Hanawalt tells us, working women were homebodies. "Their participation in the economy rarely necessitated their leaving their quarter of a city or their village. At most they went to markets several miles from their village or came from surrounding villages to find work as domestics or laborers in nearby towns"[56]

COMMERCIAL EXPANSION AND EARLY CAPITALISM

During periods of commercial trade expansion when subsistence activities gave way to home-manufactured products for local and then regional distribution, the roles of men and women everywhere came under scrutiny. Historians of these moments of transformation to a larger market worry about whether women managed to develop significant economic roles outside the family or whether their productive labor was limited to the context of the domestic environment. Alice Clark, historian of seventeenth-century England, has suggested that women moved from positions of greater economic value and independence in preindustrial, precapitalist Europe to positions of lesser value.[57] Reframed, the assertion remains the touchstone of historical debate: Did the advent of capitalism lead to a declining role for women in the labor market?

The evidence is mixed. As the diverse tasks of preindustrial work gave way to national and then international market orientations, cottage industry expanded, allowing women more scope for independent incomes while at the same time shaping their crafts to the needs of the market. This happened at different times in different places. Thirteenth-century China witnessed an expansion of women's home production of cotton, silk, and hemp, which fuelled local and national commercial growth.[58] In one seventeenth-century Turkish town, women owned about half of all the silk-spinning implements. Many supported themselves and their families with the products of their work at home—a concentration that led tax officials to reduce the tax on silk spinning because so many of its practitioners were poor women.[59] Domestic manufacture by women was so important in São Paulo, Brazil, in 1800 that it sustained more than half of all urban households—most of them headed by women.[60] But more work for the market did not necessarily increase women's autonomy.

In an effort to control production, European male artisans, threatened by wage and price restraints, formed guilds that gave them exclusive control of one occupation after another. Guild members held craft skills secret and with few exceptions denied women training or access to resources and jobs.[61] In many places such as sixteenth- and seventeenth-century Germany, guilds consolidated their power and passed regulations excluding women from traditional occupations and relegating them to the margins of the world of work. In rough economic times guilds stringently limited the access of widows to the crafts of deceased husbands. When women formed guilds of their own, they rarely possessed the same economic power to control a trade and almost never had the political voice to enforce their prices or their rules. One result was that women lost control of some of the most skilled cloth crafts, such as fine weaving and silk making.[62]

Even as workshops separated from households and men moved into more and more public spheres, most women found themselves subject to patriarchal discipline in their own or others' households. As women lost control of craft and business, ideologies of domesticity and new definitions of manliness vested in skill increasingly justified their growing economic dependence. This, as David Herlihy observes, was new: "The virtual confinement of women's labor to work within the home . . . was not an ancient arrangement. Rather, the extreme domestication of women's labor was specifically the heritage of the closing Middle Ages."[63]

Late-fourteenth-century advice manuals instructed young girls as to how to behave in this world of domestic confinement. One fifteenth-century Italian manual adjured girls to be modest, passive, deferential and retiring in all social contacts, hardly the qualities needed for success in the marketplace. Those qualities contrast dramatically with ones proposed for Parisian women a century earlier—which tolerated aggression. But they reflect the realities of a culture of men who married late after years of training and required, therefore, that girls over the age of twelve remain under tight reign to protect them from predatory single men.[64]

By the fifteenth century, women's participation in economic life had everywhere in Europe become circumscribed. Girls rarely got the benefit of full apprenticeships. When they did, they tended to be trained in food production and distribution, specialized textile skills, and in precious metal-working. Most were trained in their own homes or as servants in the households of others.[65] The vast majority of young women who earned wages did so as servants, their training designed to lead them into more efficient home lives of their own. Others learned craft skills within the households to which they were attached, gathering knowledge (generally about clothing, textiles, food provisioning, and small craft manufactures) from skilled matrons in orphanages and schools for poor girls.

In Northern England, where brewing beer and ale was a female enterprise, single women other than daughters were denied the right to brew.[66] In Spain and England women relinquished the central role they had once played in the manufacture of quality woolens. In Germany their importance in fields like medicine and administration declined. In Northern Europe they remained active as independent entrepreneurs in larger numbers than in the south but were increasingly confined to areas like provisioning and the cloth trades. Their influence retreated.[67] Even where women continued to be economically active, the increasing attachment of property to political rights tended to deny them any "magisterial" role. They could neither hold urban nor rural offices nor become guildmasters with influence over work regulations.

Yet the advent of early capitalism and the growth of towns did not so much still the income-generating activity of women as render it less visible. Women remained active in a surprising number of fields. Some managed to gain apprenticeships with masters, generally as a result of family connections and circumstances. Those from artisanal families learned transferable skills they could use to work alongside fathers and husbands in their entrepreneurial activities and which enabled them to continue family businesses long after a husband's death. Many women seem to have created limited but important roles for themselves. In London, they were butchers, bakers, flaxdressers, and feltmakers in their own right. In Lyon, they are to be found not only in every element of the food provisioning and clothing trades but also as midwives, printers, and publishers.[68]

The transformation of women's roles in Tuscany appears to be fairly typical. There, the large numbers of working women who continued to appear in local documents until late in the fourteenth century had disappeared by the fifteenth. In the late fourteenth century, women often "worked as helpers to their husbands, fathers, and brothers in workshops located in their homes."[69] Wills and bequests of fathers and husbands clearly recognized the value of this unpaid work. By the fifteenth century, women, who had been primarily responsible for weaving cloth, had disappeared, replaced by male weavers. And while "women continued to exercise certain traditionally female occupations such as midwifery, wet nursing, and domestic service, guild records, wills, property transfers, and other legal documents no longer mention the large variety of female occupations" evident in the early periods.[70] When women returned to industry in the late sixteenth and early seventeenth centuries, they entered productive enterprises organized around hired labor and outside their own households. There, they engaged in more limited tasks, generally weaving plain cloths, while men dominated the more skilled luxury crafts that required elaborate training. The transformation appears to be a result of an effort to train daughters to provide quick returns on their skills rather than to make long investments in them.

The key shift seems to have come in the ownership and control of property, and it is here that one senses the greatest loss of women's influence in early capitalist countries. In Europe, inheritance patterns changed swiftly as the need for capital became apparent. Women, who had formerly acquired a more or less equal share of their patrimony with their bothers, were provided instead with a dowry that was usually much smaller. Lacking the large capital outlay required for certain industries such as dye shops, foundries, or wood workshops, women found themselves on the fringes of entrepreneurial occupations. As markets developed and trade evolved into a distinct activity, their limited access to capital restricted their ability to participate in wholesale goods-trading or in areas that required large capital investments. They continued to predominate in areas of petty trade—as fishmongers and victuallers, for example, owning and controlling market stalls, As retailers, they sold general goods not otherwise encumbered by guilds, and they often ran small clothing or lace-making workshops.[71] Even where women did control capital, ideological inhibitions prevented them from traveling to cloth fairs or engaging in long-distance trade.

INDUSTRIALIZATION, URBANIZATION, AND DEVELOPMENT

Historians used to think that the process of industrialization (or development in the modern world) was a function largely of capital and raw material. More recent research, however, suggests the influence of custom and culture, and particularly the impact of family organization and sexual mores on how economies are shaped. Together these speak to how female labor was employed in early workshops and factories and tell much about the speed of industrialization.[72]

Unsurprisingly, those countries that most freely encouraged women to engage in "public work" were among the earliest to industrialize. Those that restrained women from engaging in wage labor inhibited the process of development by denying themselves labor and talent. Yet if women's labor seems to have been necessary for industrialization to proceed rapidly, women of different classes were variously affected by the process. Some were tempted by urban growth to leave their homes and take jobs in factories or enter domestic service; others used new educational opportunities to learn office skills and enter professions such as teaching and nursing.

In the classic industrialization scenarios of China, Japan, Western Europe, and North America, women constituted at least one-quarter of the first factory labor force and sometimes an absolute majority. Certainly, economic factors mattered. Employed first in cottage industries and home-based workshops, women found themselves working increasingly to the specifications of the middlemen who marketed their products. They entered semiskilled factory jobs when the introduction of machinery rendered their handmade products no longer competitive in increasingly complicated markets. As the division of labor became more complex, increasing numbers of new tasks required relatively little training and demanded a large and flexible workforce amenable to close supervision. Jobs opened to women in many sectors, including raw material extraction and construction, but almost everywhere women found their metier in the textile factories that constituted the dynamic heart of modern industrialization.[73] In Shanghai, women were fully two-thirds of the total industrial workforce. More than half of all women (one-third of the Shanghai proletariat in the first half of the twentieth century) worked in cotton mills.[74] At first concentrated primarily in the production of textiles and clothing, women moved quickly into manufacturing shoes, paper, and prepared foods and then into assembly-line manufacturing of all kinds.

Technological changes led women from rural to urban areas and from cottage industries to factories, but the choices they made were everywhere influenced by sociocultural considerations that simultaneously influenced economic options. In Argentina women made the move late in the nineteenth century.[75] When rural handicrafts (including wool washing, weaving, embroidery, dressmaking, and food production) no longer provided the stable incomes that had earlier sustained at least two-thirds of rural women, they were often forced into domestic service or peonage. Faced with unemployment, some migrated to coastal towns, especially Buenos Aires, where they joined immigrant women. But Argentina had virtually no textile industry and a very strong tradition of male protection, so native-born women found few job opportunities other than washing, ironing, and other forms of domestic service. By 1914 only about a quarter of them identified themselves as workers, almost all of them in urban industry. In a phenomenon that would repeat itself elsewhere, middle-class women benefited from improvements in household technology and access to the services of poor women that provided the leisure to acquire education and form the basis of a class of professional women.

If women worked primarily to sustain themselves and their families, their participation was fundamental to the growth of regional and national economies. Their household management contributed to wealth formation and, later, to the consumption that fueled continuing production. Middle-class women who worked in their own homes in nineteenth-century English cities set patterns for household production and consumption as well as for male behavior. They expected men to achieve middle-class status by hard work and thrift, engaging in competitive behavior outside but not inside the household and fostering values of accumulation among their children.[76] They also set standards of housekeeping that provided jobs for generations of domestic servants, male and female, without whose hard work middle-class households could not have existed and whose training in deference facilitated the orderly transition of Britain through the Industrial Revolution.

Women's production mattered as well. In China, at the moment of transition to a commercial economy, women's household output of cloth generally paid the taxes that allowed families to participate in the polity and fostered national progress toward a full-fledged market economy.[77] The cheap labor that women provided fueled the Industrial Revolution, and nations everywhere tried to pull them into the labor force. Britain manipulated its poor laws so as to force women to earn their livings in workshops and factories. Employers in Lowell, Massachusetts, provided ideological rationales to defuse the notion that women belonged at home. A little later, administrators in Meiji Japan sent their own daughters to work in the new textile mills to demonstrate the economic and spiritual value of women's labor outside the home. Colonial regimes everywhere fostered programs that kept women at home if they were producers and pulled them into urban labor markets to serve as domestic servants or low-level service workers.

In these ways and many others, gender-driven sociocultural norms inflected economic behavior. In Bengal, the same cultural ideals that limited women's participation in field agriculture inhibited their participation in factory work, which "never quite achieved the status of a respectable livelihood for ordinary Bengali women."[78] In parts of India, as men moved up the economic ladder and aspired to increasing status they adopted the sex and marriage codes of Brahmins. The process, sometimes called "sanskritization," resulted in removing women from productive labor within or outside the household and sometimes turning those less fortunate into the servants of others. Many Arab countries, which sequester women for religious reasons, have failed to participate in either industrialization or modernization. Turkey, Pakistan, and Egypt, which have lesser attachment to fundamentalist Muslim ideals, have, in contrast, been more readily amenable to the use of women's labor. Perhaps as a result they have also participated more fully in the industrialization process.

Cultural norms could deeply affect patterns of industrialization. Ideas of what constituted appropriate work for women governed where and how particular women sought to earn incomes; social attitudes about the relationships of men and women influenced which regions employed women in what kinds of jobs. Introduced to their workplaces by their kin and acquaintances, women as geographically remote as Shanghai, Lyon, Manchester, New Hampshire, and other industrial locations remained linked to the cultural environments from which they came. Ningbo, China, starkly reveals the intersection of cultural and economic factors on future prospects. Ningbo had been a profitable trading center when it distributed women's handicrafts in the late nineteenth century. When those goods could no longer compete with the factory products of Shanghai—just downriver—a sturdy sense of propriety prevented women from seeking work outside their homes and Ningbo from developing factories. Ningbo quickly retreated into the shadow of Shanghai, which permanently assumed a leading manufacturing role.[79]

Despite women's importance in the process, industrialization—particularly in its early stages—has not necessarily served them well. Of the many women swept into the maelstrom of factory life in industrializing economies, few would have chosen to work under the long hours and harsh conditions they typically endured. Nor would many have lived in the overcrowded and unsanitary slums that quickly developed everywhere. Most women found themselves working under horrendous conditions and living limited lives. Many new factories forced women to live in dormitories or supervised boardinghouses. In Meiji Japan, these resembled prisons. Their cramped quarters, rigid rules, and locked doors inhibited any self-expression short of escape.[80] Because contracts for women's labor were generally made with her family, the income earned by the hapless female factory worker went to her family rather than to her.

Colonial forms of capitalism and industrialization seem to have exercised a particularly negative effect on women, exacerbating the sexual division of labor and subjecting them to exploitation on account of both race and gender. As imported and machine-made goods reduced the value of women's household manufactures and crafts, women's economic contribution declined dramatically. Young women compensated by migrating to towns and cities where they might hope to join an urban labor force in workshops and factories or in domestic service. When married women joined the exodus, the consequences for indigenous culture and family life were particularly profound. The process, similar in most industrial countries, was exacerbated under colonial conditions. In Africa, it ran roughshod over a tradition of strong women whose work had long sustained households.[81] In Latin America, some scholars contend that it introduced a more rigid form of patriarchy that consistently underestimated women's productive roles.[82] And in Puerto Rico, incorporation of women into the colonial labor force produced brutal programs such as the enforced sterilization of female workers.

Although it holds the potential of relative personal and economic autonomy for workers of either sex, in many places industrialization seems more often to have enhanced than undermined patriarchal power. Countries like China and Japan and the Indonesian island of Java, which relied on agricultural economies to partially subsidize the first generations of factory workers, reinforced the family's hold on females who sought waged labor.[83] The peasant economies of China present a typical pattern. Although men produced cotton, hemp, or ramie, women turned the raw material into finished cloth. Because women worked under the direction of men who marketed the fabric, they did not threaten the patriarchal structure. Nor was that structure shattered when commercial purchase and distribution of yarn created a controlling merchant class. That process pushed land rents up, raised food prices, and increased familial cash needs. It also fuelled population expansion and the subdivision of land, rendering the economic position of the family increasingly precarious. Men took advantage of urban opportunities to hire themselves out, sometimes disappearing entirely from the family economy. Women who constituted the cornerstone of family production found themselves "defined back"—locked into domestic and reproductive roles even as men contributed less and less to the family economy.[84]

These patterns of early industrialization were soon superseded in rapidly industrializing sectors by the use of local female labor, married and unmarried, paid so little that an independent economic existence for women was nearly impossible. In this second stage, however, women who lived at home could and did contribute to the family economy. Young daughters might work in factories until they married and then engage in income-earning activities in the informal economy (like taking in boarders, laundry, or sewing) that subsidized the labor of men and sustained family life. They might continue to work in factories on a seasonal basis or engage in trade or barter—holding jobs that fitted in with their central tasks of producing and rearing the children who would constitute the next generation of workers. Although critically important in the view of family members, that labor often went uncounted by outside observers.

Even when accompanied by urbanization, full-scale industrialization served women unevenly. It encouraged them to move to factories and towns where they might evade family supervision, and it sometimes permitted them to make decisions about how to use their wages. Female workers in Lowell, Massachusetts, for example, made their own contracts, generally for a year at a time. They could save their wages or send some home to their families, and supervision was lax enough to allow occasional socializing. Women who possessed property in their own labor could (and many did) choose to use their factory careers to save for their own dowries, subsidize further education, or finance a second move to urban centers.[85] In parts of Africa, colonial administrations employed indigineous men at heavy labor in mines and heavy industry while assuming that women's agricultural production would continue to support families. When Igbo men of Nigeria were drawn into work in mines and on railroads they left their wives in charge of the family economy, where they quickly developed influential roles.[86]

But urbanization also tempted single women to leave their homes to seek their fortunes. Most found jobs as domestic servants or earned livings attending to the sexual and other needs of male workers. In South Africa, women achieved economic independence by migrating to black townships, where they provided sexual services to male laborers. Working in the houses of others until they saved enough to buy houses of their own, they could make choices about how to spend their time and incomes. Their profits sustained village families and provided a community sanctioned source of both money and autonomy.[87] Migration gave new options to many other women. Mozambique women traveled to South Africa to brew beer for miners, prostitutes in Nairobi, Kenya, came from Tanzania, and Amharic women from Ethiopia became entrepreneurs, beginning from their positions as food vendors with small market stalls.

The relative economic autonomy that resulted could and did encourage women to identify as workers. They organized into associations, guilds, and unions, with and without the help of men. And they engaged in militant workplace actions, including strikes. Some of these are legendary—Lowell mill workers struck in 1834 for shorter work days and less onerous working conditions, and immigrant women led a desperate struggle against wage reductions in Lawrence, Massachusetts, in 1912. Brazil's female textile workers took major roles in the factory commissions that improved their working conditions in the 1920s and 1930s. Women in Zambia spurned domestic service, leaving that field to men until labor shortages and wage rises in the 1940s tempted them to take jobs. South African women worked seasonally in the 1940s and 1950s; buoyed by their local working class communities they managed to develop a unified front with male workers.[88]

To the men and women who made decisions about women's work, the gendered outcomes seemed no more than natural, and gender itself constituted a rationale for the sexual division of labor. In its early stages, industrialization everywhere undermined guild restrictions, employing machinery to subdivide tasks and reduce jobs to their simplest elements. But new gendered divisions emerged as quickly as the old ones became irrelevant or unenforceable.[89] Often these relied on culturally particular notions of appropriate jobs for women.

To protect male jobs required renegotiating manly ideals and sensibilities as well. Men fought fiercely over their capacity to control the workplace; to keep the manufacture and care of machinery off-limits to women; to eliminate or prevent the use of women in "heavy" industry; and, where possible, to maintain wages that would enable them to support families—itself a key indicator of manhood in many places. These struggles reinforced myths about the relationship of femininity to home roles, contributing to negative stereotypes about women and relating their capacity to earn to "nimble fingers" rather than to the courage, physical stamina, and entrepreneurial skill commonly required of males.[90] In turn, myths about women limited their opportunities to training and education, allowed lower pay for them, and encouraged workers, employers, and policymakers to police the boundaries of women's morality. Where ideology and myth insufficiently regulated women's choices, workers sometimes resorted to sexual harassment; in more advanced industrial states, policymakers turned to protective labor legislation that regulated women but not men.

Legislation provided a widespread vehicle for restricting women's workplace expectations, aspirations, and options. In most countries such legislation came after the fact, adopted in the face of the threats posed by working women to men's jobs and by overworked wives and mothers to family life. Designed to enforce women's primary commitment to families while acknowledging their need to earn incomes, legislation regulated the hours, working conditions, and pay of women, sometimes forbidding night work and excluding women from some jobs altogether. Some countries, such as Argentina, which had a strong tradition of male protection, passed it preemptively to discourage incipient manufacturers from developing industries, like textiles, that relied on female labor. There it suggested stringent messages to men and women about the desirability of regulating women's labor in the interests of family life. Others (the former Soviet Union as an example) mandated a putative equality in the workplace but used mandatory pregnancy and maternity leaves to shape women's job options. Some provided carrots rather than sticks. France, from the late nineteenth century, subsidized community creches to care for the babies of working mothers.

Efforts to maintain the sexual division of labor in the face of economic pressures that undermined it consigned women to limited numbers of jobs, often requiring lesser skills than those demanded of men. Lacking bargaining power, women factory workers received lower pay and worked under harsher conditions than comparable male workers. Their value in the labor force diminished, women whose partners or fathers could afford to keep them at home justified their dependence by reinforcing male self-images of manhood.

But there was a trade-off. The sexual division of labor reserved some jobs for women, designating them as insufficiently manly. After short periods of adjustment, routine assembly-line work, especially with food products and small parts, and low-level clerical and office work required to sustain corporate and financial growth fell into the hands of women, providing valuable alternative sources of employment. So did many semiprofessional jobs, including teaching small children and nursing the sick. With some jobs deemed unsuitable for men and others pulling on women to leave their homes, men and women in different countries faced a continual, sometimes painful, renegotiation of gendered contracts.

Under these conditions of sharply constrained job possibilities, enforced migration for women—especially across oceans and national borders—held more limited possibilities than we might imagine. To be sure, it offered women willing to migrate relative economic independence, but it did so at the cost of personal autonomy. Irish women who emigrated as a result of the mid-nineteenth-century famine found jobs as hired help in the houses of other women. Mexico's women moved to Mexico City in large numbers at the end of the century. By the early twentieth century they constituted a third of the labor force, and it was common for married women to be employed outside their own homes. Most worked as domestic servants in the households of others. The pattern would continue as the development process rolled through countries that had been peripheral to it earlier. Caribbean and Latin American women migrated to the United States in large numbers to work as household servants, and those from the Philippines migrated to the Middle East. With and without their families, women from Turkey moved to Germany, and those from Korea went to Japan. The fact that all these women were in motion tells something about their aspirations and hopes and the economic predicaments that encouraged the women to live outside the context of traditional family life.

POSTCOLONIAL DEVELOPMENT AND GLOBALIZATION

In the modern period, the process of development has followed the classic industrialization pattern in dramatically speeded up form. First comes the separation of home and work—a result of the progressive isolation of the production of goods and services from other activities—as a result of technological change. Then the movement of jobs from home to work follows, relocating most paying jobs to factories and commercial centers.[91] The most striking effect of this process is a dramatic shift from the Western assumption that a man should be able to maintain a wife and family to the expectation that all adults will earn wages. In some countries the proportion of wage-earning women equals that of men, and the proportion of wage-earning women working to earn incomes exceeds that of men.

The change challenges old value systems as it responds to new demands of a modern world. Those who argue that women's long-standing subordination stems from a lack of job opportunities believe it can be ended if and when jobs are provided for all who want and need them. Economic development—

in the form of new industries and expanded factory production—in this view can only be good for women.[92] On the positive side, as women's value in the labor force increases, opportunities for female education expand. Literate women find jobs in government and corporate bureaucracies, social services, banking, and the emerging technological sectors as well as in traditional jobs for females. The result is a dramatic expansion of women in the semiprofessional sectors—where they now dominate. Inevitably, globalization, like nineteenth-century industrialization, challenges traditional gendered patterns of culture and patriarchy, producing increasing demands for equality among women everywhere.

Others, however, argue that if women are integrated into the development process in subordinate positions they will remain subordinate.[93] Globalization involves the control by core, or developed, countries of routine, assembly-line work, which is relegated to less-well-developed countries on the periphery of the global economy. It is characterized by the production of goods for export, so it entails little incentive to provide a wage sufficient for workers to consume the goods it produces. As capital expands and seeks to find cheap labor, it takes advantage of both the sex of workers and their ethnic or racial positions. Poor women of color tend to be drawn into production. Sometimes they work on assembly lines of large factories. At others they participate in informal sectors of the economy, where they work in small workshops or take home work and frequently sustain the households of daughters, sisters, and mothers who seek remunerative work.

In the process of expansion, technology remains in developed countries, while standardized, repetitive, assembly-line jobs move to countries on the economic periphery. Women accept these jobs as routes to survival, putting up with low wages and minimal or no social benefits, partly because family economies subsidize their wages and partly because they have little choice. Thus the jobs seem to reproduce "natural" divisions of labor. Women are hired because paying them less seems natural; men, said to need incomes to support families, often remain unemployed. The sexual division of labor is reinforced by familiar language. Women are said to have nimble hands and be more docile and willing to accept work discipline. Because they bear children, employers expect them to drop out of the workforce sporadically and therefore not to demand or expect positions of authority. In contrast, although men find it harder to find jobs in global enterprises, they tend to imagine those jobs as access routes to mobility rather than mere survival. For that reason if for no other, women often view factory work as a route to family survival; it dissolves barriers between public and private rather than builds them.[94]

Subcontracting jobs—where women work in small workshops, generally without benefit of labor regulations and subject to employers' whims—are closely connected to household labor. Often thought of by women as an extension of housework, these jobs, like those in the informal sector (including craft work), are eagerly sought by women who need or want to carry out the duties of social reproduction while contributing to the survival and maintenance of their households. The jobs save money for the entrepreneur. They are essential sources of income, especially for married, working-class women who often receive limited funds from their husbands and are impelled to take informal jobs in order to make ends meet as their children grow older.[95]

Does such work empower women? There is some evidence that it does. Malaysian women, in the view of one scholar, experience both the good and the bad parts of proletarianization. They are drawn into the workforce and then let go when their physical energies and eyesight wane. Yet while they are working, they enjoy the cash economy, they and their families benefit from consumer products, and some women earn the right to choose whom they will marry.[96] Homeworkers as well surely experience some improvements in self-respect as a result of bringing in a little money. Evidence suggests that new jobs foster resistance and tension at home and in the workplace as women's autononomy and control over their own lives increase. In the workplace, a new consciousness, sometimes active resistance, emerges.[97]

Yet, ultimately, most women must face the double shift of household and wage work. Instead of undermining the patriarchal culture, the jobs of most poor women reinforce it—reproducing in the workplace the subjugation of the household. As in the early days of the Industrial Revolution, most women find themselves consigned by a gendered division of labor to poorly paid, dead-end jobs where the resistance of unions and managers to women's organizing initiatives enhances their powerlessness.

How does their work affect family lives? That partly depends on which women go into the labor force. Diane Wolf discovered in Java, for example, that daughters who worked in textile mills were in fact subsidized by their families because they made insufficient income to feed and clothe themselves.[98] They did, however, reduce the familial burden of feeding them. There and in places like Hong Kong, Singapore, and Taiwan, where young single women predominate in the female labor force, family goals seem to remain more important than individualistic goals, and the money that women bring to their families is generally insufficient to upset patriarchal values, even when men do not have jobs. Young unmarried women reported satisfaction from meeting family obligations and increasing their individual consumption as well as from wider social contacts, but they did not earn greater respect within families or enhance their power to make decisions.[99] In Puerto Rico and the Dominican Republic, however, married women and single heads of households tended to be the majority of those entering the export production industries. There, new wage-earning opportunities for women have begun to challenge traditional family authority patterns, and more egalitarian family structures are emerging. These trends suggest a potential scenario for women's economic independence.

Occupations in Common

Observing the lines between women's public work and their private work for the household, and noting how difficult it sometimes is to mark that distinction, calls attention to the many meanings of women's work and how they have changed over historical time and space. Sometimes there appears to be a straight line from women's unpaid but productive household work to paid labor done in and through households and local markets; from there to a sharp separation between productive or paid work and reproductive, or unpaid work; and, finally, to the current stage, where reproductive work is devalued and women, like men, are pushed into the wage labor force. Yet even as we recognize the process we need to think about what it tells us in the context of different cultural experiences. Glancing at the history of a few occupations commonly held by women reveals something of the meanings of women's work.

CLOTHMAKING

Before the Industrial Revolution, the skill of clothmaking belonged to women. Counted among the basic economic functions of most cultures, it served to clothe families and as a fundamental medium of exchange.

Among all the ancient civilizations we know—including Western, Indian, African, and Chinese—women played a central role in the making of cloth. Generally, women dominated every aspect of cloth manufacture. They prepared the raw materials, spun the yarn, and wove fabric. In the case of silk, women nurtured and fed mulberry worms, harvested and processed raw cocoons into thread, and wove as well. They also fashioned and sewed clothing and embroidered finished pieces, passing down all these skills to daughters and to women of the household.

One scholar notes how little the cataclysm of Rome's fall affected the millenial association of women and clothmaking.[100] For centuries, distribution of cloth bonded households together—a material and a ritual indication of its value. As textiles contributed not only to the wealth of households but also to lineages and lords, the work of women took on different meaning. No longer a nurturing or subsistence function, clothmaking represented a critical economic asset, and the women who did it were a valuable resource. In ancient Rome as in medieval Europe, female spinners and weavers were organized into workshops by nobles and lords, and fines were levied for marrying them or removing them. Cloth became a means of exchange. The Carolingian monarchs of France demanded strips of linen from their serfs as part of their annual dues payment. These strips were assigned a monetary value and sometimes served as money. In China from the early eighth century to the end of the sixteenth, every household paid taxes "in cloth and yarn as well as grain," and by the last half of the sixteenth century "hundreds of millions of bolts of cloth were levied and redistributed directly by the Chinese State every year."[101]

Remarkably, textile production remained the province of women, even when—its value recognized—it became a vehicle for aggrandizing male power and building the prosperity of lords and kings, of regions and nations. To be sure, men occasionally worked at the loom. In medieval Europe, men who proved useless in agriculture were assigned to textile workshops. In China, where women after the tenth century were more and more excluded from field agriculture and secluded in households, their work in sericulture and at the wheel and loom came increasingly to reflect the moral order leaders sought to impose. "The training of daughters," Francesca Bray tells us, "taught diligence, orderliness and respect for labor." It enhanced the dignity of a wife and continually reminded her of her status as subject of the state.[102]

Women's culture unified women across class lines, and provided responsibility, status, and economic value. Commercialization, whenever it came, slowly pushed women out of some of the most lucrative, skilled and specialized functions and reduced their capacity to distribute the finished cloth. In Europe, women began to lose their hold on the wool trades during the fifteenth century. Although they continued to spin, they were pushed out of the weavers' trades.[103] In Tuscany, silk workers continued to raise silk worms and do the difficult job of processing cocoons into raw silk. Weaving workshops, controlled by men, formed into guilds that excluded women. Even in China, where sericulture remained critical to the economies of many regions, women slowly lost access to their skills during a sixteenth-century campaign to discourage commercial production in the interest of the self-sufficient household. When the state began once again to foster women's household manufacture during the early seventeenth century, women lost their grip on weaving the finest cloths as men began to run the workshops that used their labor.

If women lost access to the best jobs they maintained an influential presence in cloth manufacture, taking their places in factories that became the most visible symbols of the Industrial Revolution in most places. There, they participated and continue to participate in a new kind of female culture that operates outside household walls yet continues a long tradition of clothing the world.

SEX WORK

The sale of sexual services—sex work—provides a prism through which to think about the categories within which men and women work. Although men have not infrequently participated in sex for pay, words like "prostitution" conjure up a largely female sphere. And although such work has sometimes been honorable, more often it has been the source of female degradation. Women have been sold into it as slaves, assigned to it by virtue of caste and class, chosen it as a route to personal independence, and turned to it of economic necessity. In all these guises sex work is a form of labor. But because it goes to the heart of power relations between men and women, sex work serves as a barometer of moral harmony. Controlled and regulated by men, it suggests an ordered and orderly society; out of control, it provokes fears of anarchy. The status of sex work in particular societies tells us not only about relations of domination and subordination between men and women but also about its self-image and goals.

In preindustrial societies, sex work was not merely tolerated but often admired. The ancient world set aside special places for women who entertained men and provided sexual satisfaction. After the advent of Christianity in the West, the medieval Church officially condemned prostitution. But local authorities tended to treat women who violated their injunctions leniently, especially those who charged a fair price for their services.[104] The Church defined a prostitute as a woman who had more than one partner, heedless of whether or not she charged for her services. In China, the practice of concubinage identified men with the resources to pay for their sexual satisfaction, but it left women who engaged in it significant rights for themselves and their children. In contrast, the sale of daughters and wives to others left them helpless to determine their own fates, placing a premium on female attractiveness as a trading card in the sex trade. A beautiful and accomplished courtesan in the Chinese tradition, like a Japanese geisha or Korean *kisaeng*, could regulate her own sexual services while remaining the financial beneficiary of men who admired her.

The "free labor" systems that emerged with the advent of market economies left many unmarried women in control of their own destinies. It also made them victims of unfriendly labor markets. As women turned to prostitution in order to survive and male demand for their services expanded, town authorities increasingly tried to keep the sex trade as unobtrusive as possible, sometimes formally banning it while unofficially tolerating it. They confined sex workers to particular houses or streets, regulated their dress, and limited their access to public spaces. In late-medieval France, Spain, Germany, and parts of Italy, municipalities set up their own brothels and licensed the prostitutes they housed. The restraints provided enterprising women with opportunities to manage municipally owned houses and sometimes set up their own brothels, where they could either rent rooms to prostitutes or provide them with customers and reap a profit from their labors.[105] In this form as in others, the brothel became a fixture of every town and city. Its presence a mark of social order as well as a visible sign of gender inequality.

Industrialization, with its requirements for a disciplined and hard-working citizenry, not only increased the numbers of women who needed to earn their own livings but also encouraged their mobility to towns and cities where anonymity left them vulnerable to market pressures. Women without homes took to street-walking, challenging the guardians of morality to further regulate what seemed like the archetype of misbehavior.[106] If, in the interests of a disciplined workforce and prosperous state, women were enjoined to become properly educated mothers and guardians of morality in the home, prostitutes embodied the dangers of public life and the presentiment of danger. And if female thrift, morality, and self-discipline provided daily incentives for the disciplined and productive labor of the working and middle classes and the prosperity of the state, then prostitutes offered men of all classes a release of energy and an outlet for repression. They also served as a mark of danger, challenging the value system required for disciplined labor and ordered family life. Thus, the single, unemployed, and homeless women who flooded Italian cities at the end of the nineteenth century evoked a strong negative outburst from respectable citizenry, to whom they represented a flouting of state authority and moral degeneracy antithetical to the bourgeois ethic of the working class.[107]

Prostitution could, however, empower the women who engaged in it. At its best, it provided a steady source of income where otherwise there would be none. Where women could earn enough to own their own property, as in Nairobi, Kenya, they could turn houses into sanctuaries not only for women who served men sexually but also for men who benefited from the comforts of home.[108] From that perspective sex work appears in a different guise. Often the last recourse of women thrown on their own resources, it nevertheless provided a vehicle for financial mobility and economic security. Some observers report that many women now enter the industry of their own accord—in order to "stand on their own feet."[109]

And yet sex work is embedded in both gender and class inequality that subjects most of the women who do it to sexual domination and exploitation; they are vulnerable to the idiosyncracies of politics and the will of public opinion. Sex workers in Chihuahua, Mexico, had been comfortably tolerated for years before officials felt the need to act against them and "protect" their community's image. After 1900 they confined brothels to three carefully designated zones, required prostitutes to register and undergo weekly medical examinations, and insisted on decent dress and public behavior.[110] Racial and ethnic exploitation complicates the picture. In New Orleans, Louisiana, prostitution was carefully organized by both race and class, with poor black women occupying the "cribs" that constituted the lowest rungs of the ladder. The Japanese used Koreans as "comfort women" for ordinary workers long before they forcibly rounded them up during World War II to serve in that capacity. After the war, these women reported that they had been required to have sex with as many as three hundred Japanese a day—at about three minutes an occurrence.[111] That should not be surprising, however. Military bases everywhere have secured and protected locations at which soldiers could find women to serve their needs.

The commodification of women reached its nadir during the twentieth century with the emergence of an international political economy and the flowering of an international sex industry. Racial issues fuelled the importation of Chinese women to the United States during the 1860s and 1870s to serve the needs of Chinese railroad workers and were behind the fear of a white slave trade that engulfed Europe and the United States in the early twentieth century. More recently, a growing middle class that has disposable incomes (and expansion of a poor working class whose daughters are desperately in need of jobs) has fuelled sex tourism. Designed to attract foreign currency to developing countries such as Korea, the Philippines, and Thailand, sex tourism continues a long tradition in which women's sexual comforts are made available by powerful men, largely for their own purposes.[112] Sex tourism remains unregulated or only formally controlled in deference to national needs.

HOUSEHOLD WORK

In the sexual division of labor, women have traditionally worked in and around the household—a division that became more marked as specialization and the aggrandizement of technical skills drew men into larger workplaces. Although every sort of household worker was subject to the will of the household's head, generally a male, the idea of household work contains an enormous range of jobs and significant differences in power and position for the women who have held them. As wives, women could find themselves committed for life to a single household; as slaves, women were also committed for life or at the discretion of their owners but with very different access to power. Women might work as apprentices or as indentured servants, each serving a limited term and the former entitled to specialized training in some aspect of the household arts. Or women might be called in for an occasional service, like wet-nursing, of a limited duration. Depending on its temporal and geographical location, domestic service could include everything from the care of domestic animals to spinning and weaving. Typically, it involved tasks related to household maintenance, such as washing, cleaning, provisioning, and providing for the household's occupants.

Female slaves served domestic households into the late nineteenth century. They were common in late-medieval Europe, in most of Asia, in the southern states of the United States, and in many Latin American countries.[113] Often, as in the United States and Latin America, they were defined by race or ethnicity. In late-nineteenth-century Brazil, slaves worked alongside free women. Both lived in intimate relation to the family, and, as with family members, no public law intervened between the will of the master and the treatment of the servant.[114] But servants who rendered intimate family services and acquired family secrets were far from powerless. They held the power of the master in check by their capacity to deploy knowledge that could affect the householder's control over his children and servants as well as his standing in the community.

Down into the modern period, the overwhelming majority of all working women everywhere engaged in household work (either as wives or as servants) at some point in their lifetimes. Throughout the first third of the twentieth century, worldwide, most women who sought paid labor found jobs as household servants, and many still do so. Seventy percent of wage-earning women in nineteenth-century Brazil, and two-thirds in the United States during the same period, identified themselves as servants. As late as 1940, nearly 90 percent of African American women in the United States worked in some form of domestic or household service. Although household work is clearly a woman's job, men also worked as other people's slaves and servants. Yet male servants tended to hold more specialized jobs, and their numbers rapidly diminished with increasing industrialization.

The twentieth century witnessed a dramatic transformation in the nature of household labor. In industrial societies, most jobs moved outside the household. Ready-made clothing, prepared foods, widespread refrigeration, and nurseries for children have reduced the need for household services and increased the need for wives to earn cash incomes. In the most advanced industrial countries, the proportion of wives without children in the paid labor force equals that of men. And the proportion of working women with children has risen steadily. New opportunities for women have expanded, in part in sectors that substitute paid work for work formerly done at home.

Women who managed traditional households set an example for those who worked for and with them, by teaching employees the skills necessary to do their jobs. As industrialization removed privileged wives from this labor and more and more household tasks began to be farmed out, more privileged women lost their knowledge base. In an apt metaphor captured by the Chinese, they no longer wove cloth but embroidered it instead. Laundry workers, dressmakers, cooks, and nannies still served households, but they did so from outside the walls. As with factory technology, the knowledge necessary to sustain a household was increasingly located in the brains of more and more specialized workers who sometimes contracted for jobs on a daily or hourly basis. Paternalistic relations broke down. Historian Lucy Salmon observed this process in the late-nineteenth-century United States. It was characterized by a demand that employment relations between household workers and wives be regularized, with servants obtaining their training elsewhere before offering the labor for hire. In sharp contrast to the earlier notion of an integrated household all of whose occupants shared its work, Salmon raises the possibility of classifying domestic workers in terms of skill level, the better to enable them to bargain for good wages.[115] Presciently, she points to the interdependence of occupations for upper-middle-class women and work for the poor. "The pay of wage-earning women," she notes, "will never rise above the starvation point while the women of the upper and middle classes are permitted to live without work."[116]

These changes have left households not less dependent on the labor of women but differently dependent. As nineteenth-century women could create and manage their own dressmaking workshops, so twentieth-century childcare entrepreneurs and "cleaning services" provide entrepreneurial opportunities for women. More recently, economic incentives to modernization have reduced the control of traditional families, increasing the desire for autonomy on the part of all sorts of women and shifting power relationships among those who hire and those who work at household jobs. In advanced industrial countries, more and more affluent women, eager to replace their own domestic labor, willingly subscribe to contracts that call for high wages and relatively good working conditions. Pulled by the temptation of wages high enough to support their families and pushed by the absence of economic opportunity at home, women migrate, often thousands of miles, in search of incomes high enough to support their families at home.[117] Women, for all of the technology of a global economy, remain profoundly interdependent for their economic choices and personal freedom.

SHAPING THE CULTURAL MILIEU

In seventeenth-century China a few privileged women not only learned to read and write but also did so at a level that altered the literary landscape and influenced the political fortunes of their families. Although secluded within the walls of their family compounds, their words reached out into the political arena to influence the shape of national decision-making.[118] It turns out that such women were not unusual, either inside or outside of China. Although often invisible—sometimes sequestered in convents and hidden away in harems—they contributed to a variety of forms of education. Working sometimes as unpaid mothers, wives, and members of religious orders and at others as readers, teachers, writers, and patrons, women helped shape the cultural milieus within which they livid.

Education was hard come by for most women for most of historical time. Refused access to leading roles in the religious institutions and the administrative agencies that served as incentives to educate men, the rate of female literacy has historically been far lower than that of men. Yet before the onset of industrialization, privileged women who could read, write, and cipher often took their talents seriously and encouraged others to follow suit. As readers, they contributed both to the preservation of books and their continuing life. Where financial resources permitted, they purchased and collected books, carefully passing them on to daughters when they died.[119]

Because reading tended to serve no business purpose for them, women used books in a continual process of self-education, preparing themselves and their peers for the growth of a literate mentality. As readers, they also interpreted. They commented on words and patterns, sometimes altering them to suit particular sensibilities. Some Chinese women managed to publish their work and distribute it to family and friends where it sparked continuing conversation and sometimes response.

Women used the cultural capital derived from reading in both religious and secular capacities. Excluded from public religious life except as worshippers, they engaged with devotional readings in the privacy of their own homes, encouraging an iconography of literate womanhood. Portraits of the Virgin Mary reading or surrounded by books became common illustrations. Uneducated in Latin, Western European women commissioned vernacular translations of many texts (most famously "Books of Hours"), prayerbooks for daily use. Their act encouraged a broader audience for devotional and secular materials and spread spiritual engagement, perhaps cynicism as well.

As religious and secular teachers, women took on the mantle of educating the very young. Nunneries served as infant schools for boys as well as girls, and dame schools taught the small children of artisans as well as gentry. Excluded from universities and from all the scholarly professions, they learned to disseminate ideas in less formal ways as well. Some conducted seminars and salons in their living rooms or at their dinner tables. Others disseminated ideas when they moved (with marriage) to new cultural milieu; sometimes lodging manuscripts among the intimate items in their trousseaux. The eminent scholar Christine de Pisan wrote a book of moral instruction for her son before she turned her attention to the education of women.

The education of small children was so firmly a woman's field in most countries that with the advent of industrialization, and the accompanying need to teach large numbers of children at least the rudiments of literacy, women moved easily and quickly into early childhood education. Governments, religious and missionary institutions, and employers overwhelmingly chose women for what should have been important jobs. They were available because there were few other respectable job opportunities, they would work for relatively little pay, and they saw these jobs as extensions of the natural teaching they would do as mothers. Teaching could be done in the home or in sex-segregated schools in cultures that secluded women; it could also be done under the supervision of male headmasters and principals in those that did not. But women could rarely control what they taught. The result—one of the classic ironies of a gendered workforce—is that women served, by example, to introduce children to the dilemmas of occupational segregation.

Conclusion

If work is common to every human society, the factors that influence its organization are historically circumscribed. The complex layers of its construction are rooted in household and culture as well as geography and climate and in every instance are exposed only by rigorous and specific analysis. Identifying the reciprocal relationship between patterns of life and the creation of a labor force in particular societies is no simple task, yet it provides an essential ground for comparison across region and religion, environmental resources, and politics. When we begin to recognize the power of gendered ideas and habits of mind to shape particular labor force patterns—to determine who is available for what kinds of work, who may be trained and how, and who excluded—we open the door to a fuller understanding of gender. And when we start to explore the impact of gendered ideas and cultures on economic progress and social transformation, we expand our horizons to encompass new explanatory dimensions for historical change. For that reason if for no other it is worth considering how gender and work have interacted over time.

Notes

1. Judith M. Bennett et al., *Sisters and Workers in the Middle Ages* (Chicago: University of Chicago Press, 1989), 6.

2. David Landes, *The Wealth and Poverty of Nations: Why Some Are So Rich and Some Are So Poor* (New York: W. W. Norton, 1999), 413.

3. I have not attempted a historiographical survey—that would be foolhardy in this moment when the literature on women's work expands exponentially every day. But these notes contain an extensive listing of material on which I relied. I hope this list-

ing will constitute a preliminary guide for those who wish to follow the subject further and that it will be sufficient to lead those interested in particular topics or areas to the first-person literary texts written by the educated and the religious; to huge varieties of official documents such as wills, inventories, tax accounts, employment records, and occupational censuses; and to evidence of daily practice drawn from household objects, dress, and folk wisdom as well as from oral histories, folk wisdom, memoirs, and diaries.

4. Maureen Mackintosh, "Gender and Economics: The Sexual Division of Labour and the Subordination of Women," in *Of Marriage and the Market: Women's Subordination Internationally and Its Lessons*, ed. Kate Young, Carol Wolkowitz, and Roslyn McCullagh (London: Routledge, 1981), 3.

5. Ester Boserup, *Woman's Role in Economic Development* (New York: St Martin's Press, 1970), ch. 1.

6. Monica Green, "Women's Medical Practice and Health Care in Medieval Europe," in *Sisters and Workers in the Middle Ages*, ed. Judith M. Bennett et al. (Chicago: University of Chicago Press, 1989), 44; Merry E. Wiesner, *Working Women in Renaissance Germany* (New Brunswick: Rutgers University Press, 1986), 187.

7. Patricia Buckley Ebrey, *The Inner Quarters: Marriage and the Lives of Chinese Women in the Sung Period* (Berkeley: University of California Press, 1993), 173–75.

8. Kathleen Sheldon, *Courtyards, Markets and City Streets: Urban Women in Africa* (Boulder: Westview Press, 1996).

9. Richard Anker, *Gender and Jobs: Sex Segregation of Occupations in the World* (Geneva: International Labor Office, 1998), 403.

10. Jean C. Robinson, "Of Women and Washing Machines: Employment, Housework, and the Reproduction of Motherhood in Socialist China," *China Quarterly* 101 (1985): 32–57; Wendy Z. Goldman, *Women at the Gates: Gender and Industry in Stalin's Russia* (New York: Cambridge University Press, 2002)..

11. Bahnisika Ghosh, "The Role of Women in Economic Activity: A Study of Women in Rice-Farming Systems in West Bengal," in *From the Seams of History: Essays on Indian Women*, ed. Bharati Ray (New York: Oxford University Press, 1995), 255.

12. Florencia E. Mallon, "Studying Women's Work in Latin America: Reflections on the Direction of Feminist Scholarship," *Latin American Perspectives* 14 no. 2 (1987): 255–61, quotation on 256.

13. Silvia Marina Arrom, *The Women of Mexico City, 1790–1857* (Stanford: Stanford University Press, 1985), 201.

14. Boserup, *Woman's Role in Economic Development*, ch. 2. Nor did polygamy inhibit women from feeling responsible for earning incomes outside the household (Sheldon, *Courtyards, Markets and City Streets*, 144–45).

15. Manoshi Mitra, "Women in Colonial Agriculture: Bihar in the Late Eighteenth and Nineteenth Century," *Development and Change* 12 (1981): 29–54. Boserup (*Woman's Role in Economic Development*, 48) points out that secluded women who contributed little may have paid the largest dowries and that in anticipation of a huge dowry (and in respect of women's relative lack of economic value) some regions resorted to female infanticide.

16. E. Patricia Tsurumi, *Factory Girls: Women in the Thread Mills of Meiji Japan* (Princeton: Princeton University Press, 1990).

17. Thomas Dublin, *Farm to Factory* (New York: Columbia University Press, 1981); Joan Wallach Scott and Louise Tilly, *Women, Work and Family* (New York: Holt, Reinhart and Winston, 1978).

18. Barbara A. Hanawalt, ed., *Women and Work in Preindustrial Europe* (Bloomington: Indiana University Press, 1986), x.

19. Wiesner, *Working Women in Renaissance Germany*, Conclusions; Arrom, *The Women of Mexico City*, 202; Sheila Lewenhak, *Women and Work* (New York: St. Martin's Press, 1980), ch. 9.

20. Wiesner, *Working Women in Renaissance Germany*, 192; see also Lewenhak, *Women and Work*, ch. 9.

21. Elizabeth Anne Kuznesof, "The Role of the Female-Headed Household in Brazilian Modernization: São Paolo 1765–1835," *Journal of Social History* 13 (1980): 589–614.

22. Sherry Ortner, "The Problem of 'Women' as an Analytical Category,'" in *Making Gender: The Politics and Erotics of Culture*, ed. Sherry Ortner (Boston: Beacon Press, 1996), 116–231; Jo Ann McNamara, *Sisters in Arms: Catholic Nuns through Two Millennia* (Cambridge: Harvard University Press, 1996); Carol Neel, "The Origins of the Beguines," in *Sisters and Workers in the Middle Ages*, ed. Judith M. Bennett et al. (Chicago: University of Chicago Press, 1989), 240–60.

23. Wiesner, *Working Women in Renaissance Germany*, 190.

24. Ebrey, *The Inner Quarters;* Martha C. Howell, *Women, Production, and Patriarchy in Late Medieval Cities* (Chicago: University of Chicago Press, 1986).

25. Wiesner, *Working Women in Renaissance Germany*, 187.

26. Alice Kessler-Harris, *In Pursuit of Equity: Women, Men, and the Quest for Economic Citizenship in Twentieth Century America* (New York: Oxford University Press, 2001), ch. 3.

27. Naila Minai, *Women in Islam: Tradition and Transition in the Middle East* (New York: Seaview Books, 1981), 206.

28. Susan Schaefer Davis, "Working Women in a Moroccan Village," in *Women in the Muslin World*, ed. Lois Beck and Nikki Keddie (Cambridge: Harvard University Press, 1978), 419–20.

29. Angélique Janssens, "The Rise and Decline of the Male Breadwinner Family? An Overview of the Debate," *International Review of Social History* 42, sup. 5 (1997): 2.

30. Ivy Pinchbeck, *Women Workers and the Industrial Revolution, 1750–1850* (London: Routledge and Sons, 1930).

31. Lena Sommestad, "Welfare State: Attitudes to the Male Breadwinning System: The United States and Sweden in Comparative Perspective," *International Review of Social History* 42, sup. 5 (1997): 153–74.

32. Stephen Meyer, "Work, Play, and Power: Masculine Culture on the Automotive Shop Floor, 1930–1960," in *Boys and Their Toys: Masculinity, Class, and Technology in America*, ed. Roger Horowitz (New York: Routledge, 2001), 13–32; Joshua Freeman, "Hard Hats, Construction Workers, Manliness and the 1970 Pro-War Demonstrations," *Journal of Social History* 26 (1983): 725–44; Sonya Rose, "Respectable Men, Disorderly Others: The Language of Gender and the Lancashire Weavers' Strike of 1878," *Gender and History* 5 (1993): 382–97.

33. Hanawalt, *Women and Work in Preindustrial Europe*, xvii.

34. Ebrey, *The Inner Quarters*, 24–25.

35. Judith Brown, "A Woman's Place Was in the Home: Women's Work in Renaissance Tuscany," in *Rewriting the Renaissance*, ed. Margaret Ferguson, Maureen W. Quilligan, and Nancy J. Vickers (Chicago: University of Chicago Press, 1986), 215–16.

36. David Katzman, *Seven Days a Week: Women and Domestic Service in Industrializing America* (New York: Oxford University Press, 1981), 269.

37. Arrom, *The Women of Mexico City*, 203.

38. Mukul Mukherjee, "Women's Work in Bengal, 1880–1930: A Historical Analysis," in *From the Seams of History: Essays on Indian Women*, ed. Bharati Ray (New York: Oxford University Press, 1995), 234–35.

39. Leela Fernandes, *Producing Workers: The Politics of Gender, Class, and Culture in the Calcutta Jute Mills* (Philadelphia: University of Pennsylvania Press, 1997).

40. Mukherjee, "Women's Work in Bengal."

41. Wiesner, *Working Women in Renaissance Germany*, 192.

42. Davis, "Working Women in a Morroccan Village," 421–22.

43. See especially, Fernandes, *Producing Workers;* and Arrom, *The Women of Mexico City.*

44. Dorothy Ko, *Teachers of the Inner Chambers* (Stanford: Stanford University Press, 1997); Susan Mann, *Precious Records: Women in China's Long Eighteenth Century* (Stanford: Stanford University Press, 1997).

45. Minai, *Women in Islam*, 213.

46. Romans did not allow women to do the liberal arts. David Herlihy, *Opera Muliebria: Women and Work in Medieval Europe* (Philadelphia: Temple University Press, 1990), 12; Donna Guy, "Women, Peonage and Industrialization: Argentina, 1810–1914," *Latin American Research Review* 16, no. 3 (1981): 69.

47. George E. Brooks, "The Signares of Saint-Louis and Goree: Women Entrepreneurs in Eighteenth-Century Senegal," and Leith Mullings, "Women and Economic Change in Africa," both in *Women in Africa: Studies in Social and Economic Change*, ed. Nancy J. Hafkin and Edna G. Bay (Stanford: Stanford University Press, 1976), 19–44 and 239–64; Marcia Wright, "Technology, Marriage, and Women's Work in the History of Maize-Growers in Mazabuka, Zambia: A Reconnaissance," *Journal of Southern African Studies* 10 (1983): 71–85; Jack Goody and Joan Buckley, "Inheritance and Women's Labour in Africa," *Africa* 43 (1973): 108–21.

48. Mercedes Borrero Fernández, "Peasant and Aristocratic Women: Their Role in the Rural Economy of Seville at the End of the Middle Ages," in *Women at Work in Spain: From the Early Middle Ages to Early Modern Times*, ed. Marilyn Stone and Carmen Benito-Vessels (New York: Peter Lang, 1998), 11–32.

49. Barbara Hanawalt, "Peasant Women's Contribution to the Home Economy in Late Medieval England," in *Women and Work in Preindustrial Europe*, ed. Barbara A. Hanawalt (Bloomington: Indiana University Press, 1986), 3–19.

50. Mitra, "Women in Colonial Agriculture," 29–54. Nellore, India, provides an example of a moment that extended into the twentieth century when women attached themselves, along with their husbands (or other male relatives) to a land owner who provided a daily wage and an annual retainer to both male and female. But women's jobs (primarily weeding, sewing and transplanting, and harvesting grain) generally paid less than those assigned to men (which involved heavy labor, transportation, and late hours), for which women were thought not to be suited. M. Atchi Reddy, "Female Agricultural Labourers of Nellore: 1881–1981," *Indian Economic and Social History Review* 20 (1983): 67–80.

51. Quoted in Susan Mann, "Household Handicrafts and State Policy in Qing Times," in *To Achieve Security and Wealth: The Qing Imperial State and the Economy, 1644–1911*, ed. Jane Kate Leonard and John Watt (Ithaca: Cornell University Press, 1992), 88.

52. Ko, *Teachers of the Inner Chambers*

53. Herlihy, *Opera Muliebria*, xi.

54. Eileen Power, *Medieval Women* (New York: Cambridge University Press, 1975), ch. 3.

55. Power, *Medieval Women*, 56–57.

56. Hanawalt, *Women and Work in Preindustrial Europe*, viii.

57. Alice Clark, *Working Life of Women in the Seventeenth Century*, 3d ed. (London: Routledge, 1992).

58. Ebrey, *The Inner Quarters*, ch. 7.

59. Haim Gerber, "Social and Economic Position of Women in an Ottoman City: Bursa, 1600–1700," *International Journal of Middle Eastern Studies* 12 (1980): 231–44.

60. Kuznesof, "The Role of the Female-Headed Household," 590.

61. Herlihy, *Opera Muliebria*, 171, 173; Martha Howell, *Women, Production and Patriarchy in Late Medieval Cities* (Chicago: University of Chicago Press, 1986).

62. Hanawalt, "Peasant Women's Contribution."

63. Herlihy, *Opera Muliebria*, xi.

64. Ibid., 167.

65. Natalie Zemon Davis, "Women in the Crafts in Sixteenth Century Lyon," and Kathryn Reyerson, "Women in Business in Medieval Montpellier," both in *Women and Work in Preindustrial Europe*, ed. Barbara A. Hanawalt (Bloomington: Indiana University Press, 1986), 167–97 and 120.

66. Judith Bennett, *Ale, Beer and Brewsters in England: Women's Work in a Changing World, 1300–1600* (New York: Oxford University Press, 1996); *Goesaert v. Cleary*, 335 U.S. 464 (1948).

67. Howell, *Women, Production and Patriarchy in Late Medieval Cities*.

68. Davis, "Women in the Crafts in Sixteenth-Century Lyon," 167–97. There is disagreement over the question of whether capitalism disadvantaged women. Alice Clark argues that it did in Britain; Merry Wiesner (Germany) and Martha Howell (Leiden) concur.

69. For example, see Brown, "A Woman's Place Was in the Home," 216.

70. Ibid.

71. In Sweden women mercers outnumbered male mercers five to one. Grethe Jacobsen, "Women's Work and Women's Role: Ideology and Reality in Danish Urban Society, 1300–1550," *Scandinavian Economic History Review* vol. 31, no. 1 (1983): 3–20; Wendy Gamber, *The Female Economy: The Millinery and Dressmaking Trade, 1860–1930* (Urbana: University of Illinois Press, 1997), 9.

72. Landes, *The Wealth and Poverty of Nations*, 412.

73. Maxine Berg, "What Difference Did Women's Work Make to the Industrial Revolution?" in *Women's Work: The English Experience, 1650–1914*, ed. Pamela Sharpe (London: Arnold, 1998), 149–71.

74. Emily Honig, *Sisters and Strangers: Women in the Shanghai Cotton Mills, 1919–1949* (Stanford: Stanford University Press, 1986), 3.

75. The following material is drawn from Donna Guy, "Women, Peonage and Industrialization: Argentina, 1810–1914," *Latin American Research Review* 16 (1981): 65–89.

76. Leonore Davidoff and Catherine Hall, *Family Fortunes* (Chicago: University of Chicago Press, 1987); Bonnie G. Smith, *Ladies of the Leisure Class* (Princeton: Princeton University Press, 1981).

77. Francesca Bray, *Technology and Gender: Fabrics of Power in Late Imperial China*, (Berkeley: University of California Press, 1997).

78. Mukherjee, "Women's Work in Bengal," 235.

79. Susan Mann, "Women's Work in the Ningbo Area, 1930–1936," in *Chinese History in Economic Perspective*, ed. Thomas Rawski and Lillian Li (Berkeley: University of California Press, 1992), 243–70.

80. Tsurumi, *Factory Girls*.

81. Wright, "Technology, Marriage and Women's Work in the History of Maize-Growers"; Mullings, "Women and Economic Change in Africa."

82. June Nash and Helen Safa, eds., *Women and Change in Latin America* (South Hadley: Bergin and Garvey Publishers, 1986), cited in Mallon, "Studying Women's Work in Latin America," 257; Altagracia Ortiz, "Puerto Rican Women Workers in the Twentieth Century: A Historical Appraisal of the Literature," in *Puerto Rican Women's History: New Perspectives*, ed. Félix V. Matos-Rodríguez and Linda C. Delgado (Armonk: M. E. Sharpe, 1998), 40

83. Kathy LeMons Walker, "Economic Growth, Peasant Marginalization, and the Sexual Division of Labor in Early Twentieth Century China: Women's Work in Nantong County," *Modern China* 19 (1993): 354–65.

84. Honig, *Sisters and Strangers;* Walker, "Economic Growth, Peasant Marginalization, and the Sexual Division of Labor."

85. Thomas Dublin, *Women at Work: The Transformation of Work and Community in Lowell, Massachusetts, 1826–1860* (New York: Columbia University Press, 1979); Benita Eisler, *The Lowell Offering: Writings by New England Mill Women, 1840–1845* (Philadelphia: Lippincott, 1977).

86. Sheldon, *Courtyards, Markets and City Streets*, ch. 1.

87. Louise White, *The Comforts of Home: Prostitution in Colonial Nairobi* (Chicago: Chicago University Press, 1990).

88. Joel Wolfe, *Working Women, Working Men: São Paolo and the Rise of Brazil's Industrial Working Class, 1900–1955* (Durham: Duke University Press, 1993); Iris Berger, "Gender, Race and Political Empowerment: South African Canning Workers, 1940–1960," *Gender and Society* 4 (1990): 398–420.

89. Sometimes those restrictions were explicitly abolished. See Arrom, *The Women of Mexico City*, 5.

90. Fernandes, *Producing Workers*, 71–72.

91. Felicia Madeira and Paul Singer, "Structure of Female Employment and Work in Brazukm, 1920–1970," *Journal of Interamerican Studies and World Affairs* 17 (1975): 490.

92. Linda Lim, "Capitalism, Imperialism and Patriarchy," in *Women, Men, and the International Division of Labor,* ed. June Nash and Patricia Fernandez-Kelly (Albany: SUNY Press, 1983), 70–92.

93. Diane Elson and Ruth Pearson, "The Subordination of Women and the Internationalisation of Factory Production," in *Of Marriage and the Market: Women's Subordination Internationally and its Lessons,* ed. Kate Young, Carol Wolkowitz, and Roslyn McCullagh (London: Routledge, 1981), 18; and the essays in *Workers and Global Restructuring*, ed. Kathryn Ward (Ithaca: ILR Press, 1990).

94. Anker, *Gender and Jobs*, 411–16.

95. Lourdes Beneria and Martha Roldan, *The Crossroads of Class and Gender: Industrial Homework, Subcontracting, and Household Dynamics in Mexico City* (Chicago: University of Chicago Press, 1987).

96. Aiwha Ong, *Spirits of Resistance and Capitalist Discipline: Factory Women in Malaysia* (Albany: SUNY Press, 1987).

97. Rita S. Gallin, "Women and the Export Industry in Taiwan: The Muting of Class Consciousness," in *Workers and Global Restructuring,* ed. Kathryn Ward (Ithaca: ILR Press, 1990), 64–81.

98. Diane Lauren Wolf, *Factory Daughters: Gender, Household Dynamics, and Rural Industrialization in Java* (Berkley: University of California Press, 1992).

99. Helen I. Safa, "Women and Industrialization in the Caribbean," and Janet W.

Salaff, "Women, the Family, and the State: Hong Kong, Taiwan, Singapore—Newly Industrialised Countries in Asia," both in *Women, Employment and the Family in the International Division of Labour,* ed. Sharon Stichter and Jane L. Parpart (London: Macmillan, 1990), 72–97 and 93–136.

100. Herlihy, *Opera Muliebria,* 2, 34.

101. Bray, *Technology and Gender,* 187. In Tuscany, sericulture was entirely the function of women and children except that men planted and pruned mulberry trees and provided an important economic supplement, saving the family in famine years and linking the household economy to the marketplace. Brown, "A Woman's Place Was in the Home," 220.

102. Bray, *Technology and Gender,* 242.

103. Although women had established the industry at Barcelona in the thirteenth century, even a widow was forbidden to take over a master's shop unless she had a twelve-year-old son to succeed her. Only spinning remained a female venue. Seville, in contrast, still had a high proportion of women weavers. A century later women there were also mostly spinners. Jane Schneider, "The Anthropology of Cloth," *Annual Review of Anthropology* 16 (1987): 409–48.

104. James A. Brundage, "Prostitution in Medieval Canon Law," in *Sisters and Workers in the Middle Ages,* ed. Judith M. Bennett et al. (Chicago: University of Chicago Press, 1989), 79–99.

105. Ruth Mazo Karras, *Common Women: Prostitution and Sexuality in Medieval England* (New York: Oxford University Press, 1996); Wiesner.

106. Jeffrey Weeks, *Sex, Politics and Society: The Regulation of Sexuality since 1800* (New York: Longman, 1981); Judith R. Walkowitz, *Prostitution and Victorian Society: Women, Class, and the State* (New York: Cambridge University Press, 1980).

107. Mary Gibson, *Prostitution and the State in Italy, 1860–1915* (New Brunswick: Rutgers University Press, 1986).

108. Louise White, *The Comforts of Home: Prostitution in Colonial Nairobi* (Chicago: University of Chicago Press, 1990).

109. John Lie, "The Transformation of Sexual Work in Twentieth-Century Korea," *Gender and Society* 9 (1995): 323.

110. William E. French, "Prostitutes and Guardian Angels: Women, Work, and the Family in Porfirian Mexico," *Hispanic American Historical Review* 4 (1992): 529–53.

111. Lie, "The Transformation of Sexual Work in Twentieth-Century Korea," 310–27.

112. Lin Lean Lim, ed., *The Sex Sector: The Economic and Social Bases of Prostitution in Southeast Asia* (Geneva: International Labor Office, 1998).

113. See, for example, Susan Mosher Stuard, "To Town and to Serve: Urban Domestic Slavery in Medieval Ragusa," in *Women and Work in Preindustrial Europe,* ed. Barbara A. Hanawalt (Bloomington: Indiana University Press, 1986), 39–55; and Sandra Graham Lauderdale, *House and Street* (Austin: University of Texas Press, 1992).

114. Lauderdale, *House and Street,* 4.

115. Lucy Salmon, *Domestic Service* (New York: Arno Press, 1972), 268.

116. Salmon, *Domestic Service,* 272

117. Judith Rollins, *Between Women: Domestics and Their Employers* (Philadelphia: Temple University Press, 1985).

118. Ko, *Teachers of the Inner Chambers.*

119. Susan Groag Bell, "Medieval Women Book Owners: Arbiters of Lay Piety and Ambassadors of Culture," in *Sisters and Workers in the Middle Ages,* ed. Judith M. Bennett et al. (Chicago: University of Chicago Press, 1989), 135–61.

5

Race and Ethnicity in
Women's and Gender History
in Global Perspective

PAMELA SCULLY

Different societies' understandings of race, class, masculinity, and femininity critically affected and produced knowledge about appropriate behavior and aspirations of individuals at particular moments.[1] Historians are paying attention to how ideas of blackness or whiteness—or colonized or colonizer—were produced and reproduced in gender and women's history.[2] Race in particular is now seen not as a biological truth so much as a cultural classification resulting from cognition or perception.

Discrimination based upon differences in skin color or cultural affiliation is a relatively new phenomenon. In Ancient Egypt, for example, skin color or place of origin appears to have had little place in determining a person's social or economic position. Even by the European Middle Ages, when people increasingly made an association between whiteness and purity, racism as a way of excluding people solely because of their skin color did not exist. For example, people respected the legacies of scholars of African descent such as St. Augustine and Ptolemy.[3]

Likewise, when Christopher Columbus's expedition encountered the Taino of the Caribbean, race was not the category through which people understood the encounter. The Taino perhaps saw Columbus and his men as an ancestor or dead chief returning from the land of the dead across the sea rather than as a biologically different kind of person. Columbus understood his meeting with the Taino in terms of a variety of grids of understanding prevalent in the European Middle Ages. The views ranged from believing that the outer limits of the European world were populated by monsters to believing that the world was divided into the Christian world, China, and the uncivilized remainder.[4] Thus, although Columbus and his European contemporaries certainly held prejudices against indigenous people and feelings of superiority about European civilization, race as a biological category of difference was not the category through which they understood the Colombian encounter.

Some ten years earlier, across the Atlantic on the shores of Central West Africa, people of the Kongo Kingdom welcomed white spirits of the dead who emerged out of the sea near present-day Congo. The governor of the province of Soyo greeted the spirits as representatives of a new cult of the earth and water spirits and sought to be initiated into the cult.[5] The BaKongo were witnessing the first Portuguese exploration of the central African coast. They made sense of the pale men who spoke a different language not through the lens of race but through a framework of spiritual knowledge and explanation that fit with Kongo religion and cosmology.

Race, as a way of thinking about and classifying individuals by skin color and putative biology, is a product of particular historical interactions between Europe and indigenous societies around the globe, at least from the fifteenth century. A study of race and ethnicity as social historical constructs within women's and gender history thus only makes sense if one studies race, ethnicity, and gender as historically specific and within a comparative perspective. Even within Europe, the history of the idea of race as well as of the category *woman*, for example, have undergone many permutations and understandings.[6] Across time and geography, the history of women, perceptions of woman, and the intersection of race and gender are much more intricate and complex.

Ethnicity, too, has an uneasy history that spans many centuries. Forms of ethnic identification appear to have older roots than that of race. In Asia and Southeast Asia, for example, caste and ethnicity have long histories of cultural identification and exclusion. Indeed, it is sometimes difficult to distinguish clearly between ethnicity and race. In China and Japan, discrimination of ethnic minorities has long existed, with the bodies of women often being seen to represent the purity or impurity of a given ethnic group. Thus, for example, women of ethnic minorities were spared foot binding in nineteenth-century China because they were seen to be outside of the boundaries of Chinese civilization.

With the rise of a new wave of European imperialism from the 1880s, Europeans tended to perceive distinctions within putative racial groups through ethnicity. British colonialism in particular employed the concept of ethnicity, closely related to that of tribe, to accomplish rule over myriad societies within Africa, for example.[7] Ethnicity in America has been an important site of struggle in debates about immigration for well over a century. Throughout the 1920s nativists sought to limit or stop immigrants from Ireland and Southern Europe, arguing that certain ethnic groups were inferior to others. Thus the category *white* could be further subdivided into a gradation of racially coded ethnic groups.

Historiographies of Race and Racism

Historians of women's and gender history have inserted new dynamics into the historiography of race by establishing a methodology for studying race as a historical category linked to notions of gender and sexuality. In addition, they have sought to analyze race and ethnicity within Europe and the colonies, both in the Americas and in Southeast Asia, in the same frame. In so doing, feminist historians have shown that attempts are ill-advised to provide a rigid chronology for the rise of racial thinking that extends neatly across time and space. They have suggested that rather race and ethnic identities can be embraced and accentuated in one context and time period and can decline and become relatively unimportant social and economic markers in another. They have also called attention to ways in which women and men have experienced gendered racial identities as a source of empowerment and disenfranchisement in the political arena.

Historians have tended to see black identity as a synonym for race, with whiteness being "so natural, normative and unproblematic that racial identity" is seen as a "property only of the nonwhite."[8] Some historians have begun to analyze the politics of whiteness in white women's political lives, but that is a relatively new trend in women's history. During the Victorian era, women missionaries, teachers, explorers, and suffragists to some extent embraced whiteness as a way of creating a "positive female identity" for themselves "in a deeply misogynistic society."[9]

Historians of gender have shown that there is no essential womanhood to which historians and history can appeal. That has implications for the study of race in women's history, and Evelyn Brooks Higginbotham most powerfully calls for greater theorizing of race within that discipline.[10] Higginbotham charges that many white feminists have tended to conflate white woman with black womanliness and assume that all women are alike in identities and aspirations. Higginbotham argues against any kind of essentialist invocation of race. She also maintains that historians of African American women's history, by invoking concepts such as "black womenhood," are in danger of assuming that all black women are the same and somehow share the same feminine identity. Such a notion obscures differences of class experience, family experience, and geography that shape experiences of race and gender. Yet talking of black womanhood points to ways in which race and racism have powerfully affected black women's lives. It also alerts historians to how the experience of racial oppression can help create foundations for powerful identity politics.

Higginbotham instructs historians studying race and women's and gender history to understand how race was constructed or understood at different periods in history. It should not be assumed that people have always understood or recognized race. Higginbotham also advises grappling with race's power as a "metalanguage" or model that shapes concepts such as "gender, class, and sexuality."[11] By that she means seeing how ideas about blackness and whiteness operate in tandem, or in concert, with other ideas about manliness or femininity. Race, that is, cannot be examined in isolation from other categories that shape society and history. Finally, Higginbotham suggests trying to analyze the Janus face of race. It can, they say, be used as a tool of oppression and also serve as a vehicle or concept for liberation. Thus, we need to appreciate how race works in history and not naturalize race and its effects.

Other authors have also asserted the need to attend to the many sites of difference and identity within women's history. Elsa Barkley Brown argues that merely mentioning difference—that is, talking of white and black women in the same breath—does not itself constitute analysis of the discrete experiences of women. Brown suggests that historians write of women's various experiences through the idiom of jazz rather than classical music. This means that teachers and writers accept that there is no one universal historical score by which to write or teach history. "Race (and yes gender, too) is at once too simple an answer," Brown observes, "and at the same time a more complex answer than we have yet begun to make it."[12]

Part of the complexity of dealing with race lies precisely in confusion about how to account for the genesis of the concept. Historians tend to locate the rise of biological racism within the eighteenth century arising from a fifteenth-century backdrop of European colonization of the Americas and Southeast Asia. Historians of race in the Atlantic world in particular have long debated the causes of racial thinking. Winthrop Jordan argued in *White over Black* that Europeans, even before the rise of the slave trade, associated blackness with death and evil. Jordan therefore concluded that racism, or at least racial thinking, predated colonial slave systems. Settlers in the Americas enslaved Africans because they already saw them as inferior. Other historians, such as Eric Williams in *Capitalism and Slavery*, maintained instead that racism arose from the experience of slavery and the slave trade in the Americas.[13] The emergence of a system of slavery, with slaves being drawn almost exclusively from Africa, a geographical and cultural context different from that of slaveholders, gave rise to settlers' association of blackness and inferiority and the rise of formal legal racism.

More recently, scholars have again looked to Europe for explanations for the rise of race as an important marker of difference. Scholars of the Enlightenment argue that the era produced both hardened forms of gender inequality and new ideas about race. Men's increasing social and political liberty was in many instances formally dependent on their domination of women and children in the home. In addition, the rise of classification as a model for understanding the world helped produce racial thinking. The encyclopedic model of classifying things and people tied individuals to biology and the group in new ways. That fascination with categorization arose in part as a way of mastering the new information about people, biology, and cultures that Europe confronted as a result of the discovery of the Americas from the fifteenth century. Race became a primary language through which European intellectual thought sought to explain cultural difference.

Racial explanations of difference also drew on contemporary notions of gender. During the late eighteenth and early nineteenth centuries philosophers such as Jean-Jacques Rousseau as well as scientists such as George Cuvier sought to account for what they perceived as the natural differences of men and women. Race and gender became linked to the extent that a description of whiteness invoked associations with masculinity. White male scientists as well as European popular culture increasingly came to see femininity as well as blackness as forms of pathology.[14]

Ideas about women as somehow marginal, and perhaps threatening to male society, thus mirrored and came to enhance in intricate ways white racist ideas about people of African descent. The invention of race thus drew on the experiences of slaveholders in the Atlantic slave colonies, where white men had almost total power over the bodies of black women. The idea of race, however, also was informed by longer negative male understandings, rooted in European history, of women.

Historians of gender and women's history argue that languages of race, gender, and sexuality emerged not so much in either Europe or the colonies but rather across the divide of metropole and colony. Colonialism depended on racial categories of inclusion and exclusion to maintain boundaries between colonized and colonizers. Sexuality and gender were essential pillars of the construction of racial discrimination and identities within the colonial setting. Who was allowed to marry whom—and which children were counted as children of the colonizers and which were not—helped secure colonial rule. But race as a category of knowledge changes across time and space. Children of settler men and indigenous women could at one time be included within the settler definition of "white" and at another be included in a category of "mixed race."[15] In early-eighteenth-century Louisiana, for example, French authorities were very concerned about relationships between French men and Indian women. At the same time in the Dutch Cape Colony, South Africa, and in the Dutch East Indies, authorities actually encouraged concubinage as a way of maintaining colonial rule. Similarly, early in the history of the Colony of Virginia slaveholders formed ideas about blackness being an inferior racial and sexualized category. In contrast, in the slaveholding Cape Colony, although women were regarded differently according to geographic origin, race as such does not appear to have been a salient organizing category until into the nineteenth century.

In Louisiana at the turn of the eighteenth century, French colonial authorities worried that settler men, many of whom came from Canada and had long interaction with Native American communities there, were becoming too involved with indigenous communities. French-speaking men both lived in Native American villages and established relationships with Indian women. Officials believed that such relationships "retard[ed] the growth" of Louisiana in that men were less likely to settle down and become farmers, thus rendering the colony stable and profitable. Officials also worried that settlers would be drawn into the fold of Indian communities and not reproduce French culture on American soil.[16]

Whereas the French actively encouraged French women to emigrate to Louisiana, including forcibly putting prostitutes onboard ships, the VOC (Dutch East India Company) for much of its tenure as an imperial power actively discouraged white women from emigrating. The VOC established a way station in the Cape Colony in 1652 for its boats en route to the Dutch East Indies. It also discouraged any kind of formal settlement, although it had to rescind the policy within a few years. The company did allow relationships between its employees and African women, however. At the Cape, one indigenous woman named Eva was able to marry into the higher echelons of the Dutch East India Company in Cape Town. She served as a linguistic and cultural translator between the Dutch and the indigenous Khoisan.[17]

The Dutch policy of encouraging sexual relationships between Dutch men and indigenous women, and the ambivalent acceptance of children of mixed-race, continued well into the nineteenth century in the Dutch East Indies. In Malaysia, the Dutch saw colonialism as dependent upon the same sort of sexual relationships. The VOC believed that European marriage would be so costly that it would draw Europeans down into a poorer white class and thus complicate the neat divides of wealthier whites and poorer local societies. That, too, changed, however, with the rise of eugenics and racial science in the twentieth century. Ann Stoler argues that colonial authority came to rest more clearly on "European-ness" and on more racially distinct populations.[18]

The creation of "knowledge" about race appears to have been in operation much earlier on in other societies, particularly in the Americas. Virginia's early colonial history people, for example, identified themselves with local communities, with kin groups, and, perhaps, with "nations" conceived as African, Indian, and English. Yet soon after the establishment of slavery, ideas of femininity and blackness became laden with pejorative associations within a context of slaveholding. The relative openness of both ethnicity and racial categories changed in the mid-seventeenth century with the consolidation of patriarchal colonial power. Racial categorization of blackness versus whiteness became the primary social, economic, and political identifier. Kathleen Brown shows that gender ideals about good, industrious wives versus wenches, concepts settlers imported from England, underwent changing gender and racial meanings. By the late seventeenth century, the "good wife," who had the connotation of being an industrious household worker, became increasingly a white category, at least in public discourse. Black women became wenches, sexual, licentious, and unruly. "Womanhood . . . began to take on a race-specific meaning in the colony."[19]

In contrast, race in the Cape Colony was not a central feature of company rule. Like Virginia in the early years, many different status and categories of origin existed, for example, French, German, Dutch, bastard, bastard hottentot, and hottentot. The categories referred to a person's geographic origin, sometimes to the status of their parents and sometimes to their putative nationality. A "bastard hottentot," for example, was the child of a slave man and a Khoi woman. Compared to Virginia, at the Cape before the arrival of the British in the nineteenth century the "respectability" of women was determined in part by baptism as by recognition of European heritage. The conflation of slaveholding status primarily with Europeans and Christians— and the facts that most Africans were not Christian and most slaves were denied baptism by their owners—helped establish possible foundations for a kind of racialized consciousness before the nineteenth century. Scholars, however, generally consider that race at the Cape only became a fully elaborated category of exclusion or self-definition in the nineteenth century.

The British, in contrast to the Dutch, actively sought to classify everyone into racial groupings. Given the confusion about status and origin, the British found it almost impossible to keep up with the categories created by the Dutch. Thus, over the course of the nineteenth century the category *coloured* enlarged to include people recognized neither as African nor as European. With the abolition of slavery in 1838, racial identities seem to have become the primary marker of status, and "colouredness" became a cultural category into which former slaves, freed in 1838, also were absorbed. Although some children of black descent had become part of the white population before slavery, after slavery their trajectory was much more likely to lie within the category *coloured*.[20]

There is no teleological story about race and ethnicity and the history of these categories does not move from liberalism to a more racist culture or the other way around. Nor can we easily argue that racism emerged in Europe and was exported to the colonies or vice versa. Historians have also shown how messy concepts of race were affected by (and helped shape) emergent ideas about class and femininity within European society during the nineteenth century. Analogies among the Irish, the working class, or prostitutes drew on a set of ideas of laziness, immorality, and degeneracy that coded the middle classes as the norm and others as deficient. It is clear that a "repertoire of racial and imperial metaphors were deployed to clarify class distinctions in Europe at a very early date."[21] Different regional literatures, however, including those of the United States, Latin America, the Caribbean, Africa, and Southeast Asia, have developed distinctive historiographies on race and ethnicity in women's and gender history.

Historiographies of Race and Ethnicity

THE UNITED STATES

Gender identities and clan membership shaped individual and societal relations in the Native American societies that occupied what was later to become the United States. Ideas about the centrality of kinship and innate differences between men and women thus played more of a role than ethnicity or nationhood in shaping people's experiences in precolonial societies. A woman member of the Iroquois, for example, would have had quite a lot in common with a female peer in one of the Native American societies of what became New England.

Gender ideologies of male and female roles also shaped encounters among European traders, settlers, and indigenous people from the sixteenth century. Similarities in indigenous and European beliefs about women's productive, reproductive, and emotional labor helped frame the earliest cross-cultural encounters.[22] In many instances Native American women were the first mediators between Europeans and Native American communities. They acted as guides and translators and did domestic work for European traders and early settlers, relationships that in part explain why so many European men married local women and had children by them. The relationship between Pocahontas and John Smith is only the most famous example of such female work in the early period of European exploration. It was in the wake of the early relationships that officials from various colonizing enterprises in what became the United States sought to regulate and sometimes ban interracial marriages.

Racial identities became more fixed with the entrenchment of slavery and colonialism within the early colonial era. The social construction of racial stereotypes meant that black women had to fight for individuality and power within racist constructions that labeled them either asexual or hypersexual. Studies of black and white women's experiences of slavery have shown how slaveholders' racialized stereotypes of womanhood profoundly affected women's experiences. Black women on plantations were constantly confronted by racist stereotypes of the "mammy" and "Jezebel." The image of Jezebel was that of a black woman, sexually available and enticing, who lured men to have sex despite their better nature.

The idea of the hypersexual black woman emerged early in colonial American history and continued to shape interactions between black women and white men as well as within the black community. Slave mothers, for example, lived with the worry that if their adolescent daughters were considered pretty slaveholders would rape them. They thus cautioned the daughters to be modest and not openly express their sexuality. During the postbellum period, some middle-class African American women felt they had to practice a "culture of dissemblance," because, they believed, in order to be seen as respectable by their own communities and the larger, white-dominated community it was necessary to silence their sexuality, which was seen as compromising their status.[23]

The antithesis of Jezebel, the asexual, elderly black mammy, emerged during the post–Civil War era in books and memoirs that celebrated slavery and lamented the war. *Gone with the Wind* provides a striking example of the genre. The image of the mammy materialized as a way of justifying slavery and showing that everyone on a plantation was, after all, one happy family. Women slaves who fulfilled the role of nanny and or cook to the white family were remembered as special—totally dedicated to the needs of the slaveholding family. Even slaves, as Deborah Gray White points out, saw nannies as having a close association with the white household, but they were much more likely to recognize that domestic work also involved constant scrutiny and loss of privacy. In the end, as a fiction of what slavery had meant, "Mammy was . . . the perfect image for antebellum Southerners. . . . As part of the benign slave tradition and part of the cult of domesticity, Mammy was the centerpiece in the antebellum Southerner's perception of the perfectly organized society."[24]

Mythologies of black women's sexual availability continued to shape black women's relationship to their sexuality long after slavery had ended as a formal social and economic system. Black women had to negotiate womanhood through racial codes that had been established under slavery but continued to be elaborated by white society in new settings—and on into the twentieth century.[25]

Attention to class as well as race also reveals other complexities within women's and gender history. In North Carolina, for example, poor women, both black and white, were marginal to slaveholding culture. Poor white women and free black women posed a threat to the patriarchal plantation order because they did not fulfill a role in the reproduction of slavery. Poor women were more likely to break taboos against interracial sexual relations and social interaction and were thus vulnerable to prosecution by the state. Under laws designed to stop miscegenation, the state was much more likely to prosecute cases involving a white woman and a black man than cases concerning white men and black women.

Historians have also generated a sophisticated literature on the interplay of ethnic cultures and the creation of new ones in the United States. American officials promoted middle-class domestic ideals, both intentionally and unintentionally, to female immigrants during the early years of the twentieth century and at its end.[26] State and missionary officials sought to create new forms of ethnic identification among Mexican immigrant communities by making them into "Americans." Officials assumed that "American" meant English-speaking and Protestant. Americanization also was linked to dominant class notions of female domesticity in which married women were expected to stay at home and nurture the next generation. State officials saw Mexican women as having great power to shape their children and culture. Thus officials explicitly targeted women and home as places where Americanization would best be applied.

Officials saw food and domesticity as fundamental to cultural transformation. Social workers visited Chicano homes and taught mothers to make roast chicken rather than burritos, which were seen to be insufficiently "American." Drawing on widespread notions of women as "mothers of the nation," the social workers attempted to emphasize women's importance in incorporating children into the American dream.[27] Social workers taught women English songs that told of women cooking meals and sending men to work and children to school.

The Americanization programs in Texas and California both failed, in part because of the vitality of ethnicity as a form of identifying oneself and one's community. Families that resisted Americanization did not cling to a static Mexican identity but helped create a new, synthetic identity from the immigrant experience. In addition, the assumptions about femininity, domesticity, and home that governed Americanization often had little application to the lives of immigrants. The fragile economic existence of many Mexican families, which made them move frequently in order to look for work, frustrated the gendered program of Americanization.

Immigration into the United States could also fix gender ethnic identities that had hitherto been more fluid. Young women and old often came to America as dependents of men, which placed women in an especially vulnerable situation as they tried to accommodate the demands of Anglo culture and natal families. Maxine Hong Kingston documents such tensions in *The Woman Warrior.* American teachers expected her to be shy and calm as a "Chinese" girl.[28] Thus, Hong Kingston adopted a particular persona at school, which separated her from herself at home and from educational opportunities.

THE CARIBBEAN

The historiography of the race and ethnicity in gender and women's history in the Caribbean has largely charted the different experiences of black and white women under slaveholding. Enslaved men and women, as in much of the United States, also lived on plantations, although more likely with absentee landlords. Similar images of black women as being sexual and dominant mothers also prevailed, affecting black women's lives both before and after slavery. Women slaves rebelled in various ways, such as working very slowly, pretending to be ill so as to interrupt the work demands of plantations, and, sometimes, refusing to bear children. Race and slaveholding privileged white women, virtually eliminating gender solidarity among women. Although to some extent victims of patriarchal relationships within their marriages, white women benefited from their position on plantations. They disciplined slaves, sold people into slavery, and upheld the racial order.

In the French Caribbean, notably Haiti, a relatively large free black population created a different context for the experience of race and gender. Until the middle of the eighteenth century, free black women enjoyed significant economic independence and social status. Before 1763, all women who were free were considered white and thus enjoyed some legal protection. In part as a reaction to the power free black women wielded, French authorities from 1773 excluded women of color from the category *white* and increasingly also labeled free black men as men of color. During the era of instability in which factions in Saint-Domingue struggled for supremacy, men of color began to emphasize their participation in military activities as evidence of claims to citizenship.

The emphasis on a militaristic masculinity as a criterion for citizenship continued into the period of Haiti's independence, and men experienced a much more profound liberation than did women as slaves wrested the colony away from the French. Mimi Sheller maintains that men were seen as more important citizens than women because male participation in military activities was critical to warding off imperial attacks during the early nineteenth century.[29] Political culture in Haiti thus increasingly affirmed men's rights as citizens at the expense of women's. Men and women experienced blackness differently, in part because different concepts were attached to being a black man or a black woman.

Slave emancipation in the Atlantic world was a gendered process. Abolitionists and officials both in the United States and Britain and her colonies— as well as slaves themselves to some extent—agreed that the end of slavery would involve reassertion or even creation of a proper gender order. In the United States, freed men saw freedom as offering the opportunity to head a patriarchal family—an image shared, to some extent, by men who were slaves in the Caribbean as well as in the British Cape Colony. The abolitionist newspaper *South African Commercial Advertiser* celebrated such a vision in an editorial on emancipation day in the Cape Colony on December 1, 1838. Emancipation, the newspaper maintained, would make a free man the king of his family, and he could reign over the hearts and minds of loyal and willing subjects.

Male liberty built upon the subordination of women and children. Freed men to some extent embraced the idea of freedom as masculine entitlement, although they also seem to have supported a wife's right to work outside the home. In the postemancipation period across the Atlantic world, former slaves tried wherever possible to withdraw from regular work. Women in particular avoided labor on plantations and entered into more independent enterprises such as becoming laundresses and market gardeners. The gender order that freed people constructed after slavery ended thus did not necessarily coincide precisely with emancipators' visions.

Catherine Hall has shown how abolitionists such as John Angell James of Birmingham moved from being fervent supporters of abolition to imperialists after abolition.[30] Abolitionism contained within it the seeds of a new racism founded on notions of the cultural and gender superiority.[31] Even white female antislavery activists in Britain (and much the same can be said for the United States) justified their antislavery involvement on the basis of what they saw as a special ability to understand the sufferings of slaves.

White women argued that they were particularly sensitive to the plight of enslaved women. They based this claim on the fact that, as women, they shared some sense of oppression with slaves, and as middle class women they were more sensitive to morality than men. Thus, white women positioned themselves as moral saviors of the white nation and older sisters, if not mothers, to black women slaves. Embedded in this discourse on antislavery then was a view of white, middle-class femininity as a higher form of femininity than either working-class and/or black femininity. White abolitionists were ambivalent about whether women needed to be rescued back into femininity and freedom because of the degradations slavery caused or whether they had to be taught how to "become" women because blackness rendered them inferior.

The story of Mary Prince, a slave from Bermuda, encapsulates the experiences of many such women in the British Caribbean and the complicated relationships black Britons from the Empire experienced with abolitionists.[32] Prince, born into slavery in Bermuda about 1788, spent her childhood and early adulthood on various plantations in the slave economy of the British West Indies. Her various identities as a black person, a slave, and a woman in the early nineteenth century affected the choices available to her and the ways she pursued attempts to gain freedom. Although married to a free man, for example, she was rarely allowed to see him, and even though she converted to Christianity the conversion did not ameliorate her status. As a black person, her status precluded other forms of respectability in terms of white society. In addition, Prince endured beatings and probable sexual abuse at the hands of male owners.

In 1828 her owners, a couple named Woods, brought Prince with them to London. There she ran away and sought freedom. She attended Anti-Slavery Society meetings and became the first black British woman to speak in favor of general emancipation for all slaves. In 1828 she went to the Anti-Slavery Society to ask if she could return to Antigua and her husband, but not as a slave. A subsequent court case found that she could be free as long as she remained in England; upon arrival in Antigua she would again be a slave. She decided therefore to stay in London. In 1829 Thomas Pringle of the Anti-Slavery Society employed Prince as a domestic servant, and the following year she dictated her story to a friend of Pringle's, Susanna Strickland. The book was published in 1831—and to great acclaim. Three editions were published in 1831 alone. Prince ended her memoirs with a powerful appeal for the ending of slavery:

> All slaves want to be free. . . . We don't mind hard work, if we had proper treatment, and proper wages like English servants, and proper time given in the week to keep us from breaking the Sabbath. But they don't give it; they will have work—work—work, night and day, sick or well, till we are quite done up . . . I tell it to let English people know the truth; and I hope they will never leave off to pray God, and call loud to the great King of England, till all the poor blacks be given free, and slavery done up for evermore.[33]

Mary Prince's status as a black woman seems to have closed other possibilities for her once she arrived in England. She continued to be employed in domestic work although she had published a successful book. Even Thomas Pringle, her benefactor in England, perceived Prince within categories that tied white women to family and black and working-class women to labor.

LATIN AMERICA

The gender literature of Latin America, including the Spanish-speaking Caribbean, has focused on issues of honor and sexuality in the construction of colonial and colonized cultures. Brazilian society has long offered an interesting comparison to the United States for historians interested in race relations. Authors argued that race relations in Brazil have been historically more harmonious and more fluid than those in the United States. They pointed to Brazil's category of the "Mulatto" (a person of supposedly mixed race) versus the tendency in the United States to make a person who has a black ancestor fit into the category *black*. Authors also argued that the inclusive nature of Roman Catholicism and the more humane forms of slavery practiced in Brazil helped generate greater acceptance of racial difference.

That perception of the "mildness" of Brazilian slavery is no longer held. Historians maintain that Brazil's history of race relations has, in fact, been much tenser and more exploitative than hitherto acknowledged and that race was an important medium for limiting social and economic mobility.

Historians of women's history have played an important role in making the history of race in Latin America more nuanced. They have examined how concepts of honor operated within larger colonial understandings of racial purity and degeneration. In eighteenth-century Brazil, white elites practiced endogamy (marriage within the group) and thus policed the boundaries of whiteness through marriage. Sexual and intimate relationships did occur between elite men and black and subordinate women, but those relationships were not sanctified by marriage. Unlike the French Catholic Church in Louisiana, which encouraged French men to marry their Indian concubines, the Catholic Church in Brazil attempted to end the relationships all together in the interests of preserving class endogamy.

In nineteenth-century Cuba, determining who could or could not marry helped solidify and order racial categories. Up to 1864, elite white Cuban families generally accepted interracial marriages for their children. After the ending of the Civil War in the United States, however, Cuban slave owners became ever more concerned about the possibility of a slave uprising. Elite white Cubans therefore tried to stop practices such as interracial marriage that they saw as validating equality between blacks and whites. White parents invoked concerns about family honor and the threat to family blood "purity" as reasons to refuse a match if their children wanted to marry someone perceived as "not-white."

The concept of honor and the focus on marriage continue to dominate Central and Latin American women's and gender historiography, in part because the "elite, patriarchal family, held together by . . . the gender norms . . . of the honor/shame complex," was the "central economic, political, and social institution in colonial and nineteenth century Latin America."[34]

In Brazil, ideas of race and gender arose partly out of a long history of slaveholding and also, in the postemancipation period from the 1890s, in a context of discussions about sexuality, crime, and honor. Early-twentieth-century officials in Brazil understood race and explained race relations in different ways at different times. White intellectuals had viewed Brazil's mixed population as a product of black women's supposed sexual licentiousness (rather than white men's rape of black women, for example). Yet during the first three decades of the twentieth century, and as Brazilian leaders sought to articulate a "modern" identity for their nation, they silenced black women's sexuality as an index of Brazil's racial makeup. Nationalists now touted Brazil's history of miscegenation as evidence of "interracial harmony," a national characteristic that was leading to the whitening of the population and thus contributing to Brazil's ascendancy.

For Latin American and Central American history, thus, historians of women and gender have mostly written about the colonial family, sexuality, and concepts of degeneration. A focus on race and ethnicity as categories of study in and of themselves, however, is beginning to receive attention.

AFRICA

The historiography on race and ethnicity in women's and gender history is most developed for the colonial period from the 1880s through the 1950s. Dominant themes include missionaries' promotion of domesticity among African women, ways in which colonial states and African male elders sought to control black women's sexuality, and analysis of sexual panics in which white men became convinced that black men were attempting to rape white women.

Missionaries from various denominations accompanied the force of formal colonialism from the late nineteenth century. The missions offered young women some freedom from the demands of family and from unhappy marriages; outcasts and young and elderly women were often the first people to go to live on the mission stations. But missionaries came to Africa with ideas about the different capacities of men and women and about the kinds of futures to which Africans should aspire. Missionaries in colonial Rhodesia (now Zimbabwe), for example, taught African men to be teachers and preachers. In contrast, missionaries trained African women primarily in domestic service with enough English-language training to make them able to follow employers' orders. Young women were also brought up to be good wives to the small cohort of African youths being groomed to become missionary teachers or low-level clerks in the colonial civil service. Race worked in different ways for different genders, as did gender within the category *African*. Black women were to work for white women, whom colonial culture characterized as engaging in leisure. Black women were also cast as subservient to black men, who enjoyed more status, at least in the missionary setting, by virtue of being male.

British colonialism also operated according to underlying assumptions about gender and race. Historians have argued that British colonial rule in particular helped consolidate African men's power over women. The British governed through a policy of indirect rule that gave considerable power to African chiefs (often appointed by the British) to legislate on local matters in terms of so-called customary law. Ironically, this law, which was supposed to be the legal framework that had existed in precolonial Africa, was largely a colonial invention. Equally important was the fact that African male elders helped invent it. They saw in indirect rule a chance to formalize their claim to authority over young women and society in general. During the precolonial period, elders' power had been tenuous because leaders generally used consultation and consensus rather than a code of written laws. With the coming of British colonialism, however, senior men were able to claim legal rights to control women's labor and movement in the name of defending African tradition. That analysis provokes many questions for students of African history. To what extent, for example, can we see in contemporary and historical claims to African tradition another claim by men to have control over women? Moreover, how did men's and women's experiences of colonialism differ?

South Africa to some extent offers a classic case for a discussion of race and ethnicity in women and gender history. In the British Cape Colony, slave emancipation during the 1830s "liberated" women into the family and men into citizenship. The Cape was distinctive among the four settler states that were to become the Union of South Africa in 1910 in having a nonracial franchise based on property qualifications. From the 1890s, white women campaigned for the vote, arguing that if black men could vote then surely white women deserved to as well. White women gained the vote in 1930 as part of government policies to bolster the white electorate and maintain racial oppression. The twentieth century saw increasing denial of black men's tenuous civic rights in the Cape Province and extension of segregationist laws throughout the Union. African women campaigned against the extension of those laws to women and joined men in the formation of the African National Congress. Both white Afrikaans women and African women mobilized politically around ideologies of motherhood.

In 1948 the white Nationalist Government came to power and began assembling the policies of Apartheid. Apartheid involved the racial categorization of every individual in South Africa and later involved dividing all Africans into separate ethnic groups to hamper political mobilization. Apartheid built on earlier colonial practices started by the British that controlled Africans' movements in South Africa and that tried to make Africans only eligible to be in white areas if they were working there. Apartheid consolidated white racial domination of the African majority through the banning of missionary educational institutions, through the standardization of pass laws keeping Africans out of white areas, and through a host of other segregationist laws.

Shula Marks's *Not Either an Experimental Doll*, a collection of original letters, provides a poignant insight into the complicated relations between women of different races in one colonial context—South Africa during the 1950s.[35] The women involved were Lily Moya, a young Xhosa woman; Mabel Palmer, British and active in higher education for Africans in Natal Province; and Sibusisiwe Makhanya, the first black female social worker in South Africa, who tried to mediate between Moya and Palmer. The letters provide an intimate and devastating look at the cultural and political power of white supremacy.

Moya, from the Transkei, a rural area of South Africa, was the daughter of wealthy mission-educated peasant farmers. Her grandparents had been among the first Christian converts in her region of Xhosaland. She attended school and while still a teenager became a teacher at a mission school. Moya wanted to improve her lot and move to Durban in the province of Natal in order to gain a high school degree. In 1949 she began corresponding with Mabel Palmer. Originally from Britain and a Fabian Socialist, Palmer was concerned with promoting welfare policies for the poor. Palmer was known both in London and later Natal for her commitment to workers—and being abrupt and somewhat disruptive. She saw in Moya a protégé whom she could fashion and thus helped her come to Natal Province, enrolling her in a school primarily for boys.

Moya had been schooled to identify with things English, to learn English history, and to read *Jane Eyre*. Like many young men and women across colonial sub-Saharan Africa, however, she found that identification with European cultures could involve a painful psychic separation from things African and be an incomplete psychological journey. Ideologies of incorporation based on Christianity or the adequate adoption of European education did not lead to incorporation into the social or political body politic. They particularly did not do so for Lily Moya, who found herself, with Mabel Palmer's help, one of the few young women in a school in Zululand and speaking a new language. She also came to be rejected by her mentor.

Palmer seems to have been strikingly unsympathetic—if not oblivious—to the traumas and difficulties that Lilly Moya encountered in trying to make her way in apartheid South Africa. She was unwilling, and perhaps unable because of her sense of white superiority, to imagine the difficulties of Moya's cultural and psychological journey. Sibusiswe Makhanya, a social worker with whom Moya stayed while in Natal, tried to intervene but could not help. According to the letters, Moya wanted to leave school and go to work soon after she arrived in Natal, but Palmer made her stay despite Moya's protests that a teacher was being sexually abusive.

The tragedy that the letters reveal was that Mabel Palmer uncritically accepted the fact that Lily Moya must embrace British education and refused to appreciate that her entry into the Zulu, male-dominated high school would be a difficult transition. Soon after arriving at the school, Lily Moya left, and it appears that she had a nervous breakdown. In an interview before the collection of letters was published, Lily Moya recalled that her life had been "a transfer" from schools to hospitals. "Mrs Palmer," she said, "gave me a scholarship to Sterkfontein."[36] Sterkfontein was a mental institution.

The history of race and gender in Africa demonstrates the impact of colonialism on indigenous gender systems and on ideas about men and women's roles. It also shows the extent to which African and European men had similar interests in controlling women. Nonetheless, African women forged independent lives despite colonial restrictions. Luise White's work on prostitution in Kenya shows that women were able to achieve autonomy over one area of their working lives and become independent of fathers and husbands. The novels of Buchi Emecheta, particularly *The Joys of Motherhood,* which is set in Nigeria of the 1930s and 1940s, and Tsitsi Dangarembga's *Nervous Conditions,* set in Rhodesia during the 1960s and 1970s, offer more pessimistic analyses of African women's lot in contemporary Africa.[37] They detail the difficulties individual women faced, particularly during the middle decades of the twentieth century, in overcoming men's control and forging an independent path in a colonial order where African women were expected to be servants to whites. The novels also demonstrate the complicated transformations in identity and relationships in the colonial period and provide intimate portraits of women's experiences.

SOUTH ASIA

In the women's and gender history of South Asia, scholars have shown how ideas of racialized masculinity and femininity critically informed British imperial rule in India during the nineteenth century. The British perception of the supposed femininity of Bengali men, for example, shaped debates about penal law in the Raj and questions of Indian men's service in the military; it also affected debates about the age of consent at marriage. British conceptions about how Indian women related to Indian men and about the status of "native customs" also critically informed both British laws about widow burning (sati) and British Suffragists' experiences in India.

Historians have thus demonstrated particularly well in this case that gender and racial discourses had an impact on Indian agency and British rule far beyond matters obviously dealing with men and women. Both colonial rule and Indian resistance emerged from, and in turn helped create, new ideas about gender and the relationship between race and citizenship. Contests about what it meant to be Indian as opposed to British drew on ideas of femininity and masculinity. British officials justified their imperialism partly through a gendered rhetoric of the (masculine) imperial rescue of Indian women from so-called traditional customs. In so doing, British imperial discourse fractured the idea of a solidified Indian racial identity in opposition to Britishness. Instead, the British employed a racial discourse of feminine uplift to drive a wedge between Indian men and women.

In February 1883 a member of the government of India, C. P. Ilbert, proposed a bill that would allow some Indian officials to have jurisdiction over the British who lived in Indian rural towns. The Ilbert bill, as it became known, soon generated great resistance from British subjects, and, finally, accommodation was reached that stated that at least half a jury had to be made up of British individuals or Americans if a European were to be tried in a rural village. The debates about a bill that, on the face of it, had nothing to do with gender nonetheless were critically informed by ideas of the "manly Englishman" and the "effeminate Bengali."[38]

What was striking was how the debate over the degree of power an Indian official might exercise became bound up with widespread colonial ideas about Indian masculinity. Opponents of the bill argued that Bengali men were unnaturally "effeminate" and thus did not deserve—nor would they be able to handle—the responsibilities the bill promised. Indeed, opponents also said that had the bill excluded Bengali men, perceived as uniquely lacking masculine ethos in the eyes of many British in India, it would have been passed.

British racist discourse in India did not have to make sense to have powerful effects. In many ways the gendered images of Indian culture and individual were in conflict. For example, although in some moments British officials and society in India represented Bengali men as effeminate, they argued in other contexts that Indian men were brutes who ordered their widows burned on funeral pyres. Historians have concentrated on uncovering the tendencies of British imperialism, and British women in particular, to make exotic those Indian gender practices that seemed most foreign to the British. Thus, there are studies of sati as well as the practice of maintaining the zenana, or private female quarters found predominantly between the "upper and middle classes of north, northwestern, and eastern India."[39]

Thousands of parliamentary pages from the nineteenth century document and investigate the practice of sati, which British officials perceived as an Indian cultural phenomenon. Sati was prevalent, however, in only some regions of India, and even there only a very small number of women immolated themselves on their husbands' pyres. During the nineteenth century sati became more widespread in India, perhaps because the British focused on it as an "Indian" practice that had to be eradicated. Thus, sati and emergent Indian national identity became fused in a complicated relationship that put women and gender relations at the center of a struggle over the benefits of colonial rule.

Gendered and racial ideologies were thus central to the implementation of British imperialism in India. Campaigns against sati were articulated through rhetoric in which white men and women saved black women from black men. The links British administrators and the British public thus made between Indian femininity as a condition that required rescue pervaded British colonialism in India, and British suffragists pursued similar goals of recovery and recuperation in relationships with Indian women.

SOUTHEAST ASIA

The history of the Pacific and Indonesia has proved a productive arena of study for historians of race and ethnicity. The dominant story of colonial historiography is used to equate the arrival of white women in the colonies with the emergence of racism. It certainly reshaped race relations between whites and Fijians in Fiji as tensions emerged within the new domestic sphere of the colonial household. Before white women's arrival, white men either had lived with native mistresses or let servants take care of the household. Historians now suggest that the tensions that arose between white and indigenous women in domestic service positions were not because of the white women's inherent racism. Rather, racial tension was part of the growth of a plantation economy from the 1860s, with requirements for intensive labor and clearing of land. It accompanied more extreme demands of the colonial enterprise on the labor of Fijians. The arrival of white women did not create racism but coincided with the transition from one form of rule to another.

In Southeast Asian history, scholars have also analyzed the ways racial categories helped to consolidate colonial rule and reproduce colonial cultures divided between colonizer and colonized. The boundaries of colonial rule were fundamentally unstable and needed to be constantly reproduced and reimagined. Sexuality helped mark class and race in different ways. The category *mixed race,* for example, was not recognized as a legal category in colonial policy in Indochina and the Netherlands Indies, precisely because it destabilized the theories of immutable racial difference and hierarchy upon which colonial rule depended. A study of the family and sexual relations is thus not only an interesting sideline in colonial history but also an important nexus of colonial power.

Themes in Nineteenth-Century Comparative History

In turning to more explicitly comparative issues of race and ethnicity in women's and gender history, certain themes emerge. Scientific enquiry and its connection with colonial relations of power played an important role in linking femaleness, blackness, sexuality, and inferiority from the late eighteenth century. A study of slave societies and postemancipation societies shows that they invoked (and to some extent depended upon) particular associations of blackness, femaleness, and dishonor. Sexual violence had many connections to race and ethnicity, and the racial nature of the new imperialism of the late nineteenth century also offers comparative possibilities in women's and gender history. There are also significant invocations of race and gender identity in women and political movements.

RACIAL SCIENCE

The late eighteenth and early nineteenth centuries' joining of class, race, and gender through racialized visions of female sexuality is perhaps most powerfully represented in the iconography surrounding Sara Baartman, who became known as the "Hottentot Venus." Baartman was paraded through England and France as a cultural and sexualized artifact. French scientists examined her in order to determine and explicate the supposed connections between physique and racialized sexuality.

An African woman of Khoisan descent, Baartman was born on the frontier of the British colony of the Cape in the last quarter of the eighteenth century. She grew up in a war zone in which settlers raided the African communities resisting colonialism. Following her capture by settlers, Baartman was brought to Cape Town as a servant to Hendrik Cezar and Alexander Dunlop. They brought her to England in 1810, eager to make money from displaying her as a curiosity at the kind of "freak shows" then popular in Britain and France. They knew of the long-standing interest by scientists and naturalists in the bodies of Khoi women, who were said to form a kind of bridge between animals and humans. Scientists saw in the nomadic life of the Khoi, their language, and the fact that they wore few clothes evidence of a lack of civilization.

Cezar displayed Baartman at crowded freak shoes in London, and antislavery activists were outraged. In 1810 Zachary Macaulay of the antiabolitionist movement brought a case against Cezar. He suspected that Baartman was kept in a state of slavery and was being indecently exposed to the public gaze. Having no one to turn to, she was unlikely to protest her conditions of treatment. Nonetheless, the court found in favor of Cezar and refused to end her ordeal. [40] A few years later, Cezar took Baartman to France, where he sold her to an animal trainer. When interviewed, she said she was "very unhappy Sara who does not deserve her fate."[41]

Scientists and scientific culture in general also participated in her abuse and objectification. Geoffroy St. Hilaire and George Cuvier, leading French scientists, were given permission to study her and did so for three days. Shortly thereafter, at the end of December 1815, Baartman died of an illness. Even death did not bring peace. Cuvier dissected her genitals, and a plaster cast of her body was displayed in the Museum of Man in Paris until the 1980s. In an effort to make restitution, a movement developed in South Africa during the 1990s that demanded the return of Baartman's body. According to Khoi religious belief, it was bad for her spirit to be on display and not have been buried. It was also bad "for the spirit of everyone who had a hand" in the abuse of Sara Baartman.[42] In August 2002 her remains were finally returned to the Cape, where she was buried near her place of birth in a ceremony attended by hundreds of people.

Sara Baartman's life powerfully demonstrates the power of white intellectual and popular stereotypes of black femininity and sexuality in shaping the lived experiences of individuals. The Victorian era in England also witnessed intense work on definitions of femininity and masculinity, in part as an attempt to understand the "natural laws" that could explain social and political inequality between the sexes. The categories of gender and race, in fact, increasingly became linked as explanatory devices. In nineteenth-century London and elsewhere, missionaries often drew on proselytizing experiences in Africa to make sense of the British working classes.[43] Indeed, by the 1850s powerful cultural assumptions about the inferiority of blacks and women enabled scientific statements to the effect that the skulls of blacks and women were similar. That fact, scientists argued, explained women and blacks' lower economic and social status within Victorian society. In this understanding, class position became a result of physicality rather than political or economic discrimination.

This "crossing" between images of womanhood and blackness and between race and gender became increasingly evident in late-nineteenth-century England. Ideas of class behavior and class boundaries in nineteenth-century England were closely connected to, and drew power from, contemporary notions of race and gender. The relationship and illicit marriage between Hannah Cullwick, from the working class, and illustrator and social critic Arthur Munby demonstrates these connections. Both partners kept diaries recording his fascination with hard female labor. They also record his interest in the dirt and grime with which many working-class women had to contend as well as Hannah's insistence on personal autonomy.[44] After four years of marriage she refused to continue living with him and found independent employment.

Images of blackness and whiteness, elite and working-class identities, and femininity and masculinity became fetishized in Cullwick and Munby's relationship, but it demonstrates the currency of these ideas in British culture. Munby drew working-class women with black faces, grimed with dirt but also echoing contemporary stereotypes of Africans. His fascination with grime, blackness, and labor arose precisely because those things contravened the code of femininity for the women of his class, with whom he was supposed to enjoy sexual relations. His desire for dirt, working-class women, and black women contravened essential prohibitions of middle-class imperial culture in England.[45]

RACE, GENDER, AND SEXUAL VIOLENCE

The elaboration of complex sets of such invocations of racial and sexual stereotypes was solidified over the course of the nineteenth century. It is clear that in Europe and the Americas as well as in Southern Africa, at least from the nineteenth century, race became a primary way of classifying and explaining cultural difference. In slave societies across the Americas and Africa, race, ethnicity, and gender did ideological work in maintaining boundaries between free and unfree and between owners and slaves. That was even the case in Africa, where into the nineteenth century boundaries between slaves and masters were much more permeable than in the plantation economies of the New World. Particularly in patrilineal societies where kinship was determined through the male line, masters married their women slaves and the children were incorporated into the society, albeit on unequal terms to free people.

Slaves were drawn from societies perceived as being different from the slaveholding society. During the nineteenth century in parts of Central Eastern Africa, for example, certain African societies became engaged in large-scale slave ownership, in part resulting from their encounters with the Atlantic slave trade. Groups such as the Chikunda in current-day Mozambique developed slave raiding and ownership as a form of economic and political organization. They liked to enslave women from different cultural or ethnic groups as a way of maintaining the women's marginality to the social system.

All slave societies have depended upon violence to maintain distinctions between free and slave and to reproduce the dominance of slaveholders. In slaveholding cultures such as those of the United States and South Africa, slaveholding society maintained the ideological boundaries between slave and free, in part through a gendered and sexualized discourse on the capacities of men and women of different races. Yet such slaveholding societies also reproduced slavery itself through a violent crossing of those barriers. Particularly in the wake of Britain's closing of the Atlantic slave trade in 1807, race played a critical and vicious ideological part in the sexualization and abuse of women slaves. Slaveholders participated in the rape of slaves and encouraged forced marriages as a way of producing enslaved children.

In both the Cape and North American slave systems, slavery was widely dispersed throughout the white population, with most slaveholders owning fewer than eight slaves. In both systems during the early nineteenth century slaves lived at relatively close quarters to slaveholding households; masters and slaves lived in close proximity, an intimacy that created the conditions for paternalism founded also in violence and rape. White men argued that black women enticed them in to sexual relations, a construction that conceptually silenced the reality of rape. Because the women were considered to be, in contrast to white women, sexually agressive and licentious, their rapes were "justified." Moreover, they "created" the conditions for being raped.

In the Cape Colony, whites' racial interpretations of black women's sexuality were further differentiated into ethnic categories or categories of origin, although all slaveholders did not necessarily share those sexualized ethnic categories. There is some evidence that slaveholders perceived women from Indonesia, known increasingly as "Malays" at the Cape, as beautiful and sensual but not as aggressively sexual as their peers from Mozambique. Such images could affect the experiences of individual women slaves. A woman of putative Malay descent, for example, was more likely to find herself in a sexual relationship with her master than a woman of African descent. Perhaps the only possible benefit for the woman involved with a slaveholder was that she was more likely to be manumitted than were her peers. There was also a chance that her children would be freed.

What such sexualized constructions of black womanhood accomplished was to erase white men's rape of black women. White society as a whole thus enabled the maintenance of certain fictions about the gentility of white racial slavery in both the United States and the Cape Colony. In addition, it ignored the role of violence and sexual violence in reproducing that society. The denial of the power of violence in shaping relationships under slavery had important repercussions for black women and men's experience of emancipation during the nineteenth century.

Silence about white men's rape of black women during the slave period contributed to a new form of violent practice after emancipation. The entwined operations of race, gender, and sexuality became even more charged once the distinction between slave and free no longer so clearly divided society. In the United States, white opinion as well as judicial opinions upheld the notion that to be a black woman was indeed not to be a woman at all. The term *ladies' car* on segregated trains, for example, was meant not for all women but for white women, who alone in the eyes of segregationists qualified for the category *lady*.

Supposedly, neat divisions of respectability were harder to maintain, even as a fiction, in the Cape Colony. There the population included whites of many different backgrounds and geographic origins, including those from the Netherlands, Germany, and Britain. In the Western Cape, where slavery had predominated, whites distinguished between black people born in the region and Africans from the Eastern Cape who came to Cape Town and surrounding farms to work from about the 1840s.

In the aftermath of slavery, many freed people converted to Christianity or Islam to identify themselves as a distinct community of respectable people. They sought to distinguish themselves from the bondage and disrespect of slavery and from Africans from Xhosa Land to the east, whom some freed people perceived as inferior and foreign. Missionaries in particular welcomed freed people into the community of "civilization" and were thus more likely to see freed women as having the capacity to be ladies. The white community thus did not as starkly nor as uniformly represent the supposed dichotomy between white "ladies" and black "nonladies" in the Cape as in the United States. Nonetheless, in both settings ideologies of masculinity and racialized meanings of womanhood helped determine individual experiences of emancipation.

If abolitionists and enslaved men agreed that emancipation provided the title to masculinity, many white men saw such masculinity as threatening to their own status as white men in charge of society. Both the United States and the Cape were premised upon racial slavery and violence. Historians have long noted the rise of lynching during the Jim Crow era between the 1880s and the 1920s. One of whites' justifications for lynching was as a defense of white women raped by black men. Embedded in that explanation was a host of assumptions about black and white masculinity, female sexuality, and the place of women in defining cultural and racial boundaries. As anthropologists have frequently noted, women in general tend to be seen as the bearers and markers of a society's morality and culture—and after emancipation in the U.S. South the marker of white purity was the white woman. When white men lynched black men in the United States, it was, in part, as a way of creating racial loyalty and disciplining potential transgressors.

Lynching foreclosed the notion that white women might "cross the race barrier" and choose to have sex and/or a love relationship with a black man. Such a possibility had to be silenced because white women were perceived as the bearers of white morality and culture. If they transgressed the boundary of race—and, indeed, had a child of the union—then southern whiteness was destabilized and rendered a fiction rather than a natural "fact." Lynching can thus be seen as a disciplinary act. It disciplined black men to observe the social and physical boundaries of racial consciousness, it disciplined white women to remain within the fold of whiteness, and it terrorized African American society at large in the wake of Reconstruction.

The various rape scares that flourished in different colonies during the twentieth century all involved similar denials and representations of race and gender. In Southern Africa, however, rape scares did not emerge in the post-emancipation Cape Colony. Rape panics, when white men accused black men of raping white women, occurred in areas where colonialism was relatively recent and where colonists felt less sure about the ability of the state to reinforce white privilege. Rape panics, known in colonial terms as the "Black Peril," occurred in Natal Colony in the 1880s and, during the early twentieth century, in the post–Boer War Transvaal and in Southern Rhodesia. Racial violence and white understandings of possible violence by black men against white women were connected to ideological constructions of white womanhood.

Lynching and rape scares can be understood as tied to the defense of ladylike women who supposedly needed protection because white society would crumble without their "virtue" (i.e., their refusal to have sex with black men). The irony, of course, is that lynching and the accusations of rape acknowledged implicitly that white women did not refrain from relationships with black men. Under this scenario lynching, rape scares, and accusations denied that white women could desire black men and threatened them to dare to do so.

Yet if the white image of the black rapist emerged in white popular discourse in both countries, the ways in which white societies dealt with it were very different. There were deaths in the United States and men brought to court on rape charges in South Africa. Clearly, some rape panics—for example, that in the British colony of Natal in 1886—had the potential of ending in lynching. Four hundred white men reacted with vicious fury in the aftermath of an African man's alleged attack on a white woman. At a rally on the evening of the event, speakers, meeting with loud acclaim, proposed tarring and feathering, castration, and public hanging to punish black men accused of raping white women. A few days later, whites stormed a jail to try to lynch another African suspected of raping a white woman. The police, however, had already taken the prisoner elsewhere.[46] The dynamics of lynching thus existed, but in South Africa it did not become a part of the political economic landscape on the scale that it was in the South of the United States.

In part, one can see this as reflecting the particular racist cultures of the various emancipation eras. Cape emancipation occurred in the 1830s, when race had not yet emerged as an overarching descriptive and symbolic category. Reconstruction in the United States, however, occurred at a time when it was accepted that white women's purity as symbolic of racial purity needed defense.

The rape scares in South Africa that can be at least metaphorically compared to lynching also occurred well after emancipation and primarily in the new Boer republics. These states of the Orange Free State and the South African Republic had been set up during the mid-nineteenth century by Dutch-speakers who disapproved of the perceived liberalization of master and servant relations promoted by the British. Rape scares also occurred in the colony of Natal, which was taken over by the British in 1848. They only colonized Southern Rhodesia in the late 1890s and only after military resistance by Africans. The panics all occurred in contexts where white settlers were unsure of their ability to maintain power over Africans. As Ivan Evans has noted, suspicion of the state's ability to bolster white racial privilege led to extra-legal forms of lynching and rape accusations.[47]

IMPERIALISM AND MASCULINITY

The era of the new imperialism from the late nineteenth century to the early twentieth century can be helpfully conceptualized as a racialized and gendered rape narrative. The imperial project in which Europeans and Americans sought to conquer other regions was based in part on a vision of the Old World as being a masculine invader of feminine continents and subcontinents. In the United States and Britain, the imperial moment of the late nineteenth century occurred within a context in which the upper classes in particular became concerned at the feminization of upper-class men. The philosophy of Christian muscular education at schools of the elite such as Eton and Rugby, and Teddy Roosevelt's Rough Riders who went off to fight in Cuba during the Spanish American War, are examples of attempts to "firm up" middle- and upper-class men. Imperialism of the late nineteenth century was very much a product of this moment. In part it was justified by the argument that upper-class men, losing their hold on society and the economy as a result in part of the industrial revolution, would be reinvigorated in the colonies. British officials and popular culture in part justified imperialism as a way of saving black women from black men. The imperial adventure was a kind of protective fatherly and saintly endeavor rather than one involving economic and political exploitation.

A popular British example of that view of empire, Henry Rider Haggard's *King Solomon's Mines,* portrays the search of three heroes, who are white, for gold somewhere in Southern Africa.[48] The gold is hidden in an inaccessible cave guarded by the bodies of great African kings. Along the way, the men help restore an African king to his throne, in part because he is seen to have learned the habits of British liberalism. The story of gold just waiting to be found by adventurous white men obscures the central motivations and nasty facts of imperialism. The British were primarily interested in mining for riches and taking the wealth back to Britain, especially after the discovery of gold in the Transvaal in 1886. Imperialism was all about extracting gold from the earth for the benefits of whites but using poorly paid African laborers who worked in deathly conditions.

King Solomon's Mines illustrates the ways in which imperialist discourses invoked racial and gender stereotypes to justify white authority. In the novel, the land is female. The heroes first have to climb the cold breasts of Sheba, a mountain range, before they can enter (or rape) the dark space of the cave. The trope of rape plumbs the ideological work of race and gender in colonial cultures (both in the colonies and in the metropole). It links larger political economic narratives and debates about what led to the late nineteenth century's scramble for Africa and the popular portrayal of that imperial process.

WOMEN AND RACIAL POLITICS

The history of women and racial politics in the United States and the British Empire suggests, however, that we also need to see how appeals to racial identity could be Janus-faced. They could, that is, be used in often very contradictory ways. Women, for example, could invoke race as a way of bringing women together. They could also invoke racial identity as a means of excluding others, and, sometimes, women could use both forms of racial discourse simultaneously.

In the United States, in some areas as early as the seventeenth century and more generally by the nineteenth century, race became a critical category of exclusion. In political terms the constitution denied the vote to all women and to black men. As white women organized against slavery and for their own enfranchisement, they drew on the wider context of racial oppression, often accepting it even as they challenged other injustices. Women constructed themselves as white sometimes in opposition to other women in pursuit of such causes as antislavery and female suffrage. Some women created and justified a political life for themselves on the basis of seeing themselves as white with respect to black individuals.

Ambivalence among white women activists also emerged in woman suffrage politics in the United States, South Africa, Britain and other parts of the British Empire. The rise of Social Darwinism and the woman suffrage movement in the late nineteenth century created an uneasy yet fruitful alliance (for white women). White women championed their rights to the vote by embracing the notion that some women were fitter than others were for political voice and office. The identification of white North American women with modernity was widespread. In Pueblo communities at the end of the nineteenth century, for example, white women sought to "uplift" Native Americans through education and Christianity.

Similarly, in parts of the British Empire, including India and South Africa, some white suffragists articulated a racially ordered view of women's place. European women, in this formulation, would tutor "sisters" who needed uplift and education. British suffragists argued for the necessity of women's emancipation by pointing particularly to the supposedly terrible status of Indian women. The "specter of a passive and enslaved Indian womanhood" thus became an important frame of reference for feminist writers.[49]

In South Africa, some suffragists argued that white men should give white women the vote because women knew Africans better than men did. Middle-class, English-speaking women argued that they should have the vote because their experience as organizers of households, and therefore African labor, meant they brought a special level of experience to the issue of how to legislate regarding Africans. When suffragists acknowledged affiliation with black women on the basis of womanhood, they represented them as needing tutelage from more experienced "sisters" (i.e., white women). In short, racial identity in the form of whiteness often trumped the possibility of meaningful collaboration around female identity.[50]

If in white female politics of the nineteenth and early twentieth centuries women articulated notions of racial female uplift in exclusionary terms, the use of race could resonate differently in black communities. The notion of racial uplift was central to the formation and continued success of black women's clubs. In the United States black self-help organizations emerged from African Americans' exclusion from white organizations. The organizations included philanthropic groups, churches, and educational institutions. In Detroit in the 1860s, for example, African American teachers consciously worked to "aid and advance the race." By becoming teachers, women drew on wider understandings in both the white and black communities that saw women as nurturers and protectors of culture.

Self-help women's clubs were a key forum in which black women in the United States and elsewhere sought to maintain and promote a positive gendered racial identity through emphasizing progress and societal uplift. Like teaching, the sphere of women's clubs in many ways affirmed conventional middle-class beliefs in women's domestic role while challenging dominant white racism, which held that black women could not be "ladies." The club movement thus helped shape class and racial identity through an emphasis on the proper role of black middle-class women. In the United States, the 1880s witnessed the growing importance of women's clubs that drew on the rise of free black communities. The club movement consolidated even further with the formation of the National Association of Colored Women's Clubs in 1896. Women promoted the notion of racial solidarity as a method of positive identity very different to the discriminative use of race so widespread at the time.

In South Africa, the club movement as a form of racial and gender organizing also played a part, although it emerged in the twentieth century. An African American member of the "talented tenth," Madie Hall Xuma, moved to South Africa in 1940 and initiated a movement for the upliftment of black South African women.[51] She had married Dr. Alfred Bitini Xuma, soon to become the leader of the African National Congress. She also revived the Women's League of the ANC and established the Zenzele women's clubs that became affiliated with the international Young Women's Christian Association.

Madie Hall Xuma perceived a bond with African women across the line of nationality. "I regard them as my sisters" she said. "We share more or less the same background. It was my duty to share with them what we Americans know."[52] Xuma used her belief in the power and strength of African American and African culture to urge African elites to mobilize and motivate the African poor to unite against oppression. "I bring this message to you as an incentive," she urged, "so that you may not despair of your continued disabilities and fetters that hang so heavily about you—but that you will gird up your loins and unite your people for action and press on."[53]

Conclusion

In teaching about race and gender in comparative perspective, it is necessary to think constantly against the grain. Rather than seeing race as obvious or as part of common sense, we need to explore how it came to be seen as obvious—and when and why. In so doing historians must avoid projecting their own "common-sense" knowledge of the reality of race into the past. If we do not simultaneously analyze how race and ethnicity were always coded in terms of understandings of class and gender, we cannot understand the ways in which race and racism affected people. A comparative perspective demonstrates the transnational power of sexualized racial images as a foundation of colonial societies and exclusionary politics. It also, ironically perhaps, shows the revolutionary potential of such categories to help people assert humanity in the face of racial and gender prejudice.

Notes

1. For a good overview of the literature on women, class, and race, see Eileen Boris and Angelique Janssens, "Complicating Categories: An Introduction," in *Complicating Categories: Gender, Class, Race and Ethnicity*, ed. Eileen Boris and Angelique Janssens, supplement 7 of *International Review of Social History* (New York: Cambridge University Press, 1999).

2. Evelyn Brooks Higginbotham, "African-American Women's History and the Metalanguage of Race," *Signs* 17 (Winter 1992): 251–74; Ann Stoler "Rethinking Colonial

Categories: European Communities and the Boundaries of Rule," *Comparative Studies in Society and History* 31 (Jan. 1989): 134–61. A major exception is Nancy Stepan, "Race and Gender: The Role of Analogy in Science," *Isis* 77 (June 1986): 261–77.

3. Martin Bernal, "Race in History," in *Global Convulsions: Race, Ethnicity, and Nationalism at the End of the Twentieth Century,* ed. Walter Van Horne (Albany: State University of New York Press, 1997), 75–92.

4. Seymour Phillips, "The Outer World of the European Middle Ages," in *Implicit Understanding: Observing, Reporting, and Reflecting on the Encounters between Europeans and Other Peoples in the Early Modern Era,* ed. Stuart Schwartz (New York: Cambridge University Press, 1994), 23–63.

5. Wyatt MacGaffey, "Dialogues of the Deaf: Europeans on the Atlantic Coast of Africa," in *Implicit Understanding: Observing, Reporting, and Reflecting on the Encounters between Europeans and Other Peoples in the Early Modern Era,* ed. Stuart Schwartz (New York: Cambridge University Press, 1994), 249–67.

6. Denise Riley, *"Am I That Name?": Feminism and the Category of "Women" in History* (Minneapolis: University of Minnesota, 1988).

7. Leroy Vail, ed., *The Creation of Tribalism in Southern Africa* (Berkeley: University of California Press, 1989).

8. Ann duCille, "The Occult of True Black Womanhood: Critical Demeanor and Black Feminist Studies," *Signs* 19 (Spring 1994): 591–629, cited in Susan Stanford Friedman, "Beyond White and Other: Relationality and Narratives of Race in Feminist Discourse," *Signs* 21 (Autumn 1995): 1–49, quotation on 1.

9. Louise Michele Newman, *White Women's Rights: The Racial Origins of Feminism in the United States* (New York: Oxford University Press, 1999), 20.

10. Higginbotham, "African-American Women's History." This is also collected in an excellent collection edited by Darlene Clark Hine, Wilma King, and Linda Reed: *"We Specialize in the Wholly Impossible": A Reader in Black Women's History* (Brooklyn: Carlson, 1995). The volume covers the experience of black women in Africa, the Caribbean, and the United States. The first section includes some of the key theoretical pieces on race and women's history.

11. Higginbotham, "African-American Women's History," 252.

12. Elsa Barkley Brown, "'What Has Happened Here': The Politics of Women's History and Feminist Politics," in *"We Specialize in the Wholly Impossible": A Reader in Black Women's History,* ed. Clark Hine, Wilma King, and Linda Reed (Brooklyn: Carlson, 1995), 48.

13. Winthrop Jordan, *White over Black: American Attitudes toward the Negro, 1550–1812* (Chapel Hill: Published for the Omohundro Institute of Early American History and Culture at Williamsburg, Virginia, by the University of North Carolina Press, 1968); Eric Williams, *Capitalism and Slavery* (New York: Capricorn Books, 1944).

14. Stepan, "Race and Gender."

15. Ann Stoler, "Rethinking Colonial Categories: European Communities and the Boundaries of Rule," *Comparative Studies in Society and History* 31 (Jan. 1989): 134–61; Ann Stoler, "Making Empire Respectable: The Politics of Race and Sexual Morality in Twentieth-Century Colonial Cultures," *American Ethnologist* 16, no. 4 (1989): 634–60.

16. Jennifer Spear, "'They Need Wives': Metissage and the Regulation of Sexuality in French Louisiana, 1699–1730," in *Sex, Love and Race: Crossing Boundaries in North American History,* ed. Martha Hodes (New York: New York University Press, 1999), 35.

17. Julia Wells, "Eva's Men: Gender and Power in the Establishment of the Cape of Good Hope, 1652–74," *Journal of African History* 39, no. 3 (1998): 417–37.

18. Ann Laura Stoler, "Rethinking Colonial Categories: European Communities and the Boundaries of Rule," *Comparative Studies in Society and History* 31 (Jan. 1989): 134–61.

19. Kathleen Brown, *Good Wives, Nasty Wenches, Anxious Patriarchs: Gender, Race, and Power in Colonial Virginia* (Chapel Hill: Published for the Omohundro Institute of Early American History and Culture by University of North Carolina Press, 1996), 136.

20. Pamela Scully, *Liberating the Family? Gender and British Slave Emancipation in the Rural Western Cape, South Africa, 1823–1853* (Portsmouth: Heinemann, 1997).

21. Ann Stoler, *Race and the Education of Desire: Foucault's History of Sexuality and the Colonial Order of Things* (Durham: Duke University Press, 1995), 123.

22. Pamela Scully, "Indigenous Women and the Making of the Early Atlantic World" (manuscript in progress).

23. Darlene Clark Hine, "Rape and the Inner Lives of Black Women in the Middle West: Preliminary Thoughts on the Culture of Dissemblance," *Signs* 14 (Summer 1989): 915.

24. Deborah Gray White, *"Ar'n't I a Woman?" Female Slaves in the Plantation South*, rev. ed. (New York: W. W. Norton, 1999), 58.

25. Dorothy Roberts, *Killing the Black Body: Race, Reproduction, and the Meaning of Liberty* (New York: Pantheon Books, 1997) contains an examination of assumptions that still exist in medical circles and family planning practices about black women's uncontrolled sexuality.

26. Maxine Schwartz Seller's revised second edition of *Immigrant Women* (Albany: SUNY Press, 1994) contains a variety of documents dealing with women immigrants. The book includes sections on arrival in the states, work, family, and community life and includes reflections of immigrants from China, Russia, Slovenia, and Jamaica. The documents are short and could be easily used in a class. Perhaps the best compendium on ethnicity in women's history is *Unequal Sisters: A Multicultural Reader in U.S. Women's History*, edited by Vicki L. Ruiz and Ellen Carol Dubois (New York: Routledge, 1994), a collection of important articles on different ethnic and racial groups. Among its essays are analyses of women's labor organizing, the experiences of Japanese American women during World War II, and more recent developments such as the case between Equal Employment Opportunity Commission and Sears, Roebuck.

27. Anne M. Kellor, *Mothers of the Nation: Women's Political Writing in England, 1780–1830* (Bloomington: Indiana University Press, 2000).

28. Maxine Hong Kingston, *The Woman Warrior: Memoir of a Childhood among Ghosts* (1976, repr. New York: Vintage Books, 1989).

29. Mimi Sheller, "Acting as Free Men: Subaltern Masculinities and Citizenship on Post-Emancipation Jamaica," in *Gender and Slave Emancipation in the Atlantic World*, ed. Pamela Scully and Diana Paton (in press).

30. Catherine Hall, "From Greenland's Icy Mountains . . . to Afric's Golden Sand: Ethnicity, Race and Nation in Mid-Nineteenth Century England," *Gender and History* 5, no. 2 (1993): 212–30.

31. Hall, "From Greenland's Icy Mountains," 25; Catherine Hall, "Missionary Stories: Gender and Ethnicity in England in the 1830s and 1840s," in *Cultural Studies*, ed. Lawrence Grossberg, Cary Nelson, and Paula A. Treichler (New York: Routledge, 1992), 240–76; Scully, *Liberating the Family?* Introduction and ch. 2. On race and gender see also Persis Charles, "The Name of the Father: Women, Paternity and British Rule in Nineteenth Century Jamaica," *International Labor and Working Class History* 41 (1992): 4–41.

32. Mary Prince, *The History of Mary Prince, a West Indian Slave / Related by Herself*, ed. Moira Ferguson (Ann Arbor: University of Michigan Press, 1993).

33. Prince, *The History of Mary Prince*, 84.

34. Sueann Caulfield, *In Defense of Honor: Sexual Morality, Modernity and Nation in Early-Twentieth Century Brazil* (Durham: Duke University Press, 2000), 6.

35. Shula Marks, ed., *Not Either an Experimental Doll: The Separate World of Three South African Women* (London: Women's Press, 1987).

36. Marks, ed., *Not Either an Experimental Doll*, 209.

37. Luise White, *The Comforts of Home: Prostitution in Colonial Nairobi* (Chicago: University of Chicago Press, 1990); Buchi Emecheta, *The Joys of Motherhood* (Oxford: Heinemann International, 1988); Tsitsi Dangarembga's *Nervous Conditions* (Seattle: Seal Press, 1988).

38. Mrinalini Sinha, *Colonial Masculinity: The "Manly Englishman" and the "Effeminate Bengali" in the Late Nineteenth Century* (New York: St. Martin's Press, 1995).

39. Janaki Nair, "Uncovering the Zenana: Visions of Indian Womanhood in English-women's Writings, 1813–1940," in *Expanding the Boundaries of Women's History: Essays on Women in the Third World*, ed. Cheryl Johnson-Odim and Margaret Strobel (Bloomington: Indiana University Press), 29.

40. Yvette Abrahams, "Disempowered to Consent: Sara Bartman and Khoisan Slavery in the Nineteenth-Century Cape Colony and Britain," *South African Historical Journal* 35 (Nov. 1996): 89–114.

41. Quoted in *The Life and Times of Sara Baartman: "The Hottentot Venus,"* videorecording directed by Zola Maseko (New York: First Run Icarus Films, 1998).

42. Yvette Abrahams, in *The Life and Times of Sara Baartman*.

43. Susan Thorne, "'The Conversion of Englishmen and the Conversion of the World Inseparable': Missionary Imperialism and the Language of Class in Early Industrial Britain," in *Tensions of Empire: Colonial Cultures in a Bourgeois World*, ed. Frederick Cooper and Ann Laura Stoler (Berkeley: University of California Press, 1997), 238–62.

44. Anne McClintock, *Imperial Leather: Race, Gender and Sexuality in the Colonial Contest* (New York: Routledge, 1995).

45. During the twentieth century, the linkages already being developed in European culture between race, racism, and sexual science were, of course, elaborated in Nazi Germany. National socialist ideology linked ideas of social evolution and eugenics by categorizing people who did not fit the proposed ideal of the German male or female as unfit humans. As we know, that included people of Jewish descent, disabled individuals, gays and lesbians, and gypsies. As early as the 1930s, the Nazi state targeted homosexuals, both female and male, for elimination. In that decade, as Gisela Bock has outlined, the state passed a host of laws designed to prevent people considered inferior from having children. The sterilization law that aimed at preventing "lives unworthy of life," for example, came into effect in 1934. The next year, a law was introduced that allowed doctors to abort fetuses on racial grounds. If a woman was declared to be racially unfit, according to the logic of Nazi racial science, she was also sterilized.

46. Jeremy Martens, "Settler Homes, Manhood and 'Houseboys': An Analysis of Natal's Rape Scare of 1886," *Journal of Southern African Studies* 28 (June 2002): 379–400.

47. Personal communication with the author.

48. Henry Rider Haggard, *King Solomon's Mines* (New York: Oxford University Press, 1998).

49. Antoinette Burton, *Burdens of History: British Feminists, Indian Women and Imperial Culture, 1865–1915* (Chapel Hill: University of North Carolina Press, 1994), 63.

50. Pamela Scully, "White Maternity and Black Infancy: The Rhetoric of Race in the South African Women's Suffrage Movement, 1895–1930," in *Women's Suffrage in the British Empire: Citizenship, Nation, and Race,* ed. Ian Christopher Fletcher, Laura E. Nym Mayhall, and Philippa Levine (London: Routledge, 2000), 68–84.

51. Iris Berger, "An African American 'Mother of the Nation': Madie Hall Xuma in South Africa, 1940–1963," *Journal of Southern African Studies* 27, no. 3 (2001): 547–66.

52. Cited in Berger, "An African American 'Mother of the Nation,'" 555.

53. Ibid., 557.

6

Gender and Nation

MRINALINA SINHA

What does gender have to do with the study of the nation or nation with the study of gender? We might try to get at this question by pausing to consider, in the aftermath of the terrorist attack on New York and Washington, D.C., and the U.S. retaliation against the government in Afghanistan, a topical political cartoon by Pulitzer Prize–winning cartoonist Ann Telnaes, in a series entitled "Women and the Taliban."[1] The cartoon depicts a man representing the Taliban, staring at the famous World War II U.S. poster of Rosie the Riveter, flexing her muscles in a show of strength, with the words "We can do it." In the next frame, the man has painted over the poster in black, leaving only the woman's eyes uncovered.

We may be tempted to read the cartoon simply in terms of a "clash of civilizations" or as the essential marks of national or cultural difference.[2] Such a reading, however, would willfully ignore a complex history that includes the post–World War II backlash in the United States against the gender politics represented by Rosie the Riveter and the impact of the cold war between the United States and the former Soviet Union on the rise of the Taliban in Afghanistan.

My aim, however, is a much more limited one. What is striking is that the intelligibility of this cartoon depends precisely on the convergence between the apparently discrete domains of gender and of the nation. As such, therefore, women become immediately identifiable icons of their nations, gender politics becomes entangled in national politics and in the politics of war, and

"Taliban Painting over Rosie the Riveter" by Anne Telnaes. (Copyright 2002, Tribune Media Services, Inc. All Rights Reserved; Reprinted with Permission)

the boundaries of religious/cultural/national identity become defined through the mobilization of, or restrictions on, women. If the domain of the nation and gender are not so discrete after all, then what do we assume about nations and gender that inclines us to study them separately? How much does the assumption that gender has little to do with the "important" questions concerning national politics shape an understanding of nationalism? These are some of the questions that the contemporary scholarship on gender and nation is beginning to address.

Increasingly sophisticated scholarship on the nation as a historical construct (rather than a timeless community) has proliferated since the late twentieth century. That boom in scholarship coincides, on the one hand, with increased globalization and the consequent transformation of the traditional domain of the nation-state through immigration and the conspicuous transnationalization of economic forces. On the other hand, it also coincides with the simultaneous resurgence of nationalism at the close of the century in post-Soviet Europe as well as in other areas around the world.[3]

One of the most promising developments to emerge from this recent spate of scholarship has been the recognition of the extent to which gendered discourses have informed nations and nationalisms. In the wake of more than a decade of feminist scholarship on the subject it is no longer possible to ignore that nations have been, and are, constituted around culturally specific constructions of gender difference. This scholarship has gone a long way toward not only establishing the gendered character of the nation but also suggesting the mutual constitution of discourses of the nation and of modern gender identities themselves. It has been no coincidence, as some scholars have suggested, that attachments to modern gender and national identities have developed together and reinforced each other. What has followed is precisely a questioning of the seeming "naturalness" of, and an establishment of the connections between, the almost ubiquitous construction of people's identities in the modern world along the lines of gender and national difference.

Not so long ago, it would have been difficult to foresee the emergence of even this fragile scholarly consensus on the connections between discourses of gender and the nation. That was partly because, until the 1980s, much of the scholarship on both gender and nation had developed along separate and independent lines. Most theories of nationalism were thus quite content with an apparently gender-neutral analysis of the subject. On the one hand, this scholarship tended to minimize the contribution of women, whether in nationalist movements or in the construction and maintenance of national identities and communities, and to assume that the experience of modern nationhood was basically similar for men and women. On the other hand, this apparently gender-neutral analysis of nationalism treated men and masculinity as unmarked "universal" categories and tended to ignore the ways in which nationalism constitutes both "men" and "women."[4] While some were willing to acknowledge that gender, like race, class, and ethnicity, was a constituent element of the nation, they, too, tended to underestimate the potential of gender as a category of analysis.[5]

It was the scholars who wrote about anticolonial nationalisms who took the lead in calling attention to the significance of gender. Frantz Fanon's work on anticolonial Algerian nationalism was at least willing to recognize the symbolic significance of gender difference, despite his somewhat problematic treatment of the subject, in the struggle for independence from French colonial rule.[6] Fanon demonstrates how the French, in the name of protecting veiled Algerian woman from Algerian men, consolidated and legitimized colonial power over Algerian society. The French, therefore, were unprepared when they confronted modern Algerian women who chose to ally with the anticolonial movement against the French.

For the most part, however, theorists of nationalism have been slow to follow Fanon's lead in exploring the implications of gender difference for the analysis of nationalism. It would take more than a decade or so of feminist scholarship before the significance of gender was recognized for the study of the nation in metropolitan as much as in colonized and semiperipheral parts of the world.

If the scholarship on nationalism had demonstrated a certain indifference to gender as a category of analysis, feminist scholarship was equally guilty of neglecting the study of the nation and of nationalism. That was especially true of certain strands within feminist scholarship shaped by an assumption of the apparent naturalness of the nation for women in North America and Northwestern Europe. This scholarship tended to assume that women's relation to the nation was best summed up in that famous quotation from a character in Virginia Woolf's novel *Three Guineas:* "[A]s a woman I have no country. As a woman I want no country. As a woman my country is the whole world."[7]

The quotation invokes, of course, the history of Europe and North America, where women had to wage a separate struggle for the right to vote and to be included as citizens of the nation. On the basis of this particular history, moreover, the quotation also assumes that feminism has an apparently natural antipathy for, and an ability to transcend, the nation. A feminist scholarship that took this history as axiomatic tended to dismiss the salience of the nation and of nationalism for women and for feminism.

Here again, it was feminist scholarship of the "third world" (the colonized and semiperipheral areas of the world) that took the lead in engaging the study of nationalism as a feminist concern. Women's engagement in nationalist struggles against imperialism often led to a very different trajectory for feminism in the third world. At roughly the same time as the publication of Woolf's *Three Guineas,* for example, the anticolonial nationalist struggle in India produced a different dynamics for bourgeois women's investment in the nation. The dynamics of this relation were nicely captured in a popular nationalist slogan: "India cannot be free until its women are free and women cannot be free until India is free." In many colonized and semiperipheral areas of the world, the struggle for women's emancipation occurred in tandem with anticolonial nationalist struggles. It should come as no surprise, therefore, that third-world feminist scholarship once again was at the forefront in engaging with the phenomenon of nationalism.[8] More recently, feminist scholarship more generally has recognized the equally important ways in which the nation has also shaped, and been shaped by, gender relations and gender identities in the older, more established nation-states of the world. Indeed, the history of anticolonial nationalisms has played a formative role in shaping the scholarly agenda on gender and nation more generally.

What follows is a review of more than a decade of scholarship that has brought the study of gender and of the nation together and demonstrated the critical interdependence of the two. This essay is divided into three sections. The first consists of a brief historiographical overview of this contemporary scholarship on gender and the nation. This section aims to be neither exhaustive nor comprehensive. Rather, it identifies certain interpretive trends of the last several decades that have made possible the contemporary historiographical conjuncture in which gender has emerged as an important category of analysis for the study of the nation.

The second section describes how this scholarship provides new ways of conceiving the nation and its impact on, and investment in, particular constructions of masculinity and femininity. It also makes clear, however, that the ideological work of gender never rests simply on the construction of sexual difference itself. Gender is always already constituted by other forms of difference, such as those of class, race, ethnicity, religion, and sexuality as well as, of course, the nation.

The concluding section reflects on the potential of the scholarship on gender and the nation and points toward some possible directions for its future. It cautions against an a priori privileging of gender difference even when it incorporates divisions of class, race, ethnicity, and so on over other forms of organizing difference in the articulation of the nation at any given historical moment. These various categories of difference are neither equivalent nor identically constituted. The ways they mutually constitute or undercut each other can be examined only in concrete historical situations.

Historiographical Overview

The trajectory of the scholarship on nationalism has been well documented in a whole flurry of recent "readers" and anthologies on nationalism.[9] These compilations have conveniently reprinted various extracts from, as well as provided useful surveys of, important landmarks in this scholarship from the writings of Lord Acton in the nineteenth-century to that of late-twentieth-century theorists. Regrettably, however, many of these general surveys still continue to treat gender analysis as marginal and confine it, at best, to a chapter of its own, where its implications for recasting the study of the nation—and nationalism as a whole—remains safely contained. Fortunately, numerous articles, special issues of journals, and anthologies as well as monographs challenge this marginalization of gender from the study of nationalism and testify to the arrival of a rich new body of scholarship that takes the concept of "gendered nations" as the basis of analysis.[10]

Yet for all of this proliferation of scholarship, the nation itself remains a protean phenomenon that continues to elude easy scholarly generalizations. Because scholarship on gender is equally extensive and diverse, it may be useful to start with certain definitional clarifications.

DEFINITIONAL CLARIFICATIONS

Contemporary scholarship proceeds from an underlying assumption that both genders and nations are socially constructed around ideological systems of "difference" that implicate them in relations of social power. There are certain key terms in this scholarship, however, that may still need some broad clarifications. The *nation* may be defined as a group whose members, on the basis of some combination of beliefs in a common origin, a common history, and a common destiny, constitute themselves as a community and lay claim to a specified territory and political representation, ranging from cultural autonomy to political statehood. There is, however, no one universal and inevitable form of the nation. Nations are necessarily constructed around a myth of their own uniqueness.

The closest thing to a broad understanding of the nation, perhaps, is Benedict Anderson's characterization of nations as *limited imagined communities*. Nations are always limited because even the largest of nations has "finite, if elastic boundaries, beyond which lie other nations." They are necessarily imagined because the "members of even the smallest nation will never know most of their fellow-members, meet them, or even hear of them, yet in the minds of each lives the image of their communion." Nations also function as communities "because, regardless of the actual inequality and exploitation that may prevail in each, the nation is always conceived as a deep, horizontal comradeship."[11] This broad understanding of the nation provides a helpful framework for identifying the specificity of the nation as a community and its investment in gender difference.

That understanding of the nation also provides the basis for some broad definitions of such related terms as *nationalism, national identity, citizenship,* and the *nation-state.* The term *nationalism* has been used variously to cover any or all of the following: "the whole process of nation-building; a sense of national consciousness or sentiment; a symbolic and linguistic representation of the nation; an ideology; and a movement intended to realize the national will."[12] In its most general sense, therefore, scholars have defined nationalism to include both the belief in nationhood and the goal to establish statehood for the nation. The definitions of "national identity" emphasize that it is "constructed" and subject to a continuous process of articulations and rearticulations. Because the construction of national identity does not "depend on the existence of any objective linguistic or cultural differentiation but on the subjective experience of difference," it necessarily entails a continuous process of defining itself against a host of "others."[13] "Citizenship," likewise, is a "slippery concept"; it works through implicit and explicit mechanisms to exclude various groups from full citizenship, both within and from without the nation-state. The term may be broadly defined to refer to the status bestowed on those who are "full members of a community," which includes political, social, and economic rights and duties. As such, therefore, it goes beyond the legal rules that govern an individual's relationship to the nation-state to include the social relationships between individuals and the state and between individual citizens.[14]

The relation between the terms *nation* and *state* requires a little more clarification. Most scholars are at pains to point out that the two terms are in no way synonymous and should be kept analytically distinct.[15] The frequent conflation of the two terms—through an obliteration of the hyphen from the term *nation-state*—leads to considerable confusion. The state is never an automatic political extension of the nation; the fit between nation and state, in fact, is never perfect. Even the most seemingly homogenous nation-states contain within their borders people who are only partially, if at all, integrated into the hegemonic construction of the nation. Furthermore, the boundaries of a national community—as in the contemporary example of the Kurds or of nationals who live outside their specified countries—may cut across the political boundaries of a state. Finally, there are stateless nations and multinational states.

The preservation of the analytical separation between nation and state is important for any number of reasons, not the least of which is that their conflation has the effect of naturalizing the "invisibility" of certain groups and overlooking the different incorporation of groups in the nation and under the state. The history of German Jews with respect to the German nation and the German state is a case in point. Although "Jewish emancipation" in the German states occurred during the period of German national unification, the political inclusion of German Jews (in gender-specific ways) in the German state apparatus did not necessarily entail full incorporation into the German nation, which was imagined as a German *Volksfamilie* (folk family). German Jewish men, therefore, found themselves vulnerable to anti-Semitic charges that officially singled them out and cast doubts on the extent of their military contribution to the German effort in World War I. German Jewish veterans, who as men shared certain gendered rights and duties with non-Jewish German men under the German state, found both their German masculinity and their sense of belonging in the German nation under attack by anti-Semitic suspicions.[16] The analytical separation between nation and state is of special concern to scholars interested in exposing the invisibility of different groups in hegemonic constructions of the nation.

The meaning of "gender," like that of the nation, is the subject of scholarly debate. Since the 1980s, however, gender has emerged as an important "category of analysis" that is a constitutive element of all social relationships based on perceived differences between sexes as well as a primary way of signifying relationships of power.[17] Feminist scholars, of course, have long been accustomed to thinking in terms of a "sex-gender" system.[18] Here "sex" refers to the biological differences between male and female, and "gender" refers to the social meaning attached to these biological differences in culturally specific notions of masculinity and femininity.

The relation between socially constructed gender difference and biological sexual difference, however tenuous, has been demonstrated in contemporary feminist scholarship to be even further attenuated than was once assumed. Increasingly, scholars are demonstrating that the construction of biological sexual difference is no less social and ideological than that of gender. There was a gradual shift in the modern period, as some scholars have argued, from a basically "one-sex model" (in which a woman's body was widely considered to be simply a lesser homologue of a man's body) to a "two-sex model" (promoted in medical science, anatomy, and physiology) that constructed a woman's body as the polar opposite of a man's.[19] The historical emergence of a rigidly dichotomized understanding of biological sexual difference complicates the status of biological sex as a "natural" anchor for gender difference.

Hence newer feminist scholarship has demonstrated that "male" and "female," no less than "masculinity" and "femininity," are socially constructed categories. Indeed, an influential branch of feminist scholarship claims that "sex" is not the presocial category that lies behind or anchors "gender difference," but that the social and ideological elaboration of gender itself produces the binary construction of "sex." The implication is that gender is reproduced socially through regulated acts of repetition or "performativity." These repeated performances—rather than biology—are what constitute gender identities.[20]

The notion that gender is constituted through performativity has the effect of divorcing gender from biological sex and making the link between masculinity and the biological "male" and between femininity and the biological "female" historical and contingent rather than necessary or inevitable. Thus the grounding of masculinity and femininity around attributes of biological maleness and femaleness, respectively—a process in which the gendered discourse of nationalism has played an important role—has emerged as a subject for historical interrogation. As feminist scholarship is beginning to demonstrate, nations are produced by the repeated performances of certain gendered norms and behaviors such as militarism and sacrifice, honor and shame, sexual purity and impurity, and so on. The repetition of these gendered performances for the sake of the nation, in turn, helps construct gender and sexuality.[21] The contribution of nationalist discourses to the "performance" of certain notions of masculinity and femininity has thus emerged as an important arena for examining the construction of gender identities themselves.

INTERPRETIVE TRENDS

Scholars continue to debate many of the key issues in the study of nationalism: the origin and timing of its emergence; the reasons for, and mechanisms of, its spread; and the nature and classification of different types of nationalisms. These debates notwithstanding, it is possible to identify certain broad interpretive trends that have emerged in the scholarship in the last several decades. These trends may be summarized briefly as follows:

THE "INVENTED" CHARACTER OF NATIONS At least since the 1960s, scholars have emphasized the constructed or "invented" nature of the nation that is not a direct product of objective sociological criteria of language, religion, or other such commonalities. Rather, nations depend on critical intellectual and cultural mediation before people consider themselves as part of a single national community or before religious, ethnic, regional, or peasant-communal identities and communities are reshaped in distinctly "national" ways. Far from resting on a secure natural foundation, therefore, nations arise out of creative acts of human labor or imagination, including the emergence of national bureaucracies and communication systems; the creation of national histories and nationwide educational systems; and the spread of national myths, rituals, and "invented traditions" that masquerade as timeless.[22]

This view, of course, does not deny that nations are "real" in that they become instituted and renewed through countless ordinary, and extraordinary, practices that insinuate a nation into the very structure of society and the collective consciousness of people. Instead, it emphasizes the role of invention—both in the sense of fabrication and in the sense of the novel recombination of existing elements—that is necessary for the formation of national communities. Feminist scholarship has usefully pushed the analysis of the "invented" character of the nation to demonstrate its reliance on the discourse of gender. If nations are not natural, then their self-representation through gendered language and imagery acquires new significance. So, for example, the preponderance of female personifications in the representations of the nation—as in Germania (Germany), Marianne (France), or Mother India—require explanation.

THE "MODERNITY" OF NATIONS Scholars also emphasize the "modernity" of the nation.[23] If nations are indeed not "natural" but invented or imagined communities, then they would seem to require certain infrastructure and particular tools or mechanisms that create both the demand for, and the possibility of, such inventions.[24] The origins of nationalism have been linked to a given epoch in European history—the "ruptures of the eighteenth century"—from where it spread via European imperialism and colonialism to the rest of the world.

In this view, the nation both reflects and shapes the various intellectual, cultural, economic, social, and political changes in the transition from the premodern to the modern world. Yet precisely because of their relatively recent histories, most nations lay claim to a mythical continuity with an ancient and immemorial past, typically a retrospective invention. Nations, after all, cannot be conjured out of nothing. The acts of national imagination always select and reshape a variety of preexisting cultural traditions and premodern communities that provide the raw material out of which national communities are imagined.[25]

Clearly, then, the "novelty" and modernity of a nation exists in creative tension with its reliance on selected preexisting attachments and traditions. This emphasis on the historicity of the nation has allowed feminist scholars to explore its convergence with other modern developments such as the rise of a new discourse of sexuality in the early modern period or the spread of notions of bourgeois respectability from the late eighteenth century onward.[26] It has brought attention to the parallel, and interconnected, development of modern discourses of gender and nation.

NATIONS AS "CULTURAL ARTIFACTS"   Contemporary theorists of nationalism also emphasize cultural analysis and the cultural domain in the formation of nations.[27] If earlier scholars seemed primarily concerned with nationalism as a political ideology or with the social history of nation-building, contemporary scholars seem interested in the nation as a cultural artifact and in nationalism as a sentiment that constructs individual and collective identities.

The cultural reproduction and the cultural meaning of the nation have thus emerged as increasingly central in the scholarship on nationalism. It has provided new significance to a myriad of cultural forms, such as newspapers, novels, poems, songs, art, architecture, films, public rituals, and commemorations as vehicles for national imaginings.[28] It has also brought increased attention not just to the creative labor of intellectuals and political elites but also to the contributions of ordinary men and women as transmitters of the cultural values of the nation. Because women are often constructed as the symbolic "bodyguards" of a culture, those who carry the group's "honor" and are responsible for the intergenerational reproduction of its culture, they cannot be marginalized easily from cultural analyses of the nation.[29]

NATIONS AND THE "RULE OF COLONIAL DIFFERENCE"   Scholars have also emphasized the legacy of imperialism and colonialism to reframe the study of the nation in both the metropole and the colony. They argue that the history of nationalism has been directly implicated in the project of European domination of the world. As such, therefore, the "rule of colonial difference" (the maintenance of a supposedly essential difference of the rulers from the ruled) has shaped the history of the nation in the metropole as much as in the colony.[30] The direction of imperial influence flowed not just from the metropole to the colony but also in the reverse. We can, for example, learn much about the ideals of republican citizenship in revolutionary France by studying it in the context of the slave revolts in the Caribbean that expanded and tested the limits of its universalist principles.[31]

The further point, however, is that nationalisms in the colonial world did not simply replicate the "modular" form of the nation as it had been previously imagined elsewhere in Europe and the New World. The discourse of anticolonial nationalism, precisely because it was a belated and "derivative discourse," sought to construct its own nationhood not through identification with—but through a difference from—the "modular" forms of the national society in the modern West.[32]

The real imaginative labor of anticolonial nationalism, therefore, lay in constructing its project as "different but modern" in relation to the modern West. In so doing, the project of anticolonial nationalism was often mediated through a logic of gender difference. The discourse of Indian nationalism, for example, produced the figure of the "modern Indian woman" as the unique signifier of Indianness and of the national culture's absolute difference from the West. This scholarship has thus contributed in making gender central to the analysis of the nation.

NATIONS AS CONSTITUTED BY "DIFFERENCE" Finally, some scholars have built on, and extended, the idea of the cultural construction of nations by analyzing the nation as a "text" that is constructed through narrative processes.[33] Their most important contribution has been to reverse the underlying point that previous scholarship seemed to take for granted: the unifying potential of the nation. Instead, this scholarship underscores the ambivalence that marks the discourse of the nation. The narrative of the nation, because of its lack of a secure "natural" foundation, is constituted through the simultaneous acknowledgement and disavowal of "difference," both within and outside the boundaries of the nation.

Even as national narratives obsessively construct a unified and coherent "us," they remain caught by the ever-present threat of "difference" in their midst. We see this, for example, in the elaborate mechanisms for handling the ambiguities of racial gradations in the Jim Crow United States or apartheid South Africa. This constitutive ambivalence—the simultaneous recognition and disavowal of difference—makes for national narratives that are inherently unstable and for nationalist projects that always remain incomplete.

This approach squarely places the problem of difference—the construction of an "us" versus "them"—at the foundation of the nation. In so doing, moreover, it brings the various "margins" of the nations, defined through differences of gender, class, race, sexuality, religion, ethnicity, to the center of any analysis of the nation. Its further contribution has been to demonstrate the similarity in the discourses of the nation and of gender. To the extent to which nationality is always "a relational term whose identity derives from its inherence in a system of difference," it has a great deal in common with the discourse of gender. "In the same way that 'man' and 'woman' define themselves reciprocally (though never symmetrically), national identity is determined not on the basis of its own intrinsic properties but as a function of what it (presumably) is not."[34] In short, nations, like genders, are defined only through a construction of their "difference" from others.

CONTRIBUTIONS OF FEMINIST SCHOLARSHIP

The potential of these various historiographical developments notwithstanding, it was left to feminist scholars to assert the importance of gender as a category of analysis in the scholarship on nationalism. This rapidly growing scholarship has recast the understanding of the nation in a number of important ways. Given the pervasiveness of gendered imagery and gendered language in the self-representation of nations, feminist scholars have attempted to understand the reasons for the gender blindness of most theories of nationalism. The unselfconscious repetition of gendered imagery in many of the theories of nationalism has itself contributed in naturalizing the gendered discourse of the nation. One reason for the gender-blindness of much of the scholarship on nationalism has to do with the axiomatic status that the division of modern civil society into a public political domain and a private familial or conjugal domain has acquired in theories of Western politics and society.[35]

Much of the scholarship on nationalism—despite the contributions of feminist scholarship—associated nationalism typically with the domain of the "public," from which women have been excluded, and women with the domain of the "private." The contribution of women to the construction and maintenance of national communities and national identities was thus minimized in this allegedly gender-neutral scholarship on nationalism. Yet as feminist scholarship has long demonstrated, the origins and separation of the modern domains of the public and private were not "natural." The thrust of both feminist theoretical and historical scholarship has been to demonstrate a much more contingent, and interconnected, history of the gendered divisions of the modern public and private.

The constitution of the modern domains of the public and the private took place on the basis of a prior "sexual contract," which gendered these domains masculine and feminine, respectively.[36] The new public sphere in postrevolutionary France, for example, emerged as the result of a deliberate—and not just accidental—exclusion of women from the public and their relegation to a new domain of the private.[37] The postrevolutionary backlash against women in public included an attack against the salons run by aristocratic and *haute bourgeois* women precisely for confounding the newly legitimated boundaries between the gendered "public" and "private."

The ideological construction of gender difference, therefore, has historically shaped the modern "public" world of politics as much as it has the "private" world of familial relations in large parts of the world that came to be constituted as the "West." It would seem to follow, then, that even when scholars choose to limit their study of the nation only to the domain of the public, they do their work a disservice by ignoring the dependency of the modern public on the domain of the private as well as the historical contingency of their respective gendered constructions.

Furthermore, the persistence of apparently gender-neutral theories of nationalism also reflects the extent to which an ideological construction of gender difference—grounded on a supposedly natural two-sex model of biological sexual difference—has become so naturalized as not to warrant any attention. By now, however, too much scholarship has challenged the fixity of gender and the seeming self-evidence of the categories "woman" and "man" to take the gendered constructions of nationalist discourses at face value. This would mean that such terms as *mother tongue*, which is not necessarily the language of one's "real" mother, would need to be analyzed rather than taken as "natural."[38]

When scholars fail to interrogate the pervasiveness of gendered imagery in nationalist discourse, they miss the important role of nationalism itself in consolidating, and contributing to, the constitution of "men" and "women" and of "masculinity" and "femininity." Feminist scholarship on the nation has thus offered important challenges to the theoretical assumptions and methodologies that have hitherto dominated the scholarship on nationalism.

One important contribution of feminist scholarship has been the considerable body of work on women and the nation that reverses the neglect of women by previous scholarship on nationalism. This scholarship has demonstrated women's contributions to, and the nature of women's integration in, the project of modern nationhood. Although women may have been marginalized from the domain of the public, they have clearly played a significant role in the production and maintenance of national communities and national identities all over the world. Women, for example, are conspicuous in nationalist discourses as symbols of national culture and, through the control of women's sexuality, as the markers of community boundaries. Hence concerns about interracial and intercommunal sexual relations have typically centered on the access to, and availability of, women.

The most visible contribution of women to nationalist projects, of course, has been the mobilization of women, along with men, as active participants in various nationalist projects. From the peasant women whose bread riots ignited the French Revolution (1789) and the Russian Revolution (1917) to the contribution of elite and bourgeois women in various nationalist movements, the range of women's activities has been varied. Women have contributed to social reform and public education movements, they have participated in various public rituals and protests that constitute the "national public," and they have mobilized on behalf of national liberation and revolutionary struggles.

A Japanese journalist who witnessed the 1911 uprisings that brought down the Qing dynasty in China was impressed by the impact of the nationalist project on middle-class women. Compared with "modern Chinese women," he wrote, "the militant London suffragette is nothing. Daily she supplies arms and ammunitions to her brother revolutionaries and is occasionally arrested with her tunic lined with dynamite."[39] At times, moreover, women's contributions to the nationalist struggle have been more radical than men's. During the Irish Land War in 1881 and 1882, for example, the uncompromising stand of Anna Parnell's Ladies Land League, with its membership extending from Catholic middle-class to peasant women, against evictions and in favor of Irish self-determination became an embarrassment to many of the male leaders who were ready to compromise with the British.[40] Similarly, women fought alongside men as guerillas in the Land and Freedom Army during the Mau Mau uprising in Kenya (1952–59). For Elizabeth Gachika, who was in the guerilla camps in the Nyandura forest from 1952 to 1953, the experience challenged traditional gender roles: "We were doing just like men. We could shoot and so forth . . . I shot many [Europeans] . . . I went with the men on the raids."[41] Equally significant, however, is the invocation of the supposedly "traditional" roles of women—as mothers, as objects of reverence and of protection, and as signifiers or markers of a group's innermost identity—in projects of nationalism.

Feminist scholarship, indeed, has demonstrated a variety of ways in which women contribute to the project of the nation:

— as biological reproducers of the members of ethnic collectivities;
— as reproducers of the boundaries of ethnic/national groups;

— as participants in the ideological reproduction of the collectivity and as transmitters of its culture;
— as signifiers of ethnic/national difference—as a focus and symbol in ideological discourses used in the construction, reproduction, and transformation of ethnic/national categories; and
— as participants in national, economic, political, and military struggles.[42]

Yet women are themselves always differentiated by race, class, age, education, religion, ethnicity, and urban/rural residence, all of which affect the nature and extent to which they are included in the national embrace. Their contributions and commitments to the nation have been shaped not just by their difference from men but by differences among women themselves. Insofar as this scholarship has focused on women and their relation to the nation it has also raised important questions about the implications of nationalist projects for women. While some scholars emphasize the oppressive results of nationalism on women, others focus on the contribution of nationalism in creating a space for the empowerment of women. What this scholarship, despite its difference in emphasis, seems to suggest is that women's experience of the project of modern nationhood has been distinct from that of men's.

Because gender is not a synonym for women, however, a gendered analysis of the nation does not rest simply on making women visible in the project of nationalism. The challenge posed by feminist scholarship has to do not just with the visibility of "women" but, more important, with the constitution of the nation itself in the "sanctioned institutionalization of gender *difference*."[43] The discourse of the nation is implicated in particular elaborations of masculinity as much as of femininity. As such, it contributes to their normative constructions. It becomes a privileged vehicle in the consolidation of dichotomized notions of "men" and "women" and of "masculinity" and "femininity." We thus have "fathers" and "mothers," and "sons" and "daughters," of the nation, each with their own gendered rights and obligations. This is the sense in which the discourses of gender and the nation can be seen as symbiotic. On the one hand, national narratives rely heavily on the supposedly natural logic of gender differences to consolidate new political identities around the nation. On the other hand, the discourse of nationalism provides legitimacy to normative gendered constructions of masculinity and femininity.[44]

The concern of many a feminist scholar, therefore, has been as much with men and masculinity as with women and femininity.[45] Indeed, some scholars have argued that the nation—typically imagined as a gendered fraternity—is essentially a masculinist or a heterosexual male construct. Nationalisms, they argue, have "typically sprung from masculinized memory, masculinized humiliation and masculinized hope."[46] So, for example, nationalist movements often involve reasserting masculinity and reclaiming male honor, and moments of nationalist fervor frequently center around a remasculinization of national culture.[47] At the same time, as many studies have shown, women have enthusiastically supported the nation and nationalism. Although we may thus debate the extent to which nations are best understood as inherently masculinist constructs, nations in one form or another have relied on a discourse of gender difference. One of the "gender ironies" of nationalism, in fact, is that the nation, for all its emphasis on a "deep horizontal comradeship," constitutes its members differentially in distinctly gendered ways.[48]

The discourse of the nation is thus inevitably implicated in gender power. The hierarchical construction and institutionalization of gender difference in nationalist discourse has typically meant that the costs and benefits of nationhood and of national belonging fall unevenly on men and women. Even when nationalist projects have invited women to stand alongside men in sacrificing for the nation, they often reassert the "traditional" roles of women once the moment of national crisis is over. The nature and implications of the nation's constitution in gender difference have been the subject of some of the most sophisticated contemporary scholarship on the subject.

Gender itself is never constituted only through the ideological construction of sexual difference. One "becomes a woman," or for that matter a man, not just in opposition to members of the other sex but also in opposition to other women and to other men.[49] When President Theodore Roosevelt famously compared the "cowardly" and "selfish" woman who neglected her duty to be a mother with the man who "fears to do his duty in battle when the country calls him," his vision of the gendered national duties of Americans was based not just on a notion of sexual difference. His admonition, in fact, was directed very specifically to the "well-born white woman" who through "wilful sterility" was guilty of "race suicide."[50] "Womanhood" in Roosevelt's rhetoric of the nation, then, was already also a class-bound and racialized construct. Nations, indeed, are not only gendered but also simultaneously "raced" and constituted by other axes of difference. The discourse of race—the fiction of a "racial identity"—is no less constitutive than the discourse of gender in the construction of nations.[51]

The further point, however, is that the various axes of difference—of gender, race, ethnicity, class, sexuality, and of colonizer and colonized—are not only mutually constitutive but also differently constituted. Hence they often intersect in the articulation of nations in uneven and unpredictable ways. The construction of Australian national identity, for example, mobilized various forms of difference—colonizer versus colonized, elitist versus populist, urban versus rural, settlers versus indigenous populations, and men versus women—whose interaction played out in unexpected ways. The creation of the Commonwealth of Australia in 1901 from a federation of six former British colonies was frequently represented as the coming of age of a white Australian masculinity. On the one hand, the colonial context led to an elaboration of Australia's difference from the "mother-country" in a populist narrative of the nation around the "mateship" of rough and virile men in a white frontier society. The cultural representation of the nation was centered around a white masculinity that privileged the white "bushmen" at the expense of both non-Aboriginal and Aboriginal women as well as Aboriginal men. On the other hand, the heavily masculinist rhetoric of the nation was also tempered by the specific context of a colonial settler society. White Australian women were thus enfranchised only one year after the creation of the Commonwealth, well before their counterparts in Britain. The political rights and representation of white Australian women as "citizen mothers" was closely tied to a state apparatus designed to maintain a "white" Australia.[52]

To ignore the various modes of organizing "difference" in the articulation of the nation, therefore, would reproduce the "gender blindness of previous historians of nations and nationalism in another key."[53] One of the most challenging and rewarding agendas for feminist scholarship, indeed, has been to account for the mutual constitution, and the often contradictory and uneven mediation, of multiple axes of difference in the articulation of both genders and nations.

Major Themes

The gendered articulation of the nation—no less than its articulation in other forms of organizing difference—can be examined only in concrete historical situations. Nations and national identities are continuously being formed and reformed in relation to various categories of difference. All nations are gendered, but there is no one privileged narrative of the gendering of nations. At the same time, scholars have traditionally deployed various modes of classifying different types of nationalisms. The most common, perhaps, is the distinction made between the civic or political nationalism of the late-eighteenth and early-nineteenth century in the established states of Northwestern Europe and the later romantic or cultural nationalism in Central and Eastern Europe from the second half of the nineteenth century. This broad chronological and geographical categorization of different nationalisms is sometimes extended to include in the latter category the wave of decolonizing nationalisms in the second half of the twentieth century.

There are important reasons to distinguish among nationalist projects under an already established state, on the one hand, and insurgent nationalisms attempting to assert cultural autonomy or lay claim to political statehood, on the other.[54] Too often, however, the geographical and chronological classification of different types of nationalisms lead to overly simple evaluations of nationalisms as "good" in their early forms in Western Europe and as "bad" in their later incarnations elsewhere. The problems with such easy evaluations of different types of nationalisms are further compounded when gender is included in the analysis. Civic nationalisms, which are constituted around the liberal construct of citizenship, no less than romantic nationalisms, which are constituted around ethnic or cultural particularities, have historically used gendered forms of inclusion and exclusion in the nation.[55]

Yet, keeping in mind that different modes of constituting the nation emphasize different aspects of gender relations, some scholars have offered a broad threefold classificatory model for different nationalist projects:

> *Staatnation:* when political citizenship of specific states and in specific territories is the basis of the national collectivity;
> *Kulturnation:* when members of the national collectivity are identified with specific cultures or religions;
> *Volknation:* when the nation is constituted around the common origin of the people or their "race."[56]

Although the construction of nations around state citizenship may potentially be the most inclusive, all nationalist projects rely on different modes of gendered exclusions and inclusions. The Staatnation works through the gendered biases in the liberal construction of citizenship; the Kulturnation operates through gendered constructions of cultural and ethnic differences; and the Volknation is reproduced through an elaborate monitoring and control of women's reproductive capacities and of their sexuality. The point of such a classificatory model is not to suggest fixed characteristics of different nationalist movements but to focus on dimensions of nationalist projects that may become central, or may be promoted by different members of the same national collectivity, in any given historical moment. The attempt to universalize the gendered reproduction of nations—outside of concrete historical situations—is thus difficult if not futile.

Nevertheless, a decade or so of scholarship on the subject has offered some broad themes for analyzing the intersection between the discourses of gender and of the nation. These, for the sake of convenience, may be divided as the constitution of the nation in gender difference, the gendered modes of national belonging, and the relation between feminisms and nationalisms.

THE CONSTITUTION OF THE NATION IN GENDER DIFFERENCE

One of the most striking features of nationalist discourses, as numerous scholars have observed, is the pervasiveness of familial and gendered imagery. All nations are imagined as "domestic genealogies."[57] The very term *nation* comes from the Latin *natio* (to be born). People are "born" into a nation, and foreigners "adopt" a nation or are "naturalized" into national citizenship.[58] Individuals are assigned their place within the national family, and nations themselves belong within the global family of nations. The nation is often constituted as *Heimat* (homeland). The relations of people to specific lands, languages, cultures, or shared histories are expressed as motherlands or fatherlands, mother tongues, mother cultures, and "founding fathers" or "mothers of the nation." Feminist scholars, therefore, justifiably raise questions about the reasons for, and implications of, the ubiquitousness of gendered and familial imagery in nationalist discourses.

The family—constructed as a "natural" heterosexual and patriarchal unit—performs a variety of critical ideological services in the constitution of the nation. The first, perhaps most obvious, function is in representing the nation as an innate or organic community whose members, like those of the family, are constituted by "natural" ties rather than by mere accident or choice. The familial imagery thus offers the "invented" nation a powerful legitimizing language of naturalization. In order to do so, however, the institution of the family itself is first removed from history and made into a timeless and natural unit of social organization. The family is thus depoliticized in the discourse of the nation; it is constructed as prior to history and thus immune to political challenge or to change.[59]

The history of the nation, however, has been closely associated with a particular historical form of the family—the heterosexual bourgeois nuclear family—and the resulting normative constructions of sexuality and gender identities that sustain this family form. The history of their mutual reinforcement can be seen in their development in Europe. There, the rise of the middle class from the eighteenth century onward produced a unique differentiation of gender roles and a distinctive code of bourgeois "respectablity" that emphasized the control of sexual passions by both men and women and presented marriage as the only acceptable sexual relationship.[60] Nineteenth-century European nationalisms entered into a convenient marriage with bourgeois "respectability" and contributed to spreading its norms across classes. The norms of bourgeois sexual respectability, in turn, helped in the construction of the national community as a virile homosocial community whose "proper" male homosocial relations were secured through the identification and exclusion of homosexuality often figured as "effeminacy" or deviant.

The norms of sexual respectability also helped differentiate "pure" from "fallen" women. The former were constructed as the symbolic signifiers of the nation and deployed for the service of the nation in their "naturally" subordinate roles as dutiful mothers, wives, and daughters. In contrast to the "normal" sexuality of respectable men and women of the nation, European nationalisms associated "abnormal" sexuality with a variety of others—such as Jews, Africans, homosexuals, and so on—in their midst. Hence at the same time that white English womanhood was being desexualized, Sara Bartman, a Khoisan woman from the Cape of South Africa, could be brought to England and exhibited in public as an exotic specimen of exaggerated female sexuality.[61] The development of gendered European nationalisms sustained—and were themselves sustained by—the naturalization of a racialized bourgeois heterosexual and patriarchal family form.

The bourgeois ideology of gender, family, and sexuality was further sustained in the imperialist-nationalist projects of the nineteenth century. The norms of bourgeois domesticity and the resulting construction of gender difference in the colonies helped construct and maintain the ideological, economic, and political power of colonizing elites. The Western bourgeois ideal of gender difference was used as the yardstick of "civilization," and any deviation from it became further proof of the "backwardness" of indigenous people. Hence the *zenana* (secluded female quarters in certain elite Hindu and Muslim households in north India) was not the only object of the reforming zeal of British social reformers and missionaries in India. The *Marimakkathayam* (matrilineal traditions of the Nairs in southern India) were considered equally "primitive" for not conforming to the "proper" patriarchal gender-roles of the Victorian bourgeois family.[62]

The imposition of a Western bourgeois ideology of gender and family, moreover, informed such colonial initiatives as the British slave emancipation in the Western Cape of South Africa. The project of emancipation was shaped by the view of ostensibly "liberating the family" so free African men could take up their "proper" roles as fathers and heads of households, and free African women could, as wives and mothers, be brought under the natural authority of the male head of the family.[63] The pervasiveness of that ideal—to which many freed African men and women contributed—helped maintain the power of former slaveowners, missionaries, and the colonial state over African men and women even after emancipation. The ideology of gender, family, and sexuality similarly framed the colonial policies and practices of the other European nations, such as the French, the Dutch, and the Germans in their respective empires.[64] The marriage between European nationalisms and bourgeois respectability, therefore, was cemented not just in Europe but also in the imperial-nationalist process of "domesticating the empire."

The project of anticolonial nationalisms likewise deployed the bourgeois nuclear family—often constructed as distinctive through a selective appropriation of bourgeois Western forms and the adaptation of certain indigenous traditions—in its own discourse. Although national narratives from the third

world also deployed some version of the bourgeois nuclear family in constituting their own nationalist projects, these narratives were more transparent-
ly rooted in the structural transformations of elites. In other words, bourgeois
norms in the third world were not universalized—across classes—in quite the
same way as they were in nineteenth-century Europe.

The origins of modern Egyptian nationalism, for example, were closely
intertwined with the transformation of elites in the late nineteenth and early
twentieth century in Egypt.[65] The model of the bourgeois family—following the
demise of harem slavery that had been the mainstay of elite Ottoman-Egyptian
households—was the key to both these processes. On the one hand, the new
familial discourse reflected a new elite consolidation that was the result of the
upward mobility of native Egyptian elites and the "Egyptianizing" of older Ottoman-Egyptian elites. On the other, it was also the "building block" of the
modern Egyptian nation. The bourgeois family—especially through the emphasis on motherhood—offered a shared national narrative to Egyptian Copts and
Muslims and a myth of continuity for modern Egypt to the "golden ages" of the
Pharaonic past. The specifically bourgeois aspect of this process was, arguably,
more visible in the context of third-world nationalisms than in nineteenth-century European nationalisms. In the colonized world—and for a variety of complex reasons that have to do with the form of colonial capitalism—the bourgeoi-
sie was less able to represent its own interests as universal.[66]

The interconnection between national, gender, and sexual identities in
a range of nationalist projects has produced a powerful, mutually reinforcing discourse that renders these identities natural and innate. Indeed, at
moments of perceived crises the defense of national and of normative gender and sexual identities often become closely intertwined. Thus the rhetoric of anticommunism that gripped the United States at the height of the cold
war in the 1950s invoked the spectre of "Momism"—smothering mothers
guilty of weakening the manly resolve of their sons in the fight against communism—and of homosexuality as an alien and un-American infestation contracted from foreigners.[67] The pervasiveness of the links between political
subversives and homosexuals was echoed in the opening question of an article in *Life* magazine in 1964: "Do the homosexuals, like the Communists,
intend to bury us?"[68] When scholars ignore the significance of the trope of
the family for nationalist discourse, therefore, they not only foreclose an examination of the mutually reinforcing logic of nation, gender, and heterosexual identities but also underestimate the force of the representational labor
in constructing the nation—like the family—as timeless, natural, and organic.

The second, and related, function of the representation of nations as
domestic genealogies—replete with a cast of fathers, mothers, sons, and
daughters of the nation—is to provide the nation with its "instrumental pas-

sions."[69] The nation, for all its foundational ambivalence, has the capacity to inspire enormous passion and devotion from its members. Indeed, what intrigues scholars about nationalism is precisely that so many men and women have been willing not only to kill but also to die for their nation. Hence nationalism, as some scholars suggest, does not resemble modern political ideologies, like liberalism or conservatism. It is closer to the discourse of religion with its lure and promise of immortality or to the discourse of kinship and ethnicity with its emphasis on the inevitable, as opposed to the merely accidental, or chosen, connections between members of the collectivity.

The language of kinship plays a very important role in allowing the nation to appropriate for itself the kind of elemental passions hitherto associated with the ties of blood. Thus the nation in the form of an abused or humiliated mother appeals to her sons and daughters, albeit often in differently gendered ways, to come to her protection and restore her honor. Similarly, the nation as fatherland calls upon its sons and daughters to obey the father and fulfill their respective gendered duties to the nation. The representation of the nation through a language of love—an "eroticized nationalism"—helps account for the distinctiveness of nationalism as a discourse capable of arousing enormous passions from the members of nations.[70]

In this context, therefore, heterosexual desire is often mapped onto political desire as *amor patrie* (love of country). In Latin America during the nineteenth century, for example, romance novels inspired "passionate patriotism" toward the new nations.[71] The new national ideals in Latin America were reflected in tales of heterosexual desire and marriage. These "foundational fictions," through stories of love that conquers all, offered a figurative conciliation for the many political and social tensions that beset the new nation-states. Most often, perhaps, the nation is represented as a female body—"to love, to posses, and to protect"—in the discourse of nationalism. That was the form in which the nation was represented, for example, in nineteenth-century Iran.[72] Iranian nationalist discourse offered a new heterosexual love—transforming the tradition of the divine and homoerotic love of classical Perso-Islamic literature—in which the *vatan* (homeland/Iranian nation) was constructed as the female paramour of nationalist men. The image of the vatan as female lover coexisted with another, equally powerful, female incarnation of the vatan as mother. It is as female lover/mother that the vatan/Iran insinuated itself into the emotions of the people, with different implications, of course, for men and women's relation to this feminized nation. The eroticization of nationalism through the identification of the nation with a female body—and the prominence of metaphors of the feminine in the discourse of the nation—allowed women to create a place for themselves within the national family, and it also fixed them in certain relations within the national collectivity. The nation's hold on the emotions of people, indeed, would be hard to understand outside of its investment in gendered kinship relations and in the poetics of heterosexual love.

The further ideological work of the family is to make the various forms of hierarchies both within the nation and between nations seem "natural." Because the family is idealized as a domain in which individual members willingly subsume their interests within the supposedly unified interests of the family (as represented by the male head of household), it becomes a signifier of "hierarchy within unity" for the nation.[73] The myth of the family as a fundamental "unity," of course, is sustained in part through a belief in the allegedly natural subordination of women and children to adult men within the family. The nation's identification with the family to signify the fundamental "unity" of its own members similarly constructs the hierarchies of gender, class, race, and ethnicity within the national community as natural and thus without a history. The familial discourse serves precisely to leave the fundamental "unity" of the nation unchallenged even as actual social relations of power and exploitation divide the members of the nation.

This "family romance" glosses over relations of domination within the family as much as within the nation.[74] The use of the family ideal in the nationalist rhetoric of the United States—as in the rhetoric of "family values" and in the conceptualization of the U.S. nation-state as a national family—renders racial, class, gender, and heterosexual power within the nation as "natural" through invoking the gender and age hierarchies of the family. So, for example, the violence against certain groups, such as Native Americans, Mexican Americans, and African Americans, whose history in the United States was shaped by conquest and slavery rather than voluntary migration, becomes (like "domestic violence") invisible in the narrative of the national family. Similarly, the differential entitlements of citizenship—like birth order in a family— "naturally" privileges groups on the basis of their time of arrival in the United States.[75]

Age and gender hierarchies within a family were also frequently deployed in the context of a developmental narrative of colonial superiority to legitimate European domination abroad. The people of the colonized world were often represented as "children," or "childlike," who needed the benevolent and natural protection of European fathers—and occasionally of European mothers as well. The project of European imperialism and colonialism was thus incorporated within a familial discourse in which the self-representation of imperial nations was that of stern but kindly guardians over people as yet lacking requisite political maturity.

The lack of political maturity was sometimes also explained in explicitly gendered terms, as in the opposition of Sir Lepel Griffin, a diehard nineteenth-century British imperialist in India, to demands for political representation by either Englishwomen or Bengali men. Although he considered the possession of "feminine qualities" by both as grounds for their disqualification from political representation, he also noted an important difference between Englishwomen and Bengali men: "The characteristics of women which disqualify them for public life and its responsibilities are inherent in their sex and are worthy of honour, for to be womanly is the highest praise for women, as to be masculine is her worst reproach, but when men, [such] as the Bengalis are disqualified for political enfranchisement by the possession of essentially feminine characteristics, they must expect to be held in such contempt by stronger and braver races, who have fought for such liberties as they have won or retained."[76] The ideology of gender legitimated the exclusion of certain men as much as women, albeit differently, from political representation. The image of the family performs an important ideological service for the nation in representing a whole range of social inequalities—inside and outside the nation—as "natural" hierarchies. The nation, then, despite its social inequalities, can be represented as a community or a "deep horizontal comradeship."

Finally, the ideology of gender difference mediates the role of the nation as a "modern-Janus."[77] Janus was the Roman god who stood at the gates of people's homes, one head turned forward and another turned backward. The nation, too, has one face turned toward the future, representing the principle of novelty and change, and another face turned toward the past, embodying the principle of tradition and continuity. The nation thus "presents itself both as a modern project that melts and transforms traditional attachments in favor of new identities and as a reaffirmation of authentic cultural values culled from the depths of a presumed communal past."[78] The temporal contradiction of the nation—its paradoxical function as a force for both change and continuity—is negotiated, often in very complex ways, via the medium of gender difference.

One resolution of the "temporal anomaly" (the representation of the nation as both bearer of tradition and agent of modernity) has been through the identification of women with the "authentic body of national tradition" and of men with "national modernity."[79] The gendered history of the "national costume" in Icelandic and Norwegian nationalisms seems to reflect this pattern of the gendering of national tradition and modernity.[80] The nationalist project in both northern European countries in the late nineteenth century led to the "invention" of so-called traditional national costumes as the symbols of the nation. These were purportedly modeled on the rustic costume of peasants in the region but were, in fact, composites of various styles that, more accurately, amounted to nothing short of a nationalist invention.

In Norway, the national costume was initially worn both by men and women during the late-nineteenth century and became a powerful symbol of the nation. By the turn of the century, however, the wearing of the national costume became a preserve only of women. This occurred in the context of a shift in the class allegiance of the nationalist movement from the idealized rustic peasant to the progressive urban intellectual. The change in the significance of the national costume for men and women now came to represent the association of men with the force of nationalist progress and change and women with national continuity and tradition.

In Iceland, from the outset only women wore the national costume, which was designed by a man who explained it as a symbol of the nation as mother. It consisted of a tight corset that lifted women's breasts, representing the mountainous nature of Iceland; a full skirt that could be expanded during pregnancies, indicating the fertile plains and maternal womb of the nation; and an apron, pointing to the domestic duties of women. The costume for Icelandic women, which foregrounded women as mothers and emphasized their duties within the home, was in sharp contrast to the Western male suit preferred by middle-class Icelandic men and that reflected the variety of roles open to men in the modern nation.

During the early Meiji period in Japan, the Western-style short haircut became the site for a contestation over a similar association of women with national tradition and men with national modernity. The Japanese emperor, in keeping with the broader agenda of "Westernization," expressly encouraged men, especially the long-haired samurai, to cut their hair. A government ban in 1872, however, made the new short haircut illegal for women. When some Japanese feminists defied the ban and cut their hair and also discarded the traditional kimono for Western clothes, their defiance may be seen as a rejection of this gendered resolution of the "temporal anomaly" of the nation.[81]

Yet the resolution of the temporal anomaly of the nation through the gendered construction of tradition and modernity often takes on a much more complex form, especially in various third-world nationalisms. The figure of the "woman" occupies a more variable position within different nationalist projects. Womanhood has sometimes been used to signify the continuity and authenticity of national tradition (as in the previous examples from Norway, Iceland, and Japan); at others, it has been used to represent the backwardness of a past that is to be eschewed by the modernizing project of the nation.[82] Mustapha Kemal, for example, defined the modernity of the new Turkish nation through its distance from the backwardness of women in the past. In a speech in 1923 he declared, "A people which has decided to go forward and progress must realize [the emancipation of women] as quickly as possible. The failures in our past are due to the fact that we remained passive to the fate of women."[83] His project of nation-building, therefore, entailed the emancipation of women by decree from above.

In still other national projects, womanhood has been used to embody both the promise and the threat of modernity. This flexibility in the metaphorical role of women for the gendering of tradition and modernity is especially noted in various anticolonial nationalisms. This is, perhaps, itself a testimony of the complex ways in which the problem of tradition and modernity is recast in the context of colonialism and anticolonial nationalism.

The dilemma of anticolonial nationalisms was simultaneously to appropriate post-Enlightenment ideas of modernity and progress and assert the nation's cultural difference from the West.[84] The process entailed, as in the case of nineteenth-century Bengal, the construction of a spatial dichotomy in nationalist discourse between an inner/spiritual world, where the cultural authenticity of the nation was located, and an outer/material world, where the nation acknowledged its subordination to, and the need to borrow from, the modern West. This spatial division also acquired a gendered dimension in the division between the "Home" and the "World." Even the "home"—as the locus of the nation's authentic identity—was never in any simple way the site of static precolonial traditions. Instead, the middle-class Bengali "home" was subject to various reforms that included the selective appropriations of Western bourgeois domestic norms. In this context, the Bengali *bhadramahila* (respectable woman) was assigned a new identity in nationalist discourse that was defined against both the excesses of modernization associated with the Western and Westernized woman and the backwardness associated with peasant and lower-caste/class women in India. Only such a reformed and modern Indian woman—and not the "traditional" woman—could truly embody the cultural identity of the new nation in the making.

The role of women in various other third-world nationalisms demonstrates a similar complexity that goes beyond the mere alignment of women with static and unreformed tradition. Women—more often than not—have had to carry the more complex burden of representing the colonized nation's "betweenness" with respect to precolonial traditions and "Western" modernity.[85] The nationalist project both initiated women's access to modernity and set the limits of the desirable modernity for women. In this context, several early-twentieth-century feminists, such as Halide Edibe in Turkey or Hudá Sha'rawi in Egypt, constructed their dynamic public roles as a duty to the nation rather than as a right.[86] As signifiers of the nation, women needed to be modern, but they could not mark a complete break from tradition. The woman of the anticolonial nationalist imagination, then, was not necessarily a "traditional" woman. She was more likely the "modern-yet-modest" woman who both symbolized the nation and negotiated its tension between tradition and modernity.[87]

Even cultural-revivalist and fundamentalist movements in the third world are seldom traditionalist in any simple way. The call to tradition in these movements is more precisely a response to the modernization of gender relations and to the transformation of gender roles that have already been underway. As one scholar so aptly puts it, "if fundamentalists are calling for the return to the veil, it must be because women have been taking off the veil."[88] The fundamentalist attack against the modernization of gender roles, moreover, is often fueled by class tensions produced by the failure of socioeconomic development and the effects of neocolonialism. The critique of *gharbzahdegi* ("Westoxification") under Ayatollah Khomeini in the Islamic Republic of Iran, for example, reflected both gender and class conflict. The objects of that critique were mainly upper-middle-class and educated women, who, compared with poor and peasant women, had benefited under the previous Pahlavi regime.[89] The important point is that as the "true essence" of national and cultural identity—whether as signifiers of tradition or of modernity—women become vulnerable to different political agendas of the nation.

GENDERED MODES OF NATIONAL BELONGING

If the ideology of gender difference has been important in the constitution of the nation, then the nation has been equally important for the construction of gender and the performance of masculinity and femininity. Hence, as various scholars have demonstrated, the nation always relates to its members differently as "men" and "women." The project of modern nationhood has largely cast men as "metonymic" (as causes of national history) and women as "metaphorical" or symbolic (analogues of the national soul).[90] In other words, men are defined as consequential to the nation and as its agents, but women are defined as its iconic embodiments. The differential gendered construction of nationalist agency is illustrated in the mottoes of the Hitler youth movement. While boys were asked to "live faithfully; fight bravely; die laughing," girls were expected to "be faithful; be pure; be German."[91]

The trope of sacrifice—one of the most powerful in the narrative of the nation—is similarly gendered. Men are usually called to give their life or die for the nation, and women willingly to surrender their sons and husbands to die for the nation. To be sure, women have historically been agents in the project of the nation and, in some cases, have also died along with men on the battlefields for the sake of the nation. Vietnam, with a tradition of women leading armed resistance against foreign oppression going back to the famous Trung sisters (Trung Trac and Trung Nhi) in 39 C.E., produced a long list of women martyrs during all stages of its nationalist struggles against the Japanese, the French, and the United States.[92] Furthermore, not all men (and not all women) are constructed in similar ways in the project of the nation.

255

Yet the belief in the "natural" difference between men and women has been fairly constant in the constitution of nations, and the nation itself has helped construct the normative constructions of "men" and "women" and of "masculinity" and "femininity."

The focus on the nation as a site for the construction of gender difference has, first, called attention to the hitherto neglected question of the construction of "men" and "masculinity" in nationalist discourse. The nation is implicated in the construction of "men" in various ways. The nation itself is largely modeled as a brotherhood or a fraternity. This, of course, has never included all men. The homosociality of the national brotherhood has depended in large part on the exclusion of homosexuals and men otherwise constructed as deviants. The long tradition in European nationalism of the connection between the nation and male bonding reached its apotheosis in the construction of the German fascist state as a *Männerbund*.[93] The nation is not only imagined typically as a fraternity but is also defended and administered through predominantly homosocial institutions. In numerous ways, then, the project of nationhood constructs men as contiguous with each other in the making of the nation.

The discourse of nationalism, moreover, is an important site for the enactment of masculinity. The military—increasingly constructed since at least the second half of the seventeenth century in Europe as an exclusive masculine arena, from which women who traditionally accompanied soldiers to provision, cook, clean, and tend to the wounded were gradually excluded—has constituted a privileged arena in the construction of both modern masculinity and the modern nation.[94] In many cases, indeed, political rights for men have flowed directly from their eligibility to shed blood for the nation. The nationalist project, therefore, is often associated with the production of a militarized masculinity.

The discourse of Prussian nationalism during the anti-Napoleonic wars (1806–15) was founded on a gender order that assigned distinct and complementary roles to "manliness" (*Männlichkeit*) and "womanliness" (*Weiblichkeit*).[95] In the wake of Prussia's military defeat at the hands of the French in 1806 and 1807, the discourse of Prussian nationalism urged men to enlist in a "people's war" to "defend the fatherland" and reclaim German manliness, which was defined as different from and superior to the manliness of the French. The introduction of universal conscription during the Wars of Liberation, in the context of a gendered war rhetoric, was limited only to men and became the basis for the extension of civil rights and political citizenship to men. In this case, therefore, the production and demonstration of a militarized German masculinity was based on the defense of the nation. Yet this militarized German masculinity was also defined in relation to, and as a complement to, the proper "feminine" roles of German women.

The contours of patriotic masculinity, however, are also produced against, or through the self-conscious rejection of, the feminine or the feminized. That is reflected, for example, in the metamorphosis of Theodore Roosevelt from an "effete" and "weakling" New York state assemblyman to a powerful symbol of turn-of-the-nineteenth-century imperial U.S. masculinity.[96] Roosevelt's self-transformation—which began with his association with the Badlands of South Dakota and a new image as a "muscular cowboy"—was accomplished by bringing together the two dominant themes of turn-of-the-century U.S. nationalism: westward expansion and U.S. imperialism. Roosevelt's enthusiastic support of the so-called Spanish American War and the role of his "Rough Riders" captured both these themes of patriotic masculinity. The opponents of imperial U.S. intervention in the debate over the "Philippines question" were dismissed as "fossils" and "old women." The project of a patriotic imperial nationalism entailed production of a youthful virile manliness whose opponents were the effete, the feminized, and the old.

The production of nationalist masculinity in national discourse is also enacted via the control/protection of women. The politics of "colonial masculinity" (which informed both colonizers and colonized) in the British Empire illustrates the multiple dimensions in the performance of masculinity.[97] On the one hand, elite "white" British masculinity was constructed both through its difference from feminized or effeminate native men and through its role as the benevolent protector of women. The protection of "Oriental" women—the idea of "white men saving brown women from brown men"— was an important component in the self-definition of white British masculinity in the colonial context.[98] The real or imagined threat to white women from the alleged assaults of native men provided, perhaps, the most dramatic demonstrations of white imperial masculinity in the colonial domain. Even rumors of attacks on white women—as, for example, during the Rebellion of 1857–58 in India—produced a call to arms to white men to avenge the "honor" of the English race.[99] On the other hand, however, "native" men also sought to reclaim their honor and masculinity—from negative representations in colonial discourse—by claiming the right to control/protect "our" women from foreigners and foreign influence. The rhetoric of the protection of women as well as the protection of the nation—itself often represented as a woman— was thus an important component in the production of masculinity.

The nationalist constructions of "women" and "femininity," and women's complicity in those constructions, have also been the subject of much scholarly attention. Despite the historical marginalization of women from the sphere of formal national politics, women are not absent from the domain of the national public. Women, as members of the national family, enter the domain of the national public in numerous ways. The nationalist project assigns them roles not just in biological reproduction but in the larger social and cultural reproduction of the national collectivity. As such, women are called to perform certain important nationalist tasks, such as the preservation and transmission of the national language (the "mother tongue," as it were) and the national culture. Women have emerged as national actors—as mothers, educators, workers, and fighters—in various nationalist projects. The myriad ways in which they contribute to the nationalist project have been discussed. A further point, however, is that the construction of femininity within nationalist discourse has had important implications for women.

The pervasiveness of powerful female figures—especially the figure of the mother—in the discourse of nationalism provides an important context for understanding the cooperation and complicity of women with such constructions. The image of "motherhood," both in the cultural representation of the nation as "mother" and in women's roles as "mothers of the nation," has been among the most powerful and exalted images of the feminine. The dominant construction of women as mothers—as objects of both national reverence and protection—has been the most important way in which women have been integrated into various nationalist projects. In the United States, white women otherwise excluded from the construction of civic virtues in the young republic enjoyed a status as "republican mothers" who nurtured the heroic sons of the new nation.[100]

The complementary construction of machismo and *marianismo* in Latin America similarly emphasized the maternal qualities of women, mainly elite, white, and creole women in the national narratives of the various nations.[101] Yet this glorification of motherhood in nationalist discourse has also justified the exclusion of women from the civic virtues that made formal political participation in national politics possible. Nationalist projects, indeed, demonstrate tension between the exaltation of powerful female figures—especially the mother—and the marginalization of women from national politics.

The relationship between the exaltation of feminine images and the marginalization of women in nationalist projects, however, is not always so straightforward. Women have also successfully mobilized the construction of "motherhood" to stake their claims in national politics. Indeed, women are constructed by (and themselves construct the meaning of) motherhood in nationalist discourse. The meaning of motherhood is also constructed differently in different nationalist projects. In South Africa, for example, "motherhood" was deployed very differently, despite its superficial similarities, by the racially exclusive Afrikaner nationalist project and the multiracial nationalism of the African National Congress.[102] Whereas in the former the construction of motherhood remained limited to the domestic domain and did not engage the broader issues of women's situation, women in the African National Congress were able to deploy the focus on motherhood to raise general concerns about women's emancipation. Women in both nationalist projects were active in the articulation of motherhood and also deployed it to sanction their own participation in nationalist movements. The Argentine Madres de la Plaza de Mayo is, perhaps, the most famous example of women's mobilization of motherhood. This movement had counterparts not only in several Latin American countries reeling under the effects of military dictatorships in the 1970s but also in the Mothers Fronts in Sri Lanka in the 1980s.[103] Women powerfully invoked the image of "motherhood" to denounce political torture and the "disappearance" of political activists. In this sense, then, the construction of powerful female figures in nationalist projects may also empower the mobilization of women.

Yet—to the extent that constructions of "women" and "femininity" are closely bound with considerations of national/cultural identity—these constructions have important implications for women's experience of nationhood. For the sake of the nation, for example, women are often at the receiving end of a wide range of nationalist policies and practices, especially at moments of perceived national crises. The image of a vulnerable "white womanhood" as the embodiment of the honor and prestige of the white race was frequently invoked in colonial contexts to secure colonial power. It sanctioned a variety of colonial policies that entailed control of white women's sexuality in demarcating and policing racialized boundaries for the exercise of colonial power over native populations.[104] Similarly, the critique of modernization and westernization in fundamentalist and cultural revivalist movements is frequently articulated as a call for the "retraditionalization" of women. The systematic use of rape of "enemy" women as a nationalist strategy during times of war, as in the conflicts in Bangladesh in 1971 and in Bosnia-Herzegovinia in the 1990s, is the most dramatic illustration of the consequences for women of being symbols of national culture and vulnerable to violation by national enemies.

There are numerous other ways, however, in which national concerns about the health, demographic future, racial composition, or cultural identity of a nation have entailed the adoption of policies that target women. The Zionist-nationalist discourse and its project of settlement in Palestine, for example, enlists Jewish women in the state of Israel in a "demographic race" against Palestinian Arabs to bear more children. As the former Israeli Prime Minister, Golda Meir, confessed, she was afraid "to wake up every morning wondering how many Arab babies have been born in the night!"[105] The aggressive pro-natalist policies directed at Jewish women under the Israeli state were legitimated as a nationalist priority.

It is, indeed, "women" who become subject in nationalist projects to shifting definitions and redefinitions of national priorities and interests. For women, nationalist projects have often entailed a transition from a "private patriarchy," where women are under the patriarchal control of individual heads of families, to a "public patriarchy," where they experience the patriarchal control of an ethnic collectivity or a larger community of men.[106] The nationalist construct of "women," therefore, produces an anomalous experience of nationhood for women.

Finally, nationalist projects construct "women" primarily through a heterosexual relationship to men that emphasizes a supposedly "natural" hierarchy between men and women. The identification of women mainly with the private and familial sphere has been the basis for the exclusion of women as citizens or from full membership of the community. The most obvious, of course, is the denial of political rights to women as citizens. In most states in Europe and the Americas, women's suffrage followed well after most men's. It was not until the twentieth century that most of these states granted national female suffrage. Many Asian and African states, however, extended universal suffrage to men and women at the same time during the period of national independence in the twentieth century.

Yet the political disabilities in women's status as citizens go beyond the denial of the right to vote. The history of discrimination against women in relation to education, professional employment, economic independence, and rights within marriage, divorce, inheritance, and the custody of children— all the things that have qualified men for public roles—have constructed women's disqualification from a variety of public roles and made them dependent on fathers and husbands. The legacy continues to haunt women's relations to the nation and the state, well after the granting of formal legal equality.

The anomalous status of women as citizens is reflected in the dual construction of women both as individuals in their own right, subject to the general laws of the state, and as men's legal appendages, subject to the provision of special laws. The nationality and immigration laws in many countries in Europe and North America, for example, have a long legacy of being based on the model of the heterosexual nuclear family, with a male head of household and females subsumed as dependents of men. Until World War II, most countries in Europe, with the exception of the Soviet Union, did not give married women equal access to nationality and citizenship. The statutes of most European countries followed the *Code Napoleon,* which decreed that a married women's nationality followed from that of her husband. A married woman's citizenship derived not from her father or from the country of her birth, but from her husband's citizenship. When women married foreign men, therefore, they lost their nationality and had to take up the nationality of their husband. In the event of a divorce, these women often found themselves "stateless."

The anomalous position of married women's nationality and citizenship began to be addressed only in the context of international concern over the "white slave trade" in the interwar period.[107] As large numbers of European women from the last quarter of the nineteenth century began to emigrate in search of more opportunities, many of them landed in brothels in foreign ports. Their sexual availability to foreign—often racially diverse—men galvanized many European nation-states to "protect" the sexual virtue of their national women, who were now reconstructed not as prostitutes but as "white slaves" in need of protection. The so-called rescue of these women, regardless of their desire to be rescued, created an international movement that came up against the anomalous nature of married women's nationality and citizenship. Ironically, therefore, the movement concerned about the sexual virtues of "bad women" opened the way for a reconsideration of married women's citizenship rights in a number of Latin American and European countries.

The British Nationality Act of 1981 for the first time gave white British women the right to pass their citizenship to their children born abroad. Until then, British men married to foreign women could pass their nationality to their wives and to their children, but British women lost their British nationality on marriage to foreign men and were unable to pass their nationality to their children born abroad. The nationality and immigration legislations have been an important means through which nation-states maintain and preserve a gender-based as well as racialized community of citizens.[108]

In many third-world countries, the duality in the construction of women as citizens is reflected in the tension between secular law and personal law.[109] In many cases, for example, the domain of family legislation and personal law that affects marriage, divorce, child custody, and maintenance and inheritance law, is based on religious law, even when other legal codes are fully secular. The domain of personal law usually privileges the heterosexual patriarchal family and the rights of men over that of women. The nation-state, therefore, ends up colluding with the patriarchal family in circumscribing women's legal equality as citizens of the state. The Constitution of India, for example, is committed to the adoption of a uniform civil code that would eventually put an end to the colonial legacy of the separation between secular law and religious-based personal laws for different communities in India. Yet adoption of a uniform civil code in postindependent India has been mired in sectarian politics and the identification of women and femininity with the identities of religious communities.[110] Recognition by various nationalist projects of women as citizens in their own rights, therefore, is often compromised by the construction of women primarily through a heterosexual relationship to men.

THE RELATION BETWEEN FEMINISMS AND NATIONALISMS

The contemporary scholarship on gender and nationalism has raised questions about the compatibility of feminisms and nationalisms. Although some scholars have suggested that these are necessarily incompatible, the history of feminisms and nationalisms in different locations belies such easy generalizations.[111] What emerges instead is the recognition that the relationship between feminisms and nationalisms is not given but rather shaped in specific historical conjunctures.

In Europe, feminist movements for suffrage and other rights for women generally emerged after, and in response to, the projects of modern nationhood. As such, therefore, they called attention to the inequality of women in the constitution of the nation as a community. In revolutionary France, for example, modern French feminism developed against a background of the construction of a sexually differentiated national public and private and the resulting gendered exclusions in the idea of republican citizenship. In her *Declaration of the Rights of Women in 1791*, Olympe de Gouges made a case for the rights of women and challenged the exclusion of women from national politics. In doing so she stressed the fundamental complementarity between men and women based on their sexual "difference." At the same time, however, Gouges also sought to transcend the construction of sexual difference by claiming equality for men and women. Herein lay the "paradox" of feminism: Even as it challenged the construction of sexual difference on the basis of which women were excluded from political rights, it could not help calling attention to these differences and in the process securing sexual difference.[112] The development of modern feminism, especially in the West, was caught within the ideology of gender difference, which from its outset had to contend with gendered exclusions in the universalist rights of modern citizenship.

The "woman question" was by and large not part of the nationalist agenda of many early nationalist projects in Western Europe. Some scholars have gone even further in suggesting that because the history of nationalist projects in most countries in Europe quickly turned away from the democratic potential of the individual and from active political participation by the people, it did not provide an attractive or an adequate ideology for feminism. Because the nationalist programs of most Western European countries had an overall negative impact on women, some scholars have assumed that feminism and nationalism in the European context are "almost always incompatible ideological positions," with only two examples from Western European history— that of nineteenth-century Italy and twentieth-century Finland—of a temporary confluence between feminism and nationalism.[113]

Although the self-representation of European feminism may be aligned with radical ideologies that were often explicitly international—and even antinational—in orientation, that does not mean that early European feminists were not staunchly nationalist or that their feminist project was not invested in the racial and imperial politics of their nations. European feminists, as much as their counterparts in the United States and elsewhere, articulated their feminisms as explicitly racialized and imperialist projects precisely for the sake of acceptance and inclusion in the imperial nation. Victorian and Edwardian middle-class British feminists, for example, framed their demand for female suffrage in terms of their imperial-nationalist responsibility. When British feminists elaborated on the image of the supposedly helpless and degraded Indian woman, this was not merely incidental to their feminist project. Rather, they deployed the plight of Indian woman precisely to justify their own claims—as of the "white woman's burden"—for political inclusion in the imperial nation.[114]

Other scholars have similarly demonstrated that the internationalism of European and U.S. feminists did not necessarily entail the transcendence of nationalist politics. In the United States, where an organized antiblack women suffrage strategy had already emerged by the 1890s, white suffragists readily identified with the racial and imperial priorities of the nation. At the Inter-American Women's Congress in Panama in 1926, for example, feminists representing the United States abstained from voting on a resolution for woman suffrage in all American nations on the grounds that Latin American women were not ready to exercise political rights.[115]

The point is, notwithstanding the inhospitable climate for feminism within many nationalist projects in Europe, that the feminism of middle-class white European feminists, like that of their counterparts in the United States, was informed by the racial and imperial politics of their respective projects of nationhood.

In many colonized and semiperipheral regions, as also in some Eastern European countries, the development of feminism and nationalism was often self-consciously connected.[116] That was partly because here the nationalist projects stimulated the transformation of women's position through a broader concern with national rejuvenation and social reforms. These projects often sought to counter colonial portrayals of the plight of women by turning to a golden age in the ancient past where women supposedly enjoyed equality with men. The project of nineteenth-century Czech nationalism entailed a similar construction of a golden age of gender equity in the past. The mythical figures of Libuse, founder of Prague, and Vlasta, a woman warrior and leader of a woman's revolt, became appropriated as real historical persons from the nation's past. This past was then contrasted favorably to the

masculinist culture of German oppressors.[117] The "woman question," therefore, has been an important component of the national agenda for national
reconstruction in some projects. These projects afforded enhanced opportunities to bourgeois women.

The development of feminism alongside nationalism, however, does not
necessarily provide safeguards. In many third-world nationalist projects the
articulation of women's interests has often been subordinated to the interests
of the nation. Feminist demands, for example, are expected to be framed only
within the parameters of anticolonial nationalism. In some nationalist movements, moreover, feminists are advised to shelve demands until the nationalist emergency is over; they are told "not now, later."[118] In other cases, feminists
have been portrayed as "traitors to the nation" and feminism identified as a
bourgeois and Westernized project that is irrelevant to the more urgent concerns of the nation. Ironically, the nationalist project in post-Soviet Russia has
similarly delegitimized feminism for its association with the "old order" and
with state emancipation. The end of women's emancipation is thus hailed as
a positive result of the collapse of the USSR.[119] In still others, the hospitable
climate for feminism created during nationalist liberation struggles has been
overturned with the attainment of independence. The most famous example
is of the Algerian war of liberation against the French, in which approximately
eleven thousand Algerian women participated as *moudjahidates* (freedom
fighters), with some two thousand involved in the armed wing of the struggle. Whatever openings emerged for a new gender politics in the course of
the struggle were quickly foreclosed in its aftermath. Women were pushed back
from the political sphere and officially subordinated to men with the adoption of the Family Code based on the *Shariah* (Islamic canonical law).[120] There
was a similar trajectory in the relation between feminism and nationalism in
Ireland. The commitment to progressive gender politics, and the contributions of Irish women in the nationalist struggle, were conveniently forgotten
in the repressive gender regime instituted by the Irish constitution of 1937.[121]
To conclude, however, that third-world nationalist projects manipulated wom-
en cynically to garner support for nationalism would be to underestimate the
importance of the "woman question" in the ideological self-representation of
anticolonial nationalisms.

Although the relation between feminism and nationalism has almost always been complex, there is no necessary outcome of this relationship. The
more important point is that nowhere has feminism ever been autonomous
of the national context from which it has emerged. This has been clearly evident in the history of the international feminist movement. The major liber-
al-feminist international organizations of the first half of the twentieth cen-

tury were dominated by women from the United States and Northwestern Europe, many of whom not only assumed feminism's ostensible transcendence of national politics but were also invested in an ideology that insisted on the apparent separation of feminist from nationalist concerns.[122] Feminists from other parts of the world contested and exposed that view. Indian feminists such as Kamaladevi Chattopadhyay, Shareefah Hamid Ali, Dhanvanthi Rama Rau, and others, for example, never missed an opportunity to raise the question of the struggle against imperialism at international feminist conferences like the International Alliance of Women and the Women's International League for Peace and Freedom conferences, throughout the interwar period.[123]

Feminists from different parts of the world not only challenged the "maternalism" that often underwrote the ideology of the international feminist movement but also insisted on making national self-determination into a feminist issue. The real possibility of transnational feminist alliances lies in recognition, rather than transcendence, of the unequal power relations and disparate histories that divide women. That is the kind of hard political work that some women's projects are undertaking in order to build alliances between women of polarized ethnonational groups by challenging the mobilization of their ethnonational identities for war: the Women's Support Network in Belfast in Northern Ireland of Protestant and Catholic women; the Medica Women's Therapy Centre in Zenica in central Bosnia of Bosnian Serb, Croatian, and Muslim women, and Bat Shalom in Israel of Jewish and Palestinian women.[124]

Conclusion

It should be clear by now that the gendered articulation of the nation can be examined only in specific historical contexts and always in relation to a variety of forms of organizing difference. Catherine Hall's study of a critical moment in the formation of British national identity—the passage of the English Parliamentary Reform Act of 1832—is in many ways exemplary in this respect.[125] The context for the Reform Act of 1832 was framed by two preceding events: the Catholic Emancipation in 1829 that was followed by the Irish Coercion Act of 1833 (and by the attempt to reform the Irish church) and the slave rebellion in Jamaica in 1831 (also known as the "Baptist War") that was followed by the Act of 1833, abolishing slavery in most British colonies. The settlement of 1832 was shaped precisely by the historical conjuncture of the moment and entailed new definitions of citizens and subjects and of different modes of belonging in, and identifying with, the nation and the Empire. This brings together a web of relations that include Britain and Jamaica; England and Ireland; Catholics and Protestants; and aristocratic, middle-class, and working-class men and women as well as former slave men and women in the making of the settlement of 1832.

The strength of this approach comes from attention to the significance of the historical conjuncture of the 1820s and 1830s and deployment of the "rule of difference" to explore the multiple articulation of the nation. We thus see a variety of intersecting but uneven modes of identification with and belonging in the imperial nation: Protestant women claiming their right to participate in the public sphere by signing petitions to the Parliament against Catholic emancipation; Catholic Irish women succeeding in their campaign on behalf of their men in the passage of the Catholic Emancipation Act; Catholic men gaining the right to enter some public offices at the same time as many Irish Catholic men had lost the franchise; former slave men and women being partially freed as they were made apprentices for a fixed term until they could "learn" to be free; freed black women being made the property of their husbands; working-class men and women active in reform demonstrations and female political unions; and new groups of men claiming their political fitness by the assertion of their manly independence against the effeminacy of the aristocracy.

It is against this background of different definitions of citizen and subject in relation to class, gender, ethnicity, and race that the settlement of 1832 acquires significance for the national formation. The Reform Act articulated a masculine form of rule that specified for the first time that only men could vote in elections and be political citizens of the nation. Although property was made the basis for the franchise, women, including property owners, were excluded from the franchise. The very act of naming the specific exclusion of women, however, would also in succeeding decades put the question of woman suffrage on the national agenda.

This multilayered analysis of the 1832 Reform Act underscores the potential for recasting the study of gender and of the nation. The future of the scholarship on gender and the nation, indeed, may lie precisely in such densely historicized analysis of the articulation of the nation in specific historical moments. Only then will we begin to make visible the multiple, and often uneven, ways in which particular forms of difference inform, and are produced by, the nation in any given historical moment.

Notes

I would like to thank the following people for their comments on an earlier draft: Antoinette Burton, Lori Ginzberg, Clement Hawes, Seth Koven, Bonnie Smith, and Theodore Weeks. A modified version of the essay was published in *Gender and Empire: A Companion Volume of the* Oxford History of the British Empire, edited by Philipa Levine, and is reprinted by permission of Oxford University Press.

1. See http://cagle.slate.msn.com/news/TelnaesTaliban/main.asp.

2. Samuel P. Huntington, *The Clash of Civilizations and the Remaking of World Order* (New York: Simon and Schuster, 1996).

3. For Eric Hobsbawm, the flood of scholarship on nationalism since the 1980s, like Minerva's owl that takes flight only at dusk, is a sign that nationalism as a historical phenomenon might have finally passed its peak. E. J. Hobsbawm, *Nations and Nationalism since 1788* (New York: Cambridge University Press, 1990). The resurgence of nationalism as an important political force in 1989, especially in Central and Eastern Europe, suggests that a requiem for nationalism may as yet be premature.

4. For a critique of this literature, see Nira Yuval-Davis, *Gender and Nation* (Thousand Oaks: Sage, 1997).

5. Anthony D. Smith, *National Identity* (London: Penguin, 1991). Smith recognizes gender as significant for social identity but dismisses its role in collective mobilization.

6. See especially "Algeria Unveiled," in *A Dying Colonialism*, trans. H. Chevalier (1959, repr. Harmondsworth: Pelican, 1970). For an assessment of Fanon's treatment of gender, see Winifred Woodhill, "Unveiling Algeria," *Genders* 10 (Spring 1991): 112–31, and Madhu Dubey, "The 'True Lie' of the Nation: Fanon and Feminism," *Differences* 10 (Summer 1998): 1–29.

7. Virginia Woolf, *Three Guineas* (1938, repr. London: Hogarth Press, 1947), 197.

8. Kumari Jayawardena, *Feminism and Nationalism in the Third World* (London: Zed Books, 1986).

9. For some broad overviews of the scholarship on the nation and nationalism, see Gopal Balakrishnan, ed., *Mapping the Nation* (London: Verso Press, 1996); Geoff Eley and Ronald Grigor Suny, eds., *Becoming National* (New York: Oxford University Press, 1996); John Hutchinson and A. D. Smith, eds., *Nationalism* (New York: Oxford University Press, 1994); Homi K. Bhabha, ed., *Nation and Narration* (New York: Routledge, 1990); and Edward Mortimer, ed., *People, Nation and State: The Meaning of Ethnicity and Nationalism* (London: I. B. Taurus Publishers, 1999).

10. Ida Blom, Karen Hagemann, and Catherine Hall, eds., *Gendered Nations: Nationalisms and Gender Order in the Long Nineteenth Century* (New York: Berg, 2000). Scholarship in this area is vast and growing. See, for example, Yuval-Davis, *Gender and Nation;* Nira Yuval-Davis and Floya Anthias, eds., *Woman-Nation-State* (New York: St. Martin's Press, 1989); Andrew Parker et al., eds., *Nationalisms and Sexualities* (New York: Routledge, 1992); Anne McClintock, Amir Mufti, and Ella Shohat, eds., *Dangerous Liasons: Gender, Nation and Postcolonial Perspectives* (Minneapolis: University of Minnesota Press, 1997); Rick Wilford and Robert C. Miller, eds., *Women, Ethnicity and Nationalism: The Politics of Transition* (New York: Routledge, 1998); Ruth Roach Pierson and Nupur Chaudhuri, eds., *Nation, Empire, Colony: Historicizing Gender and Race* (Bloomington: Indiana University Press, 1998); Caren Kaplan, Norma Alarcon, and Minoo Moallem, eds., *Between Woman and Nation: Nationalisms, Transnational Feminisms and the State* (Durham: Duke University Press, 1999); Sita Ranchod-Nilsson and Mary Ann Tetreault, eds., *Women, States, and Nationalism: At Home in the Nation?* (New York: Routledge, 2000); and Tamar Mayer, ed., *Gender Ironies of Nationalism* (New York: Routledge, 2000). For special issues of journals, see "Nationalisms and National Identities," *Feminist Review* 44 (Summer 1993); "Gender, Nationalisms and National Identities," *Gender and History* 5 (Summer 1993); "Links across Difference: Gender, Ethnicity and Nationalism," *Women's Studies International Forum* 19, nos. 1 and 2 (1996); and "The Awkward Relationship: Gender and Nationalism," *Nations and Nationalism* 6, no. 4 (2000).

11. Benedict Anderson, *Imagined Communities: Reflections on the Origin and Spread of Nationalism* (1983, rev. ed. London: New Left Books, 1991), 15–16.

12. Rick Wilford, "Women, Ethnicity and Nationalism: Surveying the Ground," in *Women, Ethnicity and Nationalism: The Politics of Transition,* ed. Rick Wilford and Robert C. Miller (New York: Routledge, 1998), 9.

13. Peter Sahlins quoted in Lloyd Kramer, "Historical Narratives and the Meaning of Nationalism," *Journal of the History of Ideas* 58, no. 3 (1997): 526.

14. The phrase is from T. H. Marshall, *Citizenship and Social Class and Other Essays* (New York: Cambridge University Press, 1950); the discussion is from Ruth Lister, "Citizenship: Towards a Feminist Synthesis," *Feminist Review* 57 (Autumn 1997): 28–48.

15. See especially Yuval-Davis, *Gender and Nation,* 12–15.

16. The discussion is from Ruth Roach Pierson, "Nations: Gendered, Racialized, Crossed with Empire," in *Gendered Nations: Nationalisms and Gender Order in the Long Nineteenth Century,* ed. Ida Blom, Karen Hagemann, and Catherine Hall (New York: Berg, 2000), 49.

17. Joan Wallach Scott, "Gender: A Useful Category of Historical Analysis," in Joan Wallach Scott, *Gender and the Politics of History* (1986, repr. New York: Columbia University Press, 1998), 28–52.

18. The term *sex-gender system* is from Gayle Rubin, "The Traffic in Women: Notes on the Political Economy of Sex," in *Towards an Anthropology of Women,* ed. Rayna R. Reiter (New York: Monthly Review Press, 1975), 157–210.

19. Thomas Laqueur, *Making Sex: Body and Gender from the Greeks to Freud* (Cambridge: Harvard University Press, 1990).

20. Judith Butler, *Gender Trouble* (New York: Routledge, 1990).

21. Tamar Mayer, "Gender Ironies of Nationalism: Setting the Stage," in *Gender Ironies of Nationalism,* ed. Tamar Mayer (New York: Routledge, 2000), esp. 5.

22. For Hobsbawm, the nation is an important example of an "invented tradition." Eric Hobsbawm, "Introduction: Inventing Traditions," in *The Invention of Tradition,* ed. Eric Hobsbawm and Terence Ranger (New York: Cambridge University Press, 1983), 1–14.

23. For a review of nationalism and modernity, see Craig Calhoun, "Nationalism and the Contradictions of Modernity," *Berkeley Journal of Sociology* 42 (1997–98): 1–30; Kramer, "Historical Narratives"; Anthony D. Smith, "Nationalism and the Historians," *International Journal of Comparative Sociology* 33, nos. 1–2 (1992): 58–80; and Anthony D. Smith, *Nationalism and Modernism: A Critical Survey of Recent Theories of Nations and Nationalism* (New York: Routledge, 1998).

24. Hans Kohn, *The Idea of Nationalism: A Study in Its Origins and Background* (New York: Macmillan, 1944); Elie Kedourie, *Nationalism* (London: Hutchinson, 1960); Karl Deutsch, *Nationalism and Social Communication* (Cambridge: MIT Press, 1966); C. J. Hayes, *Essays on Nationalism* (New York: Macmillan, 1966); John Breuilly, *Nationalism and the State* (Manchester: Manchester University Press, 1982); Miroslav Hroch, *Social Preconditions of National Revival in Europe* (New York: Cambridge University Press, 1985); Liah Greenfield, *Nationalism: Five Roads to Modernity* (Cambridge: Harvard University Press, 1992); Ernest Gellner, *Nations and Nationalism / Ernest Gellner* (Ithaca: Cornell University Press, 1983); Anderson, *Imagined Communities.*

25. This point is made in A. D. Smith, *The Ethnic Origins of Nationalism* (Oxford: Blackwell, 1986).

26. For the emergence of the discourse of sexuality and bourgeois respectability, see

Michel Foucault, *The History of Sexuality*, vol. 1, trans. Robert Hurley (New York: Pantheon, 1978); and George L. Mosse, *Nationalism and Sexuality: Middle-Class Morality and Sexual Norms in Modern Europe* (Madison: University of Wisconsin Press, 1985).

27. Geoff Eley and Ronald Grigor Suny, "Introduction: From the Moment of Social History to the Work of Cultural Representation," in *Becoming National*, ed. Geoff Eley and Ronald Grigor Suny (New York: Oxford University Press, 1996), 3–38, esp. 24. Eley, however, is right to note that some of the most interesting new scholarship on the nation combines the approaches of social history with that of the new cultural history. Also see Geoff Eley, "Culture, Nation and Gender," in *Gendered Nations: Nationalisms and Gender Order in the Long Nineteenth Century*, ed. Ida Blom, Karen Hagemann, and Catherine Hall (New York: Berg, 2000), 27–40.

28. See, for example, Joan Landes, *Visualizing the Nation: Gender, Representation and Revolution in Eighteenth-Century France* (Ithaca: Cornell University Press, 2001).

29. Yuval-Davis, *Gender and Nation*.

30. Partha Chatterjee, *Nationalist Thought and the Colonial World: A Derivative Discourse?* (1983, repr. Minneapolis: University of Minnesota Press, 1998).

31. C. L. R. James, *The Black Jacobins: Touissant L'Ouverture and the San Domingo Revolution* (New York: Vintage Books, 1963); Laurent Dubois, "La Republique Metisse: Citizenship, Colonialism, and the Borders of French History," *Cultural Studies* 14, no. 1 (2000): 15–34.

32. Chatterjee, *Nationalist Thought and the Colonial World;* Partha Chatterjee, "Whose Imagined Community?" in *Mapping the Nation*, ed. Gopal Balakrishnan (London: Verso Press, 1996), 214–25.

33. Bhabha, ed., *Nation and Narration*.

34. Andrew Parker et al., "Introduction," in *Nationalisms and Sexualities*, ed. Andrew Parker et al. (New York: Routledge, 1992), 5.

35. This is from Nira Yuval-Davis, "Introduction," in Nira Yuval-Davis, *Gender and Nation* (London: Sage, 1997), 1–25.

36. Carol Pateman, *The Sexual Contract* (Stanford: Stanford University Press, 1988)

37. Joan B. Landes, *Women in the Public Sphere in the Age of the French Revolution* (Ithaca: Cornell University Press, 1988).

38. Etienne Balibar, "The Nation-Form: History and Ideology," in Etienne Balibar and Immanuel Wallerstein, *Race, Nation, Class: Ambiguous Identities*, trans. Chris Turner (London: Verso Press: 1991), 99.

39. Quoted in Jayawardena, *Feminism and Nationalism in the Third World*, 182; also see Tani Barlow, *Gender Politics in Modern China* (Durham: Duke University Press, 1993); and Christina K. Gilmartin et al., eds., *Engendering China: Women, Culture, and State* (Cambridge: Harvard University Press, 1994).

40. Margaret Ward, "The Ladies Land League and the Irish Land War 1881/1882: Defining the Relation between Women and Nationalism," in *Gendered Nations: Nationalisms and Gender Order in the Long Nineteenth Century*, ed. Ida Blom, Karen Hagemann, and Catherine Hall (New York: Berg, 2000), 229–48.

41. Cora Ann Presley, *Kikuyu Women, the Mau Mau Rebellion and Social Change in Kenya* (Boulder: Westview Press, 1992), 136.

42. The list is from the Introduction in *Woman-Nation-State*, ed. Nira Yuval Davis and Floya Anthias (New York: St. Martin's Press, 1989), 7.

43. Anne McClintock, "'No Longer in a Future Heaven': Gender, Race, and Nationalism," in *Dangerous Liasons: Gender, Nation and Postcolonial Perspectives*, ed. Anne McClin-

tock, Aaamir Mufti, and Ella Shohat, (Minneapolis: University of Minnesota Press, 1997), 89.

44. Mayer, "Gender Ironies of Nationalism," 1–24.

45. Joanne Nagel, "Masculinity and Nationalism: Gender and Sexuality in the Making of Nations," *Ethnic and Racial Studies* 21 (March 1998): 242–69.

46. Cynthia Enloe, *Bananas, Beaches and Bases: Making Feminist Sense of International Politics* (Berkeley: University of California Press, 1989), 44.

47. For some examples, see Joseph Massad, "Conceiving the Masculine: Gender and Palestinian Nationalism," *Middle East Journal* 49 (Summer 1995): 467–83; Frances Gouda, "Gender and Hyper-Masculinity as Postcolonial Modernity during Indonesia's Struggle for Independence, 1945–1949," in *Gender, Sexuality and Colonial Modernities,* ed. Antoinette Burton (New York: Routledge, 1999), 161–74; and Susan Jeffords, *The Remasculinization of America: Gender and the Vietnam War* (Bloomington: Indiana University Press, 1989)

48. Mayer, ed., *Gender Ironies of Nationalism.*

49. Norma Alarcon, "The Theoretical Subject(s) of *This Bridge Called My Back* and Anglo-American Feminism," in *Making Face, Making Soul = Haciendo Caras: Creative and Critical Perspectives by Feminists of Color,* ed. Gloria Anzaldúa (San Francisco: Aunt Lute Foundation, 1990), 356–69; Evelyn Brooks Higgenbotham, "African American Women's History and the Metalanguage of Race," *Signs* 17 (Winter 1992): 251–74.

50. Quoted in Ida Blom, "Gender and Nation in International Comparison," in *Gendered Nations: Nationalisms and Gender Order in the Long Nineteenth Century,* ed. Ida Blom, Karen Hagemann, and Catherine Hall (New York: Berg, 2000), 17; Yuval-Davis, *Gender and Nation,* 30.

51. Etienne Balibar, "The Nation-Form," in Etienne Balibar and Immanuel Wallerstein, *Race, Nation, Class: Ambiguous Identities,* trans. Chris Turner (London: Verso Press, 1991), 86–106. Some scholars, most notably Anderson, separate the history of racism from the principle, as opposed to the actual practices, of the nation.

52. The discussion is from Marilyn Lake, "Frontier Feminism and the Marauding White Man: Australia, 1890s to 1940s," in *Nation, Empire, Colony: Historicizing Gender and Race,* ed. Ruth Roach Pierson and Nupur Chaudhury (Bloomington: Indiana University Press, 1998), 94–105; and Marilyn Lake, "Mission Impossible: How Men Gave Birth to the Australian Nation: Nationalism, Gender and other Seminal Acts," *Gender and History* 4, no. 3 (1992): 305–22.

53. Quoted in Pierson, "Nations," 42.

54. Eley, "Culture, Nation and Gender," 27–40.

55. Glenda Sluga, "Identity, Gender, and the History of European Nations and Nationalisms," *Nations and Nationalism* 4, no. 1 (1998): 87–111.

56. The discussion is from Yuval-Davis, "Introduction," 20–21.

57. Anne McClintock, *Imperial Leather: Race, Gender and Sexuality in the Colonial Contest* (New York: Routledge, 1995), 357.

58. McClintock, "'No Longer in a Future Heaven,'" 90–91.

59. Ibid., 91.

60. Mosse, *Nationalism and Sexuality.*

61. Yvette Abrahams, "Images of Sara Bartman: Sexuality, Race, and Gender in Early-Nineteenth-Century Britain," in *Nation, Empire, Colony: Historicizing Gender and Race,* ed. Ruth Roach Pierson and Nupur Chaudhury (Bloomington: Indiana University Press, 1998), 220–36.

62. Janaki Nair, "Uncovering the Zenana: Visions of Indian Womanhood in English-women's Writings, 1813–1940," *Journal of Women's History* 2 (Spring 1990): 8–34.

63. This discussion is from Pamela Scully, *Liberating the Family? Gender and British Slave Emancipation in the Rural Western Cape, South Africa, 1823–1853* (Portsmouth: Heinemann, 1997)

64. Julia Clancy-Smith and Frances Gouda, eds., *Domesticating the Empire: Languages of Gender, Race, and Family Life in French and Dutch Colonialism* (Charlottesville: University of Virginia Press, 1998); Lora Wildenthal, "Race, Gender, and Citizenship in the German Colonial Empire," in *Tensions of Empire*, ed. Frederick Cooper and Ann Laura Stoler (Berkeley: University of California Press, 1997), 263–86.

65. The following discussion is from Beth Baron, "The Making of the Egyptian Nation," in *Gendered Nations: Nationalisms and Gender Order in the Long Nineteenth Century*, ed. Ida Blom, Karen Hagemann, and Catherine Hall (New York: Berg, 2000), 137–58.

66. For this point, see Ranajit Guha, *Dominance without Hegemony: History and Power in Colonial India* (Cambridge: Harvard University Press, 1997).

67. The following discussion is from Lee Edelman, "Tearooms and Sympathy; or, The Epistemology of the Water Closet," in *Nationalisms and Sexualities*, ed. Andrew Parker et al. (New York: Routledge, 1992), 263–84.

68. Ernest Havemann, *Life Magazine*, June 26, 1964, 76, quoted in Edelman, "Tearooms and Sympathy," 268.

69. G. Kitching, "Nationalism: The Instrumental Passion," *Capital and Class* 25 (1985): 98–116.

70. Parker et al., "Introduction," 1

71. Doris Sommer, *Foundational Fictions: The National Romances of Latin America* (Berkeley: University of California Press, 1991).

72. The following discussion is from Afshaneh Najmabadi, "The Erotic Vatan [Homeland] as Beloved and Mother: To Love, to Possess, and to Protect," *Comparative Studies in Society and History* 39 (July 1997): 442–67.

73. McClintock, *Imperial Leather*, 45.

74. Lynn Hunt, *The Family Romance of the French Revolution* (New York: Routledge, 1992).

75. This is from Patricia Hill Collins, "It's All In the Family: Intersections of Gender, Race, and Nation," *Hypatia* 13 (Summer 1998): 62–82.

76. Quoted in Mrinalini Sinha, *Colonial Masculinity: The "Manly Englishman" and the "Effeminate Bengali" in the Late Nineteenth Century* (New York: St. Martin's Press, 1995), 35.

77. Tom Nairn, *The Modern Janus: Nationalism in the Modern World* (London: Hutchinson, 1990); Tom Nairn, *Faces of Nationalism: Janus Revisited* (New York: Verso Press, 1997); see also Homi K. Bhabha, "Dissemination, Time, Narrative and the Margins of the Modern Nation," in *The Location of Culture* (New York: Routledge, 1994), 139–46.

78. D. Kandiyoti, "Identity and Its Discontents: Women and the Nation," *Millennium: Journal of International Studies* 20, no. 3 (1991): 431.

79. McClintock, *Imperial Leather*, 359.

80. The following discussion is from Blom, "Gender and Nation in International Comparison," 3–26.

81. Cited in Jayawardena, *Feminism and Nationalism in the Third World*, 241–42; also see Sharon L. Sievers, *Flowers in Salt: The Beginning of Feminist Consciousness in Modern Japan* (Palo Alto: Stanford University Press, 1983).

82. This point is made in Valentine M. Moghadam, "Introduction and Overview:

Gender Dynamics of Nationalism, Revolution and Islamization," in *Gender and National Identity: Women and Politics in Muslim Societies,* ed. Valentine M. Moghadam (London: Zed Books, 1994), 4.

83. Quoted in Jayawardena, *Feminism and Nationalism in the Third World,* 36.

84. Chatterjee, *Nationalist Thought and the Colonial World.*

85. Winifred Woodhull cited in Madhu Dubey, "The 'True Lie' of the Nation: Fanon and Feminism," *Differences* 10 (Summer 1998): 1–29.

86. This point is made in Kandiyoti, "Identity and Its Discontents," note 17; see also Hudá Sha'rawi, *Harem Years: The Memoirs of an Egyptian Feminist (1879–1924),* ed. and trans. by Margot Badran (1986, repr. New York: Feminist Press, 1987); and Margot Badran, *Feminists, Islam and Nation: Gender and the Making of Modern Egypt* (Princeton: Princeton University Press, 1995).

87. Afshaneh Najmabadi cited in Kandiyoti, "Identity and Its Discontents," 432.

88. Fatima Mernissi, *Beyond the Veil,* quoted in Valentine E. Moghadam, "Introduction: Women and Identity Politics in Theoretical and Comparative Perspective," in *Identity Politics and Women: Cultural Assertions and Feminisms in International Perspectives,* ed. Valentine E. Moghadam (Boulder: Westview Press, 1994), 15.

89. Nayareh Tohidi, "Modernity, Islamization and Women in Iran," in *Gender and National Identity: Women and Politics in Muslim Societies,* ed. Valentine M. Moghadam (London: Zed Books, 1994), 110–47; see also Valentine E. Moghadam, "Introduction and Overview," in *Identity Politics and Women: Cultural Assertions and Feminisms in International Perspectives,* ed. Valentine E. Moghadam (Boulder: Westview Press, 1994), 1–17.

90. Elleke Boehmer, cited in McClintock, "'No Longer in a Future Heaven,'" 91.

91. Claudia Koontz, *Mothers of the Fatherland* (London: Joanthan Cape, 1986), 196, cited in Yuval-Davis, "Gender and Nation," 29.

92. For examples, see Karen Gottshchang Turner with Phan Thank Hao, *Even the Women Must Fight: Memories of War from North Vietnam* (New York: John Wiley, 1998); Thi Tuyet Mai Nguyen, *The Rubber Tree: Memoir of a Vietnamese Woman Who Was an Anti-French Guerilla, a Publisher and a Peace Activist,* ed. Monique Senderowicz (Jefferson: McFarland, 1994).

93. Mosse, *Nationalism and Sexuality.*

94. Blom, "Gender and Nation in International Comparison," 15.

95. This is from Karen Hagemann, "A Valorous *Volk* Family: The Nation, the Military, and the Gender Order in Prussia in the Time of the Anti-Napoleonic Wars, 1806–15," in *Gendered Nations: Nationalisms and Gender Order in the Long Nineteenth Century,* ed. Ida Blom, Karen Hagemann, and Catherine Hall (New York: Berg, 2000), 179–206.

96. The discussion is from Nagel, "Masculinity and Nationalism," 249–51; see also Gail Bederman, *Manliness and Civilization: A Cultural History of Gender and Race in the United States, 1880–1917* (Chicago: University of Chicago Press, 1995); and Kristin Hoganson, *Fighting for American Manhood: How Gender Politics Provoked the Spanish-American and the Philippine-American Wars* (New Haven: Yale University Press, 1998).

97. Sinha, *Colonial Masculinity.*

98. The phrase is from Gayatri Chakravorty Spivak, "Can the Subaltern Speak? Speculations on Widow Sacrifice," *Wedge* 7–8 (Winter–Spring 1985): 121.

99. Jenny Sharpe, *Allegories of Empire: The Figure of Woman in the Colonial Text* (Minneapolis: University of Minnesota Press, 1993).

100. Linda Kerber, *The Revolutionary Generation: Ideology, Politics, and Culture in the Early Republic* (Washington: American Historical Association, 1990).

101. S. Radcliffe and S. Westwood, *Remaking the Nation: Place, Ideology and Politics in Latin America* (New York: Routledge, 1996), cited in Wilford, "Women, Ethnicity and Nationalism," 11–12.

102. Deborah Gaitskill and Elaine Unterhalter, "Mothers of the Nation: A Comparative Analysis of Nation, Race and Motherhood in Afrikaner Nationalism and the African National Congress," in *Woman-Nation-State,* ed. Nira Yuval Davis and Floya Anthias (New York: St. Martin's Press, 1989), 58–78.

103. Asuncion Lavrin, "International Feminisms: Latin American Alternatives," and Mary E. John, "Feminisms and Internationalisms: A Response from India," both in *Feminisms and Internationalism,* ed. Mrinalini Sinha, Donna Guy, and Angela Wollacott (Oxford: Blackwell, 1999), 175–91, 195–204; see also Malathi de Alwis, "Motherhood as a Space of Protest: Women's Political Participation in Contemporary Sri Lanka," in *Appropriating Gender: Women's Activism and the Politicization of Religion in South Asia,* ed. Amrita Basu and Patricia Jeffrey (New York: Routledge, 1997), 185–202.

104. Amirah Inglis, *The White Woman's Protection Ordinance: Sexual Anxiety and Politics in Papua New Guinea* (London: Sussex University, 1975); Ann Laura Stoler, "Making Empire Respectable: The Politics of Race and Sexual Morality in Twentieth-Century Colonial Cultures," in *Dangerous Liasons: Gender, Nation and Postcolonial Perspectives,* ed. Anne McClintock, Aaamir Mufti, and Ella Shohat (Minneapolis: University of Minnesota Press, 1997), 344–74; Ann Laura Stoler, "Sexual Affronts and Racial Frontiers: European Identities and the Cultural Politics of Exclusion in Colonial Southeast Asia," in *Becoming National,* ed. Geoff Ely and Ronald Suny (New York: Oxford University Press, 1996), 286–324.

105. Quoted in Nira Yuval-Davis, "National Reproduction and 'the Demographic Race' in Israel," in *Woman-Nation-State,* ed. Nira Yuval Davis and Floya Anthias (New York: St. Martin's Press, 1989), 92–109.

106. Sylvia Walby,"Women and Nation," in *Mapping the Nation,* ed. Gopal Balakrishnan (London: Verso Press, 1996), 235–54.

107. Donna Guy, "'White Slavery,' Citizenship and Nationality in Argentina," in *Nationalisms and Sexualities,* ed. Andrew Parker et al. (New York: Routledge, 1992), 201–17; see also Nancy Cott, *Public Vows: A History of Marriage and the Nation* (Cambridge: Harvard University Press, 2000).

108. Frances Klug, "'Oh to Be in England': The British Case Study," in *Woman-Nation-State,* ed. Nira Yuval Davis and Floya Anthias (New York: St. Martin's Press, 1989), 16–35.

109. Kandiyoti, "Identity and Its Discontents," 436–40.

110. Nivedita Menon, "State/Gender/Community: Citizenship in Contemporary India," *Economic and Political Weekly,* Jan. 31, 1998, PE3–PE10.

111. The claim about the incompatability of nationalism and feminism is implicitly endorsed in the editor's introduction—although in not all the essays—in *Feminist Nationalism,* ed. Lois A. West (New York: Routledge, 1997), xi–xxxv.

112. Joan Scott, *Only Paradoxes to Offer: French Feminists and the Rights of Man* (Cambridge: Harvard University Press, 1996).

113. Gisela Kaplan, "Feminism and Nationalism: The European Case," in *Feminist Nationalism,* ed. Lois A. West (New York: Routledge, 1997), 3–40.

114. Antoinette Burton, *Burdens of History: British Feminists, Indian Women, and Imperial Culture, 1865–1914* (Chapel Hill: University of North Carolina Press, 1994).

115. Rosalyn Terborg-Penn, "Enfranchising Women of Color: Woman Suffragists as

Agents of Imperialism," in *Nation, Empire, Colony: Historicizing Gender and Race,* ed. Ruth Roach Pierson and Nupur Chaudhury (Bloomington: Indiana University Press, 1998), 41–56.

116. Jayawardena, *Feminism and Nationalism in the Third World.*

117. Jitka Maleckova, "Nationalizing Women and Engendering the Nation: The Czech Nationalist Movement," in *Gendered Nations: Nationalisms and Gender Order in the Long Nineteenth Century,* ed. Ida Blom, Karen Hagemann, and Catherine Hall (New York: Berg, 2000), 293–310.

118. Enloe, *Bananas, Beaches and Bases,* 62.

119. Rosalind March, "Women in Contemporary Russia," in *Women, Ethnicity and Nationalism: The Politics of Transition,* ed. Rick Wilford and Robert C. Miller (New York: Routledge, 1998), 87–119.

120. Cherifa Boutta, "Feminine Militancy: Moudjahidates During and After the Algerian War," in *Gender and National Identity: Women and Politics in Muslim Societies,* ed. Valentine M. Moghadam (London: Zed Books, 1994), 18–39.

121. Breda Gray and Louise Ryan, "The Politics of Irish Identity and the Interconnections between Feminism, Nationhood, and Colonialism," in *Nation, Empire, Colony: Historicizing Gender and Race,* ed. Ruth Roach Pierson and Nupur Chaudhury (Bloomington: Indiana University Press, 1998), 121–38.

122. Leila J. Rupp, *Worlds of Women: The Making of an International Women's Movement* (Princeton: Princeton University Press, 1997); see also *Feminisms and Internationalism,* ed. Sinha et al.

123. Mrinalini Sinha, "Suffragism and Internationalism: The Enfranchisement of British and Indian Women under an Imperial State," *Indian Economic and Social History Review* 36 (Dec. 1999): 461–84, reprinted in *Women's Suffrage in the British Empire: Citizenship, Race, and Nation,* ed. Ian Fletcher, Laura E. Nym Mayhall, and Philippa Levine (New York: Routledge, 2000), 224–40.

124. Cynthia Cockburn, *The Space between Us: Negotiating Gender and National Identities in Conflict* (London: Zed Books, 1998).

125. Catherine Hall, "The Rule of Difference: Gender, Class and Empire in the Making of the 1832 Reform Act," in *Gendered Nations: Nationalisms and Gender Order in the Long Nineteenth Century,* ed. Ida Blom, Karen Hagemann, and Catherine Hall (New York: Berg, 2000), 107–36.

7

Worlds of Feminism

SUSAN KENT

The concept of feminism is at once breathtakingly simple and dazzlingly complex. The term came into English from the French in the 1890s, replacing the word *womanism*. It referred to "the doctrine of equal rights for women, based on the theory of the equality of the sexes."[1] On the face of it nothing could be more straightforward. But when one proceeds to break down the definition into its various parts, difficulties immediately arise about the nature, content, context, and constituency of the term. Equal rights to what? For all women? Who is considered a woman in the context of feminist demands? What does equality of the sexes mean? And who decides these issues?

Since the 1970s, feminists from all lands and of all persuasions have debated the definitions, issues, and problems contained in "feminism." One strand of the debate centers on whether women are "similar" to men and therefore deserving of equal treatment with no favor. Or, are they "different" from them, and do they therefore have special needs that deserve recognition and response? The disagreement has been reflected in histories of feminism that seek to gauge the relative success feminists in the past had in achieving their ends by referring to their "similarity" or their "difference." But as a number of historians and philosophers of feminism have pointed out, attempts to categorize feminists as belonging to one side or the other ignore the fact that feminism, paradoxically and inconsistently but necessarily, embraces both equality and difference positions, which are often in tension with one another to be sure but productive and powerful if acknowledged and used strategically.[2]

A second and related source of controversy derives from the assumption in much of Western feminist thinking that women, as both subject and object of feminism's program, share common natures, common needs, common wants, common desires, and a common oppression. Women of color in Britain and America and throughout the world since the 1970s have made it clear that differences in race, sexuality, class, nationality, culture, religion, age, and ethnicity must undermine any such notions of an essential femininity or womanliness upon which feminism might rest. Poststructuralist scholars have gone further, arguing that the meanings attached to that collective body of female beings called "women" are not stable over time or across or even within cultures at a particular time. Rather, they assert, the category of "women" is a contingent one, always related to other categories that help organize and inform society and culture. In the West since the eighteenth century, those categories included concepts such as "nature," "class," "reason," and "humanity," which changed over time and thus produced change in the meanings accruing to "women" as well.[3]

Feminism connotes the equal rights of women. If it is impossible to identify a constant meaning for or a stable category of "women," then it would follow that it is impossible to define feminism in any reliable way, either over time or over space. For that reason scholars have come to speak of "feminisms" rather than "feminism," acknowledging the vast complexity of women's lives across the globe and throughout history. I find the term in the plural awkward and diffuse and prefer to retain the power of the singular "feminism" and address the problem of definition by locating the content and the activities it spawned to their precise historical contexts. In other words, "feminism" is a historically contingent concept. It, like the "women" it speaks for and about, exists only in history. Defining and articulating a feminism at any given historical time and place requires understanding what the category of "women" is positioned against at that particular time and place. Just as entire worlds of women populate the universe across time and space, entire worlds of feminism exist as well.

Feminist movements arose in Europe and America in response to the exclusion of women from participation in political and public life, especially as liberal and democratic regimes obtained those rights for increasing numbers of men during the eighteenth and nineteenth centuries. Women's exclusion was argued for and justified by references to their sexual differences from men—differences, it was asserted over and over again, that derived from nature. As a consequence, Western feminists had to answer opponents in the language used to categorize women as inferior. They had to refuse the ideology of sexual difference that established their inferiority as fact, to transgress the boundaries and practices that normalized "women."

But they had also to focus on women as a collectivity on whose behalf they advocated. Paradoxically, they had to embrace as well as refuse their identities as "women." It is the job of historians to "recognize . . . that sexual difference is constructed in a variety of practices," as theorists Parveen Adams and Jeffrey Minson put it. Moreover, it is necessary to "determine which differences and which practices are oppressive" at any particular moment and in any given culture.[4] The activities and ideas that historians identify as feminist at any given time, then, are contingent on the discourses—the languages, systems of meaning, and practices—that construct "women" and on the discourses of resistance that feminists produce in their challenge to society.

Such contentions suggest a number of prickly but vital questions for historians of feminism and feminists. When women calling themselves feminists do not contest the legitimacy of prescriptions constructing "women," for example, when they do not challenge the dominant discourses about sexuality but embrace as their own constructions of masculinity and femininity that delimit their identities and roles, or when they make demands for women that may be quite radical but justify them by traditional separate-sphere arguments, can their politics continue to be regarded as feminist? Or when women explicitly eschew the label *feminist,* as many did in the interwar period in Europe no matter that they shared the fundamental tenets of what other women were promoting under the banner of feminism—what then?

I am not trying to make a case for a right feminism and a wrong one. Rather, I wish to underscore Denise Riley's contentions that the category of "women," and therefore feminism, is always contingent. Because "women" is always relative to other categories, we must be careful in analyzing movements whose critiques of the gender system necessarily depend upon the definition of "women." We must also pay attention to the languages feminists used and incorporated in advocating their positions. In addition, it is important to analyze their strategic considerations and the impact they had on achieving their ends. Feminism should be examined in the context of the discursive practices that create the gender system from which it emerged in order to discover what meanings those practices had for contemporaries.

Early Voices, 1689–1820

Although individual medieval women such as Christine de Pisan sharply criticized the misogyny of the period and formulated a comprehensive "pro-woman" argument to counter it, it was in the doctrine of liberalism, as developed by the English philosopher John Locke, that provoked the creation of a somewhat coherent argument during the late seventeenth century about women sharing in its precepts. Early-seventeenth-century Britons and American colonists understood the world in which they lived to be fundamentally, properly, and irrevocably hierarchical. They imagined their social order to be a "great chain of being," with God the Father and the angels at the top followed by monarchs, aristocrats, gentry, and then everyone else. Women held their various positions on the chain by virtue of their relationship to men as wives or daughters. As women they were inferior and subordinate to men, as God had demonstrated in making Eve out of Adam's rib. Moreover, Eve's transgressions had caused all women to be stained by her sin. Construed as insatiably lustful and with sexual appetites equal to or greater than men's, women of the seventeenth century were perceived to be potential agents of damnation and destruction. They required, it was thought, the mastery of men to preserve their propriety and honor and even the stability of the social order itself.

Hierarchies of gender mirrored those of status based on landownership in rural areas and on guild structures in towns. Subjects of the crown knew themselves to be subordinate to their monarch; farmers knew themselves to be fully subordinate to landlords, as did apprentices and journeymen to their guild masters; and women subordinated themselves to their husbands. Patriarchal rule—whether of master to man or man to woman—prevailed.

Patriarchy in state and society as well as in the family rested on the ancient presumption that a male head of household held property not just in his land and animals but in his wife and children. Although never legally classified as chattel (i.e., property) of men, married English, Welsh, and Scots women faced restrictions in common law that rendered them, for all intents and purposes, the property of their husbands. At the very least, common-law doctrines institutionalized the inferiority and subordination of women to men. Under the law of coverture unique to England and the American Colonies, married women had no legal existence apart from their husbands. They had no legal rights to property, earnings, freedom of movement, conscience, or their bodies or children. All belonged to their husbands. If a woman was raped, the crime was perceived as a form of theft, not from her but from her husband or male relatives. Cases of adultery were prosecuted only in those instances where the woman involved was married. Women lost their names when they married.

All of these circumstances combined to suggest that women were the property of men in fact if not law. Certainly, they meant that women did not enjoy the autonomy, the independence, that was a vital prerequisite for formal political participation (which most men did not possess either, although not because they were excluded by law). By 1600 only in rare and exceptional cases did individual women vote for or hold pubic office. In the Gaelic areas of Ireland, where English common law did not prevail, married women may well have enjoyed a higher legal status and greater property rights. Gaelic women, it appears, could hold property and administer it as they saw fit, independent of their husbands.

Regardless of social class, women were expected to stay within the confines of the home—the realm of "within," as some ministers put it, as opposed to the world "without." Didactic literature enjoined them to keep themselves within the private sphere of home and family, where they could best cultivate and exhibit the qualities of proper women. Proper women were expected to be modest, humble, obedient, pious, temperate, patient, silent, and, above all, chaste. That is not to say they were all of those things; indeed, the very need to enjoin them to be so may suggest that they were not. Most likely, however, once these norms of femininity became accepted as part of the "natural" order, as was the case by 1600, it would be difficult for women to transgress them with impunity. To do so would be to call down upon their heads charges of immorality and unnaturalness, which most people could not have afforded. Observations that women did not enjoy the same legal, educational, or political privileges as men, such as those put forward by Margaret Cavendish, Duchess of Newcastle, were likely to provoke outrage, culminating in diagnoses of insanity.

But the ideology of gender, like any other ideology, is never static. Changes taking place in the economy or in politics or society bring about changes in ideology as well, exposing inconsistencies and contradictions. Because ideologies are always uneven and often contradictory in their applicability to, or effect on, various people in society, they produce possibilities for resistance to them, possibilities for change. Even the most extreme forms of Protestantism, by proclaiming the *spiritual* equality of men and women (their equality, in other words, before God), opened avenues for some women to make claims for other kinds of equality as well. By the end of the seventeenth century, economic, social, and political change converged to produce a challenge to authority that would have profound implications for the relationships between men and women, ruler and ruled.

Economic changes that occurred during the seventeenth century significantly altered the economic role of women in elite and middling families. As upper and middling families prospered as never before with the expansion of the economy, wives and daughters in those families no longer played vital roles in production. More and more throughout the course of the eighteenth century, the ability of a husband and father to keep the women of his family idle became a symbol of his success. It was not long before the idea that women of elite and middling families worked would be unimaginable, a serious violation of the social code. Women became the chief and conspicuous consumers of the goods produced by capitalist methods and of the exotic items coming into Britain from overseas. The transformation of women's economic role from that of necessary economic partners in production to one of leisured, ornamental consumers reduced the real power they might exercise in a family.

A few educated elite women protested vociferously against the situation women faced as a consequence of these developments and attributed their subordination not to any "natural" inferiority but to a lack of economic rights and access to education. Mary More, writing in the 1670s, argued that economic dependence upon their husbands rendered women near slaves. The title of Aphra Behn's first play, *The Forced Marriage* (1671), suggested the constraints women faced as they struggled to achieve economic survival. The play itself, as well as other works Behn published, dealt with themes of rape and women's powerlessness. Her outrage over enslaved Africans, expressed in *Oroonoko: or, The Royal Slave* (1688), implied a link between the condition of women and that of slaves, anticipating by more than a century an association feminists would make throughout the nineteenth century. Behn, Margaret Cavendish, the Duchess of Newcastle, and Bathsua Makin advocated serious education for women, albeit elite women, urging them to develop and use their considerable mental powers. In 1686 *The Female Advocate,* written by fourteen-year-old Sarah Fyge, castigated misogynist tracts that flooded Restoration England, charging their authors with jealousy, incompetence, and a bald desire to exercise power over women.

In all of these ways, some women of the Restoration resisted contemporary beliefs about women's natural weakness and inferiority and their need to be obedient and subordinate to men. In so doing they also challenged the assumptions about masculine privilege on which such ideas about femininity rested.[5] England's Glorious Revolution of 1688, during which the landed elites overthrew James II and placed William and Mary on the throne in return for a written guarantee of parliamentary power and the rights of the individual, implemented the forerunner of a liberal regime in Great Britain.

In 1689 John Locke, in support of the passage of a bill of rights that limited the power of the monarchy, issued a work he had written ten years earlier. *Two Treatises of Government* explored the conditions in which a monarch might be overthrown by his or her own subjects. Locke proclaimed that in a state of nature all men and women are free and equal, thus undermining the arguments from nature for women's subordination. So powerful were Locke's philosophical formulations against domestic patriarchy that the Church of England felt compelled to alter its doctrine in 1705 to acknowledge the mutual and reciprocal rights and obligations of women and men in marriage. Such ideas left open the door to divorce, as Locke had anticipated in likening the contract that establishes civil society with that that creates marital union and in claiming that both could be revoked in the event of nonconformance with its terms.

But at the same time Locke's *Two Treatises*—which came to serve as the theoretical justification for the settlement of 1689 by establishing men's right to resist tyranny and which stands as a founding doctrine of liberalism—provided philosophical legitimation for closing down possibilities for women participating in political affairs. In rebutting earlier patriarchal arguments based on analogies of state and familial power Locke distinguished between the state and the family as civic entities, relegating the family to a private sphere disconnected from politics. In separating the two, and insisting that qualification for participation in the public political sphere rested on property ownership and independence of the control or influence of others, Locke effectively excluded women from political activity. Married women could not own property under common law. Moreover, even if women did own property, whether under an equity settlement or as a *femme sole*, they were considered dependent upon men within the family and therefore disqualified from public life. Henceforth women, in ideological terms, would occupy the private sphere of home and family where they could best display the virtue expected of them; men would demonstrate virtuous behavior in the public sphere of work and politics.

Because of the ambiguity of Locke's formulations he could be interpreted in at least two ways. Drawing upon his arguments for support, Elizabeth Johnson decried in 1696 the "notorious violations on the liberty of freeborn English women," while an anonymous author of *The Hardships of the English Laws* (1735) castigated the government for withholding from women their constitutional rights. Mary Astell reacted differently, focusing not on the liberatory elements of Locke's message but on the consequences for women in his separation of power in the state and power in the family. She recognized that the condition of the possessive individualism that characterizes liberalism and justifies political participation for men necessitated a concomitant narrowing of women's scope. She asked pointedly in 1700, "If absolute sovereignty be not necessary in a state, how come it to be so in a family? . . . Is it not then partial in men to the last degree to contend for and practise that arbitrary dominion in their families which they abhor and exclaim against the state? . . . If all men are born free, how is it that all women are born slaves?"[6] Astell, a Tory who opposed the revolutionary settlement, sought to weaken its ideological underpinnings by demonstrating the hypocrisy of separating public from private authority. She was no less astute about liberalism's disadvantages for all that, however.

The democratic revolutions of the late eighteenth century in America and France revealed more fully the contradictions inherent in liberalism for men and women. In America, those contradictions provoked mild private responses from a few women who felt keenly their exclusion from the political equation of liberty. The American revolutionaries declared that "all men are created equal" but classified women, slaves, and men without property, along with children and the insane, as lacking in the qualities necessary to attain citizenship. Abigail Adams appealed to her husband in a letter in 1776 to urge the passage of laws that curtailed the "unlimited power" of men over their wives, warning that "if particular care and attention is not paid to the ladies, we are determined to foment a rebellion and will not hold ourselves bound by any laws in which we have no voice, or representation."[7] She and her friend Mercy Otis Warren shared their feelings in private correspondence, and Phillis Wheatley, a former slave, used poetry to put down her desires for freedom, liberty, individual rights, and toleration. Even politically attuned women, however, did not raise their voices in public to protest their lack of rights and liberty.

The creation of the American Republic did excite comment about the need to educate virtuous citizens to serve it. Many women seized upon this need to claim the role of educator of citizens, and they helped to develop what one historian has called the "ideology of republican motherhood."[8] Mothers must be educated if they were to raise virtuous sons and daughters, proponents insisted. In so doing they argued for education for themselves and gave their domestic duties as mothers a political cast. Judith Sargent Murray, for example, in *On the Equality of the Sexes*, written in 1779 but not published until 1790, questioned the received wisdom that nature had made men mentally superior to women. What passed for women's inferiority, she insisted, was merely a lack of education. Educate women, and they would be capable of great things. "A sensible and informed woman—companionable and serious—possessing also a facility of temper and united to a congenial mind—blest with competency—and rearing to maturity a promising family of children—Surely the wide globe cannot produce a scene more truly interesting." Benjamin Rush also urged competent education upon women, arguing that the Republic's success depended upon mothers who could train their sons in patriotism and republican virtue. "To qualify our women for this purpose," he noted, "they should not only be instructed in the usual branches of female education, but they should be taught the principles of liberty and government; and the obligations of patriotism should be inculated upon them."[9]

French women more vociferously and publicly declared their objections to being excluded from the political rights promised men in the Declaration of Rights of Man and Citizen of 1789. Women had been central in the demonstrations and riots that produced the revolution of 1789, in the October Days that returned the royal family to Paris, and in the so-called second revolution that established the French Republic in the fall of 1792. They were called *citoyennes*, the feminine rendition of "citizen," acknowledged for their part in overthrowing the old regime and recognized as enjoying the same rights to happiness promised men. The revolutionaries, in fact, passed laws that gave women civil, although not civic, rights. They were granted equal inheritance rights with men, for example, and permitted, like men, to divorce, but they were excluded from participating in politics through the vote. As Talleyrand pointed out, women's rights to happiness depended utterly upon eschewing "political rights and functions." "In abstract principle," he conceded, "it seems impossible to explain that half of the human race is excluded by the other from participation in government." But nature, he insisted, had endowed women with capabilities suited to the home and family. It was within the confines of home and family, provided that they gave up any claims to political life, that they could take part in the benefits of revolution "under the empire of liberty and equality. . . . At the moment they renounced all political rights, they gained the certainty that their civil rights would be consolidated and even expanded," he declared.[10] The contradiction created by giving women civil agency while denying their existence as political actors helped produce feminism in France.[11]

Olympe de Gouge responded in outrage against the thinking of revolutionaries like Talleyrand with her own *Declaration of the Rights of Women and the Citizen* (1791). "Oh, Women!" she despaired in the preamble, "what advantages have you gained from this Revolution? A more blatant contempt, a more outright distain." She charged men with perpetuating against women all the prejudices and corruption they had claimed to have done away with in overthrowing the aristocratic old regime. "Man," she demanded, "are you capable of being just? . . . Who gave you the sovereign empire to oppress my sex?" Far from incorporating the universal rights they had asserted in 1789, revolutionaries were laying bare the very particular nature of political rights in a constitution that excluded women from politics. Women would have to assert their own political rights and insist that they be given the force of law, de Gouge insisted. Following the Declaration of the Rights of Man clause by clause, she enumerated the rights that belonged to women by nature: equal rights to property, taxation, the law, and participation in civic life. Only by explicitly including women could putatively universal rights be achieved, she declared.[12]

The French Revolution electrified radical men and women in Britain, who had been basing their claims for greater political participation on the rights of heads of households—as property owners—to citizenship. In 1791 Thomas Paine published *The Rights of Man* in which he asserted that citizenship rested not on possession of property, whether landed, mobile, or personal, but on the capacity of individuals to reason. *The Rights of Man* exploded Lockean notions of the separation of public and private spheres that granted men citizenship in part on the basis of their status as heads of households. Instead, everyone, regardless of social rank (or, as women such as Mary Wollstonecraft and Mary Hays would soon assert, of gender) possessed the ability to reason. Everyone, therefore, qualified for direct participation in the political nation.

Wollstonecraft made explicit what Paine had left abstract. In *A Vindication of the Rights of Women* (1792) she argued for women's full admission to the political nation, with all the rights and responsibilities accorded to men, on the grounds that women, no less than men, possessed reason and contributed to public virtue through the rearing of civic-minded children. She urged that women be educated in the "manly virtues" (just as men should become "chaste and modest") and learn to become industrious, independent members of society rather than dependent parasites. "My own sex, I hope, will excuse me," she wrote, "if I treat them like rational creatures, instead of flattering their fascinating graces, and viewing them as if they were in a state of perpetual childhood, unable to stand alone. . . . Every being," she insisted, "may become virtuous by the exercise of its own reason." She envisaged citizen-women taking to "the field" to "march and counter-march like soldiers, or wrangle in the senate to keep their faculties from rusting."[13] Such a society of educated and virtuous men and women would be truly enlightened.

Mary Hays, a member of the radical dissenting circle to which Wollstonecraft belonged, contended that the aims of government—the happiness of individuals (and the means by which that happiness was to be realized, or "the possession of private virtues") would come to naught if women were not admitted to its jurisdictions. In March 1797 she wrote to the editor of *Monthly Magazine* that "till one moral and mental standard is established for every rational agent, every member of a community, and a free scope afforded for the exertion of their faculties and talents, without distinction of rank or sex, virtue will be an empty name, and happiness elude our most anxious research." Hays's *Appeal to the Men of Great Britain in behalf of the Women* (1798) called upon her countrymen to "restore to woman that freedom, which the God of nature seems manifestly to have intended, for every living creature! Liberty,—rational liberty,—such as is consistent with the good order of every branch of society."[14]

A year later Mary Robinson castigated politicians for having banned women from listening to parliamentary debates. "Why are women excluded from the auditory part of the British senate?" she demanded in *A Letter to the Women of England, on the Injustice of Mental Subordination.* "The welfare of their country, cannot fail to interest their feelings." Alluding to the Enlightenment notion put forward by men like Edward Gibbon and Adam Smith that the progress of civilizations could be measured by the degree to which women were honored within them, Robinson noted with irony that "many of the American tribes admit women into their public councils, and allow them the privileges of giving their opinions, *first,* on every subject of deliberation. The ancient Britons allowed the female sex the same right: but in modern Britain women are scarcely allowed to express any opinions at all!" She urged the women of Britain to educate themselves, especially their daughters, to "expand their minds, and purify their hearts, by teaching them to feel their mental equality with their imperious rulers."[15]

The Contradictions of Liberalism and the First Wave of Feminism, 1829–1914

Liberalism, whether British, American, or French, explicitly denied women political citizenship. The contradiction between, on the one hand, a liberal ideology that had legitimated the dismantling of aristocratic power and authority and the enfranchisement of middle-class, and later working-class, men, and, on the other, the denial of the claims of women to full citizenship was resolved by appeals to biological and characterological differences between the sexes. The qualities of femininity that evolved were antithetical to those that had warranted widespread male participation in the public sphere. Men possessed the capacity for reason, action, aggression, independence, and self-interest. Women inhabited a separate, private sphere, one suitable for the so-called inherent qualities of femininity. Emotion, passivity, submission, dependence, and selflessness all derived, it was claimed insistently, from women's sexual and reproductive organization. Nineteenth-century theorists imposed a socially and culturally constructed "femininity" upon the female as a biological entity, a sexed body, and it was a gender identity derived from ideas about what roles were appropriate for women. Collapsing sex and gender—the physiological organism with the normative social creation—made it possible for women to be construed as both sexually pure and purely sexual. Although paradoxical, these definitions excluded them from participation in the public sphere and rendered them subordinate to men in the private sphere.

These arguments at one and the same time idealized women and expressed profound fear of them. Women were aligned with morality and religion, whereas men represented corruption and materialism. Women were construed as occupying the ethical center of industrial society and invested with the guardianship of social values, whereas men functioned in a world of shady dealings, greed, and vice, values generally subversive of a civilized order. Women were also identified with nature—wild and unruly yet to be explored and mastered. Men belonged to culture—controlled, systematic, and symbolic of achievement and order. Correspondingly, women were assigned an exclusively reproductive function in contrast to men, who allegedly held a monopoly on productivity.

In each case, notions of femininity, or female nature, ultimately rested upon the perceived sexual organization of women, who were construed to be either sexually comatose or helplessly nymphomaniacal. Whether belonging to one category or the other, women were so exclusively identified by their sexual functions that nineteenth-century society came to regard them as "the Sex." This in turn set up yet another dichotomy that offered two possible images: women could be either revered wives and mothers or despised prostitutes. Both roles effectively disqualified them from economic and political activity. At the same time, as middle-class feminists and working women argued, the characterization of women as "the Sex" created the potential for abuse.

The contradiction between the ideal wife and mother on the one hand and the degraded prostitute on the other was too extreme to reflect the real experiences of women. Nineteenth-century women were, indeed, participants in and agents of culture. They did operate in the material and productive world of industrial society, and their contribution to the economic sphere was not limited to having babies or servicing the sexual needs of males. Working-class women battled valiantly against enormous odds to bring in precious shillings to the household exchequer while at the same time maintaining a household in such a way as to affirm their families' respectability. Many middle-class women coopted the vision of the "angel in the house" in order to justify stepping out of it and engaging in public campaigns to end slavery, increase education, or reform the lives of poor Britons at home or colonized subjects abroad. Other middle-class women protested the image of femininity assigned to them. Borrowing the very terms liberals used to justify enfranchising men, they embarked on a movement to gain recognition for full and complete humanity, thereby eliminating the reductively sexualized definition of femininity that threatened their integrity and dignity.

Domesticity invested in women the responsibility of maintaining morality and purity. The angel in the house, ideology had it, was herself pure, without sexual feeling and passionless. Until the early eighteenth century, contemporaries believed that women's lust, as personified by Eve, was insatiable but that women could become spiritual through God's grace and hence less carnal. During the eighteenth and nineteenth centuries, the dominant definition of women as especially sexual was reversed and transformed into the view that they were less carnal and less lustful than men. The notion of woman without passion came into being. Passionlessness was, in the eighteenth century, a product of women's purported superior moral and spiritual nature, and it helped provide a higher status in society than women had enjoyed before. It undermined the identification of women with sexual treachery and countered the notion that they were primarily sexual creatures at a time when their

SUSAN KENT

social, political, and economic disabilities rendered them vulnerable to predation.

Some of the most prominent nineteenth-century writers on domesticity—Sarah Stickney Ellis in England and Catherine Beecher in America for example—incorporated the notion of women's greater spirituality and morality in calling upon them to use their influence to effect reform outside their homes. Ellis identified the domestic sphere as the proper one for women and eschewed the idea of women engaging directly in the political or economic sphere. Yet she, and others like Harriet Martineau, also believed that women's influence extended far beyond the arena of home and family and urged them to exercise their power in order to change things in the political, social, and economic realms. Women had a "mission," a duty to bring their special qualities to the immoral world outside. It was a concept that authorized women's activities outside their homes and appeared to contradict the mandate that they remain within it. And, like More, both Martineau and Ellis insisted that women required education if they were to use their talents for beneficial ends rather than fritter away their time in idle pursuits.

Convinced of their greater virtue and duty to bring their moral strengths to bear on the harsher aspects of society, women flocked to a number of campaigns that were political in nature. In Britain and America they formed moral reform associations to fight prostitution—directing their attacks on men who solicited prostitutes rather than on the prostitutes themselves. They also formed temperance societies to reduce the incidence of alcohol abuse. Above all, American and British women joined the antislavery campaign in huge numbers.[16]

The antislavery movement appeared to be the perfect arena for demonstrating women's greater spiritual and moral natures. Conceived not as a movement for rights but as an expression of women's philanthropy, the campaign could be shorn of political coloration and be represented in religious and moral terms. The Anti-Slavery Society in England exhorted women to serve the "sacred cause" of abolition in the name of Christ. "Should they, for His sake," one of its publications read, "actively engage in this labour of Christian love, they cannot fail, whatever be the issue, to inherit 'the blessing of those who are ready to perish', and the richer blessing Him who declared that even a cup of cold water given in His name shall not lose its reward." Women might go about "imbuing . . . the rising race with an abhorrence of slavery" by passing out pamphlets, writing letters, and petitioning members of Parliament "without violating that retiring delicacy which constitutes one of . . . their loveliest ornaments."[17]

Regarded as an extension of domestic duties, antislavery permitted women such as Anne Knight in Britain and Elizabeth Cady Stanton and Lucretia

287

Mott in the United States to flex their moral muscles, stretch their spiritual legs, and have an impact on a matter of immense political and economic importance. They could even do so without appearing to transgress against the strictures that barred them from such activities.

In its early manifestations, then, passionlessness seemed to offer positive rewards for women. They had a stake in its creation as an ideology and its acceptance and perpetuation by society. As physicians took up the notion of passionlessness in the mid-nineteenth century, however, they reduced it from its moral and spiritual connotations to a phenomenon involving scientific biological principles. The medical version of the passionlessness of women once again imposed an exclusively sexual characterization upon them. It placed women in a position of sexual vulnerability while justifying anew their exclusion from "male" pursuits. In denying middle-class women sexuality, nineteenth-century bourgeois society paradoxically heightened an awareness of women as primarily as reproductive and sexual beings. One aspect of the physicians' "science of sex" insisted upon women's complete lack of sexual feeling. The other asserted that women's bodies were saturated with sex.

In asserting the nonsexuality of women, doctors helped encourage the establishment of prudery in middle-class social interactions and encouraged the idea that ignorance was tantamount to innocence in sexual matters, helping to create a climate in which women had little or no knowledge of their sexual and reproductive functions. Moreover, the definition of women as pure and asexual and men as passionate and lustful set up a potentially antagonistic relationship in which men were understood to be aggressive and women as victimized by that aggression.

Although nineteenth-century physicians preached the desirability of restricting or controlling the expenditure of male sexual energies, they believed the male sex drive to be "innate." Equating respectable and pure women with motherhood and men with sexuality required a construction of female sexuality that posited its dual nature. Masculinity and male sexuality rested on the twin pillars of motherhood and prostitution. At a time when masturbation was perceived to cause a myriad of physical and mental pathologies, the only recourse for men was to create another class of women, prostitutes existing exclusively for the gratification of male sexual desires.

In fact, prostitution provided a metaphor, carried only to an extreme degree, for the predicament of women under patriarchal society, insisted nineteenth-century feminists such as Josephine Butler in England, Hubertine Auclert in France, and Victorian Woodhull in America. Marriage, they and other feminists in France, Germany, and even Russia declared, contained many similarities to prostitution.[18] The marriage contract, buttressed by the legal systems of Europe and America, gave husbands complete possession of their wives' bodies. Under the regime of domesticity, marriage and the family were firmly based on ideals of romantic love, companionship, and a spiritual equality between men and women, but the legal, economic, and social position of women had yet to affirm that fact. Under the law of coverture, married women had no rights or existence apart from their husbands. The popular aphorism "my wife and I are one and I am he" described a situation in which a married woman had no legal rights to her property, earnings, freedom of movement, conscience, body, or children. All resided in her husband.

The early supporters of women's rights frequently characterized women's position in society as analogous to slavery. Many of them, like the Americans Elizabeth Cady Stanton, Lucretia Mott, and Susan B. Anthony, had come to their feminist positions after having been part of the antislavery campaign. Without the means to become financially independent, women would forever be locked into the same vulnerability to abuse from men that African slaves experienced at the hands of their masters. Throughout the nineteenth century, women and their male allies challenged these hold-overs of aristocratic patriarchal society. They sought property rights, education and employment opportunities, and the right to divorce. These legal disabilities, they insisted, did not protect women in the domestic sphere of home and family but rather exposed them to the brutalities of the world at large.

The contradictions of separate ideology opened a space within which women could contest their positions of powerlessness. For English women such as Bessie Raynor Parkes and Barbara Leigh Smith Bodichon, women's inability to find respectable work by which they might support themselves—indeed, to actually end up owning for themselves any wages they might earn—rendered them unable to leave abusive or potentially abusive situations. Bodichon's *A Brief Summary in Plain Language of the Most Important Laws Concerning Women* (1854) laid out in a systematic fashion the legal situation that made women the chattels of men. The solution to these problems lay in increasing educational and employment possibilities for women and obtaining the passage of bills that gave married women the right to own property and retain their earnings, just as *femmes sole* might currently do. To that end, these "ladies of Langham Place," as they came to be called after the location of their London office, founded the *English Woman's Journal* in 1858. In its pages, contributors publicized "the cause" of women throughout Britain, raising issues of concern about property rights and divorce laws.

Langham Place also provided a space for the Society for Promoting the Employment of Women, founded by Jessie Boucherette in 1859 to provide a kind of clearinghouse of employment opportunities for mostly middle-class women who lacked a means of support other than the overcrowded, low-paying, and humiliating profession of governess, the only employment they might obtain without compromising their class position. The society argued that middle-class parents must recognize that their daughters might not be able to marry, given the "redundancy" of women relative to men, and must be educated for work beyond being a governess or teaching. They recognized that for women to become economically independent they must break down barriers that kept them from being educated for remunerative work in sound educational institutions.

Queen's College had been founded in 1848 and began to grant degrees to women, and Mary Frances Buss and Dorothea Beale had opened the North of London Collegiate School for Ladies and Cheltenham School, respectively, during the 1850s so single, middle-class women might qualify for more lucrative employment. The ladies of Langham Place, however, set their sights on bigger targets: British universities and medical schools. Their activities ensured that Girton College at Cambridge University in 1871, the University of London in 1878, and Newnham College at Oxford University in 1879, admitted women to examination. Anna Jellicoe, an Irish advocate for women's education, helped found Alexandria College in Dublin. The University of Edinburgh admitted five women to its medical school in 1869, and in 1874 the London School of Medicine for Women opened its doors and matriculated fourteen women.

The ladies of Langham Place also helped set in motion the campaign for women's property rights. With the passage of the Married Women's Property Acts of 1870 and 1882, married women secured the right to retain and own any property or earnings they might bring to their marriages. Husbands no longer enjoyed full and free access to their wives' assets.

Feminists charged that the rights of husbands to force sexual intercourse and compulsory childbearing on wives established a condition of "sex-slavery," as *Common Cause,* the official newspaper of Britain's National Union of Women's Suffrage Societies, described it in 1910. Hubertine Auclert, an outspoken journalist and advocate of woman suffrage, frequently attended city hall weddings in Paris in 1880, where she declaimed against the vow that entreated women to obey their husbands. "You do not owe obedience and submission to your husband," she insisted. "Be his friend, his wife, his companion, and not his slave, his servant."[19] For many, the issue was at the center of the feminist movement. Couched in rather vague terms, the issue that so inflamed the passions of feminists was marital rape. A husband's right to sexual intercourse with his wife was absolute, superseding even the right of a woman to protect herself and/or her unborn children from disease.

The feminist critique of marriage necessarily involved a critique of masculinity. Male sexuality, exemplified in microcosm by the institution of marriage, was—British feminists like Josephine Butler, Elizabeth Wolstenholme

Elmy, and Frances Swiney believed—destructive both to women and, ultimately, to the whole of humanity. The experiences of women in marriage, where, in the words of Wolstenholme Elmy, they were subject to "the excess of sexual proclivity and indulgence general on the part of man," led feminists to demand the right to control their bodies and their fertility.[20]

Yet artificial means of birth control were anathema to most mainstream nineteenth-century feminists, who believed that such devices would allow men easier, more frequent access to their wives by eliminating the fear of pregnancy. With only a few exceptions feminists opposed contraception because they feared it would "give men greater sexual license." Contraceptive knowledge did not become an explicit feminist demand in Europe or America until after the turn of the century. Even then it only rarely found its way into print until after World War I, when activists such as Emma Goldman and Margaret Sanger in the United States and Marie Stopes in Britain began to demand women's right to use birth control.

Feminists certainly favored "voluntary motherhood"—the right to abstain from sexual intercourse.[21] For some, in fact, the right to refuse intercourse was at the core of their movement. But abstinence was possible only if men agreed to it, something feminists doubted the willingness of most husbands to do. Their critique of masculinity instilled in them the conviction that only a massive transformation in the laws, customs, mores, and traditions of Britain could produce a society in which women could exercise the same freedom and liberty accorded to men. That transformation, they insisted, required that women arm themselves with the vote.

The most radical challenge of the women's movement to patriarchal control consisted of demands for enfranchisement on the same lines as men. The campaign for the vote was designed to eliminate the notions of separate spheres and "natural" differences between the sexes, insisted upon by domestic ideology. In the United States, a convention of women held in Seneca Falls, New York, in 1848 passed unanimously all of the resolutions calling for property rights, guardianship of children, inheritance rights, and the like. The clause demanding woman suffrage, however, barely achieved a majority of votes. Yet votes for women soon became the mainstay of the American feminist movement. A resolution passed at an 1856 national convention noted, "Resolved, that the main power of the woman's rights movement lies in this: that while always demanding for woman better education, better employment, and better laws, it has kept steadily in view the one cardinal demand for the right of suffrage: in a democracy, the symbol and guarantee of all other rights."[22]

Susan B. Anthony, a former teacher and temperance advocate, joined with Elizabeth Cady Stanton, an ardent antislavery activist, to spearhead the movement for woman suffrage that began after the Seneca Fall Convention. Although the movement split into the National Woman Suffrage Association and the American Woman Suffrage Association after 1869, it lasted for more than sixty years.

A few French women led by Jeanne Déroin, a utopian socialist and feminist journalist who was jailed for her opinions, demanded the vote in 1848 from the newly established provisional government. Its demise at the hands of Louis Napoleon cut short the question of women's suffrage as well. With the creation of the Third Republic in 1871 an organized women's movement resurfaced under the leadership of republican moderates Léon Richer and Maria Desraismes, who founded L.F.D.F. and Amélioration, respectively. A more militant group, Suffrage des Feminines, under Hubertine Auclert, a radical republican, emerged during the late 1870s. By the 1880s the demand for women's suffrage had become a regular aspect of French politics.

The British women's suffrage campaign as an organized movement began in April 1866, when Barbara Bodichon, Jessie Boucherette, Emily Davies, and Elizabeth Garrett, all members of prominent Liberal families, set out on a petition drive to demand votes for women. By June they had collected 1,499 signatures. John Stuart Mill, who had stood for election to Parliament on a platform that had included the enfranchisement of women, presented the petition to the House of Commons.

Mill's role in the suffrage movement went beyond that of parliamentary champion of the women's cause. His writings, and those of his wife, Harriet Taylor Mill, provided a theoretical foundation for the arguments suffragists advanced throughout their fifty-year campaign. Harriet Taylor Mill's "Enfranchisement of Women," published in the *Westminster Review* in 1851, was widely read and then circulated by the members of the Women's Suffrage Society in 1868. Her husband attributed her with most of the ideas he presented in *The Subjection of Women,* published in 1869 but written eight years earlier. The Mills pointed out that the distinctions between the sexes imposed by society were purported to be those delineated by nature. The private sphere belonged to women, and the public sphere to men, because of biological differences between the two. Separate-sphere ideology, encompassing the notion of natural differences between the sexes, justified the exclusion of women from power and reinforced and perpetuated the stereotype of women as "the Sex," making them vulnerable to abuse by men.

As Harriet Mill noted, "Many persons think they have sufficiently justified the restrictions of women's field of action, when they have said that the pursuits from which women are excluded are *unfeminine,* and that the *proper sphere* of women is not politics or publicity, but private and domestic life." She insisted that cultural constructions of masculinity and femininity bore no relation to the reality of male and female character. "We deny," she asserted, "the right of any portion of the species to decide for another portion, or any individual, what is and what is not their 'proper sphere.' The proper sphere for all human beings is the largest and highest which they are able to attain to." Harriet Mill did not attempt to deny that male and female natures, as evident in her society, differed markedly. She would not, however, concede that these differences were necessarily natural or inherent to the two sexes. "What is now called the nature of women is an eminently artificial thing," insisted her husband. "What women are is what we have required them to be."[23]

Although feminists identified the contradictions contained in domestic ideology and liberalism as they pertained to power relations between women and men, they were blind to the implications they had for inequalities based on class and race. Few feminists questioned their white bourgeois status or considered how working-class or African American women fared under their structures. Instead, they tended to embrace divisions and prejudices based on class and race that informed liberalism and their societies as a whole. In the United States, for example, the woman suffrage movement split over the question of enfranchising blacks. Anthony, Stanton, and Sojourner Truth, a former slave, were dismayed by the qualifier "male" in the Fourteenth Amendment to the Constitution, although too many women's suffragists could not entertain the idea that votes they demanded for themselves should be extended to African Americans as well.[24]

British feminists participated uncritically in an imperial discourse that cast subject Indians and Africans as savage and immoral.[25] Closer to home, European and American feminists rarely intended their dreams of a new world for men and women to extend to the working classes of their nations. Social feminists, always in a minority, made far more radical claims on behalf of women workers. The icy receptions they met from their bourgeois sisters very often reinforced their beliefs that capitalist relations of production, rather than relations between men and women in patriarchy, were at the center of women's inequalities and oppressions and would have to be removed if equality between men and women were to be attained.[26]

While feminists in the West pursued an agenda that more often than not excluded working-class women or women of color, women in other parts of the world began to address some of the same questions about equality with men that had been raised in Europe and the United States. In Egypt, for example, as the state began to modernize and make claims on the public lives of its citizens in areas like education, work, and health, officials looked to women as well as men to implement many of its goals. In doing so it ran up against the power of long-standing religious and patriarchal traditions that restricted women's activities to their homes. A number of individual feminists of the educated, urban, privileged classes challenged the strictures of religion and patriarchy, demanding a change in the practices and laws that limited women's opportunities. In 1873 the state opened a school for the daughters of governmental officials and the white female slaves of upper-class households. Drawing upon their new educations, a number of women questioned religious precepts that demanded their seclusion from society, the veiling of face as well as body (called *hijab* in Arabic), and other practices that constrained their lives. In 1892 Hind Naufal, a journalist, established a women's press in Egypt with her journal *Al Fatah* (The Young Woman), which provided an outlet for feminist discussion. By the early part of the twentieth century, women's feminist writing began to reach a wider, more mainstream audience as activists such as Malak Hifni Nasif, Bahithat Al Bad'iya, and Nabawiyya Musa published tracts demanding education, the right to employment, and legal rights for women.[27]

Throughout the nineteenth-century, Indian male reformers such as Ram Mohum Roy led movements designed to ameliorate some of the oppressive practices that Indian women experienced. Concerned about women's lack of education, the remarriage of widows, purdah, and child-marriage, these male-led and male-dominated movements sought to alleviate women's positions within the patriarchal family rather than undermine patriarchy itself. They effected changes that improved women's lives considerably but did not concern themselves with women's rights. Such demands would have to come from women themselves. Beginning in the late nineteenth century, groups and organizations of Indian women sprang up, led by feminists who had gone abroad to be educated. Swarna Kumari Devis's Ladies Association in 1886, Pandita Ramabai's Sharda Sudan in 1892, Ramabai Ranade's Hindu Ladies Social and Literary club in 1902, and others like them sought to raise awareness about education and employment for women and women's political and legal rights. Women's journals such as *Stree Bodh* appeared and articulated a feminist stance on such issues as purdah, education, employment, child marriage to adult men, women's part in the nationalist movement, and women's exploitation at the hands of men.[28]

By the beginning of the twentieth century, suffrage campaigns in the United States and Europe attained the status of mass movements. In Britain, with the advent of militancy arising out of the Women's Social and Political Union (WSPU) in 1905, the entire feminist movement centered around suffrage as a way for women to free themselves from servile bondage to men. As a symbol of civic and political personality, the vote would be an effective agent in eliminating the notion of women as "the Sex." As an instrument of power, feminists believed—as did their adversaries—that it would transform the elevating "influence" of women into a tool with which to create greater and truer morality among men by eliminating distinctions between public and private spheres. They meant to use the vote to build a sexual culture in Britain that would reflect the needs, desires, and interests of bourgeois women.

The ideology of women's private sphere rested on definitions of female sexuality. Women who challenged the ideology of separate spheres addressed the central premise of the ideology: the question of personal sexual identity. Feminists charged that in presenting women as "the Sex," ideology did not protect them and enshrine their virtue but permitted their abuse by men. As "the Sex," women had not been elevated to a pedestal as the moral guardians of hearth and home but rather dragged through the mud, either as prostitutes or "respectable" receptacles for male sexuality. Feminists sought to eliminate the stereotypes of women—both the idealized and the feared—that rendered them inhuman and to create through the weapon of the vote a society consistent with their needs, interests, and self-defined reality. "Votes for Women, Chastity for Men," Christabel Pankhurst's summation of the demands of feminist women, reflected the deeply felt conviction that the regimes of male sexuality and female subordination called into being by separate sphere ideology required transformation. The suffrage movement, she insisted, constituted "a revolt against the evil system under which women are regarded as sub-human and as the sex slaves as men."[29]

War, Revolution, and Nationalism, 1917–60

The outbreak of world war in August 1914 brought to a halt European suffragists' efforts to gain votes for women. By that time, the suffrage campaign had attained the size and status of a mass movement in many countries, commanding the time, energies, and resources of thousands and riveting public attention. Finnish women had secured the right to vote in 1906, followed by their Norwegian sisters in 1913. In early 1918, in what it defined as a gesture of recognition for women's contribution to the war effort, Parliament granted the vote to British women over the age of thirty. The measure, although welcome to feminists as a symbol of the fall of the sex barrier, failed to enfranchise some three million of eleven million adult women. French women did not gain the vote despite their contributions to the war effort, although German women were enfranchised in the creation of the Weimar Republic, and American suffragists won their fight for votes for women when the Nineteenth Amendment was ratified in 1920.

When war ended feminists continued to agitate for votes for women on the same terms as they had been granted to men. Organized feminism, however, despite the fact that a considerable portion of the potential female electorate remained disenfranchised, never again became a mass movement.

By the end of the 1920s, feminism as a distinct political and social move-ment had become insignificant. The experiences of the Great War—articulat-ed and represented in specific languages of gender and sexuality—forged dra-matically different ideas about gender and sexual identity for many men and women than those of the late-Victorian and Edwardian eras. These languages and identities they spawned provide the context within which interwar femi-nism operated and by which it was constrained. Feminists' understandings of masculinity and femininity—of gender and sexual identity—became trans-formed during the war.

Prewar feminists regarded their movement as an attack on separate-sphere ideology and its constructions of masculinity and femininity. They perceived relations between the sexes to be characterized by a state of war in which patriarchal laws, institutions, and attitudes rendered women vulnerable to sexual abuse and depredation (rather than by complementary and coopera-tion, as separate sphere ideologists so insistently claimed). For the most part, feminists believed masculinity to be culturally, not biologically, constructed and attributed women's victimization to a socialization process that encour-aged the belief in the natural, biologically determined sex drive of men. Their demand for the elimination of separate spheres incorporated an attack on the cultural construction of the female as "the Sex" and males as sexual aggres-sors. Insisting that male behavior could be changed, that masculinity and male sexuality were socially determined and not ordained by God or nature, fem-inists implied that femininity and female sexuality, too, were products of so-cialization. Challenging the dominant discourse on sexuality, they aimed finally to create a society in which the positive qualities associated with each sex could be assumed by the other. It would be a society in which the "natu-ral" equality and freedom of both men and women could be achieved.[30]

With the onset of the Great War, many feminists began to modify their understandings of masculinity and femininity. Their insistence upon equali-ty with men gradually gave way to an ideology that emphasized women's spe-cial sphere—a separate sphere, in fact, that carried with it an urgent belief that the relationship between the sexes was one of complementary. Prewar feminists had vigorously attacked the notion of separate spheres and the medical and scientific discourses about gender and sexuality upon which those spheres rested. Many feminists after World War I, by contrast, pursued a pro-gram that championed rather than challenged the prevailing ideas about masculinity and femininity that appeared in the literature of psychoanalysis and sexology. In embracing radically new—and seemingly liberating—views of women as human beings who possessed sexual identities, many feminists accepted theories of sexual difference that helped advance notions of sepa-rate spheres for men and women. The shift did not take place suddenly, and many other feminists resisted it throughout the 1920s. Acceptance of the dominant discourse on sexuality, however, represented a fundamental abandonment of prewar feminist ideology.

By the end of the 1920s feminists found themselves in a conceptual bind that trapped women in "traditional" domestic and maternal roles and limited their ability to advocate equality and justice for women. In Great Britain, for example, a faction within the largest feminist organization, the National Union of Societies for Equal Citizenship (NUSEC), declared they would now refer to themselves as "new feminists" in order to distinguish themselves from the thinking of the prewar period still held by many of their colleagues. "New feminism," explained Eleanor Rathbone, president of NUSEC in 1925, embodied the belief that the equality of women with men had been achieved. "Women are virtually free," she announced. Feminists could now turn to the needs of women as women rather than as imitators of men. "At last we can . . . demand what we want for women," she observed, "not because it is what men have got, but because it is what women need to fulfill the potentialities of their own natures and to adjust themselves to the circumstances of their own lives." Justification for new feminist demands such as the endowment of motherhood, birth control, and protective legislation for women centered on the role of women in the home and "the occupation of motherhood—in which most women are at some time or another engaged, and which no man . . . is capable of performing."[31]

The new feminist agenda was not inherently antifeminist by any means; such demands can be quite radical. Indeed, as Rathbone argued, women's needs are often very different from those of men, and a strictly egalitarian line failed sometimes to address those needs. The difficulty arose from the arguments new feminists advanced to legitimate their demands. Not the rights of women but their needs as mothers backed feminist appeals now. Not equality but sexual difference characterized the relationship between men and women as new feminists understood it.

When new feminists made demands based on women's traditional special needs and special functions, and when they ceased to challenge the dominant discourse on sexuality, their ideology became virtually indistinguishable from that of antifeminists. To "old" feminists like Emmeline Pethick-Lawrence, Cicely Hamilton, Rebecca West, Winifred Holtby, and Vera Brittain, who espoused a strictly egalitarian line, "new feminist" arguments reminded them of nothing so much as the antifeminist arguments marshaled in the nineteenth and early twentieth centuries to deny women equality with men. In 1927 NUSEC split over the change in emphasis and lost much of its momentum and status as an organization. More important, new feminism, by accepting the terms of the larger culture and putting forward a politics of sexual difference, compromised its ability to advocate equality and justice for women.

While the Great War sparked changes in understandings about gender that produced a dramatic shift in feminist positions in Europe between the wars, in other parts of the world the war strengthened revolutionary and nationalist or anticolonial movements that contained strong feminist components. In Russia, the Bolshevik Revolution of November 1917 brought to power a government committed to the emancipation of women. Ultimately seeking the dissolution of the family as the only true means by which women could make themselves the equals of men, the communist regime introduced a new family code in 1918 that raised women's status to that of men's, made marriage a civil rather than a religious matter, gave children born out of wedlock identical legal rights to those whose parents were wed, and made divorce readily available to both parties. Two years later, the government made it legal for women to obtain abortions legally if done by a physician.

Under the leadership of Alexandra Kollontai, a women's bureau—called a *zhentodel*—sought to implement the regime's vision for liberated women by establishing nurseries for children, communal dining halls, and other services that freed women from child care and housekeeping duties so they might work and engage in political affairs if they chose. The conditions created by civil war, famine, and foreign intervention severely curtailed the zhentodel's ability to carry out its program, but it did have an impact on women's lives in Russia and Central Asia and exposed millions to new possibilities for work and politics.

The family legislation, however, brought more rather than less hardship to women. Easy divorce, free sexual unions, and an inability to enforce child payments on the fathers of children born out of marriage created distress for many women abandoned by husbands and sexual partners. One party member, harkening back to the slogan of the French Revolution, declared that the new laws had brought women "liberty, equality, and maternity."[32] Joblessness rates for women soared with the implementation of the New Economic Policy in 1921, forcing thousands of women into prostitution to survive. Government bureaucrats did not always share the commitment to women's freedom that Bolshevik leaders like Lenin had espoused, and factory managers turned a blind eye to the harassment of women workers at the hands of their male comrades. Feminism might be the official party of the communist regime, and it helped bring about improvement in areas like women's literacy, but for many women it produced little positive change in their everyday lives.

With Stalin's rise to power in the late 1920s, the commitment to women's equality and emancipation vanished. The zhentodel was dismantled in 1930. The state resurrected the family as an official unit of society and made abortion illegal and divorce difficult and expensive to obtain. The Five Year Plans provided employment for women, to be sure, but they were forced into jobs that paid far less than men's and restricted from those that carried prestige and remuneration. Women had to work if their families were to survive, and the abandonment of programs designed to ease their domestic obligations ensured that they bore a double burden. Although abortion rights and easier divorce were restored to women upon Stalin's death in 1952, the weight of work and familial duties remained the same.

In China, the May Fourth movement of 1915–21 saw a significant development of feminist thinking that sought reform of marriage laws and the introduction of property and voting rights for women; access to jobs in the public sector; and prohibition of polygamy, concubinage, and prostitution. Between 1924 and 1927, the Chinese Nationalist and Communist parties joined together to try to establish a unified nation-state. Women constituted a powerful constituency advocating for revolution, and their participation in the short-lived alliance posed a challenge to patriarchal power in traditional China. The women sought to create a society in which relations between men and women might be more equal in the family, in society, in the economy, and in politics.

As was the case in Europe, feminist reforms were sometimes ancillary to nationalist or communist goals. But the leadership of both the Nationalist and Communist parties recognized that their success in creating a national government depended upon their ability to mobilize women, and they were eager to support feminist demands and help create feminist organizations. For the brief period of the Nationalist-Communist alliance, feminists commanded the attention of a significant number of people. In a symbolic gesture of defiance against the traditional order, women cut their hair short, just as men had cut off their long queues during the 1911 revolution to show their contempt for their Manchu rulers.

On March 8, 1924, a Women's Day celebration in Guangzhou attracted three thousand people who heard calls for the abolition of concubinage, prostitution, child brides, and girl bondservants, and equality in wages, education, and law for women and men. By 1926 Women's Day crowds had more than tripled in size, and women's demands escalated to include abolishing the arranged marriage system and making divorce possible. The following year, twenty-five thousand people attended the Women's Day rally. Although the featured speaker at the 1924 rally was Liao Zhongkai, the governor of Guangdong province, he was accompanied by Zeng Xing, the woman who would be named to head the National Central Women's Department. She and her department would come to dominate the subsequent women's festivals.[33]

The collapse of the Nationalist-Communist coalition in 1927 and the invasion of China by Japan in the 1930s cut short the feminist movement of the mid-1920s, although its efforts to challenge traditional patriarchy and transform gender relations continued to have effect. When the communists came to power in 1949, their indebtedness to women in the movement was acknowledged in legal codes that gave women equal rights with men. More substantively, perhaps, the communist regime offered women a positive identity based on work for wages, something denied them in traditional society. Many, although certainly not all, responded enthusiastically.

Until the nationalization of industry in 1956 women who worked in factories—who worked "outside" a family workshop that kept them out of view of strangers as opposed to those who worked "inside" a household workshop among family members who knew them—were regarded as "broken shoes," a phrase usually consigned to prostitutes or other women who appeared on the streets. Virtuous women remained inside the family system. Those who ventured outside—beggars, slaves, prostitutes, vendors, or servants—fell beyond the confines of respectability and were considered shameful and sexually loose. Women who worked in factories, where they could be seen by strangers, carried the stigma of being "broken shoes" until Mao's regime introduced a new ideology of proper womanhood to replace that based on the dichotomy of "inside/outside."

Now women who worked in factories for wages served the revolution as agents of liberation by creating surplus value upon which the state could draw. These "liberated" women were cast in opposition to those who remained in household workshops, which, in the eyes of the communist regime, constituted privatized, petty bourgeois labor units opposed to the state. Once considered fallen women, factory workers were now regarded as the most progressive members of society. The shift in representation—it did not reflect any kind of transformation in the actual working lives of women—from the most degraded to the most exalted appealed to large numbers of women who could now take pride in their existence. For them, communism proved a liberatory movement, offering them an identity they could embrace and define as feminist. A later generation of post-Maoist women rejected the feminism of their older co-workers, regarding it as an artifact of state-run, state-sanctioned policies that produced a version of proper femininity they refused to accept.[34]

Elsewhere, in places such as Egypt or India, feminist campaigns could not be extricated from the anticolonial movements of which they were a part. During the national revolution from 1919 to 1922, when Egypt secured nominal independence from Great Britain (although British troops remained on Egyptian soil until the Suez Crisis of 1956), feminist and nationalist leaders organized mass demonstrations of elite women who left the security of their harems to make clear their hatred of colonial rule. In 1920 feminists demanded the creation of a women's section of the Nationalist Party and insisted that it partake substantively in decision-making processes, making its objections loudly and publicly known when it was bypassed.

With independence, nationalists' enthusiasm for women's involvement and feminist demands such as education and employment opportunities, the right to worship in mosques, and political participation weakened appreciably. The Constitution of 1923 declared that "all Egyptians are equal before the law. They enjoy civil and political rights and equally have public responsibilities without distinction of race, language, or religion." Although that appeared to inaugurate a regime that would fully recognize women's rights, an electoral law negated them by excluding women from the suffrage. Almost immediately, the Egyptian Feminist Union, led by Huda Sha'rawi, formed. The union demanded education and work for women, reform of personal status laws that restricted their movement and comportment in public, abolition of state-sponsored prostitution, and the vote.

Women won educational rights and a minimum age of marriage, but their other demands were ignored. With the Arab socialist revolution of 1952, feminists such as Duriyya Shafiq, head of the Daughter of the Nile Union, took the opportunity to point out the contradiction between a constitution that declared equal rights for all and an electoral system that denied women the vote. Shafiq led a hunger strike and sit-in in parliament to draw attention to feminist demands.

Despite opposition from conservative and fundamentalist Muslim groups, the revolutionary government gave women the vote in 1956. At the same time, however, in a clear statement of its intentions to tolerate feminist activity, the government began to outlaw feminist organizations. By 1959 feminist groups had been shut down, and in 1964, women's organizations were legally banned from forming. Organized feminism disappeared as women were forced to retreat from public view.[35]

The first organized Indian feminist movement appeared in 1917 with the formation of the Women's Indian Association. Subsequent groups arose during the 1920s, the most visible and influential being the All India Women's Conference, whose members sought originally to open discussion of women's education but quickly realized that many other issues (e.g., purdah, dowry, child marriage, and the remarriage of widows) were intricately connected to it. All of them, in turn, were bound up in the question of British rule. Equality and opportunity for women, they knew, were inseparable from the burning issue of Indian independence. Nationalist men supported feminists' demands for suffrage, eager to demonstrate that Indian men were far more progressive than their supposedly superior British overlords.

Upon gaining independence, the ruling Congress Party included universal adult suffrage and sex, caste, and religious equality in the constitution. But when it came to sexual equality in the home, they were less able to show enthusiasm. In fact, when the All India Women's Conference proposed reform of the Hindu Code in 1934, seeking change in marriage, divorce, and inheritance laws to better serve women, the men of the Nationalist Party objected. In 1943 and 1945 the Legislative Assembly rejected a new Hindu Code that incorporated women's equality in domestic matters. After independence in 1947, opposition to it remained high despite the support of such influential men as Pandit Motilal Nehru. Only when Nehru made it an issue of his prestige and support after 1951 did the new code pass, and even then it took more than two years. Feminists had been clear from the start that their agenda depended upon the success of the Nationalist Party's agenda. When the time came for Nationalist men who had succeeded in throwing off foreign domination to agree to ending their own domination of women in personal affairs, they balked.[36]

The "Second Wave" of Feminism, from the 1960s to the Present

What is called the second wave of feminism, known at the time as women's liberation, arose in the West during the 1960s. Inspired in part by the civil rights movement in the United States and New Left movements in Europe, women in Britain, France, Germany, Italy, and America began to demand freedom from the roles, portrayals, and expectations that limited, diminished, and oppressed them. The sexual revolution of the 1960s had placed a premium on men's pleasures and the fulfillment of their sexual desires at the expense of women, whose highly sexualized images appeared in magazines like *Playboy* and *Penthouse* and on billboards and posters.

Women's liberation activists protested loudly and vividly against such depictions of women as sexual objects. One of their first actions took place in 1970 when a group of women interrupted the Miss World beauty contest in London by leaping onstage and blowing whistles, hooting, mooing like cattle, and brandishing signs that read "Miss-conception," "Miss-treated," "Miss-placed," and "Miss-judged." They lobbed stink bombs, flour bombs, and smoke bombs at contestants, judges, and the master of ceremonies Bob Hope. Their actions resembled those of the militant suffragists of the first decade of the twentieth century and earned them the same result—arrest. They created a spectacle that succeeded in garnering for the movement enormous publicity.[37]

In the United States, the National Organization for Women (NOW) mobilized the Women's Strike for Equality on August 26, 1970. Thousands of women in cities across the nation carried banners and signs demanding their rights. The visibility of the women's liberation movement increased markedly, and thousands more flocked to join NOW and various other groups. In 1975 more than three thousand feminist events took place in the United States. Some seventy women's liberation groups existed in London alone by 1969. In Paris, feminist groups with names like Psychanalyse et Politique and Elles Voient Rouge (Women See Red) formed. Publications such as *MS*, *Shrew*, *Red Rag*, and *Spare Rib* appeared, analyzing women's oppression, recounting earlier feminist efforts, spreading the feminist message, and making claims for women's personal, sexual, and familial freedom.

In the United States, a presidential order made civil service jobs open to those who qualified "without regard to sex"; the Equal Pay Act was passed in 1963; Title VII, which outlawed discrimination in employment to include "sex," was extended in 1964; and Title IX banning discrimination passed in 1972. In Britain, the Equal Pay Acts of 1970 and 1975 and the Sex Discrimination Act of 1975 made it possible for women to gain equal treatment with men in some areas of education, training, and wage-earning.

Second-wave feminists, however, looked for more than equality with men before the law. They sought changes in the law, the social and economic system, and the culture that would "liberate" them from current conceptions of femininity, which, they argued, locked them into stifling, unfulfilling, slavish positions and often made them vulnerable to sexual predations from men. Unlike contemporary liberal feminists and those of the nineteenth and early twentieth centuries, feminists seeking liberation believed that the very system in which they lived required abolition or complete overhaul.

Feminists differed in their designation of just what system it was that oppressed them. Socialist feminists hailing from New Left organizations identified capitalism as the source of conditions that rendered them inferior to men. Like Marx, explained Hilary Rose, who "was able to go behind the appearance of freedom in the labour market in which buyers and sellers freely bought and sold, to reveal the systemic relations of domination and subordination which are located within the capitalist more of production itself," socialist, or materialist, feminists should "go behind—above all in personal life— the appearance of love and the naturalness of a woman's place and a woman's work, to reveal the equally systemic relationships of the sex-gender world."[38]

It was in the family in particular, socialist feminists argued, where the understandings, assumptions, and labor force necessary to keep capitalism working were reproduced, hence the family required complete transformation. For socialist feminists, adherence to Marxist doctrine and socialist groups remained a significant aspect of their politics, the goal of which was to eliminate the unjust class system produced by capitalism and reproduced by the family. The achievement of feminist aims would follow upon its extinction.

At the same time, they insisted that women's work, experiences, and functions in a capitalist society could not be subsumed into those of men, a position that forced traditional socialists to enlarge their understandings and expand their analyses of capitalism.

Radical feminists, by contrast, saw the root of their oppression in domination by men rather than in the economic system. They insisted that if women were to be liberated they would have to arrive at a "consciousness" of their oppression. As Dale Spender put it, "A patriarchal society depends in large measure on the experience and values of males being perceived as the only valid *frame* of reference for society, and . . . it is therefore in patriarchal interest to prevent women from sharing, establishing, and asserting their equally real, valid, and *different* frame of reference, which is the outcome of different experience."[39]

In "consciousness-raising" sessions where they explored their personal lives in depth, many feminists gained understanding of how patriarchy operated in the most insidious ways to make women complicit in subservience to men. In consequence, some radical feminists—many of them lesbians ostracized by straight feminists who feared their movement would be tainted by association with lesbianism—became convinced that they would have to remove themselves from sexual and social relationships with men. As Amanda Sebestyn, a British feminist, later described radical feminism, "We wanted to leave men no matter what, we started squatting so we could live with other women, we acquired of necessity new 'male' skills of plumbing, electricity, carpentry, and car maintenance, setting up our own discos and then forming bands to dance to. We cut our hair very short and stopped wearing 'women's' clothes, we stopped smiling and being 'nice.'"[40]

Despite their differences, which would become increasingly evident and acrimonious in the mid and late 1970s, feminists of virtually every ideology agreed that women's sexual freedom—their capacity to choose the kind of intimate or social grouping in which they would live and determine for themselves the kind of work they would do—was vital to their liberation. They could readily come together to support reforms that contributed to that end: access to free and legal contraception and abortion; equal pay; health, educational, and social services; increased penalties for rape and domestic violence; nursery and day care for children; and provisions that enabled women to be legally and financially independent—divorce law reform and wages for housework. They made clear from the start that they intended their varieties of feminism to create entirely different roles, expectations, identities, and material realities for women than those currently operative. A focus on personal and family issues and social and cultural practices—the clubs, bookstores, magazines, and literature of the "sexual revolution" that gratuitously portrayed women as proper objects of male sexual desire and violence—gave their movement a broad comprehensiveness that touched the lives of subsequent generations of women—and men.

Women of color in Britain and the United States found themselves in a kind of political no-man's-land during the late 1960s and early 1970s. Disconcerted by their treatment at the hands of the male-dominated black power movement yet finding women's liberation and feminism irrelevant and blind to their needs and desires ("basically a family quarrel between White women and White men," as one African American woman put it), women of color began to form their own organizations to gain liberation for themselves.[41]

In Britain, Iyamide Hazeley graphically laid out, in a poem entitled "Political Union," the grievances that black women held within black power organizations:

> You call me "Sister" Brother yet I know
> that it is simply a psychological lever to prise apart my legs.
> "Sister, make coffee for the movement,
> Sister, make babies for the struggle."
> You raped my consciousness with your body
> my body with reason,
> and assuage your unconscious guilt by oral politicking
> make believing
> "Sister, Sister."[42]

In the United States, writers such as Alice Walker, Audre Lorde, Toni Morrison, and Angela Davis began to articulate the complicated intersections of gender, race, and sexuality in their lives and communities. When they looked toward white feminist groups, they saw a political program that addressed few of their concerns. "We felt they had different priorities to us," remarked one women instrumental in forming the Brixton Black Women's Group in 1973:

> At that time, for example, abortion was the number one issue, and groups such as Wages for Housework were making a lot of noise, too. These were hardly burning issues for us—in fact they seemed like middle-class preoccupations. To begin with, abortion wasn't something we had any problems getting as Black women—it was the very reverse for us! And as for wages for housework, we were more interested in getting properly paid for the work we were doing outside the home as nightcleaners and in campaigns for more childcare facilities for Black women workers.[43]

In order to deal with a dual oppression arising from racism and sexism, a number of women formed other local black women's groups throughout London and in cities like Leicester, Manchester, Liverpool, Sheffield, and Nottingham. Coalitions of women of color, such as the Organization of Women of Asian and African Descent (OWAAD), enabled a broader international movement to emerge. Within it issues of racism and sexism that concerned women of color could be addressed and an international dialogue established.

As Hazel Carby noted in a hard-hitting article, the structures of racism meant that black women experienced difference kinds of subjugation than white women. What white women regarded as an oppressive institution—the family—black women often found to be a place from which to resist political and cultural forms of racism. White radical feminists might espouse separatism from men; black women relied on "progressive" men in their struggles for equality and justice. "Our situation as Black people necessitates that we have solidarity around the fact of race," Carby said, "which white women of course do not need to have with white men, unless it is their negative solidarity as racial oppressors." White feminists, she argued, had not recognized their role in continuing imperialist and colonialist regimes around the world or in acting as oppressors of black people at home. If they did, they refused to acknowledge their complicity for fear "that [it] will be at the expense of concentrating upon being oppressed."[44]

Carby's critique of white women's feminism raised profoundly uncomfortable issues for many women and opened up feminism as a whole to the existence of a diversity in women's lives that compelled development of far more sophisticated understandings of gender than either socialist or radical feminism had been able to provide.

In other parts of the world the legacies of colonialism, economic predation, authoritarian dictatorships of the left and right, fundamentalist religious regimes, and economic liberalization produced situations unlike those faced by feminists in Western Europe and the United States. Feminist concerns in places like Vietnam, China, parts of the Middle East, Eastern Europe, the former Soviet Union, Latin America, and Africa differ markedly from one another and from Western feminism. The ideologies and material conditions in which they operate have provoked agendas specific to their particular contexts.

In South Africa, for instance, women's equality came a distinct second to racial equality in the fight against apartheid led by the African National Congress (ANC). As a woman member of ANC noted in 1986, "In South Africa, the prime issue is apartheid and national liberation. So to argue that African women should concentrate on and from an isolated feminist movement, focusing on issues of women in their narrowest sense, implies African women must fight so that they can be equally oppressed with African men."[45] Other members of ANC—both women and men—recognized, however, that women's liberation constituted an integral part of national liberation as a whole. The ANC, at the urging of the Federation of South African Women, issued a woman's charter and guidelines for a postemancipation state that expressly identified women's need for equality and liberation on both racial and gender terms. "The emancipation of women must be an integral part of their lives," ANC guidelines declared, "not just in legal statements, but in the reality of their lives . . . if women do not achieve equality with men, society will have failed. They have struggled within their homes, they have given their time, energy, and lives to the struggle for national liberation."[46] The central issues for feminists in an ANC-governed South Africa now concern implementation of these acknowledged principles at a time when national resources are being stretched to their limits by the need to provide education, employment, health care, homes, and food in a society devastated by apartheid.

In China, in what appears to Western feminists to be an ironic turn, younger women seem to be looking toward motherhood and domesticity as a way of transgressing dominant norms of femininity, of escaping the state's demands upon them. In the years since Mao's death, China has entered a period of economic reform, and the identity of "worker," formerly praised, has taken on connotations of laziness, lack of productivity, intransigence, and inefficiency. The state has sought to reform and modernize by placing much heavier demands on workers to increase productivity and efficiency. Bearing children—and staying at home to care for them rather than returning to work shortly after their birth—enables some women to resist the state's encroachment, contest the norms of proper womanhood, and exercise some control over their bodies and identities. Rejecting what they regard as an official feminism of the state, the women are taking their own, arguably feminist, position. In light of China's one-child policy, the decision of some women to focus on child-bearing and rearing at the expense of work becomes all the more poignant.

Other official, competing pronouncements about women compelled by economic reform in China have renewed ideas about the biological functions determining a "natural" role for women as mothers. Reformers insist that the need for efficiency overrides concerns about gender equality in the workplace that state socialism had embraced. Wages and conditions of work must respond to supply and demand rather than principles of equality or fairness. Yet when market forces make jobs difficult to come by, Chinese intellectuals seeking economic rationalization urge women to remove themselves from the workplace and return home by "choice." This development has provoked women to resist, develop a feminist position in opposition to the new ideology, and insist on conditions of equal work and pay.[47]

Identifying these two examples of what look to be entirely different sets of behavior on the part of Chinese women as being potentially feminist may seem untenable. In placing them in the material contexts within which these women live, and seeing them as forms of resistance to discourses that constrain and diminish women's lives, they take on a different coloration, however. Taking seriously Parveen Adams and Jeffrey Minson's admonition about sexual difference being created in a wide variety of practices, and insistence that feminists and historians of feminism must "determine which differences and which practices are oppressive at any particular moment in any given culture," enables appreciation of the diversity, complexity, and legitimacy of whole worlds of feminism.[48]

The advent of global feminism has considerably strengthened the ability of feminists across the world to agitate for and bring about change in women's lives. When feminists in Africa, South Asia, and Latin America observed that North American and European women enjoyed a degree of prosperity, health, safety, and political stability that most women in the world did not, it became excruciatingly clear that feminism, as it had been formulated in the northern industrialized countries of the world, had little relevance elsewhere. African, South Asian, and Latina feminists, pointing out the "North-South" divide between women, have called attention to the fundamental needs of women in poor nations and demonstrated how differences of class, sexuality, race, religion, culture, and ethnicity necessitate a broader, fuller, and more comprehensive feminist politics to encompass and address them. Global feminism, although recognizing deep and divisive differences among women, has emphasized the importance of coalition-building among diverse feminist groups and organizations. In consequence, a significantly strengthened, internationally effective, and more just and open-minded feminist politics has emerged.[49]

Conclusion

Feminist movements have helped create enormous changes in women's—and men's—lives since the 1800s. In the West, women have attained rights to property, earning, education, employment, legal standing, political participation, divorce, and reproductive choice. Challenges from the religious and political right notwithstanding, women have gained for themselves and subsequent generations of women the opportunity to make significant choices about their lives: where and how they will live, what kinds of work they will do, and how to structure and enjoy their private, personal lives in areas ranging from leisure activities to sexual practices. As a consequence of the questions feminists raised about gender roles and expectations, men, too, have found freedom to challenge traditional assumptions about their place in family and society. The change has been striking. Whereas, for example, women who created the feminist movement in the United States during the 1970s had not been permitted (or even encouraged) to participate in organized sporting events believed to be for males, in June 2000 the Women's National Basketball Association's regular season games drew a larger audience than the National Hockey League playoff semifinals.

But much remains to be done as well. Women still earn less than men for comparable work; some estimates put U.S. women's salaries at 70 percent of those of men. Poverty strikes female-headed households severely. Domestic violence directed against women and children also remains a significant problem, as does sexual abuse. In other areas of the world women still have not gained political or legal rights, or they have lost them over the course of shifts of political power and governmental regimes. Cultural and religious practices continue to operate to constrain women's opportunities—indeed, to threaten their very lives. National and international feminist organizations are trying to address the problems women face throughout the world, and the 2000 United Nations World Conference for Women, following a 1995 meeting in Beijing, seeks to ensure that the member states of the international community observe the basic rights of women affirmed in the U.N. Charter and in subsequent resolutions.

Feminism has proven to produce tough and resilient ideologies and movements, reflecting both the strength of opposition to women's demands for freedom and equality and the power of those ideals to move millions to take action to realize them. Feminists' successes have resulted from their ability to analyze the power relations obtaining between men and women in any given time and place and from challenges to the assumptions, policies, and practices that structure social, economic, political, cultural, and familial life. It is a matter for both regret and celebration that feminist movements will not soon cease to exist—regret because equality for women appears to provoke continued antagonism worldwide and celebration because women continue to find the hope, courage, resources, and savvy to try to make their lives freer, fairer, more secure, more fulfilling, and happier.

Notes

1. Richard J. Evans, *The Feminists* (London: Croom Helm, 1977), 39n1.

2. Nancy F. Cott, *The Grounding of Modern Feminism* (New Haven: Yale University Press, 1987); Claire Goldberg Moses, "'Equality' and 'Difference' in Historical Perspective: A Comparative Examination of the Feminisms of French Revolutionaries and Utopian Socialists," in *Rebel Daughters: Women and the French Revolution*, ed. Sara E. Melzer and Leslie W. Rabine (New York: Oxford University Press, 1992), 231–54; Denise Riley, *"Am I That Name?" Feminism and the Category of "Women" in History* (London: MacMillan,

1987); Joan Wallach Scott, *Only Paradoxes to Offer: French Feminists and the Rights of Man* (Cambridge: Harvard University Press, 1996).

3. Riley, *"Am I That Name?"* 1, 2, 3, 5.

4. Parveen Adams and Jeffrey Minson, "The 'Subject' of Feminism," *m/f* 2 (1978): 60.

5. For this discussion of early feminist impulses, see Moira Ferguson, ed., *First Feminists: British Women Writers, 1578–1799* (Bloomington: University of Indiana Press, 1985); Anne Laurence, *Women in England, 1500–1760: A Social History* (New York: Palgrave Macmillan, 1994); Sara Heller Mendelson, *The Mental World of Stuart Women: Three Studies* (Amherst: Harvester, 1987); Ruth Perry, "Mary Astell and the Feminist Critique of Possessive Individualism," *Eighteenth-Century Studies* 23 (Summer 1990): 444–57; and Hilda Smith, *Reason's Disciples: Seventeenth-Century English Feminists* (Urbana: University of Illinois Press, 1982).

6. Perry, "Mary Astell," 444–57.

7. Quoted in Sara Evans, *Born for Liberty: A History of Women in America* (New York: Free Press, 1989), 58. See also Linda K. Kerber, *Women of the Republic: Intellect and Ideology in Revolutionary America* (Chapel Hill: University of North Carolina Press, 1980).

8. Kerber, *Women of the Republic.*

9. Jane Rendall, *The Origins of Modern Feminism: Women in Britain, France, and the United States, 1780–1860* (Chicago: Lyceum Books, 1985), 38 (first quotation), 39 (second quotation).

10. Elisabeth G. Sledziewski, "The French Revolution as the Turning Point," in *Emerging Feminism from Revolution to World War,* vol. 4 of *A History of Women in the West,* ed. Genevieve Fraisse and Michelle Perrot (Cambridge: Harvard University Press, 1993), 39 (first quotation), 40 (second quotation).

11. Scott, *Only Paradoxes to Offer,* 20.

12. Sledziewski, "The French Revolution," 43–44; Bonnie G. Smith, *Changing Lives: Women in European History since 1700* (Lexington: D. C. Heath, 1989), 101.

13. Quoted in Ferguson, ed., *First Feminists,* 413–19.

14. Ibid.

15. Vivien Jones, ed., *Women in the Eighteenth Century: Constructions of Femininity* (London: Routledge, 1990), 231–42.

16. This discussion of antislavery depends on the work of Claire Midgley, *Women against Slavery: The British Campaigns, 1780–1870* (London: Routledge, 1992).

17. Susan Kingsley Kent, *Gender and Power in Britain, 1640–1990* (London: Routledge, 1999), 186.

18. Barbara Alpern Engel, *Mothers and Daughters: Women of the Intelligensia in Nineteenth-Century Russia* (New York: Cambridge University Press, 1983); Evans, *Born for Liberty;* Ute Frevert, *Women in German History: From Bourgeois Emancipation to Sexual Liberation* (Oxford: Berg Publishers, 1989); Alfred G. Meyer, *The Feminism and Socialism of Lily Braun* (Bloomington: Indiana University Press, 1985); and Claire Goldberg Moses, *French Feminism in the Nineteenth-Century* (Albany: State University of New York Press, 1984).

19. Scott, *Only Paradoxes to Offer,* 100.

20. Susan Kingsley Kent, *Sex and Suffrage in Britain, 1860–1914* (Princeton: Princeton University Press, 1987), 112.

21. Linda Gordon, "Voluntary Motherhood: The Beginnings of Feminist Birth Control Ideas in the United States," *Feminist Studies* 1 (Winter-Wpring 1973): 5–22; Moses, *French Feminism,* 231.

22. Ellen Carol Dubois, *Feminism and Suffrage: The Emergence of an Independent Women's Movement in America, 1848–1869* (Ithaca: Cornell University Press, 1978), 41.

23. Kent, *Sex and Suffrage*, 190.

24. Dubois, *Feminism and Suffrage*, ch. 2.

25. Antoinette Burton, *Burdens of History: British Feminists, Indian Women, and Imperial Culture, 1865–1915* (Chapel Hill: University of North Carolina Press, 1994).

26. Marilyn J. Boxer and Jean H. Quataert, eds., *Socialist Women: European Socialist Feminism in the Nineteenth and Early Twentieth Centuries* (New York: Elsevier, 1978).

27. Margot Badran, "Competing Agenda: Feminists, Islam, and the State in Nineteenth and Twentieth Century Egypt," in *Global Feminisms since 1945*, ed. Bonnie G. Smith (London: Routledge, 2000), 13–44.

28. Vir Bharat Talwar "Feminist Consciousness in Women's Journals in Hindi, 1910–1920," in *Recasting Women: Essays in Indian Colonial History*, ed. Kumkum Sangari and Sudesh Vaid (New Brunswick: Rutgers University, 1990), 205–6.

29. Kent, *Sex and Suffrage*, 205.

30. Ibid., passim.

31. Susan Kingsley Kent, *Making Peace: The Reconstruction of Gender in Interwar Britain* (Princeton: Princeton University Press, 1993), 116–17.

32. Beryl Williams, "Kollantai and After: Women in the Russian Revolution," in *Women, State, and Revolution: Essays on Power and Gender in Europe since 1789*, ed. Sian Reynolds (Amherst: University of Massachusetts Press, 1987), 76.

33. Christina K. Gilmartin, "Gender, Political Culture, and Women's Mobilization in the Chinese Nationalist Revolution, 1924–1927," in *Engendering China: Women, Culture and the State*, ed. Christina K. Gilmartin et al. (Cambridge: Harvard University Press, 1994), 201–2.

34. Lisa Rofel, "Liberation Nostalgia and a Yearning for Modernity," in *Engendering China: Women, Culture and the State*, ed. Christina K. Gilmartin et al. (Cambridge: Harvard University Press, 1994), 234–38, 245.

35. Badran, "Competing Agenca," 13–44.

36. Joanna Liddle and Rama Joshi, *Daughters of Independence: Gender, Caste and Class in India* (New Brunswick: Rutgers University Press, 1986), 21, 36–38.

37. Barbara Caine, *English Feminism, 1780–1980* (New York: Oxford University Press, 1997), Afterward.

38. Hilary Rose, "Women's Work: Women's Knowledge," in *What Is Feminism? A Reexamination*, ed. Juliet Mitchell and Ann Oakley (New York: Pantheon Books, 1986), 161.

39. Dale Spender, *Women of Ideas (and What Men have Done to Them)* (London: Pandora, 1982), 4–5.

40. Quoted in Caine, *English Feminism*, 266.

41. Quoted in Evans, *Born for Liberty*, 297.

42. Beverley Bryan, Stella Dadzie, and Suzanne Scafe, *The Heart of the Race: Black Women's Lives in Britain* (London: Virago, 1985), 147.

43. Bryan, Dadzie, and Scafe, *The Heart of the Race*, 149–50.

44. Hazel Carby, "White Women Listen! Black Feminism and the Boundaries of Sisterhood," in *The Empire Strikes Back: Race and Racism in Seventies' Britain*, ed. Centre for Contemporary Cultural Studies, (London: Hutchinson/The Centre for Contemporary Cultural Studies, University of Birmingham, 1982), 231, 221.

45. Quoted in Zengie A. Mandaliso, "Gender and Nation-Building in South Africa," in *Global Feminisms since 1945*, ed. Bonnie G. Smith (London: Routledge, 2000), 69.

46. Mandaliso, "Gender and Nation-Building," 73.

47. Lin Chun, "Finding a Language," in *Transitions, Environments, Translations: Feminisms in International Politics,* ed. Joan W. Scott, Cora Kaplan, and Debra Keates (New York: Routledge, 1997), 12–13.

48. Adams and Minson, "The Subject of Feminism," 60.

49. Bonnie Smith, Introduction to *Global Feminisms.*

Contributors

MARJORIE WALL BINGHAM received her B.A. from Grinnell College and her M.A. and Ph.D. from the University of Minnesota. Most of her history teaching career took place at St. Louis Park, Minnesota, Senior High School, although more recently she has taught in the Graduate School of Hamline University. Among her teaching awards is the 1994 Nancy Roelker Mentor Award from the AHA. She has served on a variety of national committees concerned with history and the schools, including the Bradley Commission, and was one of the founders of the National Council for History Education. With Susan Gross she coauthored a series of thirteen books on women in world cultures, designed for world history classes, and founded the Upper Midwest Center for Women's History. She is also a senior consultant for the NEH project "Women, World History and the Web" and for a Korea Society project on the Silla dynasty.

JULIA CLANCY-SMITH is an associate professor of history at the University of Arizona. She holds a Ph.D. from the University of California, Los Angeles. She has published *Rebel and Saint: Muslim Notables, Populist Protest, Colonial Encounters (Algeria and Tunisia, 1800–1904)* (1994), which received three book awards; was coeditor of *Domesticating the Empire: Gender, Race, and Family Life in the Dutch and French Empires* (1998); and has been editor of *North Africa, Islam, and the Mediterranean World from the Almoravids to the Algerian War* (2001). She is coediting a special issue of *French Historical Studies* devoted to the French Empire and completing a book on trans-Mediterranean settlement in nineteenth-century North Africa. She has another book underway on colonial education for girls in French North Africa. Her extended essay in comparative women/gender history and colonial cultures, "European Imperialism and Colonial Knowledge on Women in Islamic Cultures, c. 1750–1900," is part of the six-volume *Encyclopedia of Women and Islamic Cultures* edited by Suad Joseph.

SUSAN KENT is professor of history and women's studies at the University of Colorado at Boulder. She is the author of *Sex and Suffrage in Britain, 1860–1914*, *Making Peace: The Reconstruction of Gender in Interwar Britain*, and *Gender and Power in Britain, 1640–1990*. She is at work on a book on the impact of the Great War on British subjectivity.

ALICE KESSLER-HARRIS is the R. Gordon Hoxie Professor of American History at Columbia University. She is the author of several books and many articles on wage-earning women, including *"Out to Work": A History of Wage-Earning Women in the United States* and *In Pursuit of Equity: Women, Men, and the Quest for Economic Citizenship in Twentieth-Century America*. Her current project is a biographical study of the playwright Lillian Hellman.

MARY JO MAYNES is professor and chair of history at the University of Minnesota. Her specialty is modern European history, which she approaches with an interdisciplinary and comparativist bent. She is involved in two research projects, one on the history of girlhood in modern Europe (around the topics of work and sexuality) and an interdisciplinary project on the use of personal narratives in the social sciences. She and Ann Waltner have cotaught a freshman world history course at the University of Minnesota since the early 1990s. Among her works are *Secret Gardens, Satanic Mills: Placing Girls in European History, 1750–1960* (coedited with Christina Benninghaus and Birgitte Søland) and *Taking the Hard Road: Life Courses in French and German Workers' Autobiographies in the Era of Industrialization*.

PAMELA SCULLY is an assistant professor of history at Denison University. She is the author of *Liberating the Family? Gender and British Slave Emancipation in the Rural Western Cape, South Africa, 1823–1853* and "White Maternity and Black Infancy: The Rhetoric of Race in the South African Women's Suffrage Movement, 1870–1930" in *Women's Suffrage in the British Empire: Citizenship, Nation, and Race,* edited by Ian Fletcher, Laura Mayhall, and Philippa Levine. With Diana Paton she is coeditor of *Gender and Slave Emancipation in the Atlantic World* and, with Clifton Crais, is at work on a biography of Sara Baartman, the "Hottentot Venus."

MRINALINI SINHA is an associate professor of history and women's studies at the Pennsylvania State University. She is the author of *Colonial Masculinity: The "Manly Englishman" and the "Effeminate Bengali"* and *Katherine Mayo's Mother India*.

BONNIE G. SMITH is Board of Governors Professor of History at Rutgers University. She is the author of *Changing Lives: Women in European History since 1700*, *The Gender of History: Men, Women, and Historical Practice*, and other books and articles. She has edited *Global Feminisms since 1945* and coedited *Gender Meets Disability Studies*. She is also general editor of *The Oxford Encyclopedia of Women in World History*.

MARGARET STROBEL is interim director at Jane Addams Hull-House Museum at the University of Illinois at Chicago, where she has a faculty appointment as professor of gender and women's studies and history. She is writing a book about the Chicago Women's Liberation Union and is a member of the editorial board for *Women Building Chicago, 1790–1990: A Biographical Dictionary*, edited by Rima Lunin Schultz and Adele Hast. She has published in the areas of African women's history; gender, race, and empire; the development of the fields of women's history and women's studies from a personal perspective; oral history; and public history. She is series coeditor of *Restoring Women to History*, with volumes on Africa, Asia, Latin America and the Caribbean, the Middle East, and North Africa, and her book *Muslim Women in Mombasa, 1890–1975* won the Herskovits Award from the African Studies Association.

ANN WALTNER is professor of history at the University of Minnesota. She serves as editor of the *Journal of Asian Studies* and is the author of a number of articles on gender, kinship, and religion in late imperial China. She and Mary Jo Maynes have cotaught a freshman world history course at the University of Minnesota since the early 1990s.

Index

The University of Illinois Press
is a founding member of the
Association of American University Presses.

———————————————————

Composed in 9.5/12.5 New Baskerville
with ITC Stone Sans display
by Barbara Evans
at the University of Illinois Press
Designed by Copenhaver Cumpston

University of Illinois Press
1325 South Oak Street
Champaign, IL 61820-6903
www.press.uillinois.edu